LIBRARY OF HEBREW BIBLE/
OLD TESTAMENT STUDIES

703

Formerly Journal for the Study of the Old Testament Supplement Series

Editors
Claudia V. Camp, Texas Christian University, USA
Andrew Mein, Durham University, UK

Founding Editors
David J. A. Clines, Philip R. Davies and David M. Gunn

Editorial Board
Alan Cooper, Steed Davidson, Susan Gillingham, John Goldingay,
Norman K. Gottwald, James E. Harding, John Jarick, Tracy Lemos,
Carol Meyers, Daniel L. Smith-Christopher, Francesca Stavrakopoulou,
James W. Watts

EZEKIEL AND THE WORLD
OF DEUTERONOMY

Jason Gile

LONDON • NEW YORK • OXFORD • NEW DELHI • SYDNEY

T&T CLARK
Bloomsbury Publishing Plc
50 Bedford Square, London, WC1B 3DP, UK
1385 Broadway, New York, NY 10018, USA
29 Earlsfort Terrace, Dublin 2, Ireland

BLOOMSBURY, T&T CLARK and the T&T Clark logo
are trademarks of Bloomsbury Publishing Plc

First published in Great Britain 2021
This paperback edition published 2023

Copyright © Jason Gile, 2021

Jason Gile has asserted his right under the Copyright, Designs and Patents Act, 1988, to be identified as Author of this work.

All rights reserved. No part of this publication may be reproduced or transmitted in any form or by any means, electronic or mechanical, including photocopying, recording, or any information storage or retrieval system, without prior permission in writing from the publishers.

Bloomsbury Publishing Plc does not have any control over, or responsibility for, any third-party websites referred to or in this book. All internet addresses given in this book were correct at the time of going to press. The author and publisher regret any inconvenience caused if addresses have changed or sites have ceased to exist, but can accept no responsibility for any such changes.

A catalogue record for this book is available from the British Library.

Library of Congress Control Number: 2021930666.

ISBN: HB: 978-0-5676-9430-0
PB: 978-0-5677-0133-6
ePDF: 978-0-5676-9431-7

Series: Library of Hebrew Bible/Old Testament Studies, volume 703
ISSN 2513-8758

Typeset by: Trans.form.ed SAS

To find out more about our authors and books visit www.bloomsbury.com and sign up for our newsletters.

For Melody

אשה אשר אהבתי כל־ימי חיי

Contents

Acknowledgments	viii
List of Abbreviations	xv

Chapter 1
INTRODUCTION	1
Ezekiel's Use of Texts and Traditions	3
Citing Scripture in an Oral World	7
Ezekiel's Relationship to Deuteronomy	10
The Terms "Deuteronomic" and "Deuteronomistic"	11
The Status of Deuteronomy at the Time of Ezekiel	11
Scholarly Views on Ezekiel and Deuteronomy	12
Ezekiel the Prophet, Ezekiel the Book	16
The Unity of the Book	16
Ezekiel's Role in Producing the Book	18
A Widespread Deuteronomistic Redaction of Ezekiel?	22
The Septuagint and Scribal Expansion	24
Preview of This Study	25

Chapter 2
METHOD FOR ASSESSING INFLUENCE	26
Recognizing Influence	28
Explaining Verbal Parallels	29
Defining Deuteronomic Influence	32
Identifying Literary Dependence	33
The Significance for Interpreting the Book of Ezekiel	37

Chapter 3
IDOLATRY	39
The Basis for Ezekiel's Indictment against Idolatry	40
Ezckiel and the Pentateuchal Descriptions of Idolatry	41
Deuteronomic Language for Idolatry in Ezekiel	47
שקוצים, "Detestable Things"	47
תועבות, "Abominations"	47

  העביר בנים באש, "Passing Children through the Fire"   49
  הכעיס, "Provoke to Anger"   50
  הלך אחרי אלהים / גלולים, "Going after Gods / Idols"   51
  עיניו נשא, "Lifting One's Eyes (to גלולים)"   51
  קסם, "Divination"   51
 Worshiping Idols in Exile   52
 Non-Centralized Worship   58
  "On Every High Hill, Under Every Leafy Tree"   61
  על ההרים אכל, "Eating on the Mountains"   62
  גדע, "Cut Down"   63
  נתץ, "Tear Down"   64
  Centralized Worship in the Renewed Jerusalem   64
 Ezekiel's Temple Vision (Chapter 8)   65
  Scene 1: The Image of Jealousy (8:5-6)   65
  Scene 2: The Elders and Their Images (8:7-13)   67

 Excursus: *A Marzēaḥ in Ezekiel 8:7-13?*   69

  Scene 3: The Women Weeping "the Tammuz" (8:14-15)   71
  Scene 4: Astral Worship (8:16-18)   72
  Ezekiel's Vision and Manasseh's Sins   72
 Ezekiel and Deuteronomy 4   74
  Literary Links   74
  Dating Deuteronomy 4   74
 Idolatry and Defilement   77
 Summary   78
 The Rhetoric of Allusion   79

Chapter 4
EZEKIEL 16 AND THE SONG OF MOSES   80
 Plot Structure and Thematic Links   81
  Yahweh's Discovery of Israel (Deut. 32:10 // Ezek. 16:6)   82
  Yahweh's Lavish Care (Deut. 32:10b-14 // Ezek. 16:7-13a)   84
  Israel Prospers (Deut. 32:15a // Ezek. 16:13b-14)   86
  Israel Forsakes Her God (Deut. 32:15b // Ezek. 16:15a)   86
  Israel's Idolatry (Deut. 32:16-17 // Ezek. 16:15b-22)   86
  Israel Forgets Her Origins (Deut. 32:18 // Ezek. 16:22)   87
  Israel Angers Yahweh (Deut. 32:16, 21 // Ezek. 16:26)   87
  Israel's Indictment and Punishment (Deut. 32:19-25 //
   Ezek. 16:35-43)   88
  Israel's Restoration (Deut. 32:35-36, 41-43 //
   Ezek. 16:53-55, 59-63)   88
 Literary Dependence?   89

Could Ezekiel Have Known and Used the Song?	92
Linguistic Considerations	92
Historical Context	93
Intertextual Links	94
Is It Likely Ezekiel Would Have Known and Used the Song?	95
Did Ezekiel Know and Use the Song?	96
רעב, חצים, "Arrows, Famine" (Ezek. 5:16-17 // Deut. 32:23-25, 42)	96
חרבי, "My Sword" (Ezek. 21 // Deut. 32:41-42)	97
קנא, "To Make Jealous" (Ezek. 8:3 // Deut. 32:16, 21)	98
Ezekiel's Programmatic Use of Scripture	98
Ezekiel's Prophetic Transformation	99
The Rhetoric of Transformation	101

Chapter 5

EZEKIEL 20: ISRAEL'S HISTORY	103
Deuteronomic Elements in Ezekiel 20	104
The Election of Israel (vv. 5-6)	105
Yahweh Scouting the Land (v. 6)	106
Detestable Things (v. 7)	106
Rebellion (vv. 8, 13, 21)	106
Yahweh's Anger (vv. 8, 13, 21)	107
"My Eye Spared Them" (v. 17)	108
The Scattering of Israel (v. 23)	108
Worship on the High Places (vv. 27-29)	108
"Make Your Children Pass Through the Fire" (v. 31)	109
Worshiping Wood and Stone (v. 32)	109
With a Strong Hand and Outstretched Arm (vv. 33-34)	109
"Gather You Out of the Countries Where You Have Been Scattered" (v. 41)	110
A Polemic Against Deuteronomic Theology?	110
Polemical Language in Ezekiel 20?	111
Conclusion: Ezekiel and Deuteronomy/Dtr	126
Do the Not-Good Laws (Ezekiel 20:25-26) Refer to Deuteronomy?	127
The Traditional Interpretation	127
Deuteronomy as the "Not-Good" Laws	129
Evaluation of Hahn and Bergsma	130
The Referent of the Not-Good Laws	133
Ezekiel 20 and Israelite Tradition	137
Summary	139

Chapter 6
THE SCATTERING OF ISRAEL — 140
Scattering Language in Ezekiel and Deuteronomy — 142
- Ezekiel's Scattering Language — 142
- Similarities with Deuteronomy — 143
- The Fusion of Traditions in Ezekiel — 145
- Ezekiel's Technique of Literary Appropriation — 145
- Ezekiel's Awareness of the Deuteronomic Exile Passages? — 148
- Ezekiel's Knowledge of an Exile Tradition Reflected in Ezekiel 20:23? — 149

Excursus: *Does Ezekiel 20:23 Depict an Oath?* — 149
- Ezekiel 20:23 and the Pentateuchal Traditions — 153
- Ezekiel's Theology of Exile — 158

The Origin of the Scattering Motif in Ezekiel — 161
The Direction of Influence — 162
- Threats of Exile before 597/587 BCE? — 162
- Ezekiel's Literary Appropriation — 171
The Rhetoric of Allusion — 172

Chapter 7
THE GATHERING OF ISRAEL — 173
Gathering Language in Ezekiel and Deuteronomy — 174
- Ezekiel's Gathering Language — 177
- Similarities with Deuteronomy 30 — 179
- Is Ezekiel Instead Influenced by Jeremiah or Another Prophet? — 177
- Ezekiel and Yahweh's Compassion — 182
The Direction of Influence — 184
- Ezekiel's Literary Appropriation — 184
- Other Allusions to Deuteronomy 30:3-5 — 186
- The Theology of Restoration — 187
- Dating Deuteronomy 30:3-5 — 190
The Origin of the Gathering Motif in Ezekiel — 197
- A Sensible Context for the Gathering Motif — 197
- Restoration in Ezekiel — 198
- Modified Vocabulary — 203
- Gathering in Oracles against the Nations — 204
- A Counterpart to the Scattering Motif — 204

Excursus: *Contested Restoration Passages* — 205

The Rhetoric of Allusion — 213

Chapter 8
CONCLUSION 214
   Summary 214
   Ezekiel and Scribal Expansion 216
   Deuteronomy as Divine Torah for Ezekiel 217
   Ezekiel's Use of Scripture 218
   Ezekiel's Relation to the Holiness and Deuteronomic Traditions 219
   Ezekiel as Theologian and Rhetorician 220

Bibliography 221
Index of References 244
Index of Authors 257

Acknowledgments

I am grateful to many who have supported my studies throughout the years. First, I thank my parents, who have encouraged my education at every stage. I acknowledge my primary teachers at the University of Wisconsin–Madison, Professors Michael V. Fox and Cynthia Miller-Naudé, who first taught me how to read and interpret the Hebrew Bible. The family of L. John and Marjorie Look Buyse generously provided a doctoral fellowship for my time at Wheaton College. I thank my dissertation examiners, Professors Margaret S. Odell and Michael Graves, and the two anonymous reviewers for LHBOTS, who provided valuable feedback that improved this work in many ways. I wish to thank Michael Lyons, Paul Joyce, and John Bergsma who have encouraged my work at various stages. Most of all, I wish to express gratitude to my advisor and mentor Daniel I. Block whose commentary has been my companion and guide to the book of Ezekiel. This work is much better because of his input and direction.

I dedicate this book to my wife Melody. I am forever grateful for her sacrifices, along with her constant support and encouragement. Few people match her character and virtues.

List of Abbreviations

AB	Anchor Bible
ABD	*Anchor Bible Dictionary*. Edited by David Noel Freedman. 6 vols. New York, 1992
ACEBTSup	Amsterdamse Cahiers voor Exegese van de Bijbel en zijn Tradities: Supplement Series
AJIL	*American Journal of International Law*
AnBib	Analecta Biblica
ANET	*Ancient Near Eastern Texts Relating to the Old Testament*. Edited by J. B. Pritchard. 3rd ed. Princeton, 1969
ANET Supp	*The Ancient Near East: Supplementary Texts and Pictures Relating to the Old Testament*. Edited by J. B. Pritchard. Princeton, 1969
AOAT	Alter Orient und Altes Testament
AOTC	Apollos Old Testament Commentary
ARAB	*Ancient Records of Assyria and Babylonia*. Daniel David Luckenbill. 2 vols. Chicago, 1926–1927
ATD	Das Alte Testament Deutsch
ATSAT	Arbeiten zu Text und Sprache im Alten Testament
AYB	Anchor Yale Bible
BA	Biblical Archaeologist
BBB	Bonner biblische Beiträge
BBR	*Bulletin for Biblical Research*
Bib	Biblica
BibInt	*Biblical Interpretation*
BibLeb	*Bibel und Leben*
BibOr	Biblica et orientalia
BIS	Biblical Interpretation Series
BJS	Brown Judaic Studies
BPC	Biblical Performance Criticism
BWANT	Beiträge zur Wissenschaft vom Alten und Neuen Testament
BZAW	Beihefte zur Zeitschrift für die alttestamentliche Wissenschaft
BETL	Bibliotheca Ephemeridum Theologicarum Lovanienium
BN	*Biblische Notizen*
BOT	De Boeken van het Oude Testament
BZ	*Biblische Zeitschrift*
CahRB	Cahiers de la Revue Biblique
CBC	Cambridge Bible Commentary

CBET	Contributions to Biblical Exegesis and Theology
CBQ	*Catholic Biblical Quarterly*
CBQMS	Catholic Biblical Quarterly Monograph Series
CBR	*Currents in Biblical Research*
CC	Continental Commentaries
COS	*Context of Scripture*. Edited by W. W. Hallo. 3 vols. Leiden, 1997–2003
DDD	*Dictionary of Deities and Demons in the Bible.* 2nd ed. Edited by K. van der Toorn. Leiden, 1999
DJD	Discoveries in the Judaean Desert
EdF	Ertrage der Forschung
EHS	Europäische Hochschulschriften
ETL	*Ephemerides theologicae lovanienses*
EvT	*Evangelische Theologie*
FAT	Forschungen zum Alten Testament
FOTL	The Forms of the Old Testament Literature
FRLANT	Forschungen zur Religion und Literatur des Alten und Neuen Testaments
FzB	Forschung zur Bibel
GKC	*Gesenius' Hebrew Grammar*. Edited by E. Kautzsch. Translated by A. E. Cowley. 2nd ed. Oxford, 1910
JM	P. Joüon and T. Muraoka. *A Grammar of Biblical Hebrew*. 2nd ed. Rome, 2006
HAT	Handbuch zum Alten Testament
HAR	*Hebrew Annual Review*
HBS	Herders biblische Studien
HeBAI	*Hebrew Bible and Ancient Israel*
HR	*History of Religions*
HS	*Hebrew Studies*
HSM	Harvard Semitic Monographs
HSS	Harvard Semitic Studies
HTIBS	Historic Texts and Interpreters in Biblical Scholarship
HTR	*Harvard Theological Review*
HUCA	*Hebrew Union College Annual*
IBHS	*An Introduction to Biblical Hebrew Syntax*. Bruce K. Waltke and Michael O'Connor. Winona Lake, Indiana, 1990
ICC	International Critical Commentary
Int	*Interpretation*
JAAC	*Journal of Aesthetics and Art Criticism*
JAJ	*Journal of Ancient Judaism*
JANESCU	Journal of the Ancient Near Eastern Society of Columbia University
JBL	*Journal of Biblical Literature*
JETS	*Journal of the Evangelical Theological Society*
JHS	*Journal of Hebrew Scriptures*
JNSL	*Journal of Northwest Semitic Languages*
JQR	*Jewish Quarterly Review*

JSOT	*Journal for the Study of the Old Testament*
JSOTSup	Journal for the Study of the Old Testament: Supplement Series
JSS	*Journal of Semitic Studies*
JTS	*Journal of Theological Studies*
KAT	Kommentar zum Alten Testament
LHBOTS	Library of Hebrew Bible/Old Testament Studies
LNTS	Library of New Testament Studies
LSTS	Library of Second Temple Studies
MCAAS	Memoirs of the Connecticut Academy of Arts and Sciences
MDOG	*Mitteilungen der Deutschen Orient-Gesellschaft*
MSU	Mitteilungen des Septuaginta-Unternehmens
NCB	New Century Bible
NIBC	New International Biblical Commentary
NICOT	New International Commentary on the Old Testament
NIVAC	NIV Application Commentary
NSBT	New Studies in Biblical Theology
OBT	Overtures to Biblical Theology
OTL	Old Testament Library
OTM	Oxford Theological Monographs
OtSt	Oudtestamentische Studiën
PTL	*PTL: A Journal for Descriptive Poetics and Theory of Literature*
PTMS	Princeton Theological Monograph Series
RB	*Revue biblique*
RevQ	*Revue de Qumran*
SAA	State Archives of Assyria
SBB	Stuttgarter biblische Beiträge
SBLAIL	Society of Biblical Literature Ancient Israel and Its Literature
SBLDS	Society of Biblical Literature Dissertation Series
SBLSBL	Society of Biblical Literature Studies in Biblical Literature
SBLSCS	Society of Biblical Literature Septuagint and Cognate Studies
SBLSymS	Society of Biblical Literature Symposium Series
SBT	Studies in Biblical Theology
SBTS	Sources for Biblical and Theological Study
SCS	Septuagint and Cognate Studies
SHANE	Studies in the History of the Ancient Near East
Siphrut	Siphrut: Literature and Theology of the Hebrew Scriptures
SJOT	*Scandinavian Journal of the Old Testament*
SSN	*Studia semitica neerlandica*
TB	Theologische Bücherei: Neudrucke und Berichte aus dem 20 Jahrhundert
TCS	Texts from Cuneiform Sources
TDOT	*Theological Dictionary of the Old Testament*. Edited by G. J. Botterweck and H. Ringgren. Translated by J. T. Willis, G. W. Bromiley, and D. E. Green. 16 vols. Grand Rapids, 1974–2018
UBL	*Ugaritisch-biblische Literatur*
UF	*Ugarit-Forschungen*

VT	*Vetus Testamentum*
VTSup	Supplements to Vetus Testamentum
WBC	Word Biblical Commentary
WMANT	Wissenschaftliche Monographien zum Alten und Neuen Testament
WZKM	*Wiener Zeitschrift für die Kunde des Morgenlandes*
ZABR	*Zeitschrift für altorientalische und biblische Rechtsgeschichte*
ZAH	*Zeitschrift für Althebräistik*
ZAW	*Zeitschrift für die alttestamentliche Wissenschaft*

Chapter 1

INTRODUCTION

Recent studies on the book of Ezekiel reflect an increasing awareness that the prophet drew extensively from the deep reservoir of Israel's texts and traditions.[1] Yet, in the history of modern scholarship, Deuteronomy is virtually absent among the sources said to have influenced Ezekiel in any significant way. This is remarkable, since it is universally accepted that "the style of [Deuteronomy] is one of the most original and distinctive in the OT" and can be discerned in much of biblical literature.[2] In light of Ezekiel's Priestly (specifically, Holiness School) heritage and the marked Priestly nature of the book, connections with Deuteronomy are often minimized. In his influential commentary, Walther Zimmerli, for example, claimed: "Overall the smallness of contact of Ezekiel with the language and ideas of the well-defined world of Deuteronomy is striking."[3]

To be sure, whereas Jeremiah and the Deuteronomistic historians interpret history and their present circumstances primarily through the lens of Deuteronomy, the chief influence for Ezekiel is the Holiness Code of Leviticus 17–26. However, this distinction should not be understood in absolute terms, as R. E. Clements, for example, seems to do when comparing the book of Ezekiel with that of Jeremiah: "Whereas all the theological connections of the book of Jeremiah are with the

---

1. Note especially a volume of essays titled *Transforming Visions: Transformations of Text, Tradition, and Theology in Ezekiel*, ed. William A. Tooman and Michael A. Lyons, PTMS 127 (Eugene, OR: Pickwick, 2010); see below for a review of other works.

2. Millar Burrows, *The Literary Relations of Ezekiel* (Philadelphia: Jewish Publication Society, 1925), 21.

3. Walther Zimmerli, *Ezekiel: A Commentary on the Book of the Prophet Ezekiel*, trans. Ronald E. Clements, 2 vols., Hermeneia (Philadelphia: Fortress, 1979), 1:46.

Deuteronomic movement, those of Ezekiel are to be found in the work of the emergent Priestly school."[4] Baruch Schwartz similarly describes the Priestly character of Ezekiel's theology in nearly absolute terms:

> Everything the prophet says is determined by [his Priestly pedigree]. He explains what went wrong, depicts the results of what went wrong, and predicts the eventual rectification of everything that went wrong, from a thoroughly priestly standpoint.[5]

Some scholars seem not to expect influence from Deuteronomy on Ezekiel, as if the Priestly character of his theology would preclude his acceptance of Deuteronomic ideas.

This study argues that Deuteronomy did influence Ezekiel in significant ways as he formulated his theological response to the crisis surrounding the events of the early sixth century BCE. Although Deuteronomic language may be "relatively muted"[6] in comparison to the pervasive Priestly influence in the book, an examination of Ezekiel's use of Deuteronomy's language and concepts reveals that the prophet not only accepted distinctive elements of Deuteronomic theology but in some cases alluded to specific texts. This study does not attempt an exhaustive comparison of the differences between Ezekiel and Deuteronomy (which are acknowledged). Instead, I focus on the ways in which Ezekiel was influenced by Deuteronomic words and ideas and offer some reflection on how Ezekiel appropriates them through the lens of his Priestly-Holiness tradition. Deuteronomy's influence is discernible not in every area but nevertheless in areas that are significant for his prophetic message. In various ways, it shaped how he saw Israel's past history of rebellion against Yahweh, the present situation of divine judgment, and the future hope of restoration.

---

4. R. E. Clements, "The Ezekiel Tradition: Prophecy in a Time of Crisis," in *Israel's Prophetic Tradition: Essays in Honour of Peter R. Ackroyd*, ed. Richard Coggins, Anthony Phillips, and Michael Knibb (Cambridge: Cambridge University Press, 1982), 126.

5. Baruch Schwartz, "A Priest Out of Place: Reconsidering Ezekiel's Role in the History of the Israelite Priesthood," in *Ezekiel's Hierarchical World: Wrestling with a Tiered Reality*, ed. Stephen L. Cook and Corrine L. Patton, SBLSymS 31 (Atlanta: Society of Biblical Literature, 2004), 62.

6. Paul M. Joyce, *Ezekiel: A Commentary*, LHBOTS 482 (New York: T&T Clark, 2007), 38.

Ezekiel's Use of Texts and Traditions

Ezekiel's knowledge and use of a wide array of earlier biblical literature will be a working assumption of this study.[7] Many have recognized the extent of Ezekiel's knowledge of Israel's texts and traditions. According to Brevard Childs:

> Surely one of the most important aspects of Ezekiel's message was its dependence upon the activity of interpretation within the Bible itself. Not only was Ezekiel deeply immersed in the ancient traditions of Israel, but the prophet's message shows many signs of being influenced by a study of Israel's sacred writings. The impact of a collection of authoritative writings is strong throughout the book.[8]

Similarly, Moshe Greenberg spoke of "the encyclopedic range of Ezekiel's references," explaining that "since he was a priest, we may suppose that in principle everything contained under the rubrics of 'literature' and 'traditions' in the sixth-century BCE kingdom of Judah was accessible to him. And in fact he does allude to almost every genre of literature known from the Bible."[9]

---

7. One exception is John H. Choi, who challenges the notion that pentateuchal traditions influenced non-pentateuchal traditions. He argues that not just Ezekiel, but writers of many non-pentateuchal texts like Ezra, Nehemiah, Chronicles, and the historical Psalms, were unaware of pentateuchal source traditions (*Traditions at Odds: The Reception of the Pentateuch in Biblical and Second Temple Period Literature*, LHBOTS 518 [New York: T&T Clark, 2010], e.g., 243). His treatment of Ezekiel was superficial, amounting only to a brief analysis of the supposed differences between Ezekiel's history in ch. 20 and the pentateuchal historical traditions—a topic that will be treated further in Chapter 6 of this study. He did not analyze Ezekiel's relationship to the Holiness Code or engage scholarship on the topic.

8. Brevard S. Childs, *Introduction to the Old Testament as Scripture* (Philadelphia: Fortress, 1979), 364; cf. John F. Kutsko, *Between Heaven and Earth: Divine Presence and Absence in the Book of Ezekiel*, Biblical and Judaic Studies from the University of California, San Diego 7 (Winona Lake, IN: Eisenbrauns, 2000), 10–14.

9. Moshe Greenberg, *Ezekiel 21–37: A New Translation with Introduction and Commentary*, AB 22A (Garden City, NY: Doubleday, 1997), 395; cf. Kutsko, *Between Heaven and Earth*, 13–14: "Ezekiel belonged to a priestly circle prior to his exile but probably also to a circle that continued within the exilic community…and some of the traditions that are encountered in their final literary form in the Priestly sources of the Pentateuch were also available to Ezekiel in some form, oral or written." Similarly, Jonathan Stökl argues that Ezekiel's apparent awareness of Mesopotamian traditions may indicate he was trained in cuneiform scribal literature ("'A Youth Without Blemish, Handsome, Proficient in All Wisdom, Knowledgeable and Intelligent':

Scholars have further observed that Ezekiel does not mindlessly copy his sources, but in many cases creatively reformulates them. As Corrine Patton (Carvalho) observes, "Ezekiel is known to manipulate well-known texts and motifs. The creative and theological freedom with which this author turns and extends traditions extant in earlier literature marks him as brilliantly creative."[10] Similarly, according to Gerhard von Rad, "the use which he makes of this material, and the way in which he grafts and fuses it into quite dissimilar elements in his preaching, point to an unusual intellectual ability to integrate material."[11]

Furthermore, Ezekiel's use of antecedent texts is not simply ornamental but instead carries a rhetorical force for his prophetic message. While dealing with the physical and emotional trauma of exile, Ezekiel's audience wrestled with theological and existential questions, such as: "Why did this happen to us? What is the status of our relationship with Yhwh?"[12] In this context, Ezekiel's rhetorical goals were, as Lyons summarizes, "to explain the reason for the exile, justify the destruction of Jerusalem as Yhwh's punishment for the people's behavior, prevent assimilation and despair, and convince his fellow-exiles that national restoration is possible."[13] As this study will argue, Ezekiel's creative use of scriptural texts was a significant tool to persuade his audience.

Studies of Ezekiel's relationship to other biblical books appeared as early as 1925 with Millar Burrows' Yale dissertation *The Literary Relations of Ezekiel*.[14] His work constitutes an early recognition of the many literary connections between the book of Ezekiel and other biblical literature. Burrows thought that in most cases the book of Ezekiel was

Ezekiel's Access to Babylonian Culture," in *Exile and Return: The Babylonian Context*, ed. Jonathan Stökl and Caroline Waerzeggers [Berlin: de Gruyter, 2015], 223–52).

10. Corrine L. Patton, "Pan-Deuteronomism and the Book of Ezekiel," in *Those Elusive Deuteronomists: The Phenomenon of Pan-Deuteronomism*, ed. L. S. Schearing and S. L. McKenzie, JSOTSup 268 (Sheffield: Sheffield Academic, 1999), 205; cf. idem, "Priest, Prophet, and Exile: Ezekiel as a Literary Construct," in Cook and Patton, eds., *Ezekiel's Hierarchical World*, 75–6: "The author of Ezekiel was a highly literate scribe, familiar with a wide range of stories and traditions."

11. Gerhard von Rad, *The Message of the Prophets*, trans. D. M. G. Stalker (New York: Harper & Row, 1968), 190; trans. of *Die Botschaft der Propheten*, Siebenstern Taschenbuch 188 (Munich: Gütersloher, 1967).

12. Michael A. Lyons, "Persuasion and Allusion: The Rhetoric of Text-Referencing in Ezekiel," in *Text and Canon: Essays in Honor of John H. Sailhamer*, ed. Robert L. Cole and Paul J. Kissling (Eugene, OR: Pickwick, 2017), 77.

13. Ibid., 78.

14. Burrows, *The Literary Relations of Ezekiel*.

dependent, but with his teacher C. C. Torrey he regarded the book as a product of "the late pre-Maccabean period."[15] Thus, in his view, the literary borrowing was the work of a late author, not the sixth-century prophet.

A half-century later, Keith Carley examined Ezekiel's relationship to various streams of tradition in ancient Israel. Unlike Burrows, Carley found the literary connections in the book to be a product of the prophet himself. Focusing especially on the biblical prophetic tradition, he concluded that Ezekiel knew himself to be "the heir to a long prophetic heritage…and he strove to maintain it."[16] After giving some attention to links with Deuteronomy and the Holiness Code, Carley concluded by affirming the significant role of earlier traditions for Ezekiel: "In his attempt to come to terms with the tragic fate of his people, Ezekiel drew on and developed many other strands of Israelite tradition."[17]

The commentaries of Moshe Greenberg and Daniel Block stand out by their special attention to Ezekiel's relationship to ancient texts and traditions.[18] In many cases, they did not simply identify shared language but also addressed the way in which the prophet alluded to his sources and his purposes for doing so. Greenberg devoted an article to analyzing special examples in greater detail, including the backgrounds for Ezekiel's lion imagery in ch. 19, the figure of the vine in ch. 15, and the image of Israel as faithless wife in ch. 16.[19] Like other scholars, he affirmed that Ezekiel employed tradition freely, "shaping it for his particular purposes and inventing new features in it to suit them."[20]

In her 2002 study *A New Heart and a New Soul: Ezekiel, the Exile, and the Torah*, Risa Levitt Kohn examined the affinities between the book of Ezekiel and the Priestly and Deuteronomic sources of the Pentateuch.[21]

---

15. Ibid., 101–5; C. C. Torrey, *Pseudo-Ezekiel and the Original Prophecy* (New Haven: Yale University Press, 1930).

16. Keith W. Carley, *Ezekiel among the Prophets: A Study of Ezekiel's Place in Prophetic Tradition*, SBT 2/31 (London: SCM, 1975), 77.

17. Ibid., 80.

18. Moshe Greenberg, *Ezekiel 1–20: A New Translation with Introduction and Commentary*, AB 22 (Garden City, NY: Doubleday, 1983); idem, *Ezekiel 21–37*; Daniel I. Block, *The Book of Ezekiel*, 2 vols., NICOT (Grand Rapids: Eerdmans, 1997, 1998).

19. Moshe Greenberg, "Notes on the Influence of Tradition on Ezekiel," *JANESCU* 22 (1993): 29–37.

20. Ibid., 36.

21. Risa Levitt Kohn, *A New Heart and a New Soul: Ezekiel, the Exile and the Torah*, JSOTSup 358 (Sheffield: Sheffield Academic, 2002).

Her study sought to demonstrate that the verbal parallels with Israel's literary traditions are best explained as Ezekiel's purposeful use of earlier texts. After identifying shared locutions, she concluded that Ezekiel draws from both the Priestly and Deuteronomic literature for various purposes, including the indictment of the people based on their legal prescriptions.[22] According to Levitt Kohn, the result was a unique synthesis of Priestly and Deuteronomic ideas. Her study was seminal insofar as it recognized a degree of Deuteronomic influence on Ezekiel. On the shortcomings of Levitt Kohn's work, see below in the section "Scholarly Views on Ezekiel and Deuteronomy."

The most significant study of Ezekiel's use of earlier texts is Michael Lyon's *From Law to Prophecy: Ezekiel's Use of the Holiness Code*.[23] Using sophisticated methods for determining the direction of literary dependence, he argues convincingly that the numerous verbal parallels between the Holiness Code (H) and Ezekiel are best explained by Ezekiel's appropriation of H's legal material for his prophetic oracles.[24] The significance of Lyons' work for this study is wide ranging. First, quite simply, Lyons has shown that Ezekiel drew extensively from an authoritative Israelite text as a resource for his prophetic message. Second, Lyons does not simply identify verbal parallels but shows how Ezekiel uses the earlier text in distinct ways that may be classified as techniques of literary modification. Third, Lyons has outlined the rhetorical functions of Ezekiel's use of the Holiness Code, namely, to appropriate its language in order to issue indictment, announce judgment, and predict restoration for Israel.

---

22. Ibid., 113. Cf. Yehezkel Kaufmann, *The Religion of Israel: From Its Beginnings to the Babylonian Exile*, trans. Moshe Greenberg (Chicago: University of Chicago Press, 1960), 435: "The priesthood was particularly inclined to this idea, attributing the national calamity to violation of God's Torah. Ezekiel gives it prophetic expression."

23. Michael A. Lyons, *From Law to Prophecy: Ezekiel's Use of the Holiness Code*, LHBOTS 507 (New York: T&T Clark, 2009). See my review in *BBR* 21 (2011): 111–12. Note also Lyons, "Marking Innerbiblical Allusion in the Book of Ezekiel," *Bib* 88 (2007): 245–50.

24. Drawing upon the method of Richard Schultz (*The Search for Quotation: Verbal Parallels in the Prophets*, JSOTSup 180 [Sheffield: Sheffield Academic, 1999]), Lyons shows how the text of Ezekiel sometimes (1) reflects modification of the source text in line with the prophet's distinctive style and theology; (2) only partially integrates the source text and therefore displays indications of its original context that are incongruous with the new context; (3) shows conceptual dependence on H that requires the reader to supply information from the source text in order to understand the borrowing text; and finally (4) introduces expansions that interpret the source text.

A volume of essays titled *Transforming Visions* is devoted specifically to Ezekiel's creative use of texts and traditions. Edited by William Tooman and Michael Lyons, the volume includes essays on the prophet's transformation of antecedent texts and his innovations relating to subjects in Israelite tradition and theology.[25] The essays that treat Ezekiel's use of texts are most relevant to this study, including Michael Lyons' condensation of his monograph *From Law to Prophecy* and Tova Ganzel's study of Ezekiel's language of idolatry and its relationship to pentateuchal descriptions.[26] The latter serves as a point of departure for Chapter 3 of this study. The volume represents an important example of the growing recognition of Ezekiel as a prophet who drew extensively from Israel's texts and traditions.

Citing Scripture in an Oral World

But what does it mean to say that Ezekiel knew and alluded to literary traditions? I do not presuppose Ezekiel had a written copy of Deuteronomy (in whatever form) before him. Although as a priest in the upper-echelon of society the prophet may have had access to written scrolls,[27] alternatively it may be that Ezekiel knew parts of Deuteronomy and other literary traditions from memory—whether from earlier reading written texts or from hearing the texts read aloud by orators. Scholars increasingly recognize the ancient Near Eastern world was an oral

---

25. Tooman and Lyons, eds., *Transforming Visions*. I have summarized and evaluated the various essays elsewhere (see my review in *JHS* 11 [2011], online: http:// www.jhsonline.org).

26. Michael A. Lyons, "Transformation of Law: Ezekiel's Use of the Holiness Code (Leviticus 17–26)," in Tooman and Lyons, eds., *Transforming Visions*, 1–32; and in the same volume, Tova Ganzel, "The Transformation of Pentateuchal Descriptions of Idolatry in Ezekiel," 33–49.

27. See Ellen F. Davis, *Swallowing the Scroll: Textuality and the Dynamics of Discourse in Ezekiel's Prophecy*, JSOTSup 78, Bible and Literature 21 (Sheffield: Sheffield Academic, 1989), 39–41. On degrees of literacy in the ancient world, see Susan Niditch, *Oral World and Written Word: Ancient Israelite Literature* (Louisville: Westminster John Knox, 1996), 39–41.

On Ezekiel as a priest in exile (away from the Jerusalem temple), see Andrew Mein, "Ezekiel as a Priest in Exile," in *The Elusive Prophet: The Prophet as Historical Person, Literary Character and Anonymous Artist*, ed. Johannes C. de Moor, OtSt 45 (Leiden: Brill, 2001), 199–213; Marvin A. Sweeney, "Ezekiel: Zadokite Priest and Visionary Prophet of the Exile," in *Form and Intertextuality in Prophetic and Apocalyptic Literature*, FAT 45 (Tübingen: Mohr Siebeck, 2005), 125–43.

culture in which written copies of literary traditions functioned primarily for oral performance.[28] In David M. Carr's words, "copies of texts served as solidified reference points for recitation and memorization of the tradition."[29] Indeed, the memorization of literary traditions was a staple of scribal education:

> Students in a culture such as Israel's learned the *written* tradition in an *oral-performative* and *communal* context. Whether this took the form of a beginning student singing the alphabet or a scribal master orally presenting the written Torah to a broader audience, the writing-reading process for literary texts was supported by and oriented toward a process of memorization of tradition by the individual and performance of the tradition and adaptation of it for a community or sub-community.[30]

The implications for this study are significant. As an educated and presumably highly literate member of society, Ezekiel likely knew parts of Israel's written traditions by memory,[31] or may have been exposed to oral recitations of the traditions by those who had memorized them. In either case, Ezekiel could have used and cited literary traditions without a written text before him.

---

28. See, e.g., Niditch, *Oral World*, 5–6; Karel van der Toorn, *Scribal Culture and the Making of the Hebrew Bible* (Cambridge, MA: Harvard University Press, 2007), 2, 5, 11–16: "To the public at large, the books of the Bible were icons of a body of knowledge accessible only through the oral instruction presented by religious experts" (p. 2); Robert S. Miller II, "The Performance of Oral Tradition in Ancient Israel," in *Contextualizing Israel's Sacred Writings: Ancient Literacy, Orality, and Literary Production*, ed. Brian B. Schmidt, SBLAIL 22 (Atlanta: SBL, 2015), 161–74; idem, *Oral Tradition in Ancient Israel*, BPC 4 (Eugene, OR: Cascade, 2011).

On the interplay between orality and textuality, see Walter Ong, *Oral World and Literacy*, 2nd ed. (London: Routledge, 2002); Graham Furniss, *Orality: The Power of the Spoken Word* (New York: Palgrave Macmillan, 2004); Ruth Finnegan, *Literacy and Orality* (Oxford: Basil Blackwell, 1988); Jack Goody, *The Interface between the Written and the Oral* (Cambridge: Cambridge University Press, 1987).

29. David M. Carr, *Writing on the Tablet of the Heart: Origins of Scripture and Literature* (Oxford: Oxford University Press, 2005), 6; see also idem, "Orality, Textuality, and Memory: The State of Biblical Studies," in Schmidt, ed., *Contextualizing Israel's Sacred Writings*, 161–73.

30. David M. Carr, *The Formation of the Hebrew Bible: A New Reconstruction* (Oxford: Oxford University Press, 2011), 5 (author's italics).

31. Carr claims that "an oral-written mastery of a body of texts…was something that *separated* the members of an elite from their contemporaries" (*Writing on the Tablet*, 13).

Understanding the oral culture of ancient Israel helps us understand the intertextual nature of a biblical book like Ezekiel.[32] As Carr explains: "It is increasingly clear how much of Israelite literature is…'intertextual.' But it is not intertextual in the sense that early Israelite authors were constantly engaged in a process of *visually* consulting, citing, and interpreting separate written texts."[33] Susan Niditch states that "even if [people in oral cultures] have read the works themselves, they quote from memory."[34] Carr elaborates:

> Ancient authors…did not require the ancient texts to be before them. Instead, they had already ingested such texts in the process of their education-enculturation. These ancient texts were part of their vocabulary… [and therefore] they could cite or consciously 'allude' to them.[35]

Since manuscripts "would have frequently been unwieldy, lengthy rolls of leather, in which simply finding 'the right place' would have been difficult,"[36] ancient writers or speakers "most likely would have drawn on their verbatim memory of other texts in quoting, borrowing from, and significantly revising them."[37]

Carr's words provide a powerful explanation for the many verbal parallels between Ezekiel and Israel's literary traditions when he states that Israel's scribes and orators used memorization to create "new works that often echo those works in which the scribal author was trained."[38] Carr explains that, as "fully educated literate specialists,"

---

32. Here I use "intertextual" in a diachronic sense, not as it is used by Julia Kristeva and in much of modern literary criticism (see the section on "Influence" below).

33. Carr, *Writing on the Tablet*, 159 (italics mine).

34. Niditch, *Oral World*, 5, see also 18–19. Cf. Carr, *Writing on the Tablet*, 40.

35. Carr, *Writing on the Tablet*, 159.

36. Niditch, *Oral World*, 41.

37. Carr, *Writing on the Tablet*, 161–2. Cf. idem, *Formation of the Hebrew Bible*, 6: "scribes referred to and adapted earlier written traditions *in memorized form*" (author's italics); idem, "Orality, Textuality, and Memory," 168.

38. Carr, *Writing on the Tablet*, 159; cf. Ziony Zevit: "Originality in ancient Israel may have consisted in drawing liberally from stores of memorized, partially memorized, and incompletely recalled materials deemed traditionally acceptable… All of this would have been common knowledge in the public domain. New authors, if talented, altered old templates for better, or for worse, if they were not. They attired their thoughts in literary and stylistic hand-me-downs, very much aware of the cultural attitudes affecting their use of generic patterns and language" ("Echoes of Texts Past," in *Subtle Citation, Allusion, and Translation in the Hebrew Bible*, ed. Ziony Zevit [Sheffield: Equinox, 2017], 8).

[the scribes'] training in verbatim memorization in a text-supported environment gave them tools for exact or semiexact repetition that allowed them to produce works that featured remarkably precise parallels… Though occasionally an author might have consulted an earlier locus in a scroll, such echoing did not require visual copying. An author could construct elaborate (semi)repetitions through memorization skills learned in having multiple texts 'inscribed on [his or her] heart.'[39]

Since scribal training would have been included in Ezekiel's preparation as a priest (see further below in the section "Ezekiel's Role in Producing the Book"),[40] Ezekiel's familiarity with Israelite and Near Eastern traditions can be attributed to his "priestly, cosmopolitan training."[41] Ellen Davis explains:

A Zadokite priest, he presumably prepared from an early age for the rigorous task of interpreting and pronouncing the law, and this preparation undoubtedly involved the careful study of texts. Ezekiel demonstrates "intellectualist training" which is not only exacting but broad: he draws upon historical and prophetic traditions as readily as legal ones, and the ease with which he manipulates mythic elements and calls forth vivid images bespeaks intimacy with the literary heritage of Israel and its neighbors.[42]

To conclude, the book of Ezekiel owes much of its intertextual character to the prophet's deep familiarity with Israel's literary traditions and his ability to adapt them creatively from memory.

Ezekiel's Relationship to Deuteronomy

The aforementioned studies provide appropriate context in which to view the prophet's relationship to Deuteronomy. Ezekiel is known to appropriate and adapt earlier literary traditions, and thus it is worth investigating whether he uses Deuteronomy in similar ways and for similar purposes.

The Terms "Deuteronomic" and "Deuteronomistic"

It is necessary at this point to define the meaning of "Deuteronomic" in this study, since scholars use the terms "Deuteronomic" and "Deuteronomistic" in different ways. Despite Martin Noth's introduction of

---

39. Carr, *Writing on the Tablet*, 159–60 (italics mine).
40. Ibid., 152; van der Toorn, *Scribal Culture*, 85.
41. Stephen L. Cook, *The Apocalyptic Literature*, Interpreting Biblical Texts (Nashville: Abingdon, 2003), 96.
42. Davis, *Swallowing the Scroll*, 40.

the term "Deuteronomistic" (*deuteronomistiche*),[43] some use the terms interchangeably,[44] so that the historical work of Deuteronomy–Kings, for example, can be described as the "Deuteronomic" or "Deuteronomistic" History. In this study, I maintain a distinction between the two by reserving the term "Deuteronomic" for the language and theology of Deuteronomy proper and "Deuteronomistic" for the set of theological ideas, related to Deuteronomy, that produced the Deuteronomistic History (DtrH) in the late monarchic and exilic periods.[45] Of course, the study of Deuteronomy and DtrH are intertwined and cannot be easily separated. Nevertheless, this study focuses more on Ezekiel's relationship to Deuteronomy as a literary tradition than to Deuteronomistic theology broadly.

The Status of Deuteronomy at the Time of Ezekiel

By most accounts of Deuteronomy's provenance, the book originated during the monarchic period, and therefore existed in some form at the time of Ezekiel.[46] Regardless of its origins before Josiah's reform in 622 BCE, the book—or some *Urdeuteronomium*—significantly shaped the religious

---

43. Martin Noth, *The Deuteronomistic History*, JSOTSup 15 (Sheffield: Sheffield Academic, 1981).

44. E.g., Raymond F. Person Jr., *The Deuteronomic School: History, Social Setting, and Literature*, SBLSBL 2 (Atlanta: Society of Biblical Literature, 2002), 6–7.

45. Cf. Richard Coggins, "What does 'Deuteronomistic' Mean?" in *Words Remembered, Texts Renewed: Essays in Honour of John F. A. Sawyer*, ed. Jon Davies, Graham Harvey, and Wilfred G. E. Watson, JSOTSup 195 (Sheffield: Sheffield Academic, 1995), 135–48; repr. in Schearing and McKenzie, eds., *Those Elusive Deuteronomists*, 22–35.

46. E.g., Albrecht Alt, "Die Heimat des Deuteronomiums," in *Kleine Schriften zur Geschichte des Volkes Israel*, 3 vols. (Munich: Beck, 1953), 2:250–1; Gerhard von Rad, *Deuteronomy: A Commentary*, trans. Dorothea Barton, OTL (Philadelphia: Westminster, 1966), 23–7; E. W. Nicholson, *Deuteronomy and Tradition: Literary and Historical Problems in the Book of Deuteronomy* (Philadelphia: Fortress, 1967), 58–82; Richard D. Nelson, *Deuteronomy: A Commentary*, OTL (Louisville: Westminster John Knox, 2002), 7–8; Eckart Otto, "The Pre-Exilic Deuteronomy as a Revision of the Covenant Code," in *Kontinuum und Proprium: Studien zur Sozial- und Rechtsgeschichte des Alten Orients und des Alten Testaments* (Wiesbaden: Harrassowitz, 1996), 112–22; Bernard M. Levinson and Jeffrey Stackert, "Between the Covenant Code and Esarhaddon's Succession Treaty: Deuteronomy 13 and the Composition of Deuteronomy," *JAJ* 3 (2012): 123–40.

This study does not attempt to evaluate studies that place Deuteronomy in the exilic or postexilic periods (e.g., Ernest Nicholson, *Deuteronomy and the Judaean Diaspora* [Oxford: Oxford University Press, 2014]; Juha Pakkala, "The Date of the

world of Judah, particularly Jerusalem, in the twenty-five year period before Ezekiel's exile. Ezekiel likely would have been exposed to the book in some form at the turn of the sixth century, whether in Jerusalem before the deportation of 597 BCE or after in Babylonian exile.[47] The exact shape of the book at that time is a matter of debate, but many scholars—particularly those in North America—agree that the version known in Ezekiel's time would likely have been comparable to its final form. The major exceptions might be the passages commonly attributed to an exilic redactor (Dtr2), which will receive special attention later. While I will argue that Ezekiel could have known parts of Deuteronomy 4 and 30, I do not assume that Deuteronomy had reached its final form by Ezekiel's time. Even if it can be shown that Ezekiel knew or alluded to parts of Deuteronomy, this study does not claim that he therefore knew the book in its entirety or in its final form. Nor, as argued above, does it claim that Ezekiel necessarily had access to written copies of Deuteronomy, since the prophet may have alluded to Deuteronomy from memory or from his familiarity with these texts from oral performance.

Scholarly Views on Ezekiel and Deuteronomy

While some scholars have identified a limited number of locutions shared by the two books, no study has attempted an extensive investigation of Deuteronomy's influence on Ezekiel. A few scholars have made passing remarks about the subject, in most cases asserting the limited extent of Deuteronomic influence compared to Priestly influence. Without citing any specific links with Deuteronomy, Yehezkel Kaufmann simply acknowledges that Ezekiel "is influenced by Deuteronomy, but more by the Priestly Code."[48] Jacob Milgrom grants the presence of Deuteronomic thought, but asserts that "Deuteronomy's language is hardly recognizable in Ezekiel."[49] For Milgrom, this is understandable, because "Ezekiel is a

---

Oldest Edition of Deuteronomy," *ZAW* 121 [2009]: 388–401), except to argue that some verbal parallels between Deuteronomy and Ezekiel are best explained by the priority of Deuteronomic texts and Ezekiel's allusion to them.

47. Cf. Menahem Haran, "Ezekiel, P, and the Priestly School," *VT* 58 (2008): 214; Johanna Stiebert, *The Exile and the Prophet's Wife: Historic Events and Marginal Perspectives* (Collegeville, MN: Liturgical, 2005), 16 n. 31.

48. Kaufmann, *Religion of Israel*, 433; similarly, Carol A. Newsom, "Moral 'Recipes' in Deuteronomy and Ezekiel: Divine Authority and Human Agency," *HeBAI* 6 (2017): 502.

49. Jacob Milgrom, "The Nature and Extent of Idolatry in Eighth-Seventh Century Judah," *HUCA* 69 (1998): 6.

priest and would be expected to clothe his ideas in priestly language."[50] Robert Wilson similarly finds some Deuteronomic ideas in Ezekiel, but asserts that they are expressed in Priestly ("Jerusalemite") rather than Deuteronomic ("Ephraimite") language.[51] Some speak of Ezekiel's familiarity with the Deuteronom(ist)ic school of thought, but not the book of Deuteronomy specifically.[52] Others acknowledge verbal or conceptual similarities between the two books but refrain from making conclusions about a direct literary relationship.[53]

One of the few early scholars to posit direct Deuteronomic influence in Ezekiel did so based in part on his belief that the book of Ezekiel is a product of the Hellenistic period. In *The Literary Relations of Ezekiel*, Burrows devoted a few pages to connections between Deuteronomy and Ezekiel,[54] listing about eight possible literary links, some more convincing than others. Although Burrows believed it was a later author who drew from Deuteronomy and not the prophet himself, he offered another reason for the priority of Deuteronomy, stating: "It is universally accepted that the style of Dt is one of the most original and distinctive in the OT and has exercised a wide-spread influence. Ez, on the contrary, is constantly reminiscent; therefore his dependence upon Dt is to be inferred unless strong evidence should appear to the contrary."[55]

Carley also discussed Ezekiel's relationship to Deuteronomy, citing some noteworthy links that led him to conclude that Ezekiel was by no means in conflict with Deuteronomy.[56] Nevertheless, he found little evidence of Deuteronomy's direct influence. He appealed to the alleged Northern provenance of Deuteronomy and Jerusalemite provenance of the

---

50. Ibid.

51. Robert R. Wilson, *Prophecy and Society in Ancient Israel* (Philadelphia: Fortress, 1980), 284.

52. E.g., Corrine Patton, "'I Myself Gave Them Laws That Were Not Good': Ezekiel 20 and the Exodus Traditions," *JSOT* 69 (1996): 84.

53. E.g., Kutsko, *Between Heaven and Earth*, 11. Cf. Ken-ichi Nogi, "The Main Theological Concepts of the Book of Deuteronomy and Their Influence on Jeremiah and Ezekiel" (MA thesis, Columbia Theological Seminary, 1971), who found only "a slight influence of Deuteronomy" in Ezekiel. Regarding the possibility of dependence, he concluded: "There are similarities between Deuteronomy and Ezekiel, but we can not decide whether they are really due to the direct influence of Deuteronomy or not." Nogi's conclusion reflects the common consensus, but the work did not use clear methodological criteria.

54. Burrows, *Literary Relations of Ezekiel*, 19–23.

55. Ibid., 21.

56. Carley, *Ezekiel Among the Prophets*, 57–62.

Holiness Code for an explanation, suggesting that "it would have been natural for Ezekiel to draw on a tradition from his own area whenever it was parallel to Deuteronomy."[57]

More recently, Baruch Schwartz has downplayed the alleged shared language that has been recognized by other scholars, concluding that "the Deuteronomic contribution amounts to nothing more than a few expressions."[58] "To enrich his prophetic *rhetoric*," argued Schwartz, "Ezekiel has made use of a cluster of words he picked up from the Deuteronomic circles, but these have had not the slightest effect on his prophetic *message*." Schwartz makes the strong claim that Ezekiel "has categorically rejected D's theology":

> [H]e accepts absolutely none of the essentials of Deuteronomic theology: not the Deuteronomic depiction of Israel's origins (election out of love, Israel as God's inherently holy, treasured people, the Exodus as a redemption from slavery to freedom), not the Deuteronomic hope for Israel's future (the exile as a catalyst for spontaneous repentance, followed by the ingathering of the exiles as an act of grace and mercy), and none of D's laws. Ezekiel shows no sign of having been influenced in the least by D's doctrine of transgenerational, inherited and accumulated guilt and merit.

While Schwartz's assertion that Ezekiel draws only minimally from Deuteronomic language exemplifies the common view that Ezekiel stands outside of the Deuteronomic movement, his explicit claim that the prophet *rejects* outright the most characteristic tenets of Deuteronomic theology represents a step further than what has previously been proposed.

The most focused study of Deuteronomy and Ezekiel is Miroslav Varšo's dissertation from the University of Vienna, titled "Das Deuteronomium mit Ezechiel lesen: eine intertextuelle Studie."[59] The work consists of essays on topics such as foreign gods, abominations, life and death, and righteousness and wickedness. However, the dissertation is not interested in the diachronic phenomenon of influence, preferring instead a synchronic approach. Varšo explains that his research began with diachronic questions in mind, but gradually moved to a

---

57. Ibid., 57.
58. Baruch Schwartz, "Ezekiel, P, and the Other Pentateuchal Sources" (paper presented at the annual meeting of the Society of Biblical Literature, Washington, DC, 19 November 2006), no page numbers.
59. Miroslav Varšo, "Das Deuteronomium mit Ezechiel lesen: eine intertextuelle Studie" (PhD diss., University of Vienna, 2002).

"kanonisch-intertextuellen Lektüre" of the books,⁶⁰ modeled after Georg Steins' application of Bakhtinian dialogism to biblical literature.⁶¹ Varšo cites similarities between Ezekiel and Deuteronomy, in some cases referring to a "gegenseitigem Verhältnis" or a "lexematische Brücke" between the two books,⁶² but he rarely makes conclusions about literary dependence and its direction. In one instance, he simply remarks: "Die Beziehung der Belege in Ezechiel zu jenen im Deuteronomium ist fraglich."⁶³ Varšo deals with some of the connections treated in this study, but his discussions have limited value for the objective here, namely, ascertaining Deuteronomic influence on Ezekiel.

The most notable attempt to assess the extent of Deuteronomic influence in Ezekiel is Levitt Kohn's *A New Heart and a New Soul: Ezekiel, the Exile, and the Torah*, which devoted one chapter to Ezekiel's use of Deuteronomic language.⁶⁴ She offered a list of twenty-one terms shared by D/Dtr⁶⁵ and Ezekiel and concluded that Ezekiel was influenced by both Deuteronomic concepts and language, fusing them with Priestly ideas to create a unique synthesis.⁶⁶ Levitt Kohn's work has raised the scholarly consciousness regarding Ezekiel's use of Deuteronomic words and concepts. However, further study is required for a number of reasons. First, since her consideration of Deuteronomic language in Ezekiel was only one part of her work, her work was not a thorough treatment of Deuteronomic influence. Second, Levitt Kohn did not use a well-defined method to distinguish literary borrowing from coincidental similarities.⁶⁷ Third, the mere identification of shared language does not begin to explain *how* Ezekiel might have used the borrowed language. She does not describe the literary techniques by which Ezekiel appropriates

---

60. Ibid., 10.
61. Georg Steins, *"Bindung Isaaks" im Kanon (Gen 22): Grundlagen und Programm einer Kanonisch-Intertextuellen Lektüre*, HBS 20 (Freiburg: Herder, 1999).
62. Varšo, "Das Deuteronomium mit Ezechiel," 42 n. 110, 43, respectively.
63. Ibid., 40.
64. Levitt Kohn, *New Heart*, 86–95.
65. For Levitt Kohn, D roughly corresponds to the book of Deuteronomy and Dtr to the Deuteronomic redactor(s) of Deuteronomy–Kings.
66. Levitt Kohn, *New Heart*, 94–6.
67. Cf. Michael Konkel's evaluation of her treatment of Ezek. 20: "Ezekiel 20 is one of the key references for the fusion of Priestly and Deuteronomistic traditions. A much more sophisticated and careful approach is necessary to understand how this fusion has taken place" (review of *Ezekiel's Hierarchical World: Wrestling with a Tiered Reality*, *RBL* 2005, online: http://www.bookreviews.org).

Deuteronomic language, nor how Ezekiel incorporates it rhetorically into his prophetic message. Fourth, Levitt Kohn did not sufficiently describe Ezekiel as a creative theologian who adapts Israel's tradition and forges his own unique path.[68] For these reasons, to determine the extent of Deuteronomic influence in Ezekiel, a full-scale study that goes much deeper than Levitt Kohn's preliminary work on the relationship between these two books is needed.

Ezekiel the Prophet, Ezekiel the Book

The Unity of the Book

Is it possible to speak of Deuteronomy's influence on the prophet himself, or only Deuteronomic language in the book that bears his name? To answer this question, we must consider the extent to which the book reflects the message of the sixth-century prophet. To begin, it is important to recognize the canonical prophets are not authors in the modern sense. In fact, the modern conception of an author as an individual artist who solitarily creates a book is foreign to the ancient world.[69] In the case of prophetic books, normally it was a scribe who wrote and compiled a prophet's messages, not the prophet himself (cf. Jer. 36).[70] The books were then preserved and shaped by the scribal class, a group of professional scholars who produced and copied Israel's written traditions.[71] Over time, as biblical books were copied and performed aloud to a listening public, the texts continued to be shaped by the complex interplay between the written text and oral-performative reading traditions.[72] Thus, it is imperative to understand the formation of biblical literature in light of ancient modes of text production, not modern conceptions of individual authorship. Even if we remain cautious about the ability of modern scholars to uncover pre-canonical literary stages with any degree of certainty, it is clear many books of the Hebrew Bible bear witness to a complex compositional process before arriving at their final form.

---

68. Cf. Joyce, *Ezekiel*, 38: "Her picture of Ezekiel as synthesizer and reconciler stands at odds with the evidence that he was an intensive and distinctive figure, influenced by various traditions (as we have seen) but far from being a 'lowest common denominator' person."

69. On the stark differences between modern and ancient conceptions of authorship, see van der Toorn, *Scribal Culture*, 27–49.

70. See ibid., 182, 184–8, 203.

71. Ibid., esp. 75–6.

72. Carr, *Formation of the Hebrew Bible*.

Although the book of Ezekiel, like other biblical books, certainly developed over time,[73] Ezekiel stands out among the prophetic books of the Hebrew Bible for its remarkable degree of literary and theological coherence, leading many scholars to believe the book by and large represents the message of the prophet. Unlike many other prophetic books, which "are not the kind of literary works which follow from the master plan of a single creative mind,"[74] the book of Ezekiel exhibits a remarkably coherent design and structure. In English-speaking scholarship, recent decades have witnessed broad agreement on the theological and literary unity of the book,[75] due in part to the work of Moshe Greenberg, who critiqued scholarly attempts to reconstruct the book's composition history.[76] While Greenberg took a staunchly conservative approach to the

---

73. While scholars disagree about the level of expansion in the book, at a minimum the MT of Ezekiel appears to reflect a degree of textual growth in comparison to the slightly shorter LXX version of the book (see below).

74. William McKane, "Prophecy and the Prophetic Literature," in *Tradition and Interpretation: Essays by Members of the Society for Old Testament Study*, ed. George W. Anderson (Oxford: Clarendon, 1979), 181; cited in van der Toorn, *Scribal Culture*, 177.

75. Cf. Konkel, review of *Ezekiel's Hierarchical World*: "The holistic approach, represented by the commentaries of M. Greenberg and D. I. Block, is the dominant paradigm of North American Ezekiel scholarship." According to Lyons, "there is a significant difference of opinion between Continental scholarship (which tends to find multiple redactional layers) and non-Continental scholarship (which tends to be skeptical about the existence of multiple layers, and to label attempts to recover them as 'overly complex'" (*Introduction to the Study of Ezekiel*, 65). One significant exception is Volkmar Premstaller, who follows the holistic approach (*Fremdvölkersprüche des Ezechielbuches*, FzB 104 [Würzburg, Echter, 2005]).

76. Greenberg questioned scholarly assumptions regarding style, repetition, and consistency ("What Are Valid Criteria for Determining Inauthentic Matter in Ezekiel?" in *Ezekiel and His Book: Textual and Literary Criticism and Their Interrelation*, ed. J. Lust, BETL 74 [Leuven: Leuven University Press, 1986], 123–35, esp. 128–34) and advised that "a priori expectations of how prophets express themselves cannot serve in place of descriptions of the stylistic habits of given prophetic collections" (Greenberg, *Ezekiel 21–37*, 598). He argued that instead of analyzing biblical literature by the canons of ancient literature, modern critics often judge texts based on their personal standards of literary unity, which differ among scholars and thus produce varied results. Cf. Walther Eichrodt's criticism of Gustav Hölscher, who denied most of the book to Ezekiel: "Because of his ideal picture of what a poet-prophet ought to do, he fails to do justice to the actual characteristics of the prophet with whom we have to deal" (Walther Eichrodt, *Ezekiel: A Commentary*, trans. Cosslett Quin, OTL [Philadelphia: Westminster, 1970], 202–3).

authorship of the book, recognizing few secondary elements, mainstream critical scholarship in North America and Britain largely follows a path between Zimmerli and Greenberg, highlighting the overall literary unity of the book while acknowledging a degree of redactional activity.[77]

In the book of Ezekiel, the primary argument against widespread and extensive redactional activity lies in its overall stylistic and theological uniformity. Paul Joyce, for example, argues that the book resists textual stratification because of the "marked homogeneity of the Ezekiel tradition, in which secondary material bears an unusually close 'family resemblance' to primary."[78] While acknowledging some interpolations in the book, Joyce raises doubts about the validity of the criteria typically used to distinguish secondary material from primary material, including: Deuteronomistic affinities, repetition, and hopeful conclusions to oracles of judgment.[79] Due to the inconclusive nature of these criteria, he suggests a broad range of evidence must be garnered to identify secondary material with any degree of confidence. To Joyce and many others, a moderately holistic approach seems appropriate for this prophetic book, one that takes seriously the presence of redactional activity but finds overly optimistic textual stratifications unconvincing.[80] This study adopts a similar approach due to the book's remarkable degree of literary and theological unity.

Ezekiel's Role in Producing the Book

How do we account for this unity? The distinct "Ezekielian" nature and style of even the material that may appear secondary has caused a number of scholars to postulate a major role for the prophet in the production of the book.[81] Nathan MacDonald describes the book of Ezekiel as "a consummate literary product," which, "unlike Isaiah or Jeremiah…may have been so from the very beginning. No book in the Old Testament has escaped questions about its literary integrity, but the hypothesis that Ezekiel was the product of one mind has proved itself

---

77. See Karl-Friedrich Pohlmann's discussion of a "middle way" (*Ezekiel: Current Debates and Future Directions*, ed. William A. Tooman and Penelope Barter, FAT 112 [Göttingen: Mohr Siebeck, 2017], 6–7).

78. Joyce, *Ezekiel*, 12.

79. Ibid., 7–16; see further my review in *BibInt* 18 (2010): 178–9.

80. Cf. what Greenberg calls "minute literary analysis and hyper-minute editorial stages" ("Valid Criteria," 130).

81. Terrence Collins, *The Mantle of Elijah: The Redaction Criticism of the Prophetical Books*, Biblical Seminar 20 (Sheffield: JSOT, 1993), 92–3; Block, *Ezekiel*, 1:20; Wilson, *Prophecy and Society*, 283; cf. Joyce, *Ezekiel*, 16.

to be quite hardy."⁸² In his monograph on redaction criticism in the prophetic books, Terrence Collins explains the potential role of Ezekiel himself in editing the book:

> There are good grounds for concluding that the work of rewriting was done either under the supervision of Ezekiel himself or that of a like-minded disciple, who kept tight control of the production of the book at every stage. The general uniformity of style, imagery and contents is more easily explained if we suppose that initially the work of expanding the original book was carried out under the supervision and control of Ezekiel himself. There is certainly nothing improbable about the idea… The idea for the book could well have been conceived by the same man who uttered the original sermons from which it is constructed, even though the subsequent expansions to the 'first edition' may have been the work of his followers.⁸³

Similarly, Leslie Allen sees the hand of Ezekiel in much of the "secondary" material in the book:

> The evidence seems to suggest that Ezekiel himself cannot be excluded from the process of ordering his oracles in a literary medium. In the discerning of literary layers, in case after case there exists a closeness of perspective to the basic oracle that suggests the same inspired mind at work.⁸⁴

Even Zimmerli, who believed Ezekiel's disciples (the school of Ezekiel) redacted the book,⁸⁵ suggested "the prophet himself undertook the secondary work of learned commentary upon and further elaboration of his prophecies."⁸⁶

The idea that Ezekiel significantly shaped his own book may seem at odds with how other prophetic books were produced. For the preexilic period in particular, biblical scholars generally assume it was the scribes

---

82. MacDonald does not rule out the contribution of a "scribal school" ("The God that the Scholarship on Ezekiel Creates," in *The God Ezekiel Creates*, ed. Paul M. Joyce and Dalit Rom-Shiloni, LHBOTS 607 [New York: Bloomsbury T&T Clark, 2015], 193).

83. Collins, *The Mantle of Elijah*, 92–3.

84. Leslie C. Allen, *Ezekiel 20–48*, WBC 29 (Dallas: Word, 1990), xxv.

85. Zimmerli, *Ezekiel*, esp. 1:70–1. Challenging the explanatory usefulness of this theory, Rainer Albertz, for example, reasoned: "If the disciples had nothing substantial to add to what their master had said, the heuristic advantage of distinguishing the two is slight" (*Israel in Exile: The History and Literature of the Sixth Century BCE*, trans. David Green, SBLSBL 3 [Atlanta: Society of Biblical Literature, 2003], 348, citing Davis, *Swallowing the Scroll*, 15–19).

86. Zimmerli, *Ezekiel*, 1:71.

and not the prophets themselves who wrote their oracles and shaped them into books.[87] However, Ellen Davis sees Ezekiel as a transition point toward what Karel van der Toorn calls the "scribalization of prophecy" in the postexilic period.[88] Ezekiel's significant place in this transition owes something not only to the rise of prophecy as a written genre, but also to Ezekiel's unique background as a professionally trained priest.

If Ezekiel's priestly training included expertise in reading and writing,[89] it seems plausible that—unlike most other prophetic books—the prophet himself played a significant role in the writing of his oracles and the design of the book. There are many reasons to conclude that priests were among the scribal elite in ancient Israel. As Carr observes,

> Priests in the ancient world were among the most literate members of the populace, and priests, particularly Levites, are often depicted in biblical narratives as the keepers of the texts (e.g. Deut 31:9-11; cf. Num 5:23) and the teachers of Israel (Hos 4:6; Deut 17:9-12; 31:10-13; 2 Chr 19:8-11; Neh 8:8-9).[90]

Van der Toorn similarly argues that priests needed writing skills to do their work:

> They wrote down curses (Num 5:23) and teachings (Hos 8:12; cf. Jer 8:8), certified written records (Isa 8:2; compare Jer 32:10-12), and read the Torah (Jer 2:8; 2 Kings 22). Priests recited formulary prayers for worshippers to repeat; they also wrote down private prayers of thanksgiving in fulfillment of a vow. Literacy was simply a tool of their trade.[91]

Indeed, van der Toorn proposes Israel's sacred literature was composed by priest-scribes affiliated with the temple of Jerusalem.[92] Consequently,

---

87. Van der Toorn, *Scribal Culture*, 203.
88. Davis, *Swallowing the Scroll*, 37–9; van der Toorn, *Scribal Culture*, 203.
89. On high literacy as a possession of the elites, see also Christopher Rollston, *Writing and Literacy in the World of Ancient Israel: Epigraphic Evidence from the Iron Age*, Archaeology and Biblical Studies 11 (Atlanta: Society of Biblical Literature, 2010), 133.
90. Carr, *Writing on the Tablet*, 152, see also 116–19.
91. Van der Toorn, *Scribal Culture*, 85.
92. Ibid., 85–8. Even if the scribal workshop of the temple was not the *only* place for the production of Israel's sacred literature, as van der Toorn argues, he has successfully shown that the temple was one of the main centers of scribal activity in ancient Israel. See, e.g., William M. Schniedewind, who argues that some books were likely composed in the royal court (see his review of van der Toorn, *Scribal Culture*

it is natural to conclude Ezekiel likely gained expertise in reading and writing as part of his priestly education.[93] The book itself claims Ezekiel had the ability to write, not only at a rudimentary level (24:2; 37:16), but at a literary level as well (43:11).[94]

This brief overview of scholarly opinion is intended to demonstrate that, given the present state of Ezekiel scholarship, it is reasonable to speak of Deuteronomic influence not simply on the book of Ezekiel, but indeed on the prophet himself.[95] Nevertheless, in this study, I will not merely assume Ezekiel is responsible for the entire book that bears his name, nor adopt a synchronic approach.[96] I do not rule out the likelihood of contributions from writers other than Ezekiel, whether the prophet's disciples during his lifetime or other editors at a later time. Possible interpolations will be evaluated on a case-by-case basis in an effort to determine to what extent Deuteronomic language and ideas derive from Ezekiel or later editors. In due course, I will examine in more detail criteria for identifying secondary material, including the juxtaposition of judgment and restoration, explain other compositional features of the book, including the role of *Fortschreibung* (editorial furthering or conceptual extension), and consider further the potential role of Ezekiel in editing his own book.

Ultimately, it is impossible to know with certainty whether each instance of Deuteronomic influence in the book of Ezekiel came from the prophet himself. As Zimmerli observed, "in individual cases it is often not possible to define the borders at which the prophet's own work passes over into that of the school [of Ezekiel]."[97] That does not affect

in *JHS* 10 [2010], online: www.jhsonline.org; and idem, *How the Bible Became a Book: The Textualization of Ancient Israel* [Cambridge: Cambridge University Press, 2004]).

93. Davis, *Swallowing the Scroll*, 40; Carr, *Writing on the Tablet*, 149, who cites A. Demsky, "Education, Jewish," *Encyclopaedia Judaica* 6 (1971): 396–7.

94. Although it is possible the reference to Ezekiel "writing" may imply the use of a scribe, the prophet's priestly training and knowledge of Israelite and Near Eastern traditions support the probability that he himself wrote.

95. This study presupposes the accuracy of the biographical information about the prophet presented in the book, namely, that Ezekiel was born of priestly lineage, exiled with Jehoiachin in 597 BCE, and called to prophetic ministry in Babylon. For a defense of the prevailing view that Ezekiel's ministry took place entirely in Babylon, see Andrew Mein, *Ezekiel and the Ethics of Exile*, OTM (Oxford: Oxford University Press, 2001), 27–38.

96. Joyce rightly criticizes the holistic approach on grounds that it "too easily slides from a healthy agnosticism about editorial layers into an implicit assumption of authorship by the prophet himself" (*Ezekiel*, 15).

97. Zimmerli, *Ezekiel*, 1:71.

the overarching thesis presented here. The overall unity of the book and the likelihood that Ezekiel was a highly literate, priestly scribe should give us confidence that, despite the uncertainty of any individual passage or locution, the Deuteronomic influence in the book comes largely from Ezekiel himself.

A Widespread Deuteronomistic Redaction of Ezekiel?

Some scholars have regarded signs of Deuteronom(ist)ic language and ideas in Ezekiel as de facto evidence of redaction.[98] Hölscher, who ascribed most of the book to a redactor, spoke of the Deuteronomistic character of the alleged redaction: "Vor allem ähnelt seine Ausdrucksweise derjenigen der deuteronomistichen Schriftsteller, und auch mit dem Deuteronomium selber berührt er sich mannigfach in Sprache und Tendenz."[99] Siegfried Herrmann proposed that the hopeful passages in the book were the result of later Deuteronomistic redaction in Palestine.[100] His student Rüdiger Liwak advanced the idea of a Deuteronomistic redaction, finding Deuteronomistic insertions in his analysis of other texts.[101] Frank-Lothar Hossfeld postulated six layers of redaction in the book, the fourth of which was characterized by Deuteronomistic language and concepts.[102] Indeed, Hossfeld does not attribute any Deuteronom(ist)ic language or concepts to Ezekiel himself:

---

98. For an overview, see Frank-Lothar Hossfeld, "Ezechiel und die deuteronomisch-deuteronomistiche Bewegung," in *Jeremia und die deuteronomistische Bewegung*, ed. Walter Gross, BBB 98 (Weinheim: Beltz Athenäum, 1995), 271–95. The theory of a Deuteronomistic redaction is most common in German speaking scholarship, or what Hossfeld refers to as "die mitteleuropäische Ezechielexegese" (p. 294).

99. Gustav Hölscher, *Hesekiel: Der Dichter und das Buch*, BZAW 39 (Giessen: Alfred Töpelmann, 1924), 28.

100. Siegfried Herrmann, *Die prophetischen Heilserwartungen im Alten Testament*, BWANT 85 (Stuttgart: W. Kohlhammer, 1965), 241–91. After identifying the characteristic features of the salvation oracles in Ezekiel, Herrmann finds the ideology of the Deuteronomistic school in the following motifs: (1) die Friedensbund, (2) neues Herz, neuer Geist, Herz von Fleisch, (3) notwendige Umkehr von bösem Wandel, (4) Ablegen der Unreinigkeit, (5) Beseitigung fremder Götter, (6) Wandel in Gesetz und Recht, and (7) Jahwe Israels Gott, Israel sein Volk (p. 287).

101. Rüdiger Liwak, "Überlieferungsgeschichtliche Probleme des Ezechielbuches: eine Studie zu post-ezechielischen Interpretationen und Kompositionen" (Ph.D. diss., Universität Bochum, 1976). Liwak claimed Deuteronomistic redaction in 2:2b–3:11; 5:4b-17; ch. 6; 11:14-21; and ch. 20.

102. Frank-Lothar Hossfeld, *Untersuchungen zu Komposition und Theologie des Ezechielbuches*, 2nd ed., FzB 20 (Würzburg: Echter, 1983). He finds this layer in 6:11-13; 17:16-17; 20:27-29, 41-42; 22:7, 9bα, 10; 34:7-8, 16, 17-24; 36:23bβ-28, 31-32; 37:13b-14; 38:17; 39:8-10 (pp. 526–27).

Intensive Beziehungen zur deuteronomisch-deuteronomistichen Literatur findet man nicht im authentischen ezechielischen Gut, wahrscheinlich auch nicht in der frühen Fortschreibung der ezechielischen Schule, sondern eher in späteren Fortschreibungen, die sich vornehmlich mit Fragen der inneren wie äußeren Restitution Israels im Heimatland befassen.[103]

Zimmerli rejected such approaches. In his view, Herrmann's theory overemphasizes the Deuteronomic element in the salvation oracles "over against the features that are expressly distinctive of Ezekiel in this school."[104] He also criticized Liwak's literary-critical study for its limited scope,[105] preferring instead to see the Deuteronomistic elements as a product of Ezekiel himself or his school.[106]

Many scholars today rightly reject a widespread Deuteronomistic redaction of the book for several reasons. First, recent decades have seen widespread criticism of the tendency to find pervasive Deuteronomistic redaction throughout the Hebrew Bible, a phenomenon known as "pan-Deuteronomism."[107] Second, the proponents of a Deuteronomistic redaction in Ezekiel seem to assume the prophet himself would not have been influenced by Deuteronomy or Deuteronom(ist)ic theology. However, Paul Joyce has rightly questioned this assumption, stating: "There is no reason to believe that Ezekiel himself would have been immune to the influence of deuteronomistic theology and style either in his native Jerusalem or in Babylonian exile."[108] Third, as Corrine Patton (Carvalho) reasons, if Ezekiel had undergone a large-scale Deuteronomic redaction, one would "expect a fuller example of the Deuteronomic program, more blatant and pervasive use of Deuteronomic language and theology, and more connection with Deuteronomic history."[109] Fourth, Robert Wilson observes that the Deuteronomic features are "an integral part of the book at all redactional levels. It is not possible to isolate a

---

103. Hossfeld, "Ezechiel und die deuteronomisch-deuteronomistiche Bewegung," 294.

104. Zimmerli, *Ezekiel*, 1:71; so also Paul M. Joyce, *Divine Initiative and Human Response in Ezekiel*, JSOTSup 51 (Sheffield: Sheffield Academic, 1989), 122.

105. Zimmerli, *Ezekiel*, 2:xv; so also Friedrich Fechter, *Bewältigung der Katastrophe: Untersuchungen zu ausgewählten Fremd-völkersprüchen im Ezechielbuch*, BZAW 208 (Berlin: de Gruyter, 1992), 280.

106. Zimmerli, *Ezekiel*, 2:xv.

107. See L. S. Schearing and S. L. McKenzie, eds., *Those Elusive Deuteronomists: The Phenomenon of Pan-Deuteronomism*, JSOTSup 268 (Sheffield: Sheffield Academic, 1999).

108. Joyce, *Ezekiel*, 10.

109. Patton, "Ezekiel 20 and the Exodus Traditions," 84 n. 36.

specifically Deuteronomic editorial layer."[110] Finally, as Levitt Kohn states, "it is no longer tenable to speak of a Deuteronomistic redaction of the book of Ezekiel, or even of a 'Deuteronomistically influenced' redaction of the book," precisely because Ezekiel is known as "a creative author and a shaper of Israelite traditions." Thus, it would not be surprising that he "adapts Deuteronomistic motifs and expression[s]."[111] The present study will reinforce the last of these by showing not only that Ezekiel used Deuteronomic ideas, but that he sometimes drew from Deuteronomy in ways similar to his use of other biblical literature, particularly the Holiness Code.

The Septuagint and Scribal Expansion

A related issue is whether the Septuagint bears witness to an early form of Ezekiel that had not received Deuteronomizing editorial activity. Recent studies have highlighted the importance of LXX Ezekiel as a witness to the book's early textual history.[112] Since the translator(s) of LXX Ezekiel used a relatively literal approach to render its Hebrew *Vorlage*,[113] it cannot be assumed the differences between the LXX and the MT result from the translator(s) modifying their source text. Consequently, omissions in LXX Ezekiel often (though not always) attest to expansions in the MT.[114] However, since the content of these expansions cannot be

---

110. Wilson, *Prophecy and Society*, 284.

111. Risa Levitt Kohn, "Ezekiel at the Turn of the Century," *CBR* 2 (2003): 14.

112. See Emanuel Tov, "Recensional Differences Between the Masoretic Text and Septuagint of Ezekiel," in *The Greek and Hebrew Bible: Collected Essays on the Septuagint*, VTSup 72 [Leiden: Brill, 1999), 397–410; Johan Lust, "The Use of Textual Witnesses for the Establishment of the Text: The Shorter and Longer Texts of Ezekiel," in Lust, ed., *Ezekiel and His Book*, 7–20; Daniel O'Hare, *"Have You Seen, Son of Man?" A Study of the Translation and* Vorlage *of LXX Ezekiel 40–48*, SBLSCS 57 (Atlanta: Society of Biblical Literature, 2010), esp. 33–71. On the importance of Papyrus 967, see Chapter 7 of this study.

113. Emanuel Tov, *Textual Criticism of the Hebrew Bible*, 3rd ed. (Minneapolis: Fortress, 2012), 299–300. On the adjectives "literal" and "free" to describe translations, see James Barr, *The Typology of Literalism in Ancient Biblical Translations*, MSU 15 (Göttingen: Vandenhoeck & Ruprecht, 1979).

114. Timothy P. Mackie, *Expanding Ezekiel: The Hermeneutics of Scribal Addition in the Ancient Text Witnesses of the Book of Ezekiel*, FRLANT 257 (Göttingen: Vandenhoeck & Ruprecht, 2015); idem, "Transformation in Ezekiel's Textual History: Ezekiel 7 in the Masoretic Text and the Septuagint," in Tooman and Lyons, eds., *Transforming Visions*, 249–78; Jake Stromberg, "Observations on Inner-Scriptural Scribal Expansion in MT Ezekiel," *VT* 58 (2008): 68–86. For a brief list of possible examples, see Ronald L. Troxel, *Prophetic Literature: From Oracles to Books* (Oxford: Wiley-Blackwell, 2012), 237–8.

described broadly as Deuteronomic, they do not indicate a widespread Deuteronomic redaction of the book.[115]

Among the Deuteronomic words, concepts, and ideas discussed in this study, a few significant examples are lacking in the LXX and may be the result of scribal expansion: תבנית רמש ובהמה in Ezek. 8:10 and וישבו להכעיסני in Ezek. 8:17 (both treated in Chapter 3 of this study), as well as the entirety of Ezek. 28:25-26, בגוים אשר אדיחם שם in Ezek. 4:13, and וכנסתים על־אדמתם ולא־אותיר עוד מהם שם in 39:28 (cited in Chapter 7). As I will argue, these cases would be best understood as secondary expansions that continue the trend of Ezekiel's allusions.

Preview of This Study

This study begins with methodological considerations for discerning Deuteronomic influence in Ezekiel and then subsequent chapters frame the discussion under five main categories: Ezekiel's language and conception of idolatry, the rise and fall of Israel in ch. 16, Ezekiel's review of Israel's history in ch. 20, the scattering of Israel as an image for exile, and the related motif of gathering as an image for return to the land. This work does not intend to furnish an exhaustive comparison of Deuteronomy's and Ezekiel's theology, but to show the areas where Deuteronomy exerted an influence on Ezekiel. In each case, I will show first how Ezekiel used its language and theology and then conclude with reflections on the rhetorical function for his message.

---

115. Two examples discussed later may be mentioned here: (1) In Ezek. 6:13, the words missing in the LXX resemble most closely Hos. 4:13, whereas those shared by the MT and the LXX are closest to Deut. 12:2. (2) Although the language of the gathering motif in 39:28 is different than other occurrences of the motif in Ezekiel and appears to be secondary, the language is not distinctively Deuteronomic.

Chapter 2

METHOD FOR ASSESSING INFLUENCE

The goal of this study is to investigate the extent of Deuteronomy's influence on Ezekiel by analyzing the role of Deuteronomic language and ideas in the prophetic book. Consequently, the approach adopted here is fundamentally diachronic, to be distinguished from synchronic approaches such as Julia Kristeva's intertextuality, which built from Mikhail Bakhtin's dialogism.[1] In modern literary criticism, the discussion of influence focuses on an author's relationship to the existing body of classic literature,[2] particularly a poet's artistic or aesthetic use of the works of his forebears, often to demonstrate poetic skill.[3] Described this way,

---

1. See Julia Kristeva, "Word, Dialogue, and Novel," in *Desire in Language: A Semiotic Approach to Language and Art*, ed. Leon S. Roudiez, trans. Tom Gora and Alice Jardine (New York: Columbia University Press, 1980), 64–91; first published in Σημειωτιχη: *Recherches pour une sémanalyse* (Paris: Seuil, 1969), 143–73; Mikhail Bakhtin, *Rabelais and His World*, trans. Helene Iswolsky (Cambridge, MA: MIT, 1965); idem, *Problems of Dostoevsky's Poetics*, trans. R. W. Rotsel (Ann Arbor, MI: Ardis, 1973). On the distinction between intertextuality (synchronic) and influence and allusion (diachronic) in biblical studies, see David M. Carr, "The Many Uses of Intertextuality in Biblical Studies: Actual and Potential," in *Congress Volume Helsinki 2010*, ed. Marti Nissinen, VTSup 148 (Leiden: Brill, 2012), 505–35. Gregory Machacek proposes using the word "intertextuality" in the broadest sense for both diachronic and synchronic studies ("Allusion," *PMLA* 122 [2007]: 525).

2. E.g., T. S. Eliot, "Tradition and the Individual Talent," in *The Sacred Wood: Essays on Poetry and Criticism* (London: Methuen, 1920), 42–7; repr. in *Influx: Essays on Literary Influence*, ed. Ronald Primeau (Port Washington, NY: Kennikat, 1977), 16–18.

3. Cf. Louis A. Renza, "Influence," in *Critical Terms for Literary Study*, ed. Frank Lentricchia and Thomas McLaughlin, 2nd ed. (Chicago: University of Chicago Press, 1995), 188.

The work of Harold Bloom looms large in discussions of influence in modern literature (see *The Anxiety of Influence: A Theory of Poetry* [New York: Oxford

the concept of influence might seem trivial and inconsequential. Indeed, some might regard the identification of a writer's influences to be of secondary importance for interpreting his or her work. However, Ezekiel's relationship to Deuteronomy is unlike the relationship of modern poets to classic literature, principally because Ezekiel regarded Israel's legal traditions, including Deuteronomy, as authoritative statutes given by God and consequently the primary lens to interpret Israel's relationship with God. They held a unique status for Ezekiel and his contemporaries. Therefore, the nature of Deuteronomy's influence on Ezekiel is quite different than, for example, the influence of Homer's *Iliad* on Milton. While Ezekiel's use of literary traditions exhibits a high degree of literary artistry, he used Deuteronomy's language and concepts not simply to demonstrate poetic skill, but often to add rhetorical force to his message by leveraging the authoritative status of Israel's legal traditions—even if we cannot know with certainty whether Ezekiel's immediate audience in fact shared his convictions about these legal traditions. At the end of this chapter, I will return to the significance of Deuteronomic influence for understanding Ezekiel's message.

The concept of influence requires a few clarifications. First, since, as Haskell M. Block explains, "too frequently influence has been employed in a simple and simple-minded way as the determining cause and unique source of a literary creation,"[4] it is important to affirm that Ezekiel's message and theology cannot be reduced to a description of his sources and influences. Second, influence need not imply a lack of originality.[5] In the case of Ezekiel, the opposite is true. The prophet does not simply mimic his sources, but, as observed earlier, alludes to and borrows from Israel's literary traditions with remarkable creativity. Third, the influence of earlier traditions on Ezekiel need not mean the prophet adopts their

---

University Press], 1973; *The Anatomy of Influence: Literature as a Way of Life* [New Haven: Yale University Press], 2011). Bloom focuses on what he calls the "anxiety of influence," that is, the insecurity of poets as they struggle to find identity in the shadow of their predecessors. However, setting aside its merits for modern poetry, Bloom's model is ill-suited for this study, since anxiety does not characterize Ezekiel's relationship to the literary traditions that, as I will argue, he regarded as divine statutes. His use of Deuteronomy's language and concepts most often functions rhetorically for his message.

4. Haskell M. Block, "The Concept of Influence in Comparative Literature," in Primeau, ed., *Influx*, 80; cf. in the same volume Claudio Guillén, "The Aesthetics of Influence," 56; Göran Hermerén, *Influence in Art and Literature* (Princeton: Princeton University Press, 1975), 4.

5. Guillén, "Aesthetics of Influence," 56; Hermerén, *Influence*, 4–5.

perspective wholesale. Ezekiel feels free to construct his own theology, sometimes synthesizing various theological traditions. In some cases, the prophet borrows the language from a literary tradition but departs from its theology in certain ways.[6] In other cases, Ezekiel might adopt the words of an earlier source but use them in different ways. Thus, influence does not necessarily imply the later work shares the exact viewpoint of the earlier work,[7] but instead can connote, as Ihab Hassan argued, the development of a tradition.[8]

Recognizing Influence

According to Jay Clayton and Eric Rothstein, influence refers to "relations built on dyads of transmission from one unity (author, work, tradition) to another."[9] Although the word connotes a movement from an earlier to a later unity, one identifies influence by the later writer's use of the earlier work. In other words, the influence of A on B is evident by B's use of A, as Clayton and Rothstein explain:

> The line of intentionality runs from the later to the earlier author…since one usually does not intend to be influenced by another. T. S. Eliot did not choose to be influenced by San Juan de la Cruz in the same way that he chose to employ San Juan's ideas and words.[10]

Thus, in this study Deuteronomic influence on Ezekiel will be evident by the prophet's use of Deuteronomy's ideas and words.

According to P. Cheney, influence encompasses a wide range of relationships, including "imitation, invention, citation, and many other modes of appropriation and creation."[11] Therefore, it is a broader phenomenon

---

6. See, e.g., Lyons' explanation of Ezekiel's theology of restoration (*From Law to Prophecy*, 85–8), which is discussed in Chapter 7 of this study.

7. Hermerén, *Influence*, 235–7.

8. Ihab H. Hassan, "The Problem of Influence in Literary History: Notes towards a Definition," *JAAC* 14 (1955): 75.

9. Jay Clayton and Eric Rothstein, "Figures in the Corpus: Theories of Influence and Intertextuality," in *Influence and Intertextuality in Literary History*, ed. Jay Clayton and Eric Rothstein (Madison: University of Wisconsin Press, 1991), 3.

10. Ibid., 7; cf. Hassan, "The Problem of Influence," 68; "Introduction," in Primeau, ed., *Influx*, 8.

11. P. Cheney, "Influence," in *The Princeton Encyclopedia of Poetry and Poetics*, ed. Roland Greene et al., 4th ed. (Princeton: Princeton University Press, 2012), 703.

than literary citation.[12] Michael Baxandall lists numerous terms that may describe the action of the later writer on the earlier work, including: to draw on, to appropriate from, to have recourse to, to adapt, to pick up, to take on, to engage with, to react to, to align oneself with, to copy, and to transform.[13] Therefore, Ezekiel's use of distinctively Deuteronomic language and ideas may be a sign of its influence on him even when he does not intend to refer overtly to Deuteronomy as a text.

Explaining Verbal Parallels

Scholars have used various models for describing and categorizing verbal parallels.[14] Drawing on the work of John Hollander, many studies of intertextual relationships in biblical literature use a diachronic methodological approach that distinguishes three modes of literary reference: quotation, allusion, and echo.[15] However, since not every case of shared language in the Hebrew Bible results from a writer's intentional *reference* to an earlier text, it seems appropriate to begin with more basic categories. This study proposes four theoretical explanations for verbal parallels between Ezekiel and Deuteronomy: coincidence, indirect usage, literary borrowing, and literary reference. To compare with Hollander's categories, quotation and allusion would be subcategories of the last, literary reference.

First, the presence of similar language in two texts could simply result from *coincidence*. This explanation is most likely when the shared element is a common concept or theme or a formulaic expression in biblical literature. In this case, the shared language is not due to the influence of an

---

12. Benjamin Sommer, *A Prophet Reads Scripture: Allusion in Isaiah 40–66* (Stanford, CA: Stanford University Press, 1998), 14–15.

13. Michael Baxandall, *Patterns of Intention: On the Historical Explanation of Pictures* (New Haven: Yale University Press, 1985), 59; quoted in Clayton and Rothstein, "Figures in the Corpus," 6–7.

14. For an overview, see Schultz, *Search for Quotation*, 183–5; Russell L. Meek, "Intertextuality, Inner-Biblical Exegesis, and Inner-Biblical Allusion: The Ethics of a Methodology," *Biblica* 95 (2014): 280–91. See Schultz, *Search for Quotation*, 20–55, for a review of how scholars have approached verbal parallels among the biblical prophetic books.

15. John Hollander, *The Figure of Echo: A Mode of Allusion in Milton and After* (Berkeley: University of California Press, 1984), 64; for a seminal application to biblical literature, see Richard B. Hays, *Echoes of Scripture in the Letters of Paul* (New Haven: Yale University Press, 1989), esp. 19–21; also Jonathan Gibson, *Covenant Continuity and Fidelity: A Study of Inner-Biblical Allusion and Exegesis in Malachi*, LHBOTS 625 (London: Bloomsbury T&T Clark, 2019), 39–43.

earlier text on a later writer.[16] Relatedly, two similar texts could both be dependent on a third source. This study addresses the possibility that in some instances Ezekiel draws what might be considered "Deuteronomic" language from Jeremiah and other sources. Second, shared language could be a result of *indirect usage*. In this case, a writer or speaker adopts words or ideas from common discourse, not directly from the text itself—even if the words or ideas are uniquely associated with a particular tradition.[17]

The last two categories reflect the writer's direct literary dependence on the earlier work. Thus, third, *literary borrowing* describes a writer drawing directly from an earlier text without intending to call the reader's attention to the text.[18] Evidence for the writer's knowledge of the source text provides the best evidence to differentiate literary borrowing from indirect usage, although it may not always be possible to distinguish. Fourth, *literary reference* describes a writer's attempt to draw the reader's attention to an earlier text. Unlike simple borrowing, literary reference exhibits a rhetorical purpose for referring to the source text.

Many scholars distinguish two types of literary reference: quotation and allusion.[19] What distinguishes the two is not the presence of a citation formula, which are rare in the Hebrew Bible,[20] but the degree of syntactic correspondence. Quotation is characterized by a writer's conscious repetition of words from an earlier text that exhibits identical or minimally

---

16. I often use the term writer instead of author, since the modern concept of authorship is foreign to the ancient world (see van der Toorn, *Scribal Culture*, 27–49). By using this term, I do not mean to imply that Ezekiel's use of literary traditions, or prophetic activity in general, was exclusively textual and not oral.

17. On indirect influence, cf. Hermerén, *Influence*, 32–42, 220; Richard Altick, *The Art of Literary Research*, 4th ed. (New York: W. W. Norton, 1993), 111–12.

18. See Schultz, *Search for Quotation*, 184, who cites Hermann Meyer, *Das Zitat in der Erzählkunst: Zur Geschichte und Poetik des europäischen Romans* (Stuttgart: J. B. Metzlersche Verlagsbuchhandlung, 1961), 14–15.

19. In common usage, "echo" describes a still more subtle connection. According to Hollander, an echo of an earlier text may be unconscious or inadvertent. Unlike allusion and quotation, an echo is not intended to point the reader to the source text (*Figure of Echo*, 64; Christopher A. Beetham, *Echoes of Scripture in the Letter of Paul to the Colossians*, BIS 96 [Leiden: Brill, 2008], 19–20). As such, echo offers a potential window into the author's verbal repository, influenced as it may be by earlier literature, but should not, in my view, be categorized as a type of reference. It may be closer to the second category described above, *indirect usage*.

20. See Kevin L. Spawn, *"As It Is Written" and Other Citation Formulae in the Old Testament: Their Use, Development, Syntax, and Significance*, BZAW 311 (Berlin: de Gruyter, 2002); and examples cited below in the section "Identifying Literary Dependence."

divergent wording.²¹ In my view, most literary references in the book of Ezekiel—and in the Hebrew Bible generally—do not display verbatim or near verbatim syntactic correspondence and thus would best be labeled allusions.²²

Like quotation, allusion is an intentional reference to an earlier text; but instead of word-for-word repetition, allusions exhibit a "partial reuse of a sequence of words."²³ Gregory Machacek helpfully describes allusion as:

> a textual snippet reminiscent of a phrase in an earlier author's writing but smoothly incorporated into the new context of the imitating author's work... [It] is distinguishable primarily by being brief, discrete, and local and evoking a single text that the culture of the alluding writer associates with an identifiable earlier author.²⁴

Often, the alluding author adapts or modifies the language of the source text.²⁵ The absence of strict word-for-word repetition should not be surprising. As Stead explains:

> When a source text is picked up and reused by an author there will sometimes be an unavoidable change in the grammatical form, at the very least, if not the sequence and syntax of repeated words. This is because the author may employ the lexemes in a newly creative way or may adjust the grammar and syntax in the process of integrating the quotation into his own sentence construction... [Instead of "word-for-word repetition,"] there is, rather, inversion and fragmentation, which serve the author's rhetorical purpose. Yet this still constitutes a case of intentional dependence, just as much as does an exact citation of another biblical text.

---

21. Cf. Schultz, *Search for Quotation*, 19.

22. Cf. Michael Fishbane, *Biblical Interpretation in Ancient Israel* (Oxford: Clarendon, 1985), 285, who speaks of implicit or virtual citations. Despite the rarity of explicit citation markers, one may still find quotations in the Hebrew Bible. In his study of verbal parallels in the prophetic books, Schultz finds instances of shared language with a sufficiently high degree of syntactic correspondence to be regarded as quotations (e.g., Isa. 2:2-4 and Mic. 4:1-3) (see *Search for Quotation*, 222–39).

23. Michael R. Stead, *The Intertextuality of Zechariah 1–8*, LHBOTS 506 (New York: T&T Clark, 2009), 22; cf. R. Wetzsteon, who describes allusion as indirect and uncited, but nevertheless intentional ("Allusion," in Greene et al., eds., *The Princeton Encyclopedia of Poetry and Poetics*, 42).

24. Machacek, "Allusion," 525.

25. The kinds of allusions in this study fall under Machacek's category of "phraseological adaptations." Machacek uses the term "echo" for this phenomenon, which is a subcategory of allusion (ibid., 526–7). This definition of "echo" is different than Hollander's.

In place of verbatim or near verbatim wording, an allusion requires a sufficiently distinctive element—what Ziva Ben-Porat calls a "marker"[26]—that points the reader to the source text.

Thus, the terms quotation and allusion "indicate their relative position along a continuum, with a [quotation] having greater congruence of syntax and words than an allusion."[27] While some scholars have arbitrarily chosen a minimum number of shared words to distinguish quotation and allusion,[28] in reality the line between the two is fuzzy. While it seems natural to distinguish quotation and allusion at the theoretical level, labeling each potential literary reference in Ezekiel as either quotation or allusion—based on its relative position on a continuum of syntactic correspondence—holds little value. Not only is it unclear where to draw the line between the two, but what profit would come from it? The more fundamental question is whether or not verbal or thematic parallels are the result of literary dependence (either *literary borrowing* or *literary reference*), which is the focus of this study.

Defining Deuteronomic Influence

Certainly not every instance of Deuteronomic language in Ezekiel implies the prophet's literary dependence on Deuteronomy, since words and concepts may be known to him simply from the religious discourse of his time. However, Deuteronomic influence, as defined here, is not limited to Ezekiel's *literary use of Deuteronomy*—that is, his knowledge of and reference to Deuteronomy as a text.[29] As explained above, this study distinguishes between the simple presence of Deuteronomic language used by Ezekiel (*indirect usage*) and his literary dependence on Deuteronomy, whether simply to adopt its language (*literary borrowing*) or to refer to it (*literary reference*). All three of these categories point to Deuteronomy's

26. Ziva Ben-Porat, "The Poetics of Literary Allusion," *PTL* 1 (1976): 108.

27. Cf. Rikk E. Watts, "Isaiah in the New Testament," in *Interpreting Isaiah: Issues and Approaches*, ed. David G. Firth and H. G. M. Williamson (Downers Grove, IL: InterVarsity, 2009), 214. On the limits of a quantitative approach to shared language, see Stead, *Intertextuality of Zechariah 1–8*, 40–1.

28. E.g., Beetham, *Echoes of Scripture*, 17, who defines a quotation as "an intentional, explicit, verbatim or near verbatim citation of a former text of six or more words in length."

29. Cf. Dalit Rom-Shiloni, who asserts that influence "does not depend on specific verbal connections between the texts, and in this respect it is even more remote from a literary allusion" ("Ezekiel and Jeremiah: What Might Stand behind the Silence?" *HeBAI* 1 [2012]: 215).

influence on him. Many of Deuteronomy's terms and concepts are highly distinctive in the Hebrew Bible, and by implication we may presume they would have been considered "Deuteronomic" in the religious discourse of Ezekiel's time. Therefore, even when Ezekiel does not draw directly from the text of Deuteronomy, his indirect use of language and ideas *uniquely associated with* Deuteronomy for his prophetic message (*indirect usage*) testifies to its influence on him. Thus, barring some polemical intent, the presence of Deuteronomic language would indicate a closer connection between Ezekiel and the world of Deuteronomy.

Identifying Literary Dependence

Still, the possibility of literary dependence on Deuteronomy is of particular interest, since Ezekiel is known to draw from Israel's literary traditions. The attempt to identify literary dependence with confidence has many perils, especially because the writers of the Hebrew Bible rarely announced when they were referring to an earlier text. Unlike the New Testament,[30] literary references are rarely marked with a citation formula.[31] Most often, there is no "overt mention of the act of referencing, the title of the literary work referenced, or the name of its author."[32] Fortunately, scholars have developed helpful criteria to assess the likelihood of true dependence in cases of verbal or conceptual similarity. The extent to which a parallel meets these criteria allows us to postulate dependence on a scale of confidence ranging from possibility to probability.[33]

---

30. E.g., "as it is written in the prophet Isaiah" (Mk 1:2), "it is written in the law of Moses" (1 Cor. 9:9), or simply, "Isaiah said" (Jn 12:39).

31. See Spawn, *'As It Is Written' and Other Citation Formulae*. Two examples may be noted, both in the Deuteronomistic History, where regulations from Deuteronomy are cited with phrases such as "as it is written in the book of the Torah of Moses" (משה תורת בספר ככתוב) and "just as Moses commanded" (משה צוה כאשר). See Josh. 8:31 (quoting Deut. 27:5) and 2 Kgs 14:6 (quoting Deut. 24:16). Other ככתוב, "as it is written," formulae refer generally to the Torah of Moses or a specific part thereof but never introduce a quotation of a specific textual unit, e.g., Josh. 1:8; 23:6; 1 Kgs 2:3; 23:21; 2 Chron. 35:12; Ezra 3:4; 6:18; Neh. 10:36; Dan. 9:13. S. R. Driver proposed that יהוה אמר כאשר in Joel 3:5 marks a citation of Obad. 17 (*Introduction to the Literature of the Old Testament* [New York: Charles Scribner's Sons, 1913], 313). Sommer suggests the phrase דבר יהוה פי כי in Isa. 58:11-14 may mark an allusion to Deut. 32:9-13 (*A Prophet Reads Scripture*, 135).

32. Lyons, "Persuasion and Allusion," 77.

33. Cf. Schultz, *Search for Quotation*, 223.

An obvious prerequisite for literary dependence is the *availability* of the supposed source text to the writer.[34] Since the dating of biblical books is a complex and contested matter, it is often necessary to address clearly the dating of both the source text and the alluding text. For the present study, this involves a consideration of both the composition of Deuteronomy and the unity of Ezekiel, which were addressed above. Beyond this initial prerequisite, however, one must examine whether similarities between an earlier and later text are the result of purposeful borrowing or are simply coincidental. Though such a task is as much an art as a science,[35] and certainly scholars want to avoid "parallelomania,"[36] several criteria are available to help distinguish dependence from coincidental similarities.[37]

The strongest evidence of literary dependence is a high degree of *syntactic correspondence* between two texts, that is, shared phrases, not simply shared words.[38] This is the defining feature of quotation. However, since extensive quotation is uncommon in the Hebrew Bible, a quantitative measurement of shared language alone is inadequate for determining literary dependence.[39] In the absence of verbatim wording, we must have qualitative criteria to evaluate whether a writer alludes to an earlier text. Citing Christopher B. Hays, Joseph Kelly argues scholars should not set the bar for shared language too high when identifying allusion.[40] According to Earl Miner, an allusion may consist of a single

---

34. Cf. Hermerén, *Influence*, 157, 164; Dennis R. MacDonald, "Introduction," in *Mimesis and Intertextuality in Antiquity and Christianity*, ed. Dennis R. MacDonald (Harrisburg, PA: Trinity Press International, 2001), 2.

35. See Benjamin D. Sommer, "Exegesis, Allusion and Intertextuality in the Hebrew Bible: A Response to Lyle Eslinger," *VT* 46 (1996): 485–6, and the sources cited therein; see also Jeffery M. Leonard, "Identifying Inner-Biblical Allusions: Psalm 78 as a Test Case," *JBL* 127 (2008): 264.

36. Samuel Sandmel, "Parallelomania," *JBL* 81 (1962): 1–13.

37. For example, Schultz, *Search for Quotation*, 222–39; Hays, *Echoes of Scripture*, 29–30; Beetham, *Echoes of Scripture*, 27–34; Hermerén, *Influence*, 156–262; Lyons, *From Law to Prophecy*, 47–75; Leonard, "Identifying Inner-Biblical Allusions," 241–65; Geoffrey D. Miller, "Intertextuality in Old Testament Research," *CBR* 9 (2011): 294–8; MacDonald, "Introduction," 2.

38. Schultz, *Search for Quotation*, 222–4; Leonard, "Identifying Inner-Biblical Allusions," 252–3; cf. Hays' "volume" (*Echoes of Scripture*, 29–32); Gibson, *Covenant Continuity*, 33–5.

39. Stead, *Intertextuality in Zechariah 1–8*, 41.

40. Joseph Ryan Kelly, "Identifying Literary Allusions: Theory and the Criterion of Shared Language," in Zevit, ed., *Subtle Citation*, 32. Kelly calls "shared language" a nonessential criterion for allusion and cites Christopher B. Hays who argues for

shared word or even just a shared concept.[41] What matters is that the parallel is sufficiently distinctive to suggest dependence.[42] Thus, the first main criterion for identifying allusion is the presence of a *unique or distinctive word or concept*—what Christopher Beetham calls *rare concept similarity*.[43] As the opposite of a common motif, the presence of a distinctive word or rare concept in two texts suggests that one may be drawing from the other.

A second criterion for dependence is *density*, which refers to the frequency of parallels within two passages.[44] The more parallels within two defined passages, the greater the possibility they are the result of purposeful borrowing and not just chance similarity.[45] Although some individual parallels may lack definitive evidence for dependence and may therefore vary on the scale of possibility to probability, numerous potential allusions mutually corroborate each other as evidence of literary borrowing. Of course, numerous weak links together provide a weak case for dependence. However, the presence of a few probable allusions, marked by a high degree of verbal and syntactic correspondence or a

---

the importance of identifying the "quieter echoes": "Other criteria might outweigh sheer volume… One should not despair or set the bar unduly high for 'commensurate terms'" (Christopher B. Hays, "Echoes of the Ancient Near East? Intertextuality and the Comparative Study of the Old Testament," in *The Word Leaps the Gap: Essays on Scripture and Theology in Honor of Richard B. Hays*, ed. J. Ross Wagner, C. Kavin Rowe, and A. Katherine Grieb [Grand Rapids: Eerdmans, 2008], 37).

41. Earl Miner, "Allusion," in *The New Princeton Encyclopedia of Poetry and Poetics*, ed. Alex Preminger and T. V. F. Brogan (Princeton, NJ: Princeton University Press, 1993), 38–9.

42. So also O'Brien, *Use of Scripture*, 32.

43. Beetham, *Echoes of Scripture*, 29; cf. Leonard, "Identifying Inner-Biblical Allusions," 251–2; Hermerén, *Influence*, 177, 207; MacDonald, "Introduction," 2; Kelly, "Identifying Literary Allusions," 35–6; David P. Wright, "Method in the Study of Textual Source Dependence: The Deuteronomic Code," in Zevit, ed., *Subtle Citation*, 161; Gibson, *Covenant Continuity*, 35.

44. MacDonald, "Introduction," 2; Wright, "Method in the Study of Textual Source Dependence," 160.

45. Cf. Fishbane, *Biblical Interpretation*, 285, who states that the probability of inner-biblical interpretation "is proportionally increased to the extent that multiple and sustained lexical linkages between two texts can be recognized"; Richard Altick, *The Art of Literary Research* (New York: W. W. Norton, 1963), 87: "A small, isolated similarity of phrase proves little if anything. But the likelihood of direct relationship grows if two passages virtually match, or contain peculiarities (unusual words or idioms, out-of-the-way images or images with unaccustomed details or uses)."

sufficiently distinctive motif or idea, lends credence to other parallels that alone would be considered only possible allusions.[46]

In some cases, the frequency of links is corroborated by their consistent or unique *distribution*, suggesting that a later writer follows a pattern in an earlier work or even structured his composition on it.[47] Jeffery Leonard has identified cases of "narrative tracking," which refers to "the process by which one text alludes to another by mimicking its narrative structure."[48] Together the frequency and distribution of allusions create a cumulative argument for literary dependence, as summarized by Benjamin Sommer:

> The argument that an author alludes, then, is a cumulative one: assertions that allusions occur in certain passages become stronger as patterns emerge from those allusions. In any one passage that may rely on an older text, the critic must weigh evidence including the number of shared terms and their distinctiveness, [and] the presence of stylistic or thematic patterns that typify the author's allusions.[49]

It is also useful to consider other factors that might support the *likelihood*—or *historical plausibility*—that the writer would allude to the

---

46. The same point is made by Jacob Stromberg: "It is necessary to stress this cumulative aspect of the argument only because such words and phrases that echo DI [Deutero-Isaiah] might be regarded, when viewed in isolation from one another, as mere coincidence" ("An Inner-Isaianic Reading of Isaiah 61:1-3," in Firth and Williamson, eds., *Interpreting Isaiah*, 263).

47. So also MacDonald, "Introduction," 2; Wright, "Method in the Study of Textual Source Dependence," 161, who uses the term "textual organization." Drawing on Robert Alter's narrative "type-scene," Paul R. Noble makes a similar case for allusions within biblical narratives: "A catalogue of individual, unrelated points of resemblance between two texts is not, in general, a sufficient criterion for identifying a probable authorial or redactional allusion of one text to the other. But…a common pattern in two texts *is* a sufficient criterion for postulating intentional allusion—unless the pattern is a very simple one (consisting, say, of only two or three elements, with little or no interconnection between them) it is difficult to believe that it should happen to occur in two different locations just by chance" ("Esau, Tamar, and Joseph: Criteria for Identifying Inner-Biblical Allusions," *VT* 52 [2002]: 251).

48. Jeffery M. Leonard, "Identifying Subtle Allusions: The Promise of Narrative Tracking," in Zevit, ed., *Subtle Citation*, 91–113.

49. Sommer, "Exegesis, Allusion and Intertextuality," 485. So also Leonard, "Identifying Inner-Biblical Allusions," 253–4; Rex Mason, "Zechariah 9–14," in *Bringing Out the Treasure: Inner Biblical Allusion in Zechariah 9–14*, ed. Mark J. Boda and Michael H. Floyd, with a major contribution by Rex Mason, JSOTSup 370 (Sheffield: Sheffield Academic, 2003), 201; Cynthia Edenburg, "How (Not) to Murder a King: Variations on a Theme in 1 Sam 24; 26," *SJOT* 12 (1998): 72.

alleged source.⁵⁰ A further criterion that bolsters the case for dependence is *recurrence*, or, the frequency with which a writer borrows from or alludes to a text not in a single passage but throughout his or her work.⁵¹ Other allusions to the same text confirm that the writer in fact knows it.

Lastly, for cases when the direction of dependence is in doubt,⁵² Richard Schultz has shown that evidence of *interpretive reworking* is the major criterion for determining which text borrowed from the other.⁵³ In some cases, it is possible to demonstrate that one text (re)interprets or transforms the other. To this, I would add *literary modification*: evidence that the later writer has appropriated the words of his source text and adapted them for his own literary or rhetorical purposes.⁵⁴

The Significance for Interpreting the Book of Ezekiel

While the concept of influence might seem inconsequential for some works, ascertaining Deuteronomy's influence on Ezekiel is significant for multiple reasons. To begin, it allows us to understand Ezekiel's message in its historical-theological context. Deuteronomy represents one of the major theological traditions in ancient Israel. By examining the prophet's use of its language and concepts, we are able to locate his message in relation to what Zimmerli called the "well-defined world of Deuteronomy,"⁵⁵ the distinctive theology that influenced many other biblical writers. Even more, we understand better how Ezekiel's message would have been heard by his audience in the sixth century BCE.

Second, Deuteronomy is in a special category of literary traditions for Ezekiel. As noted above, since Ezekiel and his contemporaries regarded Israel's legal traditions as torah from God (see Ezek. 20:10-11, 18), the

---

50. Sommer, "Exegesis, Allusion and Intertextuality," 485; Hays, *Echoes of Scripture*, 29–32.

51. Hays, *Echoes of Scripture*, 30.

52. See also Carr, *Formation of the Hebrew Bible*, 425–8, for criteria used to establish the direction of dependence between Proverbs and Deuteronomy; also idem, "Method in Determination of Dependence: An Empirical Test of Criteria Applied to Exodus 34:11-26 and Its Parallels," in *Gottes Volk am Sinai. Untersuchungen zu Ex 32–34 und Dtn 9–10*, ed. Matthias Köckert and Erhard Blum (Gütersloh: Kaiser Gütersloher, 2001), 107–40.

53. Schultz, *Search for Quotation*, 231. Cf. Fishbane, *Biblical Interpretation*, 285, who speaks of using the source text "in a lexically reorganized or topically rethematized way."

54. Lyons, *From Law to Prophecy*, 61–2.

55. Zimmerli, *Ezekiel*, 1:46.

study of Ezekiel's use of Deuteronomy has much more value for the interpretation of the book of Ezekiel than the study of a modern poet's use of earlier poetic works. His use of its language and concepts in some cases may have carried rhetorical force, even in cases of *indirect usage* or *literary borrowing* when he did not refer explicitly to Deuteronomy. To cite an example, even when Ezekiel does not overtly identify Deuteronomy when stating that Israel violated Yahweh's decrees, his use of Deuteronomy's distinctive language in his oracles of indictment might have implied as much.

Third, the identification of Ezekiel's *literary references* is essential for the exegesis of the book. Since writers intend quotations and allusions to be recognized by the reader, identifying them is a necessary part of fully understanding the quoting or alluding text. According to Schultz, "if a quotation's source is not recognized, there is an unfortunate semantic loss, even if the passage in itself is comprehensible."[56] Explaining allusion, Ben-Porat asserts that a correctly identified marker significantly alters the interpretation of the alluding text when the reader brings elements of the evoked text to bear on it.[57] Therefore, if a loss of meaning occurs when readers do not recognize literary references, then identifying Ezekiel's allusions to Deuteronomy will result in a fuller understanding of the book of Ezekiel.

Thus, Deuteronomy's influence on Ezekiel means more than some vague sense that Deuteronomy inspired Ezekiel. He used Deuteronomy's language and concepts not simply for aesthetic reasons, but—as I will demonstrate—in many cases for rhetorical purposes. We should not stop after merely identifying cases of literary dependence, but must proceed to interpret how they function rhetorically in the author's message.[58] By showing *how* Ezekiel used an authoritative text—indeed, the statutes and regulations given to Israel by God (20:11)—for his prophetic message, we come to understand the rhetorical techniques the prophet used to move his audience to change their beliefs and their behavior.

---

56. Schultz, *Search for Quotation*, 225.

57. Ben-Porat, "Poetics of Literary Allusion." See also Kelli S. O'Brien, *The Use of Scripture in the Markan Passion Narrative*, LNTS 384 (New York: T&T Clark, 2010), 24–6.

58. So also Stead, *Intertextuality in Zechariah 1–8*, 43–4. Cf. Christopher D. Stanley, "Rhetoric of Quotations," in *Exploring Intertextuality: Diverse Strategies for New Testament Interpretation of Texts*, ed. B. J. Oropeza and Steve Moyise (Eugene, OR: Cascade, 2016), 42–62.

Chapter 3

IDOLATRY

Idolatry constitutes the gravest sin against Yahweh in the book of Ezekiel, as in other biblical literature.[1] Indictments against idol worship pervade the prophetic book, suggesting idolatry was a special concern for Ezekiel. Looking back on Israel's history at the beginning of the sixth century, the prophet identified idolatry as the primary cause of Israel's present situation, namely, divine judgment resulting in the destruction of the land and the Babylonian exile.[2]

---

1. According to Moshe Halbertal and Avishai Margalit, "The central theological principle of the Bible [is] the rejection of idolatry" (*Idolatry*, trans. Naomi Goldblum [Cambridge, MA: Harvard University Press, 1992], 10).

2. Kutsko identifies idolatry as "the quintessential cause of the Babylonian exile" in the book of Ezekiel (*Between Heaven and Earth*, 25); cf. Middlemas, "Transformation of the Image," 114–15. According to Andrew Mein, "the prophet conceives of idolatry as the root sin…the sin that explains the others" (Mein, *Ethics of Exile*, 109). Similarly, in Ka Leung Wong's words, "the practice of idolatry is seen as the sin *par excellence* in Ezekiel" (Wong, *Idea of Retribution*, 155).

For surveys of the scholarly discussion surrounding the broader phenomenon of aniconism in ancient Israel, see Brian B. Schmidt, "The Aniconic Tradition: On Reading Images and Viewing Texts," in *The Triumph of Elohim: From Yahwisms to Judaisms*, ed. D. V. Edelman, Contributions to Biblical Exegesis and Theology 13 (Kampen: Kok Pharos, 1995), 75–105; Ronald S. Hendel, "The Social Origins of the Aniconic Tradition in Early Israel," *CBQ* 50 (1988): 365–83. On aniconism in Ezekiel, see Jill Middlemas, "Exclusively Yahweh: Aniconism and Anthropomorphism in Ezekiel," in *Prophecy and the Prophets in Ancient Israel*, ed. John Day (London: T&T Clark, 2010), 309–24.

While idolatry properly refers to the use of images in religious worship,³ whether of Yahweh or other gods,⁴ this chapter will also treat a few instances of worship of other gods when images are not explicitly mentioned, as in the descriptions of "weeping the Tammuz" in ch. 8, and child sacrifice in chs. 16, 20, and 23.⁵

The Basis for Ezekiel's Indictment against Idolatry

Unlike the extended polemics against idolatry in other biblical books, which ridicule the futility of idol worship or cite other theological criticisms,⁶ Ezekiel offers little logical rationale against such practices.⁷ For Ezekiel idolatry is foremost an offense against the חקות and משפטים, the "statutes and regulations,"⁸ which, according to 20:10-11, are the

---

3. According to Frederick E. Greenspahn, "if 'idolatry' is to have any identifiable content at all, it must entail the use of physical objects and not just the worship of some god other than YHWH... Clarity of meaning requires that an idol be an object that is itself worshipped and thus idolatry the practice of worshipping images" ("Syncretism and Idolatry in the Bible," *VT* 54 [2004]: 481). On the Bible's occasional ambiguity between "idols" and "other gods," see Thomas A. Judge, *Other Gods and Idols: The Relationship between the Worship of Other Gods and the Worship of Idols within the Old Testament*, LHBOTS 674 (New York: Bloomsbury T&T Clark, 2019).

4. José Faur distinguishes idolatry as worship of strange gods and iconolatry as the use of images in the worship of Yahweh ("The Biblical Idea of Idolatry," *JQR* 69 [1978]: 13). For the possible evidence of anthropomorphic images of Yahweh used in Israelite religion, see Stuart Weeks, "Man-made Gods? Idolatry in the Old Testament," in *Idolatry: False Worship in the Bible, Early Judaism and Christianity*, ed. Stephen C. Barton (London: T&T Clark, 2007), 13; see n. 16, where Weeks discusses possible cases.

5. Middlemas, "Transformation of the Image," 120: "With few exceptions child sacrifices in Ezekiel are made to idols (גלולים), rather than to Yahweh (16:20-36; 20:31; 23:37)."

6. E.g., Deut. 4:15-19; Isa. 40:18-20; 44:9-20; 46:1-7; cf. 2:6-8, 20; Jer. 10:1-16; Hab. 2:18-20; Pss. 97:7-9; 115:3-8; 135:15-18.

7. Cf. C. R. North, who observes that in comparison to other prophets "Ezekiel is too filled with indignation to busy himself with any rationale or 'philosophy' of idolatry" ("The Essence of Idolatry," in *Von Ugarit nach Qumran: Festschrift für Otto Eissfeldt*, ed. Johannes Hempel and Leonhard Rost, BZAW 77 [Berlin: Töpelmann, 1958], 158). However, Ezekiel expresses the futility of idols in more subtle ways. For example, as John Kutsko has noted, Ezekiel refuses to legitimize idols by calling them אלהים (Kutsko, *Between Heaven and Earth*, 35–9; also Middlemas, "Transformation of the Image," 116, 122).

8. On Israel's sins as a failure to observe the statutes and regulations, see, for example, Ezek. 5:5-6 (cf. Mein, *Ethics of Exile*, 106; Zimmerli, *Ezekiel*, 1:175:

instructions given by Yahweh in the wilderness: "I led them out of the land of Egypt and brought them into the wilderness, and I gave them my statutes (חקות) and made known to them my regulations (משפטים)."

Sometimes in Ezekiel, חקות and משפטים refer generically to the sum of cultic and social responsibilities outlined in Israel's legal traditions, as in ch. 18 (vv. 9, 17, 19, 21).[9] However, חקות and משפטים are often associated with idolatry, as in Ezek. 20:15-16, where they refer explicitly to Israel's failure to keep the proscriptions against idolatry: "they rejected my regulations (משפטים) and did not walk in my statutes (חקות) and profaned my Sabbaths—*for their heart went after idols*" (emphasis added). Here the substance of Israel's disobedience against divine instruction is identified with idolatry. Ezekiel 20:24 presents a nearly identical counterpart to 20:16, but alternatively ends with ואחרי גלולי אבותם היו עיניהם ("and their eyes were set on their fathers' idols"). In this instance, the phrase likely constitutes an epexegetical clause,[10] so that idolatry is not an additional and separate offense, but the explanation of Israel's failure to keep Yahweh's instructions. Idolatry is central in all of ch. 20, Ezekiel's account of Israel's history of rebellion against Yahweh. Indeed, in the midst of the repeated references to the חקות and משפטים in the historical account of 20:5-26, no other sin except Sabbath violation is explicitly cited. In other passages as well where the violations against the חקות and משפטים are not identified explicitly as idolatrous practices, idolatry nevertheless features in the surrounding context (e.g., 36:27; 37:24).

Ezekiel and the Pentateuchal Descriptions of Idolatry

Since for Ezekiel idol worship constitutes an offense against divine instruction, it makes sense to compare his language for idolatry with that of Israel's legal traditions in order to determine whether Ezekiel may have drawn from their prohibitions against idolatry. Some scholars have noted the special concern for idolatry shared by Deuteronomy and Ezekiel. Jill Middlemas, for example, asserts that "Ezekiel's stance on the worship of other gods appears to follow the line of the Deuteronomic Code that

---

"Jerusalem's sin is not something vague, but an affront to the clear, revealed law of God"). Block identifies the חקות and משפטים in Ezekiel as references to Yahweh's covenant stipulations outlined in the Priestly writings and Deuteronomy (*Ezekiel*, 1:199).

9. For example, in 18:9 the terms ומשפטי חקותי serve either to summarize the previously mentioned cultic and social virtues in 18:5-8 or to encapsulate all the other covenant stipulations not mentioned.

10. See *IBHS* §39.2.4.

forbids the worship of other deities and representations of deities."[11] In an essay, Tova Ganzel has argued more specifically that Ezekiel drew almost exclusively from Deuteronomic rather than Priestly literature for his terminology and conception of Israel's idolatry.[12] This chapter will build upon Ganzel's treatment.

Ezekiel's affinity with Deuteronomy may be due in part to the Holiness Code's relative silence on the subject. The Holiness Code (H) mentions idolatry only a few times (Lev. 19:4; 26:1, 30), two of which are prohibitions.[13] Milgrom observes that "other than these two tangential citations, there is no polemic in H against idolatry... What is totally missing in H is the frontal attack, like the repeated gunfire of D."[14] By contrast, Deuteronomy mentions idolatry thirty-six times, leading Milgrom to speak of "D's obsession with idolatry."[15] Therefore, Deuteronomy places a far greater emphasis on idolatry than the Holiness Code. One particular example reinforces the point: whereas in Lev. 20:23 (20:22-26) the people are warned against the customs of the Canaanites on grounds of purity

11. Middlemas, "Transformation of the Image," 115.

12. Ganzel, "Transformation of Pentateuchal Descriptions," 34: "Ezekiel's descriptions of [idolatrous] practices, surprisingly, reflect a far more notable connection to D and to Dtr than to the Priestly literature." Ganzel's discussion of Deuteronomic vocabulary in Ezekiel corrects Milgrom, who asserted that Ezekiel was influenced by the thought, but not necessarily the language, of Deuteronomy ("Nature and Extent of Idolatry," 6).

While otherwise minimizing Deuteronomy's influence on Ezekiel, Baruch Schwartz grants Ganzel's conclusion and offers an explanation: "As demonstrated in Ganzel's doctoral dissertation [see now Ganzel, "Transformation"], Ezekiel has a penchant for using the Deuteronomic terms for the Israelites' idolatrous practices—presumably, I would say, because the terms provided by P were anachronistic and unconnected with the historical reality as it had transpired, a natural outgrowth of the same feature of P I mentioned above: it is cast in the distant past" (Schwartz, "Ezekiel, P, and the Other Pentateuchal Sources"). Apparently, for Schwartz the writers of Deuteronomy were less successful at making the book appear Mosaic than the writers of P.

13. Milgrom, "Nature and Extent of Idolatry," 4. In addition, Num. 33:50-53, traditionally regarded as a Priestly passage, instructs the Israelites to "drive out the inhabitants of the land from before you and destroy all their images [משכית] and destroy all their metal images [מסכה] and demolish all their high places." Note also child sacrifice to Molech in Lev. 20:2: איש איש ... אשר יתן מזרעו למלך מות יומת.

14. Jacob Milgrom, "Does H Advocate the Centralization of Worship?" *JSOT* 88 (2000): 67–8.

15. Milgrom, "Nature and Extent of Idolatry," 6. Cf. idem, "Does H Advocate the Centralization of Worship?" 68: "What is totally missing in H is the frontal attack [against idolatry], like the repeated gunfire of D (4.19, 25; 6.13-14; 7.4; 8.12; 11.16; 13.2-19, and so on)."

and separateness, in Deuteronomy they are repeatedly warned against the customs of the Canaanites because of their idols (e.g., Deut. 12:2-4). This difference suggests idolatry was not the primary concern for P/H and highlights the fact that Ezekiel shares Deuteronomy's polemic against idolatry.

To be sure, Ezekiel uses a couple of H's words for idolatry.[16] One may be the prophet's favorite term גלולים, which occurs thirty-nine times in Ezekiel.[17] It is difficult to determine the origins of the term, which appears elsewhere only in Lev. 26:30; Deut. 29:16[17]; Jer. 50:2; and six times in DtrH.[18] While some have suggested Ezekiel adopted the term from common parlance or even invented it,[19] Ezekiel may have known it from Lev. 26:30, a covenant curse that promises the destruction of Israel's גלולים.[20] Another shared word is חמנים, which Lev. 26:30 and Ezek. 6:4-6 use to describe the destruction of incense altars.[21]

---

16. Treated by Ganzel, "Transformation," 43–5.

17. Ezek. 6:4, 5, 6, 9, 13; 8:10; 14:3, 4, 5, 6, 7; 16:36; 18:6, 12, 15; 20:7, 8, 16, 18, 24, 31, 39; 22:3, 4; 23:7, 30, 37, 39 (2×), 49; 30:13; 33:25; 36:18, 25; 37:23; 44:10, 12. For a detailed discussion of the word's meaning and possible etymologies, see Kutsko, *Between Heaven and Earth*, 32–4; Daniel Bodi, "Les *gillûlîm* chez Ézéchiel et dans l'Ancien Testament, et les différentes pratiques cultuelles associées à ce terme," *RB* 100 (1993): 481–510. Johan Lust argues that the meaning of גלולים in the book of Ezekiel is broader than idols ("Idols? גלולים and εἴδωλα in Ezekiel," in *Florilegium Lovaniense: Studies in Septuagint and Textual Criticism in Honour of Florentino García Martínez*, ed. H. Ausloos, B. Lemmelijn, and M. Vervenne, BETL 224 [Leuven: Peeters, 2008], 317–33). However, his argument is based on the Septuagint, whose understanding of גלולים is not determinative for the meaning of the word in the sixth century BCE.

18. 1 Kgs 15:12; 21:26; 2 Kgs 17:12; 21:11, 21; 23:24. Weinfeld lists the word among Deuteronomic terms for idolatry (Moshe Weinfeld, *Deuteronomy and the Deuteronomic School* [Oxford: Clarendon, 1972, repr., Winona Lake, IN: Eisenbrauns, 1992], 323).

19. H. D. Preuss, "גלולים, *gillûlîm*," *TDOT* 3:1; Bodi, "Les *gillûlîm*," 482; Patton, "Pan-Deuteronomism," 210; cf. Zimmerli, *Ezekiel*, 1:187: "Since Isaiah and Jeremiah refer to idols with a completely different terminology, we may ascribe the formation of the term [גלולים] to the sphere of life to which Ezekiel belonged; i.e., to the circles of the Jerusalem priesthood. Since it is used in the book of Ezekiel without any closer definition, Ezekiel must have taken it up as a term already coined."

20. The phrase ונתתי את פגרי בני ישראל לפני גלוליהם in Ezek. 6:5 cites virtually verbatim Lev. 26:30's גלוליכם פגרי על פגריכם את ונתתי. However, the locution is absent in LXX Ezekiel and may be secondary (Lyons, *From Law to Prophecy*, 139).

21. Note the broader connections between Lev. 26:30-31 and Ezek. 6:4-7 cited in ibid., 62–3; Block, *Ezekiel*, 1:218–19). Note also פגרים ("corpses") in Ezek. 43:7, 9.

Although Ezekiel's use of the Holiness Code broadly is well established, his use of its two prohibitions against idol worship in Lev. 19:4 and 26:1 is not obvious.

> Lev. 19:4   Do not turn to idols (אלילים) or make cast images
> (מסכה אלהי) for yourselves: I am Yahweh your God.
> Lev. 26:1   You shall make for yourselves no idols (אלילם) and erect
> no carved images (פסל) or pillars (מצבה), and you shall
> not place figured stones (משכית אבן) in your land, to
> worship at them; for I am Yahweh your God.

Idol terminology from these verses appears only twice in Ezekiel, and in both instances dependence is uncertain. The word משכית occurs in Ezek. 8:12, but without אבן, as it appears in Lev. 26:1 (אבן משכית).[22] Also, אלילים occurs in Ezek. 30:13, but in reference to Egypt's idols, not Israel's.[23] Remarkably, Ezekiel does not use the Holiness Code's terms מסכה and מצבה for idolatry,[24] nor the word פסל.[25]

Given the prophet's widespread literary use of the Holiness Code, his limited use of its idol language is surprising.[26] Instead, as I will outline in the next section, Ezekiel exhibits a marked preference for the idol vocabulary typical of Deuteronomy.[27] As Ganzel observed, "even in those cases where a Priestly alternative exists, Ezekiel shows a predilection for the Deuteronomic terminology."[28]

---

22. Cf. כל־משכיתם in Num. 33:52.

23. This term is a favorite of Isaiah (2:8, 18, 20; 10:10, 11; 19:1, 3; 31:7). As in Ezek. 30:13, Isa. 19 uses the word in an oracle against Egypt. Also Pss. 96:5; 97:7; cf. Jer. 14:14 (*Qere*).

24. The word מצבה appears in Ezek. 26:11 in an oracle against Tyre, but not in reference to idolatry (see further Elizabeth C. LaRocca-Pitts, *"Of Wood and Stone": The Significance of Israelite Cultic Items in the Bible and Its Early Interpreters* (Winona Lake, IN: Eisenbrauns, 2001), 111, 205–29. Note also Deut. 7:5; 12:3; 16:22; 1 Kgs 14:23; 2 Kgs 3:2; 10:26, 27; 17:10; 18:4; 23:14; Mic. 5:12[13]; Jer. 43:13.

25. The word פסל is common to several pentateuchal traditions, including the Decalogue (Exod. 20:4), the Holiness Torah (Lev. 26:1), and Deuteronomy (Deut. 4:16, 23, 25; 5:8; 27:15).

26. To be complete, we may also mention his use of a term not found in H but typically considered Priestly: צלם in Ezek. 7:20; 16:17; 23:14 (Num. 33:52; cf. Gen. 1:26-27).

27. So also Ganzel: "by and large, [Ezekiel's] terminology is unique to Deuteronomy and is not found in the Priestly literature" ("Transformation," 44).

28. Ibid., 44.

Beyond simply using Deuteronomy's language for idols, in 20:18 the prophet might overtly mention Deuteronomy's instructions.[29] After referring to the statutes given to the exodus generation (vv. 11-12), along with their rebellion and judgment (vv. 13-17), v. 18 describes Yahweh's exhortation to "their children in the wilderness" *not to worship idols*. While some might propose the command here is simply required for the pattern of Ezekiel's highly structured history in ch. 20, since each section of the overview includes a divine command to Israel,[30] v. 18 could refer to some part of Ezekiel's received historical traditions, conceivably the idol prohibitions in Num. 33:52 or Deuteronomy. If so, a couple of factors would support identifying it with Deuteronomy. First, Ezekiel regularly uses Deuteronomy's language for idols, not the language of Num. 33:52. Second, Ezekiel likely regarded the setting of Deuteronomy as "in the wilderness" (as v. 18 puts it), since Deuteronomy itself draws a close connection between its setting and Israel's sojourn in the wilderness. The narrative context of the Deuteronomic instruction names the second generation as Moses' audience (Deut. 2:14-16). According to Deut. 3:29 and 4:44-49, the Israelites were camped near Beth-Peor, the site of the second generation's wilderness tryst with Baal of Peor (Hos. 9:10; Num. 25:1-9).[31] Third, in Ezek. 20:18, Yahweh instructs the second generation to give up the idols that their parents worshiped in the wilderness. This fits Deuteronomy, where the wilderness rebellion is understood as the background to its instructions (1:32-45; 9:6-29). In Deuteronomy 4, the idolatry of Baal-Peor is cited (vv. 3-4) before Moses' exhortation to the second generation not to worship idols (vv. 16-19, 23).

---

29. Presuming that the command to the second generation in v. 18 must have come from a prophet, Greenberg asserted that no such thing is found in the pentateuchal traditions (*Ezekiel 1–20*, 367).

30. The three parts are: Israel in Egypt (vv. 5-9), the first desert generation (vv. 10-17), and the second desert generation (vv. 18-26) (see Block, *Ezekiel*, 1:620–4).

31. Moshe Weinfeld, *Deuteronomy 1–11: A New Translation with Introduction and Commentary*, AB 5 (New York: Doubleday, 1991), 192; Scott Walker Hahn and John Sietze Bergsma, "What Laws Were 'Not Good'? A Canonical Approach to the Theological Problem of Ezekiel 20:25-26," *JBL* 123 (2004): 206: "The relation of Deuteronomy to the second generation and particularly to the apostasy at Beth-Peor is underscored by the fact that, according to the narrative of Deuteronomy, Israel has not moved from Beth-Peor when Moses imposes on them the Deuteronomic laws."

Thus, although this identification remains uncertain,[32] it is plausible Ezek. 20:18 refers to laws given to the second generation in Deuteronomy. If so, this verse would suggest Ezekiel does not simply use Deuteronomic language but knows of the second-generation torah tradition we now call Deuteronomy. Even if this interpretation of v. 18 is incorrect, Ezekiel still seems to regard idolatry as a violation of Deuteronomy's instruction in a more indirect way. Since for Ezekiel idolatry is a violation of Yahweh's חקות and משפטים, by using Deuteronomy's idol language he effectively identifies these statutes and regulations with Deuteronomy's prohibitions of idolatry. In either case, he does not simply adopt Deuteronomy's terminology, but appeals to its very prohibitions, which are presented as divine commandments.[33]

Lastly, a corollary to this thesis relates to Ezekiel's use of the word pair חקות ומשפטים. Whereas Deuteronomy regularly refers to God's statutes with the grammatically masculine חקים,[34] Ezekiel follows H's preference for the grammatically feminine חקות.[35] When paired with משפטים, one consistently finds חקים ומשפטים in Deuteronomy and חקות ומשפטים in the Holiness Code.[36] Consequently, Ezekiel's use of Deuteronomy's idol language indicates that although he follows the Holiness Code's locution חקות ומשפטים, he uses it to refer not only to the Holiness Code, but to the totality of divine regulations, including Deuteronomy.

---

32. One dissimilarity is that v. 18 comes before the rebellion of the second generation in v. 21, which may refer to the incident at Baal-Peor in Num. 25. In the pentateuchal tradition, both Num. 33:52 and Deuteronomy come after the idolatry at Baal-Peor. Dennis Olson, on the other hand, argues that the idolatry of Baal-Peor involved the first generation (*The Death of the Old and the Birth of the New: The Framework of the Book of Numbers and the Pentateuch*, BJS 71 [Chico, CA: Scholars Press, 1985]).

33. So also Ganzel, "Transformation," 39–40. On Yahweh as the ultimate source of Deuteronomy's instructions, see, e.g., Deut. 6:1; 12:1. To be sure, Lev. 19:4 and 26:1 are also presented as divine instruction, but as we have seen Ezekiel does not appeal to them in his indictment against Israel's idols.

34. On חקים ומשפטים in Deuteronomy, see Georg Braulik, "Die Ausdrücke für 'Gesetz' im Buch Deuteronomium," *Bib* 51 (1970): 62, who argues that the terms denote the teaching of the entirety of the book (chs. 5–26), not simply a part thereof.

35. The difference is not absolute, since Deuteronomy uses חקות in conjunction with מצות (Deut. 6:2; 10:13; 28:15, 45; 30:10; see Weinfeld, *Deuteronomy and the Deuteronomic School*, 337).

36. Compare Deut. 4:1, 5, 8, 14; 5:1; 11:32; 12:1 and Lev. 18:4, 5, 26; 19:37; 20:22; 25:18; 26:3, 15 (Mein, *Ethics of Exile*, 107; Levitt Kohn, *New Heart*, 99 n. 24; Gordon H. Matties, *Ezekiel 18 and the Rhetoric of Moral Discourse*, SBLDS 126 (Atlanta: Scholars Press, 1990), 176–9.

Deuteronomic Language for Idolatry in Ezekiel

Ezekiel adopts many of Deuteronomy's terms for idols and related religious practices.[37] We begin with examples of the prophet's use of distinctively Deuteronomic language that may not be literary references in every case. Without evidence of literary dependence, his use of these terms would be characterized as *indirect usage*. Later in this chapter, we will consider more examples of Deuteronomy's idol language and concepts in Ezekiel that may be literary references to Deuteronomy.

שקוצים, *"Detestable Things"*

The word שִׁקּוּץ, "detestable thing," occurs eight times in the book of Ezekiel, and in each instance it refers unequivocally to idols.[38] The noun also appears in Deut. 29:16[17] for idols, while the verbal root שקץ is used in Deut. 7:26, which states that carved images are to be utterly detested (שַׁקֵּץ תְּשַׁקְּצֶנּוּ). Since the term often refers to idols in DtrH and Jeremiah[39] and is lacking in the Priestly literature, it may be regarded as a Deuteronomic term for idolatry.[40] Leviticus uses the related noun שֶׁקֶץ to refer to animals unfit for human consumption, but this word never refers to idolatry.[41] It can therefore be concluded that Ezekiel adopts the distinctly Deuteronomic meaning of this term for his polemic against idols.[42]

תועבות, *"Abominations"*

The word תועבה occurs frequently in the Hebrew Bible to describe all kinds of abhorrent behavior. For example, in Deuteronomy alone the word is used for prohibited food (14:3), defective sacrifice (17:1), invalid payment for a vow (23:19[18]), divination (18:12), transvestism (22:5), remarried divorcees (24:4), and false weights (25:13-16).[43] In Ezekiel, the

---

37. Cf. Ganzel's list in "Transformation," 40–2.
38. Ezek. 5:11; 7:20; 11:18, 21; 20:7, 8, 30; 37:23. The related noun שֶׁקֶץ in Ezek. 8:10 will be considered below.
39. 1 Kgs 11:5, 7 (2×); 2 Kgs 23:13 (2×), 24; Jer. 4:1; 7:30; 13:27; 16:18; 32:34; cf. Hos. 9:10; Isa. 66:3.
40. Weinfeld, *Deuteronomy and the Deuteronomic School*, 323.
41. Lev. 7:21; 11:10, 11, 12, 13, 20, 23, 41, 42. See Levitt Kohn, *New Heart*, 90.
42. So also ibid., 89–90; Ganzel, "Transformation," 40; Weinfeld, *Deuteronomy and the Deuteronomic School*, 323.
43. Kutsko, *Between Heaven and Earth*, 30; Milgrom, *Leviticus 17–22*, 1569. The ability to apply the word to varied practices is illustrated nicely by Jer. 7:9-10: "Will

word is used similarly in the context of diverse transgressions or generic rebellion.⁴⁴ Indeed, as LaRocca-Pitts has observed, Ezekiel's use of תועבה displays "a semantic range most like that found in Deuteronomy." She notes:

> Both Deuteronomy and Ezekiel use the term to refer to sexual aberrations [Deut 22:5; 24:4; Ezek 22:11; 33:26], illegitimate ritual practices including child sacrifice [Deut 18:9-12; Ezek 8:15-17; 16:22, 36], as a general term for any aberrant practices of other nations [Deut 20:18; Ezek 5:9; 16:47], and as an evaluation of the use of cultic statuary [Deut 13:15(14); 17:4; 27:15; 32:16; Ezek 5:11; 7:20; 8:6, 9, 13; 14:6; 16:36; 22:2; 23:36].⁴⁵

Varšo similarly observed:

> Deuteronomische und ezechielische Texte weisen demnach auf der Ausdrucks- wie auch auf der Inhaltsebene eine nicht geringe Zahl an Parallelen auf. Der Verstoß gegen die Gesetze aus jedem der drei Bereiche wird in Ezechiel und im Deuteronomium als תועבה bezeichnet. Die Abfolge der einzelnen thematische Bereiche - kultisch, sexuell und sozial - wird in beiden Büchern beibehalten.⁴⁶

However, it is idolatry as תועבה that represents the most distinctive link between Deuteronomy and Ezekiel. The use of תועבה for idolatry is a distinctively Deuteronomic phenomenon, according to Weinfeld,⁴⁷ and central to its anti-idolatry polemic.⁴⁸ In Deuteronomy, תועבה occurs nine times for idolatry, in reference both to idols themselves⁴⁹ and to idolatrous practices in general.⁵⁰ In DtrH, it is used *only* for idolatry, most often in the Deuteronomistic evaluations of Israel's kings.⁵¹ This contrasts with

---

you steal, murder, commit adultery, swear falsely, make offerings to Baal, and go after gods that you have not known...*to do all those abominations*?" So also Ezek. 18:13, 24.

44. Ezek. 5:9; 6:11; 7:3, 4, 8, 9; 9:4; 12:16; 16:2, 22, 43, 47, 50, 51, 58; 18:12, 13, 24; 22:2; 33:26, 29; 36:31; 43:8; 44:6, 7, 13. When specific activities are mentioned, they include sexual sin (22:11) and ethical failures (18:10-13). For a fuller treatment of Ezekiel's use of the term, see P. Humbert, "Le substantif *tô'ebâ* et le verbe *t'b* dans l'Ancien Testament," *ZAW* 72 (1960): 227–31.

45. LaRocca-Pitts, *"Of Wood and Stone,"* 113.
46. Varšo, "Das Deuteronomium mit Ezechiel lesen," 153–4.
47. Weinfeld, *Deuteronomy and the Deuteronomic School*, 323.
48. Block, *Ezekiel*, 1:203.
49. Deut. 7:26; 27:15; 32:16.
50. Deut. 7:25; 12:31; 13:15[14]; 17:4; 20:18.
51. 1 Kgs 14:24; 2 Kgs 16:3; 21:2, 11; 23:13; cf. Jer. 16:18; 32:35; 44:4.

the Holiness Code, where the term appears in only two passages and is restricted to sexual sins.⁵²

As in Deuteronomy, תועבה occurs frequently in Ezekiel to refer to idolatry. The term is applied five times to idolatrous practices (all in ch. 8),⁵³ and several times to idols themselves,⁵⁴ with the unique phrases צלמי תועבתם in 7:20 and גלולי תועבותיך in 16:36 standing out. In other passages, the direct identification of the term with idolatry is not certain but is suggested by the immediate context.⁵⁵ For example, in Ezek. 20:4 Yahweh commands Ezekiel to make known to Israel the abominations of the ancestors, and the ensuing oracle elaborates on Israel's history of idolatry. The same can be said for Ezek. 23:36. Moreover, because Ezekiel often uses תועבה for idolatry, it is possible that just as some of the non-specific references to the failure to obey the חקות and משפטים may have idolatry in mind, so some of the occurrences of תועבה in Ezekiel that do not explicitly identify a referent may in fact refer to idolatry. In summary, Ezekiel's use of תועבה for idolatry, otherwise unique to Deuteronomy and DtrH, strongly suggests Deuteronomic influence.⁵⁶ This hypothesis would seem to be corroborated by a further distinctive link, namely, the pairing of תועבה and שקץ/שקוצים. As LaRocca-Pitts observes: "Both Deuteronomy and Ezekiel use the terms *tôʿēbāh* and *šiqqûṣ* together in verses that suggest a reference to the use of [a] cultic statuary [Deut. 7:25-26; Ezek. 11:18, 21]."⁵⁷ Lastly, Carly Crouch has argued that for both Deuteronomy and Ezekiel, תועבה functions to preserve the boundaries of Israel's ethnic identity, "the fundamental marker" of which is "the exclusive commitment to YHWH" as opposed to "non-Yahwistic cultic practices, or even the outright worship of deities other than YHWH."⁵⁸

העביר בנים באש, *"Passing Children through the Fire"*

Child sacrifice is associated in Ezekiel with deities other than Yahweh.⁵⁹ When speaking of child sacrifice, Ezekiel prefers the Deuteronomic

---

52. Lev. 18:22-30 (5×); 20:13. See Milgrom, *Leviticus 17–22*, 1569.
53. Ezek. 8:6, 9, 13, 15, 17.
54. Ezek. 5:11; 7:20; 11:18, 21; 14:16; 16:36.
55. Ezek. 6:9; 20:4; 23:36.
56. Block, *Ezekiel*, 1:203; Greenberg, *Ezekiel 1–20*, 113.
57. LaRocca-Pitts, *"Of Wood and Stone,"* 113.
58. C. L. Crouch, "What Makes a Thing Abominable? Observations on the Language of Boundaries and Identity Formation from a Social Scientific Perspective," *VT* 65 (2015): 535.
59. On child sacrifice, see Francesca Stavrakopoulou, *King Manasseh and Child Sacrifice: Biblical Distortions of Historical Realities*, BZAW 338 (Berlin: de

phrase העביר בנים באש ("pass children through the fire") over the Priestly phrase נתן למולך ("give to Molech") in 16:21; 20:31; and in slightly variant forms, 20:26; 23:37.[60] Granted, these phrases are not mutually exclusive, since in one instance the Priestly material includes העביר with נתן,[61] and 2 Kgs 23:10 and Jer. 32:35 use the Deuteronomic phrase but add למלך ("to Molech"). However, in most cases the Deuteronomic literature strictly uses העביר בנים באש (Deut. 18:10; 2 Kgs 16:3; 17:17; 21:6; 23:10; cf. Deut. 12:31) and Leviticus נתן למולך (Lev. 20:2, 3, 4). Thus, Ezekiel's language for child sacrifice provides an example of his preference for Deuteronomic language, even when a Priestly alternative exists.

הכעיס, "Provoke to Anger"

Absent in the Priestly literature, the Hiphil form of the verb כעס appears throughout the Deuteronomic literature for the notion of provoking Yahweh to anger.[62] Most often the word occurs in the context of Israel's idolatry.[63] Other times the causes of Yahweh's anger are transgressions generally (חטאות)[64] or doing evil (הרע),[65] but these may also refer to or include idolatry.[66] This word occurs three times in Ezekiel to describe the provocation of Yahweh: for idolatry and violence in the land (8:17), foreign relations (16:26), and illegitimate places of worship (20:28). In the

---

Gruyter, 2004), 141–300; Ed Noort, "Child Sacrifice in Ancient Israel: The *Status Quaestionis*," in *The Strange World of Human Sacrifice*, ed. Jan N. Bremmer; Studies in the History and Anthropology of Religion 1 (Leuven: Peeters, 2007), 103–25; idem, "Genesis 22: Human Sacrifice and Theology in the Hebrew Bible," in *The Sacrifice of Isaac: The Aqedah (Genesis 22) and Its Interpretations*, ed. Ed Noort and Eibert Tigchelaar (Leiden: Brill, 2002), 1–20; Jill Middlemas, *The Troubles of Templeless Judah*, OTM (Oxford: Oxford University Press, 2005), 97–105; Milgrom, *Leviticus 17–22*, 1379–80, 1551–65; cf. also Otto Eissfeldt, *Molk als Opferbegriff im Punischen und Hebräischen und das Ende des Gottes Moloch* (Halle: Niemeyer, 1935); Heider, *The Cult of Molek*; John Day, *Molech: A God of Human Sacrifice in the Old Testament* (Cambridge: Cambridge University Press, 1989).

60. Ganzel, "Transformation," 41.
61. Lev. 18:21: למלך להעביר לא־תתן ומזרעך.
62. Weinfeld, *Deuteronomy and the Deuteronomic School*, 340.
63. Deut. 4:25; 31:29; 32:16, 19, 21; Judg. 2:12; 1 Kgs 14:9, 15; 16:13, 26, 33; 22:54; 2 Kgs 17:11, 17; 21:6; 22:17; Jer. 7:18, 19; 8:19; 11:17; 25:6, 7; 32:29, 30; 44:3, 8. Cf. Deut. 6:14-15, which does not use הכעיס, but speaks of idolatry inciting Yahweh's anger (אף).
64. 1 Kgs 15:30; 16:2; 21:22.
65. Deut. 9:18; 31:29; 1 Kgs 16:7; 2 Kgs 21:15; Jer. 32:32.
66. E.g., Deut. 31:29.

first instance, the phrase וישבו להכעיסני is lacking in the LXX Ezek. 8:17 and likely a deliberate scribal evaluation of what is going on in the temple—perhaps a continuation of the prophet's own use of Deuteronomic language in Ezekiel 8 outlined below in the section on Ezekiel's temple vision.[67] The last indictment, which reflects influence from Deuteronomic centralization, finds a parallel in 2 Kgs 23:19, which speaks of the high places (במות) provoking Yahweh to anger. In the next chapter of this study, I will argue that Ezekiel's use of כעס in ch. 16 reflects borrowing from Deuteronomy 32.

הלך אחרי אלהים / גלולים, *"Going after Gods / Idols"*

Perhaps the most common Deuteronomic phrase for idolatrous practices is הלך אחרי אלהים אחרים, "go after other gods."[68] Though Ezekiel never uses this exact phrase, he does use the similar phrase הלך אחרי גלולים, "go after *gillûlîm*," in 20:16 (cf. 20:24).[69] Since Kutsko has shown that Ezekiel avoids all words for idols that might grant them the status of deity, especially אלהים, it appears the prophet appropriated this common Deuteronomic phrase, but adjusted it for theological reasons.[70]

עיניו נשא, *"Lifting One's Eyes (to גלולים)"*

Several times Ezekiel speaks of "lifting one's eyes" (נשא עיניו) to גלולים (Ezek. 18:6, 12, 15; 23:27; 33:25). The use of the phrase נשא עינים in the context of idolatry appears elsewhere only in Deut. 4:19, which prohibits "lifting one's eyes" to the astral bodies: the sun, the moon, and the stars.

קסם, *"Divination"*

While divination is not idolatrous per se, this illegitimate religious practice is a shared concern of Ezekiel and Deuteronomy. The word קסם

---

67. Credit to anonymous reviewer for this monograph series. See Zimmerli, *Ezekiel*, 1:221; Tov, "Recensional Differences," 408.

68. Occurring 18 times in Deuteronomy, 20 times in DtrH, and 18 times in Jeremiah: Deut. 5:7; 6:14; 7:4; 8:19; 11:16, 28; 13:3, 7, 14; 17:3; 18:20; 28:14, 36, 64; 29:25; 30:17; 31:18, 20; Josh 23:16; 24:2, 16; Judg. 2:12, 17, 19; 10:13; 1 Sam. 8:8; 26:19; 1 Kgs 9:6, 9; 11:4, 10; 14:9; 2 Kgs 5:17; 17:7, 35, 37, 38; 22:17; Jer. 1:16; 7:6, 9, 18; 11:10; 13:10; 16:11, 13; 19:4, 13; 22:9; 25:6; 32:29; 35:15; 44:3, 5, 8, 15; also Exod. 20:3; 23:13; Hos. 3:1.

69. Note also זנה אחרי גלולים / שקוצים, "to go whoring after *gillûlîm/šiqqûsîm*," in 6:9 and 20:30 (cf. Exod. 34:15, 16; Lev. 20:5; Deut. 31:16; Judg. 2:17; 8:33), and תעה אחרי גלולים, "to go astray after *gillûlîm*," in 44:10.

70. Kutsko, *Between Heaven and Earth*, 38–9.

appears many times in Ezekiel,[71] and is found among the pentateuchal legal traditions only in Deuteronomy (18:10, 14). The word occurs twice in the Balaam narrative, but in verses that are not traditionally considered P (Num. 22:7; 23:23). The practice is mentioned five times in the Deuteronomistic History and three times in Jeremiah as well.[72] Zimmerli suggested that Jeremiah influenced Ezekiel, since the phrase יהוה לא שלחם, "Yahweh did not send them," in Ezek. 13:6 echoes Jer. 14:14 (cf. 23:21).[73] However, it may be just as likely that Ezekiel influenced Jeremiah, leaving open the possibility of more direct influence of Deuteronomy on Ezekiel.

Worshiping Idols in Exile

Among Deuteronomy's many references to idolatry, one stands out as especially relevant to Ezekiel and his audience in Babylonian exile. Although Deuteronomy threatens destruction and eventual exile for disloyalty to the covenant, it identifies one particular image of idolatry with Israel's state *after* the punishment of deportation. In three of the four texts that threaten expulsion from the land, Deuteronomy declares that in exile the people will worship idols, using the distinctive word pair עץ ואבן ("wood and stone").[74] In the context of exile, serving wood and stone amounts to worshiping the local gods, and perhaps the resulting assimilation and loss of Israel's religio-national identity.[75] This statement occurs in ch. 4 after Moses predicts that Israel will fall into idolatry and be scattered among the peoples (vv. 25-28) and twice in the warnings of exile in the covenant curses of Deuteronomy 28 (vv. 36, 64).[76]

---

71. Ezek. 13:6, 9, 23; 21:26, 27, 28, 34[21, 22, 23, 29]; 22:28.

72. Josh. 13:22 (in reference to Balaam); 1 Sam. 6:2 (of the Philistines); 1 Sam. 15:23; 28:8; 2 Kgs 17:17; Jer. 14:14; 27:9; 29:8.

73. Zimmerli, *Ezekiel*, 1:293.

74. Weinfeld, *Deuteronomy and the Deuteronomic School*, 324. Outside of Deuteronomy the word pair only appears here and in 2 Kgs 19:18 (= Isa. 37:19).

75. Tigay, *Deuteronomy*, 53, cited in Dalit Rom-Shiloni, "Facing Destruction and Exile: Inner-Biblical Exegesis in Jeremiah and Ezekiel," *ZAW* 117 (2005): 198.

76. Deut. 29:16[17] also mentions "wood and stone," along with "silver and gold," in the context of the idols of Egypt (ותראו את־שקוציהם ואת גלליהם עץ ואבן כסף וזהב אשר עמהם). Also 2 Kgs 19:18 (= Isa. 37:19). Note the inverted order את האבן ואת העץ in Jer. 3:9; cf. Jer. 2:27.

Deut. 4:27-28

And Yahweh will scatter you among the peoples, and you will be left few in number among the nations where Yahweh will drive you.	והפיץ יהוה אתכם בעמים ונשארתם מתי מספר בגוים אשר ינהג יהוה אתכם שמה
And there you will serve gods, the work of human hands—*wood and stone*—that neither see, nor hear, nor eat, nor smell.	ועבדתם שם אלהים מעשה ידי אדם עץ ואבן אשר לא יראון ולא ישמעון ולא יאכלון ולא יריחן

Deut. 28:36

Yahweh will bring you and your king whom you set over you to a nation that neither you nor your fathers have known. And there you shall serve other gods—*wood and stone*.	יולך יהוה אתך ואת מלכך אשר תקים עליך אל גוי אשר לא ידעת אתה ואבתיך ועבדת שם אלהים אחרים עץ ואבן

Deut. 28:64

And Yahweh will scatter you among all peoples, from one end of the earth to the other, and there you shall serve other gods which neither you nor your fathers have known—*wood and stone*.	והפיצך יהוה בכל העמים מקצה הארץ ועד קצה הארץ ועבדת שם אלהים אחרים אשר לא ידעת אתה ואבתיך עץ ואבן

In these texts, עץ ואבן functions as a fixed word pair, which is confirmed by its syntactical position in all three texts, namely, apposition: "the works of human hands—wood and stone" (4:28); "other gods—wood and stone" (28:36); "other gods that neither you nor your fathers have known—wood and stone" (28:64).

The locution עץ ואבן appears at a key point in Ezekiel 20.[77] In the beginning of the chapter, the elders of Israel approach Ezekiel to inquire of Yahweh. After the prophet's extended account of Israel's history of idolatry, Ezekiel says:

What comes into your mind will not happen, when you say: "We will be like the nations, like the tribes of the lands, serving *wood and stone*." (v. 32)	והעלה על רוחכם היו לא תהיה אשר אתם אמרים נהיה כגוים כמשפחות הארצות לשרת עץ ואבן

---

77. This verse plays an integral (and contested) function in the structure of ch. 20, serving as the hinge between the two main sections (vv. 2-31, 33-38).

Based on the rarity of this word pair, Ezekiel appears to borrow it from Deuteronomy, or at least adopt what would have been known as a distinctively Deuteronomic concept.[78] But the Deuteronomic concept of worshiping עץ ואבן in exile functions more fundamentally in the dialogue between Ezekiel and the elders. Its mention in the present exilic context suggests the prophet is alluding to Deuteronomy's prediction that the people would serve idols in exile. Now in exile, Ezekiel and the elders consider whether it will come to pass in the current generation in Babylon. Ezekiel declares unwaveringly that they will not (or need not) worship the local gods, because Yahweh will deliver them by bringing them out from the peoples, gathering them from the lands, and returning them to their homeland (vv. 33-38).

However, Ezekiel's disposition toward this Deuteronomic idea is contested. Dalit Rom-Shiloni agrees that Deuteronomy's unique association of exile with worshiping עץ ואבן is under discussion in Ezek. 20:32, but she argues Ezekiel ultimately rejects it.[79] Following Zimmerli, who understood נהיה כגוים as an indicative statement ("we will be like the nations"),[80] she interprets the elders' thought as an expression of worry that—per Deuteronomy's prediction—they will necessarily succumb to idolatry in exile. Unlike Zimmerli, who viewed v. 32 as a reaction to the preaching of vv. 1-26, Rom-Shiloni, regards v. 32 as "a genuine component of the Elders' inquiry [described in v. 3],"[81] not cited by the prophet until after his historical review (vv. 5-26).[82] Thus, the elders came to Ezekiel seeking guidance about "the traditional concept of [idolatry in] exile and their present existence in Babylon."[83] She writes:

---

78. So also Ganzel, "Transformation," 41; Levitt Kohn, *New Heart*, 92. Kutsko observes that Ezekiel purposely avoids אלהים as it occurs in Deut. 4:28; 28:36, 64: עבד אלהים...עץ ואבן, "to serve [other] gods...wood and stone" (*Between Heaven and Earth*, 39–40).

79. Dalit Rom-Shiloni, "Ezekiel as the Voice of the Exiles and Constructor of Exilic Ideology," *HUCA* 76 (2005): 22.

80. E.g., Zimmerli, *Ezekiel*, 1:414: "an expression of deep despair."

81. Rom-Shiloni, "Facing Destruction," 196. In contrast to Zimmerli, who viewed v. 32 as a reaction to the preaching of vv. 1-31, Rom-Shiloni sees v. 32 as the impetus for Ezekiel's historical review.

82. Ibid., 199: "Within the inclusio repetition of the refusal of the Elders' inquiry (v. 3, 31), the prophet proclaims first the abhorrent deeds of 'their fathers' (v. 4-26). Getting to his contemporaries (v. 30-32a), Ezekiel then quotes their words (v. 32b), and rebukes them with a unique prophecy of deliverance."

83. Ibid., 202.

3. *Idolatry*

> The quotation [in v. 32] presents the Elders' own interpretation of this Deuteronomic concept of exile. In their minds, their present [situation] is a fulfillment of [Deuteronomy's] threats of destruction and dislocation. This interpretation leads the Exiles to a tremendous despair, since they face a terminal break in their religio-national identity and in their covenantal bond with God.[84]

In Rom-Shiloni's interpretation, Ezekiel responds by dispelling with an analogy the "traditional" notion that idolatry was inevitable in exile: just as Yahweh was with the people outside the land in the Sinai and wilderness periods (vv. 5-26), so he would be with them in exile also (vv. 33-38).

However, this interpretation of Ezek. 20:32 is doubtful. Most importantly, the idea that v. 32 reflects the despair of the elders is problematic, not least because it interprets their motivation in pious, orthodox terms. Zimmerli cites the remorse of the people generally in 33:10 and 37:11 for support;[85] but the depiction of the elders in ch. 14 provides a closer parallel. There the elders in exile are not pious Yahwists repulsed by the thought of idolatry. According to Ezekiel, they do in fact worship idols: "these men have taken their idols into their hearts" (14:3).[86] Furthermore, Yahweh's wrathful response in 20:33 is consistent with the people's continued rebellion, not their exclusive devotion to Yahweh.[87] Rom-Shiloni rightly observes that Ezekiel sees the exiles as the future of Israel, but this does not mean he considered them above reproach.[88] For Ezekiel, his exilic audience was idolatrous and deserved indictment. Thus, as most commentators prefer, the elders' "thought" reflects their willful desire to worship idols and should be understood in an optative sense: "let us be like the nations…worshiping wood and stone."[89] This interpretation finds

---

84. Ibid., 198.
85. Zimmerli, *Ezekiel*, 1:414.
86. Chapter 20 as well may accuse the elders of idolatry. Without seeing a tension with her thesis, Rom-Shiloni herself regards 20:30 as an accusation of idolatry, citing Greenberg, who translates: "you defile yourselves in the manner of your fathers" (Greenberg, *Ezekiel 1–20*, 362; cited by Rom-Shiloni, "Facing Destruction," 200). So also Allen, *Ezekiel 20 48*, 3 4, who cites the exclamatory function of the *heh* interrogative (JM §161b) and translates: "Are you contaminating yourselves the same way your ancestors did!"; cf. Zimmerli, *Ezekiel*, 1:402.
87. Block, *Ezekiel*, 1:649.
88. So also Andrew Mein, "Ezekiel: Structure, Themes, and Contested Issues," in *The Oxford Handbook of the Prophets*, ed. Carolyn J. Sharp (Oxford: Oxford University Press, 2016), 199.
89. Thus, for example, Eichrodt, *Ezekiel*, 277; Greenberg, *Ezekiel 1–20*, 371, 386; Block, *Ezekiel*, 1:648–51; Joyce, *Ezekiel*, 152; Davis, *Swallowing the Scroll*, 112; cf. Lust, "Ezekiel Salutes Isaiah," 371–5.

further support in Ezek. 20:32's allusion to 1 Samuel 8, where an earlier group of Israel's elders sought to be like the nations. Not only does the thought "to be like the nations" in Ezek. 20:32 clearly resemble the earlier elders' desire "to be like the nations" (1 Sam. 8:20; cf. 8:5), but Yahweh's declaration to "be king over you" (אמלוך עליכם) in the following verse (Ezek. 20:33) confirms the link to 1 Samuel 8, a central theme of which was the people's rejection of Yahweh as king over them (1 Sam. 8:7, אתי מאסו ממלך עליהם).[90]

So what then was Ezekiel's attitude toward Deuteronomy's idea of idolatry in exile? Whereas Rom-Shiloni asserts that v. 32 constitutes a quotation of the elders' actual inquiry,[91] the text itself does not state as much. Significantly, Ezekiel is the one who describes the "thought" of the elders in exile rather than the elders themselves, and, as Eichrodt asserted, it seems likely that the elders "did not say any such thing in their discussion with the prophet."[92] Thus, the elders did not come to the prophet specifically concerning "the traditional concept of [idolatry in] exile," as Rom-Shiloni argued. Rather, it is Ezekiel who knows Deuteronomy's notion of worshiping עץ ואבן in exile and interprets the elders' determination to worship idols in these Deuteronomic terms.[93] If this interpretation is correct, Ezekiel sees the elders' motivations as the actualization of Deuteronomy's curse.[94] His declaration that the thought "will never come

90. See Block for further links (*Ezekiel*, 1:649 n. 176).
91. Rom-Shiloni, "Facing Destruction," 194.
92. Eichrodt, *Ezekiel*, 277; cf. Block, *Ezekiel*, 1:648: "the verse leaves the impression that Ezekiel is able to look into the minds of his audience."
93. So also now, Michael A. Lyons, *An Introduction to the Study of Ezekiel* (New York: Bloomsbury T&T Clark, 2015), 105: "he places Deuteronomy's image of idolatry as punishment for covenant violation into the mouths of his contemporaries as an expression of intent." David Halperin similarly affirmed the influence of Deuteronomy on Ezekiel's description of the elders' desire to worship idols: "Where, then, did Ezekiel get his conviction that his 'sinful' contemporaries were plotting *en masse* to some crude idolatry? I suggest that he found it prophesied in the 'Mosaic' teachings that are now part of the Book of Deuteronomy." However, his conclusion that Ezekiel's accusation was "fantastically wrong" does not take into account Ezek. 14:3 (*Seeking Ezekiel: Text and Psychology* [University Park, PA: Pennsylvania State University Press, 1993], 113).
94. Block, *Ezekiel*, 1:649: "Ezekiel may have interpreted his compatriots' defiant comment as evidence that this prediction [of idolatry in exile in Deut. 4:28] is fulfilled in the present experience of exile, since the description of idols follows an extended exposition on the prohibition of idolatry of any sort in Israel (Deut. 4:9-25)." Cf. Greenberg, *Ezekiel 1–20*, 386: "In Deut 4:28; 28:64 such inane worship [of wood and stone] is held over the people as degrading punishment; here, in their degeneracy, they deliberately propose to embrace it."

about" does not mean he rejects the Deuteronomic idea,[95] but simply functions rhetorically to persuade his audience not to worship idols (cf. Ezek. 14:6), because Yahweh will be king over them and will ultimately bring his people back to their land (20:33-44).

Among the three occurrences of עץ ואבן in Deuteronomy, might Ezekiel have known Deuteronomy 4 or 28? The evidence suggests an allusion to Deuteronomy 4. Below I will address the date of Deuteronomy 4 and argue that Ezekiel appears to allude to Deuteronomy 4 in other instances as well. His dependence on the blessings and curses of Deuteronomy 28, on the other hand, is difficult to establish.[96] Verbal parallels with Deuteronomy 28 are present but uncommon:

1. In the curse of Deut. 28:20 (cf. 7:23), Yahweh sends מהומה ("panic") on his people. In Ezek. 7:7 the prophet describes the day of judgment with מהומה, and in 22:5 he describes the city as full of מהומה.
2. Twice in Deuteronomy 28 the curses themselves are said to "pursue" (רדף) the people. In v. 22 the curses (קללות) generally are the subject, and in v. 45 the curses are named: "fever, inflammation, with fiery heat and drought...will pursue you." Similarly, Ezek. 35:6 speaks of "blood pursuing you" (ודם ירדפך).
3. Although containing no shared words, in the context of divine judgment both Deut. 28:37 and Ezek. 36:3 speak of Israel becoming the talk of the nations.

In two more examples, Ezekiel's language is similar to that of Deuteronomy 28 but may be dependent on Leviticus 26:[97]

---

95. Indeed, Deut. 4:28; 28:36, 64 do not simply constitute "predictions" to be fulfilled, but rather punishments for covenant disobedience (J. Gordon McConville, *Deuteronomy*, AOTC 5 [Downers Grove, IL: InterVarsity, 2002], 110, 406; Greenberg, *Ezekiel 1–20*, 386).

96. Contrast the many links between Jeremiah and Deut. 28 (see Jack R. Lundbom, *Deuteronomy: A Commentary* [Grand Rapids: Eerdmans, 2013], 41–2).

97. Although Brian Neil Peterson argues that Ezekiel's message presupposes the biblical covenant and curse tradition (*Ezekiel in Context: Ezekiel's Message Understood in Its Historical Setting of Covenant Curses and Ancient Near Eastern Mythological Motifs*, PTMS 182 [Eugene, OR: Pickwick, 2012], esp. 61–76), potential links with Deut. 28 are far fewer than with Lev. 26. In most cases, when the curse lists of Deuteronomy and the Holiness Code share themes, Ezekiel's language most closely resembles the Holiness Code (e.g., the unburied dead in Ezek. 6:1-7, 13; Lev. 26:30; Deut. 28:26). On the connections between Ezekiel and Lev. 26, see Wong, *Idea of Retribution*, 78–119; Milgrom, *Leviticus 23–27*, 2348–52.

4. Deuteronomy 28:26 speaks of the people's "corpses as food for the birds of the air and beasts of the land" (והיתה נבלתך למאכל לכל עוף השמים ולבהמת הארץ, cited verbatim in Jer. 7:33; 16:4; 19:7; 34:20). Similar language appears in Ezek. 29:5 and 34:28,[98] but like Lev. 26:6, Ezekiel uses חיה instead of בהמה.
5. In the same verse (28:26), Deuteronomy uses the phrase אין מחריד, "there will be no one to frighten." Ezekiel uses the same phrase in two restoration passages, 34:28 and 39:26. Indeed, Deut. 28:26 and Ezek. 34:28 share two themes: corpses as food for animals and the אין מחריד locution. However, Ezekiel may borrow this locution from Lev. 26:6 as well, its single occurrence in the Holiness Code. Whereas the implied objects of אין מחריד in Deut. 28:26 are the feasting animals ("no one shall frighten them [away]"), the implied objects in Ezekiel and Lev. 26:6 are the people ("no one shall frighten you").

There is no conclusive evidence that these parallels with Deuteronomy 28 are the result of literary dependence. If Ezekiel knew Deuteronomy's curses, he rarely used their language. More substantial parallels with Deuteronomy 4 suggest he may have drawn from it instead.

Non-Centralized Worship

In the Hebrew Bible, the centralization of sacrifices is most closely associated with Deuteronomy.[99] A discussion of its influence on Ezekiel is fitting in this chapter, since for both Deuteronomy and Ezekiel, worship outside of the central sanctuary is often associated with idolatry—whether that of the Canaanites in Deuteronomy 12 or the Israelites in Ezekiel 6. Most commentators agree that Ezekiel's language was influenced by Deuteronomy's language for centralized worship,[100] even

---

98. Cf. Rom-Shiloni, "Ezekiel and Jeremiah," 219.

99. This study focuses on Deuteronomy's notion of centralized cultic activity and worship, not the notion of a chosen, protected city in Samuel–Kings. On this discontinuity between Deuteronomy and Joshua–Kings, see Rannfrid Irene Thelle, *Approaches to the "Chosen Place": Accessing a Biblical Concept*, LHBOTS 564 (New York: T&T Clark, 2012).

100. E.g., Greenberg, *Ezekiel 1–20*, 385: "Ezekiel's formulation of Israel's cultic offenses appears to derive from the law of centralized worship in Deut 12"; Milgrom, "Nature and Extent of Idolatry," 6: Ezekiel advocates "cultic centralization (e.g., 20:40), an innovative deuteronomic doctrine"; cf. Kaufmann, *Religion of Israel*, 434: "Ezekiel's concepts are influenced by those of D: he condemns the high places (which

if his conception is blended with the Priestly notion of temple-centered stratified holiness. To be clear, the condemnation of other worship sites by itself does not necessarily demonstrate influence from Deuteronomy's law of centralization. In Ezekiel's time, as Mein observes, for both Priestly and Deuteronomic theology, "the centrality of the Jerusalem sanctuary is an immovable datum of the religion."[101] There are other possible ways to explain Ezekiel's view of centralized worship besides attributing it to Deuteronomic influence. For example, Ezekiel may simply have been influenced by Josiah's cult reform, not the book of Deuteronomy directly. Or one might hypothesize Ezekiel received the principles of centralized worship from Priestly or Holiness theology, perhaps as reflected in a non-Deuteronomic text such as Leviticus 17, which requires sacrifice at the wilderness Tabernacle.[102]

Ezekiel's dependence on the judgment of במות in Lev. 26:30 illustrates the point. Since Ezek. 6:3-7 draws heavily from the language of Lev. 26:30-31,[103] Ezekiel's indictment against the "high places" clearly derives in part from the Holiness Code.

| Lev. 26:30 | והשמדתי את במתיכם |
| Ezek. 6:3 | ואבדתי במותיכם |

Nevertheless, we should be cautious to conclude Ezekiel received the concept of centralized worship only from Priestly theology and not also from Deuteronom(ist)ic theology.[104] We must recognize that Lev. 26:30

P ignores); he recognizes only one legal sanctuary of YHWH (P knows many, Lev. 26:31); he knows the idea of one sacred site in the land (P does not)"; also Joyce, *Divine Initiative*, 119.

101. Mein, *Ethics of Exile*, 115; cited in Joyce, *Ezekiel*, 38.

102. Following Kaufmann, Milgrom argues that the Holiness Code does not advocate a sole sanctuary ("Does H Advocate the Centralization of Worship?"), but see the incisive critique by Elizabeth Keck, "Glory of Yahweh, Name Theology, and Ezekiel's Understanding of Divine Presence" (Ph.D. diss., Boston College, 2011), 87–95. Julius Wellhausen made the connection between Lev. 17 and Deut. 12, but argued that P was a later response to D (*Prolegomena to the History of Ancient Israel*, trans. J. Sutherland Black and Allan Menzies [Cleveland: Meridian, 1965], 376–85; see more Christophe Nihan, *From Priestly Torah to Pentateuch: A Study in the Composition of Leviticus*, FAT 2/25 [Tübingen: Mohr Siebeck, 2007], 402–30).

103. See Lyons, *From Law to Prophecy*, 182.

104. Contra Mein, *Ethics of Exile*, 115: "Given the close parallels between Ezekiel 6 and Leviticus 26 it seems reasonable to deduce that Ezekiel's polemic is taken from the milieu of priestly rather than Deuteronomistic theology…in both cases the

is not a divine decree that prohibits high places, but rather a judgment against the high places.[105] Because Leviticus 26, like Ezekiel 6, indicts the במות for their idolatry,[106] it is impossible to conclude that either advocates "centralized worship" as such. It is unclear that they would deny the legitimacy of high places outright, apart from the idolatry that took place there.

So how might we identify influence from Deuteronomy specifically? In several instances, Ezekiel uses clear Deuteronomic language for illegitimate worship outside of the Jerusalem temple. The term במות will not be listed among these for a couple reasons.[107] First, although Ezekiel and the Deuteronomistic writers share a fundamental concern for the במות (Ezek. 6:3, 6; 16:16; 20:29; 43:7;[108] 1, 2 Kings passim),[109] the word does

centrality of the Jerusalem sanctuary is an immovable datum of the religion." But he grants that it is hasty to excise the "more obviously Deuteronomistic passages in 6:13 and 20:27" (p. 116).

105. Milgrom regards Num. 33:50-56, which requires Israel to destroy the Canaanites' idols and destroy their high places, as H, for him a redactor of P (*Leviticus 23–27: A New Translation with Introduction and Commentary*, AB 3B [New York: Doubleday, 2001], 2317). The same idea is found in Deut. 12:2-3, but Deuteronomy takes the command a step further by instructing the Israelites to worship at a specific place, "the place that Yahweh your God will choose" (12:5).

106. Milgrom, *Leviticus 23–27*, 2317; Zimmerli, *Ezekiel*, 1:186; LaRocca-Pitts, "*Of Wood and Stone*," 109; Mein, *Ethics of Exile*, 116.

107. For the discussion about the meaning of במה, especially the validity of the traditional association with rural, open-air altars located at natural elevations, see Patrick H. Vaughan, *The Meaning of* Bamah *in the Old Testament: A Study of Etymological, Textual, and Archaeological Evidence* (Cambridge: Cambridge University Press, 1974); W. Boyd Barrick, "The Word BMH in the Old Testament" (Ph.D. diss., University of Chicago Divinity School, 1977); idem, "High Place," *ABD* 3:196–200; Matthias Gleis, *Die Bamah*, BZAW 251 (Berlin: de Gruyter, 1997); LaRocca-Pitts, "*Of Wood and Stone*," 127–59; note also Mein, *Ethics of Exile*, 110–12.

108. Most commentators read the MT's בָּמוֹתָם ("their high places") in Ezek. 43:7 as בְּמוֹתָם ("at their death"), against the Masoretic vocalization (see Zimmerli, *Ezekiel*, 2:409, who mentions Gese, Toy, Bertholet). However, W. F. Albright understood במותם as an abbreviated form of בבמותם, "at their high places" ("The High Place in Ancient Palestine," in *Volume du Congrès: Strasbourg 1956*, ed. G. W. Anderson, VTSup 4 [Leiden: Brill, 1957], 247). On the meaning of פגרי במותם מלכיהם in Ezek. 43:7, see Block, *Ezekiel*, 2:583–6.

109. Mein, *Ethics of Exile*, 110: "Ezekiel, like the Deuteronomists, rejects utterly the worship at the so-called high places." In DtrH failure to destroy the במות is a characteristic indictment against Judah's kings (see Iain Provan, *Hezekiah and the Book of Kings: A Contribution to the Debate about the Composition of the Deuteronomistic History*, BZAW 172 [Berlin: de Gruyter, 1988], 57–90).

not appear in Deuteronomy.[110] And second, as shown above, Ezekiel's use of the term may reflect influence from the Holiness Code. Therefore, we must look elsewhere for evidence of Deuteronomy's influence on Ezekiel.

"On Every High Hill, Under Every Leafy Tree"

Among Ezekiel's indictments against worship outside of Jerusalem, Ezek. 6:13 and 20:28 reflect a distinctive Deuteronomic theme variously expressed in Deuteronomy, DtrH, and Jeremiah:[111]

Ezek. 6:13	אל כל־גבעה רמה	on every high hill,
	בכל ראשי ההרים	on all the mountain tops,
	ותחת כל־עץ רענן	under every green tree,
	ותחת כל־אלה עבתה	and under every leafy oak
Ezek. 20:28	כל־גבעה רמה וכל־עץ עבת	any high hill or any leafy tree

In the Deuteronomistic literature, the hill country is often associated with places of illegitimate worship after the construction of the Jerusalem temple. Deuteronomy 12:2 instructs the Israelites to destroy the worship sites where the nations served their gods, that is, "on the mountain heights, on the hills, and under every leafy tree" (על־ההרים הרמים ועל־הגבעות ותחת כל־עץ רענן). The Deuteronomistic historians and Jeremiah indicted Israel for worshiping at these locations, in three instances using the same expression: "on every high hill and under every leafy tree" (על כל־גבעה גבהה ותחת כל־עץ רענן in 1 Kgs 14:23; 2 Kgs 17:10; Jer. 2:20). Slightly variant expressions appear in 2 Kgs 16:4 and Jer. 3:6 as well.

As William Holladay has shown, the language of Ezek. 6:13 and 20:28 corresponds more closely to Deut. 12:2 than to its occurrences in DtrH and Jeremiah.[112] Whereas DtrH and Jeremiah describe the height of the hills with the adjective גבעה ("high"), the two instances in Ezekiel (6:13 and 20:28) follow Deut. 12:2 by using the adjective רמה ("high"). Without

---

110. Cf. Thelle, *Approaches to the "Chosen Place,"* 142–3.

111. Weinfeld, *Deuteronomy and the Deuteronomic School*, 322; John Bright, "The Date of the Prose Sermons of Jeremiah," *JBL* 70 (1951): 35, appendix B, no. 2. On the close association of this language with the במות in Ezekiel, see LaRocca-Pitts, *"Of Wood and Stone,"* 156–7. On the authenticity of this indictment in the book of Ezekiel, see my discussion in Chapter 5.

112. Holladay, "On Every High Hill," 175; see also Kasher, *Ezekiel*, 54–6; Rom-Shiloni, "Ezekiel and Jeremiah," 219; Varšo, "Das Deuteronomium mit Ezechiel lesen," 105: "Die literarischen Zusammenhänge zwischen Deuteronomium [12,2] und Ezechiel [6,13] sind viel stärker als zwischen Hosea [4,13] und den beiden untersuchten Stellen."

its parallel phrases (lacking in the LXX), Ezek. 6:13 displays virtually identical language with Deut. 12:2, albeit in a slightly variant order.

Ezek. 6:13	אל כל־גבעה רמה [ ]	on every high hill,
	ותחת כל־עץ רענן [ ]	and under every leafy tree
Deut. 12:2	על־ההרים הרמים ועל־הגבעות	on the high mountains, on the hills,
	ותחת כל־עץ רענן	and under every leafy tree

The parallel phrases in Ezek. 6:13 that are missing in the LXX, on the other hand, display notable links with Hos. 4:13, particularly the locutions ראשי ההרים ("the mountain tops") and אלה ("oak"), which are unique to these two passages among the "high hill and leafy tree" passages of the Hebrew Bible. Are these two parallel phrases (בכל ראשי ההרים and ותחת כל־אלה עבתה) simply the work of a later Deuteronomistic hand influenced by Hos. 4:13? The presence of עבתה as a synonym for רענן (also in 20:28) suggests that it was not Deuteronomistic redactors who created the parallelistic lines, but either Ezekiel or his disciples,[113] since עבת seems to be the Priestly equivalent of the Deuteronomic term רענן (see Lev. 23:40). Ezekiel 6:13 would appear to be a combination and conflation of Deut. 12:2 and Hos. 4:13 in parallel lines, a known phenomenon among Ezekiel's techniques of literary appropriation,[114] which will be explored further in Chapter 6.

על ההרים אכל, *"Eating on the Mountains"*

In chs. 18 and 22, Ezekiel lists "eating on the mountains" (על ההרים אכל) as a characteristic activity of the wicked person (Ezek. 18:6, 11, 15; 22:9). The phrase has no exact parallel in the Hebrew Bible outside Ezekiel. Given the similar locution אכל על־הדם ("eat with the blood") in Lev. 19:26 and Ezek. 33:25,[115] it might be tempting to emend ההרים to הדם, but most commentators affirm the authenticity of "eating on the mountains" in its four occurrences in Ezekiel.[116] Indeed, emending Ezek. 33:25 to bring it in line with Ezekiel 18 and 22 would be more likely,[117] even if unnecessary,

---

113. So also Weinfeld, *Deuteronomy and the Deuteronomic School*, 366.

114. Lyons, *From Law to Prophecy*, 95–7; see further Chapter 6 of this study.

115. LXX Lev. 19:26 επι των ορεων appears to be a harmonization with Ezek. 18:6, 11, 15; 22:9 (so ibid., 2, 13 n. 40).

116. E.g., Zimmerli, *Ezekiel*, 1:380; Greenberg, *Ezekiel 1–20*, 328–9: "It is perverse to adjust a repeated, unusual, textually firm expression to a single, commonplace, and hence textually dubious one."

117. C. H. Cornill, *Das Buch des Propheten Ezechiel* (Leipzig: Hinrichs, 1886), 396.

since ההרים ("the mountains"), like "every high hill," appears elsewhere in the imagery of ch. 34, which claims that "my sheep wandered over all the mountains" (34:6). While ch. 34 speaks metaphorically about God's people as lost sheep without their shepherd, the language also alludes to Israel's illegitimate worship "on all the mountains."

As most commentators agree, "eating on the mountains" appears to refer to the sacrificial meals that took place outside of Jerusalem.[118] Thus, Ezekiel's condemnation corresponds to Deuteronomy's instructions to "eat" in the single, chosen place: "eat there in the presence of Yahweh" (12:7), "the place that Yahweh your God will choose" (12:18; also 15:20).

גדע, *"Cut Down"*

In Ezek. 6:6, the prophet uses the verb גדע to describe the destruction of items of improper and idolatrous worship outside Jerusalem: "the cities shall be laid waste and the high places ruined, so that your altars will be laid waste and ruined, your idols broken and destroyed, and your incense altars cut down [ונגדעו חמניכם]." The verse resonates with both the Holiness Code and Deuteronomy. On the one hand, Lev. 26:30 expresses the same idea: "I [Yahweh] will destroy your high places and cut down your incense altars [חמניכם]."[119] The word חמן, "incense altar," does not appear elsewhere in the pentateuchal literature or in DtrH, suggesting—in light of Ezekiel's widespread references to the Holiness Code—the influence of Lev. 26:30 on the prophet. On the other hand, Ezekiel uses the verb גדע of Deut. 12:3 rather than H's כרת (Hiphil).[120] This, along with the shared word שבר and the similar syntactic construction of short phrases comprising verbs of annihilation and nouns referring to different cultic sites and artifacts, leads Rom-Shiloni to conclude that Ezekiel was dependent on Deut. 12:3.[121] In judgment, Yahweh will accomplish what the people, as commanded in Deuteronomy, failed to do: "you shall break down their altars and dash in pieces their pillars and chop down [גדע] their Asherim and burn their carved images with fire" (Deut. 7:5), and "tear down their altars and dash in pieces their pillars and burn their Asherim with fire. You shall chop down [גדע] the carved images of their gods and destroy their name out of that place" (Deut. 12:3).[122]

---

118. Zimmerli, *Ezekiel*, 1:380; Block, *Ezekiel*, 1:571; Allen, *Ezekiel 1–19*, 274; Milgrom, "Nature and Extent of Idolatry," 6; Carley, *Ezekiel among the Prophets*, 58.

119. See Lyons, *From Law to Prophecy*, 62–3.

120. Other shared locutions between Deut. 7:5; 12:3 and Ezek. 6:6 include מזבח and שבר.

121. Rom-Shiloni, "Ezekiel and Jeremiah," 218.

122. So also Ganzel, "Transformation," 42.

נתץ, *"Tear Down"*

Like גדע, the verb נתץ also occurs in Deut. 7:5 and 12:3 to refer to the destruction of the Canaanites' cultic sites. Ganzel does not decide whether its occurrence in Ezek. 16:39 is more likely influenced by Deuteronomy or instead by Lev. 11:35; 14:45, where it refers to the destruction of unclean objects. However, the potential overtones of idolatry in 16:39 might suggest Deuteronomy over Leviticus. In Ezek. 16:39, Jerusalem's "lovers" tear down (נתץ) her "mounds" (גב) and "platforms" (רמה) used for prostitution.[123] Although the precise meanings of גב and רמה are uncertain,[124] רמה in particular might have a dual connotation, signifying not only a platform for prostitution, but also a high place used for idolatrous practices.[125] After all, the extended metaphors of chs. 16 and 23 commonly vacillate between the language of metaphorical vehicle (adultery) and tenor (improper worship).

Centralized Worship in the Renewed Jerusalem

Ezekiel 20:33-44 offers an important window into the prophet's view of ideal worship. In the restoration period, worship will take place "there," that is, in Jerusalem "on my holy mountain, the mountain height of Israel" (20:40). The location for proper worship identified by Ezekiel recalls one of Deuteronomy's typical methods of describing Yahweh's chosen place, the deictic שם ("there," e.g., Deut. 12:5). Like Deuteronomy, which identifies a central sanctuary as the place of worship because of its status as the special location of Yahweh's presence,[126] for Ezekiel

---

123. See also Ezek. 26:9, 12.
124. See Block, *Ezekiel*, 1:494.
125. Mein, *Ethics of Exile*, 115.
126. See especially Stephen L. Cook, "God's Real Absence and Real Presence in Deuteronomy and Deuteronomism," in *Divine Presence and Absence in Exilic and Post-Exilic Judaism*, ed. I. J. de Hulster and N. MacDonald, FAT II/61 (Tübingen: Mohr Siebeck, 2013), 121–50, esp. 121–4. Recent scholarship has significantly undermined the traditional understanding that Deuteronomy's "name" theology expresses Yahweh's transcendence in contrast to the Priestly literature's כבוד theology, which highlights his immanence (see, e.g., Ian Wilson, *Out of the Midst of the Fire: Divine Presence in Deuteronomy*, SBLDS 151 [Atlanta: Scholars Press, 1995]). For an overview, see Sandra L. Richter, *The Deuteronomistic History and the Name Theology: lᵉšakkēn šᵉmô šām in the Bible and the Ancient Near East*, BZAW 318 (Berlin: de Gruyter, 2002), 7–40. Based on its cognate in Akkadian, she argues the phrase *lᵉšakkēn šᵉmô šām* likely means "to put his name there," not "to cause his name to dwell there" (see ibid., 207–18).

Israel will worship on Yahweh's "holy mountain" in Jerusalem (20:40),[127] because "Yahweh is there" (יהוה שמה, Ezek. 48:35; cf. 37:26b-28; 43:7).[128] Similarly, Ezekiel's vision in chs. 40–48 describes the temple in the city as the cultic center for the nation and significantly does not mention local sanctuaries.[129]

In conclusion, Ezekiel's use of Deuteronomy's language and ideas for centralization bears witness to its influence on him. At the same time, as expected, Ezekiel appropriates Deuteronomic concepts through his Priestly-Holiness lenses, as evident in his Priestly conception of the temple's stratified holiness.

Ezekiel's Temple Vision (Chapter 8)

The depictions of idolatry in the temple vision of Ezekiel 8 display significant similarities to Deuteronomy, particularly ch. 4, as observed by Ganzel.[130] The vision can be divided into four scenes: the image of jealousy (8:5-6), the elders and their images (8:7-13), women weeping "the Tammuz" (8:14-15), and astral worship (8:16-18).[131] In what follows, I will outline the affinities to Deuteronomy and consider the possibility of literary dependence. Afterward, I will address possible connections with the account of Manasseh's sins in 1 Kings 21.

Scene 1: The Image of Jealousy (8:5-6)

Ezekiel's vision begins with his transportation to the entrance of the north gate of the inner court of the Jerusalem temple, the location of the מושב סמל הקנאה המקנה, traditionally rendered, "the seat of the image of jealousy that provokes to jealousy" (8:3). The first abomination seen by the prophet is the "image of jealousy" (סמל הקנאה, 8:5). The word סמל occurs only here and in Deuteronomy 4 in the Hebrew Bible (besides

---

127. In my view, Yahweh's "holy mountain" can refer to Jerusalem while using language of the archetypal cosmic mountain and/or Eden (contra Stephen L. Cook, *Ezekiel 38–48: A New Translation with Introduction and Commentary*, AYB 22B [New Haven: Yale University Press, 2018], 125–6).

128. Greenberg, *Ezekiel 1–20*, 385: "Ezekiel's model for pure, acceptable worship of the future, described in 20:40f., is likewise the chosen site of the future whose worship is ordained in Deut 12." Also Milgrom, "Nature and Extent of Idolatry," 6 (= verbatim idem, *Leviticus 17–22*, 1385–6).

129. Carley, *Ezekiel among the Prophets*, 58.

130. Ganzel, "Transformation," 37–40.

131. Following Block, *Ezekiel*, 1:283.

2 Chron. 33:7, 15),[132] where it appears among the forms of worship prohibited by Yahweh: פסל תמונת כל־סמל, "a carved image in the form of any image" (Deut. 4:16).[133]

Given the rarity of סמל in the Hebrew Bible, it is possible Ezekiel was influenced by Deuteronomy's use of the term, irrespective of the exact referent of the "image of jealousy" in Ezekiel 8. Some sort of idol seems likely in light of the use of סמל in Deuteronomy and its theme of idolatry provoking Yahweh to jealousy (Deut. 32:16, 21; cf. אל קנא in Exod. 20:5; Deut. 4:23-24; 5:9).[134] Many scholars have identified Ezekiel's image of jealousy with Asherah,[135] particularly the "statue of Asherah" (פסל האשרה) set up by Manasseh in the Jerusalem temple (2 Kgs 21:7).[136]

---

132. On the meaning of the word see Christoph Dohmen, "Heißt סמל 'Bild, Statue'?" *ZAW* 96 (1984): 263–6; Susan Ackerman, *Under Every Green Tree: Popular Religion in Sixth-Century Judah*, HSM 46 (Atlanta: Scholars Press, 1992), 55–7.

133. Deut. 4:25 exhibits the similar phrase פסל תמונת כל, "a carved image in the form of anything," but without סמל.

134. Connecting Ezek. 8:5-6 with 43:7-9 Margaret S. Odell proposes that the סמל is not an idol, but a substitutionary offering or votive statue for child sacrifice, a practice known from Phoenicia ("What was the Image of Jealousy in Ezekiel 8?" in *The Priests in the Prophets: The Portrayal of Priests, Prophets, and Other Religious Specialists in the Latter Prophets*, ed. Lester L. Grabbe and Alice Ogden Bellis, JSOTSup 408 [New York: T&T Clark, 2004], 134–48). This hypothesis does not necessarily undermine Ezekiel's dependence on Deut. 4, since Ezekiel could have drawn from Deuteronomy's language but used it in unique ways. However, the theory is questionable. First, even if פגרי מלכיהם in Ezek. 43:7-9 should be interpreted in light of the Phoenician substitutionary offering, a connection to the סמל in Ezek. 8:3, 5 seems tenuous. Odell cites only the presence of statues and the alleged similarity of the סמל's "seat" (מושב) in 8:3 and the במות in 43:7, which she regards as pedestals. Second, she proposes that סמל הקנאה, "image of jealousy," symbolically expresses human zeal, not Yahweh's jealous response to the image. However, there is reason to question the claim that "the expression 'image of X' requires that the image embody or express the characteristics of X, and not emotional reactions to it" (p. 137). Waltke and O'Connor describe a *genitive of effect* (e.g., "the bowl of staggering," or "the bowl that causes staggering," in Isa. 51:17), which fits perfectly the understanding of סמל הקנאה as "the image that causes jealousy" (*IBHS* §9.5.2c). On the theme of idolatry provoking Yahweh to jealousy (Deut. 32:16, 21; Ps. 78:58), see Ackerman, *Under Every Green Tree*, 59–60.

135. On Asherah worship, see Day, *Yahweh and the Gods*, 42–67; Milgrom, "Nature and Extent of Idolatry," 11–13; on a Deuteronomic polemic against Asherah, see Saul M. Olyan, *Asherah and the Cult of Yahweh in Israel* (Atlanta: Scholars Press, 1988), 73; T. Binger, *Asherah, Goddess in Ugarit, Israel and the Old Testament*, JSOTSup 232 (Sheffield: Sheffield Academic, 1997), 125.

136. Eichrodt, *Ezekiel*, 122–3; Greenberg, *Ezekiel 1–20*, 168; Kaufmann, *Religion of Israel*, 144; Ackerman, *Under Every Green Tree*, 60–2; cf. Milgrom, *Leviticus*

Although any identification remains speculative,[137] this interpretation seems to be ancient, inasmuch as the Chronicler's version of Manasseh's sins refers to the statue of Asherah with סמל, perhaps dependent on Ezekiel 8.[138] However, since the statue erected by Manasseh was later destroyed in Josiah's reform, according to 2 Kgs 23:6,[139] this theory requires that either Ezekiel's vision represents the sins of Manasseh's time[140] or the image of jealousy was an Asherah statue reintroduced after Josiah.[141]

Scene 2: The Elders and Their Images (8:7-13)

In the second scene, Ezekiel enters a hidden room in the temple complex and inside finds images inscribed on the walls. Ezekiel 8:10 MT reports that the prophet sees "every form of creeping thing and beast" (כל־תבנית רמש ובהמה). Many scholars have noted the striking verbal similarity to Moses' warning in Deut. 4:16-18 not to make idols, "the form of any beast...or the form any creeping thing."

    Deut. 4:16-18
        תבנית כל־בהמה   The form of any beast...
        תבנית כל־רמש   The form of any creeping thing

    Ezek. 8:10
        כל־תבנית רמש ובהמה   Every form of creeping thing and beast

---

17–22, 1390–1. An identification with Asherah is possible without H. C. Lutzky's improbable emendation and reinterpretation of מושב סמל הקנאה המקנה. For the MT phrase, סמל המקנה הקנאה, she proposes that for הקנאה, the verse originally had a form of the root קנה, yielding "the image of the Creatress," which corresponds to the Ugaritic epithet used for Asherah (IIAB [*CTA* 4] I, 23, IV, 32) (see H. C. Lutzky, "On the 'Image of Jealousy,'" *VT* 46 [1996]: 121–4). However, John Day has rightly observed: "There are no adequate grounds for rejecting the MT, and although Asherah is called *qnyt 'ilm*, 'Creatress of the gods' in Ugaritic, it would be extraordinary for Ezekiel to refer to what was for him an abomination by such a positive sounding epithet as 'the Creatress'" (*Yahweh and the Gods*, 62–3); cf. Ziony Zevit, *The Religions of Ancient Israel: A Synthesis of Parallactic Approaches* (London: Continuum, 2001), 556–7 n. 150.

    137. Middlemas, *Troubles*, 91–3.
    138. Note הסמל פסל and הסמל in 2 Chron. 33:7, 15, respectively.
    139. Cf. Block, *Ezekiel*, 1:281.
    140. On the possibility that the sins of Ezek. 8 reflect the time of Manasseh, see below.
    141. E.g., Eichrodt, *Ezekiel*, 122–3.

The language is too similar to be coincidental.¹⁴² Furthermore, the use of the word תבנית for idols represents a unique link between Ezekiel and Deuteronomy 4. A similar use occurs only in Ps. 106:20, which is a postexilic psalm known to draw from Ezekiel.¹⁴³ Elsewhere in the Hebrew Bible, תבנית often refers to the plan of the sanctuary or altar.¹⁴⁴

There is some question whether this clear allusion to Deut. 4:16-18 should be attributed to the prophet or to a later redactor. The LXX of Ezek. 8:10 omits the phrase in question, תבנית רמש ובהמה, leading many scholars to regard it as a later gloss.¹⁴⁵ Leslie Allen, for example, explains:

> An annotator has identified the subjects of the engravings with the prohibited images of Deuteronomy 4:17-18 and may also have had in mind the ritually unclean creatures of Leviticus 11. The note is a valuable ancient interpretation, filling out what is left tantalizingly unexplained in the basic text.¹⁴⁶

---

142. Contra Margaret Odell, who claims discontinuity between Ezek. 8:10 and Deut. 4:17-18: "The prohibition against idols in Deuteronomy [e.g., 4:17-18] is explicitly concerned with representations of YHWH, not with rival entities as in Ezek. 8:10. Second, unlike Ezek. 8:10, which is concerned only with beasts and creeping things, Deuteronomy catalogues the entire repertoire of possible representations—male and female, created beings, and heavenly luminaries" ("Creeping Things and Singing Stones: The Iconography of Ezek. 8:7-13 in Light of Syro-Palestinian Seals and *The Songs of the Sabbath Sacrifice*," in *Images and Prophecy in the Ancient Eastern Mediterranean*, ed. Martti Nissinen and Charles E. Carter [Göttingen: Vandenhoeck & Ruprecht, 2009], 198). Odell's first point may be questioned, since Deut. 4:19 speaks of the images (in this case, astral bodies) "allotted to all the people under the whole heaven." Regardless, neither argument necessarily undermines a connection to Deut. 4, because Ezekiel may use his source text's language without the exact same referent.

143. See further Chapter 6 of this study.

144. Exod. 25:9, 40; Josh. 22:28; 1 Chron. 28:11; cf. 2 Kgs 16:10; note also תבנית in MT Ezek. 43:10, which some emend to תבנית.

145. Kenneth S. Freedy, "The Glosses in Ezekiel i–xxiv," *VT* 20 (1970): 150; G. A. Cooke, *A Critical and Exegetical Commentary on the Book of Ezekiel*, ICC (Edinburgh: T. & T. Clark, 1936), 102; Greenberg, *Ezekiel 1–20*, 169; J. W. Wevers, *Ezekiel*, NCB (London: Nelson, 1969), 69; Zimmerli, *Ezekiel*, 1:219; Ackerman, *Under Every Green Tree*, 43 n. 22, 69; Allen, *Ezekiel 1–19*, 143; Middlemas, *Troubles*, 110–11; Tov, "Recensional Differences," 404; Varšo, "Das Deuteronomium mit Ezechiel lesen," 42 n. 110: "Die Argumente für die Ergänzung des Satzes in Ez 8,10 unter dem Einfluss von Dtn 4 sind überzeugend. Es zeigt sich aber, dass beide Einheiten schon seit frühesten Zeiten als in gegenseitigem Verhältnis stehend gesehen worden sind."

146. Allen, *Ezekiel 1–19*, 143.

While differences between MT and LXX Ezekiel often reflect a tendency toward expansions in the MT, the central question for Ezek. 8:10 is whether the absence of the phrase in the LXX is by itself determinative, since in my view the alleged syntactic "awkwardness" of MT Ezek. 8:10 is inconclusive.[147]

The identification of the images in Ezekiel's temple vision with the כל־תבנית רמש ובהמה ("very form of creeping thing and beast") of Deut. 4:16-18 fits a larger pattern of similarities between Ezekiel 8 and Deuteronomy 4, as summarized below. If this allusion in Ezek. 8:10 comes from later redactors, it shows a trajectory of literary borrowing. Because Ezekiel was influenced by Deuteronomy, we might expect it motivated additional coordination between the two books by later redactors. If the redactors (perhaps Ezekiel's disciples) understood the prophet's literary references and advanced them, Ezek. 8:10 would be an example when textual referencing begets more referencing.[148]

* * *

Excursus: A Marzēaḥ in Ezekiel 8:7-13?

Susan Ackerman has argued that the activity of the elders in the secret room depicts a *marzēaḥ* (מרזח),[149] known from numerous written sources from the Near East spanning nearly two millennia. The texts from Ugarit reveal the most information

---

147. It is commonly asserted that the syntax of Ezek. 8:10 makes better sense without the locution, leaving simply: ישראל בית גלולי וכל שקץ כל והנה ואראה ואבוא ("I entered and looked, and behold, every detestable thing and all the idols of the house of Israel"). The problem arises in part from the difficulty of making sense of כל תבנית שקץ ובהמה רמש (e.g., Ackerman, *Under Every Green Tree*, 69). For example, Cooke wrote: "the last word שקץ must be in [apposition] to the two preceding nouns, an awkward construction which suggests that ובהמה רמש תבנית have been inserted as a gloss from Dt. 4:17f." (Cooke, *Ezekiel*, 102; cf. Odell, "Creeping Things," 196). Others render שקץ as an adjective modifying בהמה (NRSV: "loathsome animals"; Greenberg, *Ezekiel 1–20*, 169). However, as it stands, MT Ezek. 8:10 might be construed as a series of pairs: "every form of creeping thing and beast, detestable thing and all the idols of Israel." The Hebrew Bible provides many other instances of series in which the *waw*-conjunction functions similarly, for example: "a mockery and a taunt, a warning and a horror" (Ezek. 5:15) and "burnt offering and grain offering, sacrifice and drink offering" (Lev. 23:37); cf. Deut. 29:16[17]; Isa. 19:13[14], 15; Exod. 1:4; Gen. 43:11; Hos. 2:7. Further, compare a similar double use of כל at the beginning and end of a series in Ezek. 12:14: וכל אשר סביבתיו עזרו וכל אגפיו, "all those around him, his helpers, and all his troops."

148. Credit to the anonymous reviewer of this monograph series.

149. Susan Ackerman, "A *MARZĒAḤ* in Ezekiel 8:7-13?" *HTR* 82 (1989): 267–81, which appeared slightly revised in idem, *Under Every Green Tree*, 67–79.

about the *marzēaḥ*, but the concept remains enigmatic due to the often fragmentary or inexplicable nature of the sources.[150] In his monograph on the *marzēaḥ* in the Bible and the ancient Near East, John McLaughlin has set forth three constitutive features of the *marzēaḥ* based on the evidence not only from Ugarit, but also the few texts from Ebla, Emar, and Moab, the post-biblical texts from Elephantine, Phoenicia, Nabatea, and Palmyra, and the Rabbinic references: (1) the *marzēaḥ* involved a definable upper-class membership; (2) the *marzēaḥ* had a religious component reflected in the consistent association with one or more deities; (3) alcohol consumption (usually wine) is the only activity regularly connected to the *marzēaḥ*.[151]

Although the word מרזח does not appear in Ezekiel 8, Ackerman argues that when תבנית רמש ובהמה in v. 10 is deleted based on its absence in the LXX, the scene appears remarkably like a *marzēaḥ*. The שקץ may then be understood as unclean food, as in Leviticus 11, rather than detestable animals, resulting in Ackerman's translation: "And there was every kind of unclean food, and all the idols of the house of Israel were engraved on the wall round about."[152] Consequently, the presence of unclean food together with the "idols of the house of Judah" (גלולי בית ישראל) leads her to see in the passage a ritual meal to the gods depicted on the wall. The passage contains two of McLaughlin's constitutive features, namely the presence of a definable upper-class consisting of "seventy men of the elders of the house of Israel" and a religious component represented by idols (גלולים) and the burning of incense.[153]

However, McLaughlin has rejected Ackerman's proposal for three reasons.[154] First and foremost, the scene in Ezek. 8:7-13 lacks the most defining feature of the

---

150. The Ugaritic texts include references to the "men of the *marzēaḥ*" as a prominent group, the *marzēaḥ* itself as an association and as a room located in part of a house functioning as the meeting place for the association. The *marzēaḥ* has a leader (*rabbu*) who, at least in one instance, hosts the association in part of his house. If the mythological texts depicting the gods in the *marzēaḥ* reflect actual practice, then the *marzēaḥ* functioned as an association that met in a specific location for heavy drinking—a feature bolstered by the proximity of *marzēaḥ*s to vineyards reflected in some texts. Finally, the *marzēaḥ* was connected with or dedicated to a particular deity.

151. John L. McLaughlin, *The Marzēaḥ in the Prophetic Literature: References and Allusions in Light of the Extra-Biblical Evidence* (Leiden: Brill, 2001), 65–70. Cf. Dennis Pardee: "The only constant in the documentation regarding the *marziḥu*, the primary sources for which spread over nearly a millennium and a half, is the consumption of wine; the next most frequently attested phenomenon in the prose sources is the association between a *marziḥu* and a particular deity" ("*Marziḥu, Kispu*, and the Ugaritic Funerary Cult: A Minimalist View," in *Ugarit, Religion and Culture: Proceedings of the International Colloquium on Ugarit, Religion and Culture; Edinburgh, July 1994. Essays in Honour of Professor John C. L. Gibson*, ed. N. Wyatt, W. G. E. Watson, and J. B. Lloyd, UBL 12 [Münster: Ugarit-Verlag, 1996], 278).

152. Ackerman, *Under Every Green Tree*, 71.

153. Ibid., 76.

154. McLaughlin, *Marzēaḥ*, 196–213, esp. 202–3. Others doubting any connection with a *marzēaḥ* include Middlemas, *Troubles*, 110–14; Mein, *Ethics of Exile*, 125–6.

institution: alcohol consumption. Ackerman gave little attention to this missing element, instead emphasizing the role of feasting in some of the *marzēaḥ* texts, including *CAT* 1.114, in which "the gods eat and drink," and Amos 6:1-7, where the people "eat lambs from the flock and calves from the fattening stall." Second, McLaughlin criticizes Ackerman's understanding of שקץ in v. 10 as unclean food. Ackerman related the word to its occurrences in Leviticus 11, where it refers to various types of animals unfit for consumption.[155] On the other hand, McLaughlin follows the majority of interpreters, arguing that this sole occurrence of שֶׁקֶץ in Ezekiel is merely a variant of שִׁקּוּץ, which occurs frequently in the book to refer to idols.[156] Significantly, if שֶׁקֶץ does not refer to food, any sign of a ritual meal disappears.[157] Lastly, McLaughlin contends that the secretive nature of the activity in Ezek. 8:7-13 does not correspond to the *marzēaḥ* as known from other texts.[158]

* * *

Scene 3: The Women Weeping "the Tammuz" (8:14-15)

The depiction of women weeping in the cult of the god Tammuz (Sumerian *Dumuzi*)[159] is unattested elsewhere in the Bible. As such, the third scene in Ezekiel's vision does not allude to Deuteronomy or any other part of Israel's written traditions. The practice is well known in Mesopotamia, where ritual mourning over the death of the deity, performed specifically by women, was central to the Tammuz cult.[160] Rather than Ezekiel simply

---

155. Ackerman, *Under Every Green Tree*, 70–1. Her thesis thus presumes that the gloss of ובהמה רמש תבנית, perhaps based on Deut. 4:17-18, is an incorrect interpretation of שֶׁקֶץ.

156. See Block, *Ezekiel*, 1:292 n. 47; Odell, "Creeping Things," 3; Middlemas, *Troubles*, 114. Perhaps שקץ here reflects a defective spelling of שקוץ, later vocalized incorrectly by the Masoretes (cf. the defective spelling שִׁקֻּץ in 1 Kgs 11:5, 7; 2 Kgs 23:13).

157. McLaughlin, *Marzēaḥ*, 202–3: "The word [שֶׁקֶץ] actually refers to hybrid animals that are forbidden as food *because* they are detestable… In other words, שֶׁקֶץ refers to the essential nature of such things, not their status as food; it is the former that makes them unsuitable as the latter."

158. Ibid., 204–5.

159. Block proposes that מבכות את־התמוז, with the article and the direct object marker את ("weeping the Tammuz"), here signifies that Tammuz refers not to the deity himself but rather to a special lament related to the deity (*Ezekiel*, 1:294–6).

160. See Ackerman, *Under Every Green Tree*, 79–82. On Tammuz see Bendt Alster, "Tammuz," *DDD* 828–34; Edwin M. Yamauchi, "Tammuz and the Bible," *JBL* 84 (1965): 283–90; O. R. Gurney, "Tammuz Reconsidered: Some Recent Developments," *JSS* 7 (1962): 147–60; Thorkild Jacobsen, "Toward the Image of Tammuz," *HR* 1 (1961): 189–213; repr. in *Toward the Image of Tammuz and Other Essays on*

being exposed to such practices in Babylon, Ackerman has argued for the diffusion of this east Semitic cult to the west Semitic world.[161]

Scene 4: Astral Worship (8:16-18)

In the fourth scene of Ezekiel's vision, at the entrance of the temple the prophet sees "about twenty-five men, with their backs to the temple of Yahweh, and their faces toward the east, bowing down to the sun toward the east" (v. 16). The scene recalls the prohibition of astral worship in Deut. 4:19 (also a concern in Deut. 17:3):[162]

> When you lift your eyes [נשא עיניך] to the heavens and see the sun, the moon, and the stars, all the host of heaven, do not be led astray and bow down [השתחוה] to them and serve them, things that Yahweh your God has allotted to all the peoples everywhere under heaven.

Both Deuteronomy 4 and Ezekiel 8 mention the sun (שמש) and use the verb "bow down" (השתחוה), which has led Ganzel to posit a purposeful link between these two passages.[163] Ezekiel's use of the distinctive phrase נשא עיניו ("to lift one's eyes") elsewhere adds further support that Deuteronomy 4 influenced Ezekiel (Ezek. 18:6, 12, 15; 23:27; 33:25).

Ezekiel's Vision and Manasseh's Sins

Ezekiel's temple vision also appears to have links with the description of Manasseh's sins in 2 Kings 21. This observation depends partly on the questionable identification of the "statue of jealousy" as Manasseh's

---

Mesopotamian History and Culture, ed. William L. Moran, HSS 21 (Cambridge, MA: Harvard University Press, 1970), 73–103; Raphael Kutscher, "The Cult of Dumuzi/Tammuz," in *Bar-Ilan Studies in Assyriology Dedicated to Pinhas Artzi*, ed. Jacob Klein and Aaron Skaist (Ramat-Gan: Bar Ilan University Press, 1990), 29–44.

161. Ackerman, *Under Every Green Tree*, 82–92.

162. On sun worship, see Glen Taylor, *Yahweh and the Sun: Biblical and Archaeological Evidence for Sun Worship in Ancient Israel*, JSOTSup 111 (Sheffield: JSOT, 1993). Contra Mark S. Smith ("The Near Eastern Background of Solar Language for Yahweh," *JBL* 109 [1990]: 29–39), John Day has argued that solar worship in the biblical literature is idolatrous, not Yahwistic (*Yahweh and the Gods*, 151–63). Cf. Ackerman, *Under Every Green Tree*, 98: "what is crucial to Ezekiel is that those who practice the sun cult in the courtyard of Yahweh's temple turn their backs to the temple as part of their worship. In turning their backs on the temple, they turn their backs on Yahweh. Ezekiel interprets this gesture as a rejection of the Israelite national god in favor of another deity."

163. Ganzel, "Transformation," 38.

Asherah statue (2 Kgs 21:7), but 2 Kings 21 also describes Manasseh's astral worship, a practice that features prominently in Ezekiel 8. Second Kings 21:3-5 report that Manasseh "worshiped all the host of heaven" (וישתחו לכל צבא השמים) and built altars for them. The altars were erected in the temple courts (שתי חצרות בית יהוה), the very location where Ezekiel sees the men worshiping the sun in 8:16 (חצר בית יהוה).

While it is possible Manasseh's sins are in view in Ezekiel's temple vision,[164] the closest links remain with Deuteronomy 4. First, whether or not the outrageous statue represents Asherah, it is Deuteronomy 4, not 2 Kings 21, that shares the rare word סמל with Ezekiel 8.[165] Second, among the references to astral worship in the Hebrew Bible, the language of Ezek. 8:16 most closely resembles Deut. 4:19. Second Kings 21 does not explicitly name the sun as an object of worship, and other references in 2 Kings and Jeremiah use such verbs as "sacrificing to" (קטר ל), "loving" (אהב), and "serving" (עבד) the astral bodies (2 Kgs 23:5, 11; Jer. 8:2), rather than "bowing down" (השתחוה) to them, as in both Deut. 4:19 and Ezek. 8:16. Therefore, 2 Kings 21 does not provide a sufficient alternative literary source to invalidate the distinctive links with Deuteronomy 4.

---

164. This study is not directly interested in whether the idolatry in Ezek. 8 reflects practices in Ezekiel's time or during the reign of Manasseh. Since Ezek. 8 represents an explicitly visionary experience (במראות אלהים), such an endeavor seems futile. Following Kaufmann (*Religion of Israel*, 406–9), Greenberg suggests that Ezek. 8 refers to Manasseh's day (*Ezekiel 1–20*, 202). Ackerman argues for Ezekiel's time (*Under Every Green Tree*, 47–51), so also Middlemas: "Part of the rhetoric of the book of Ezekiel, particularly with regard to the temple vision of chs. 8–11, is to emphasize the judgement on the population that remains behind in Judah… Were the vision harking back to the time of Manasseh, the thrust of the polemic would be neutralized. The vision in its entirety, therefore, more naturally falls at a time contemporaneous with the prophet, on the eve of the destruction of the temple" (*Troubles*, 93).

This issue is related to the historical question of whether idolatry persisted after Josiah's reforms. On the one hand, Milgrom claims that the presence of figurines in the archaeological record, even in the City of David near the Jerusalem temple, confirms the persistence of idolatry in the period after Josiah. On the other, the polemic on idolatry apparently persuaded many to abandon their idolatrous practices, since by 586 the exilic generation could protest that they were being punished for the sins of previous generations (Jer. 31:28; Ezek. 18:2; cf. Lam. 5:7). The Deuteronomists similarly blamed Manasseh for the exile (2 Kgs 23:26-27; Milgrom, "Nature and Extent of Idolatry," 10–11; cf. idem, *Leviticus 17–22*, 1389–90).

165. For Ezekiel's dependence on Deuteronomy here, see Ganzel, "Transformation," 36; Block, *Ezekiel*, 1:281.

Ezekiel and Deuteronomy 4

This study has identified several links between Ezekiel and Deuteronomy 4, a chapter often considered one of the later additions to Deuteronomy.

Literary Links

Of the three visionary scenes in Ezekiel 8 that exhibit parallels with other biblical texts, all find their most distinctive links with Deuteronomy 4. The first scene describes a statue with סמל, a word that occurs only in Deut. 4:16 among the literary traditions potentially known to Ezekiel. The second scene describes "every form of creeping thing and animal" engraved on the wall, an allusion to the forbidden images of Deut. 4:17-18. And the fourth scene describes astral worship using language (השתחוה and שמש) that resembles most closely Deut. 4:19. It would appear Ezekiel's vision deliberately depicts the fundamental transgression of the torah as depicted in Deuteronomy 4.

Earlier, I argued that in Ezek. 20:32, the prophet alludes to Deuteronomy's conception of worshiping "wood and stone" in exile, which appears in Deut. 4:28; 28:36, 64. Based on the limited connections between Ezekiel and Deuteronomy 28 noted above, Ezekiel likely drew from Deut. 4:28 specifically. Later, in Chapter 6 of this study, I will argue that Ezek. 20:23 explicitly cites the threat of exile found in Deut. 4:25-28. The recurrence of links provides cumulative evidence that Ezekiel may have known and used Deuteronomy 4.

Dating Deuteronomy 4

The suggestion that Ezekiel knew Deuteronomy 4 might seem to be at odds with the widely held view that the chapter dates to the exilic period.[166] But Ezekiel could have known some form of Deuteronomy 4—whether in oral or written form—even if it was roughly contemporaneous with him. Nevertheless, it seems plausible Deuteronomy 4 should be dated before 587 BCE. First, some criteria cited in discussions of the composition and redaction of Deuteronomy 4 do not directly fix its date to the period of the exile. For example, change of number (*Numeruswechsel*)—even if it

---

166. Despite the inadequacy of the terms preexilic, exilic and postexilic, I use them in this study to refer to the periods before, during, and after the Babylonian exile of 597/587–539 BCE. This paradigm oversimplifies Israel's history, because both the Southern and Northern Kingdoms experienced exiles at the hands of the Neo-Assyrian and Neo-Babylonian empires before 587. However, since the fall of Jerusalem marked a significant crisis in Israel's faith and identity, it is still useful to date biblical texts according to these broad categories.

could be used as a sign of redaction[167]—does not prove the date of the material. The case for dating the text to the exilic period rests primarily on two bases: the references to exile[168] and restoration[169] (vv. 25-28, 29-31) and explicit monotheism[170] (vv. 35, 39). Since Deuteronomy 4 refers to exile, scholars who regard the text as a literary unity therefore consider the entire passage exilic.[171] Others argue that these parts of the chapter reflect exilic additions to a preexilic composition. For example, Richard Elliott Friedman regards vv. 1-24 as preexilic and the reference to deportation and return in vv. 25-31 as an exilic addition.[172] C. Begg dates vv. 1-28, including the threat of deportation (vv. 25-28), to the period before the exile, but regards the restoration language of vv. 29-30 as exilic.[173] In the preceding section, I identified a concentration of links between Ezekiel 8 and Deut. 4:16-19. In the dating of Friedman and Begg, this part of Deuteronomy 4 would have been available to Ezekiel.

167. Many scholars have rejected this criterion for determining compositional layers (e.g., Jon D. Levenson, "Who Inserted the Book of the Torah?" *HTR* 68 (1975): 204–7; A. D. H. Mayes, "Deuteronomy 4 and the Literary Criticism of Deuteronomy," *JBL* 100 [1981]: 27–30; Norbert Lohfink, *Das Hauptgebot: Eine Untersuchungliterarischer Einleitungsfragen zu Dtn 5–11*, AnBib 20 [Rome: Pontifical Biblical Institute, 1963], 239–58; Georg Braulik, *Die Mittel deuteronomistischer Rhetorik erhoben aus Deuteronomium 4,1-40*, AnBib 68 [Rome: Pontifical Biblical Institute, 1978], 146–50).

168. E.g., Richard Elliott Friedman, "From Egypt to Egypt: Dtr1 and Dtr2," in *Traditions in Transformation: Turning Points in Biblical Faith*, ed. Baruch Halpern and Jon D. Levenson (Winona Lake, IN: Eisenbrauns, 1981), 180; von Rad, *Deuteronomy*, 50; Noth, *Deuteronomistic History*, 34. For further discussion, see Chapter 6 of this study.

169. Hans Walter Wolff, "The Kerygma of the Deuteronomistic Historical Work," in *The Vitality of Old Testament Traditions*, ed. Walter Brueggemann and Hans Walter Wolff (Atlanta: John Knox, 1975), 96 (trans. of "Das Kerygma des deuteronomistischen Geschichtswerk," *ZAW* 73 [1961]: 171–86 (emphasis original); Frank Moore Cross, *Canaanite Myth and Hebrew Epic: Essays in the History of the Religion of Israel* (Cambridge, MA: Harvard University Press, 1973), 278; von Rad, *Deuteronomy*, 50; Nelson, *Deuteronomy*, 4.

170. E.g., Weinfeld, *Deuteronomy 1–11*, 230.

171. E.g., Norbert F. Lohfink, *Höre, Israel! Auslegung von Texten aus dem Buch Deuteronomium*, Die Welt der Bibel 18 (Düsseldorf: Patmos, 1965), 87–120; Levenson, "Who Inserted the Book of the Torah?" 203–7, 215; Braulik, *Die Mittel*; Mayes, "Deuteronomy 4," 25–31.

172. Friedman, *Exile and Biblical Narrative*, 17; idem, "From Egypt to Egypt," 180–2.

173. C. Begg, "The Literary Criticism of Deut 4,1-40: Contributions to a Continuing Discussion," *ETL* 56 (1980): 43–5.

Still, the validity of using exile and return and alleged monotheistic statements as criteria for dating biblical texts remains open to question, and the evidence for an exilic date is not as conclusive as many assume. In Chapters 6 and 7 of this study, I will consider in more detail the likelihood that biblical passages threatening exile and promising return may precede 587 BCE. For now, it will suffice to note that many scholars reject the notion that the mere mention of exile means a text comes from the period of the Babylonian exile, not least because exile was a known tool of imperial subjugation in the ancient Near East before 587.[174] Even promises of return from exile may also date to the period before 587. If a historical exile is required to speak of a return—an assumption open to question—then the deportation of the Northern Kingdom in 722 provides a suitable context for the biblical writers to speak of return well before 587. Second, the use of monotheistic statements to date biblical texts is itself circular, inasmuch as it relies on reconstructions of the history of Israel's religion. But more importantly, the phrase אין עוד in Deut. 4:35, 39 is not "monotheistic" in the strict sense. Nathan MacDonald and others have argued convincingly that the phrase "there is no other" does not deny the existence of other deities but emphasizes Yahweh's incomparability.[175]

Since Martin Noth, the dating of Deuteronomy 4 has been central to the larger discussion of the Deuteronomistic editing of Deuteronomy. Noth himself regarded ch. 4 as the work of the exilic Dtr (or a later editor) composed as a transition between the historical overview of chs. 1–3 and the law corpus beginning in ch. 5.[176] Scholars commonly assert the exilic date of Deuteronomy 4 by citing parallels with other texts that are considered exilic.[177] Often ch. 4 is seen as part of an envelope

---

174. E.g., Cross, *Canaanite Myth*, 287; Duane Christensen, *Deuteronomy 1–11*, WBC 6A (Dallas: Word, 1991), 93; Richard D. Nelson, *The Double Redaction of the Deuteronomistic History*, JSOTSup 18 (Sheffield: JSOT, 1981), 23; Carsten Vang, "The So-Called '*Ur-Deuteronomium*': Some Reflections on Its Content, Size and Age," *Hiphil* 6 (2009): 11–15.

175. Nathan MacDonald, *Deuteronomy and the Meaning of "Monotheism*,*"* FAT II/46, 2nd ed. (Tübingen: Mohr Siebeck, 2012), 79–85, who cites three problems with Rechenmacher's interpretation of אין עוד as an "exclusivity formula" (Hans Rechenmacher, *"Außer mir gibt es keinen Gott!" Eine sprach- und literarurwissenschaftliche Studie zur Ausschließlichkeitsformel*, ATSAT 49 [St Ottilien: EOS, 1997]). See also Michael Heiser, "Monotheism, Polytheism, Monolatry, or Henotheism? Toward an Assessment of Divine Plurality in the Hebrew Bible," *BBR* 18 (2008): 5–13, esp. 5–6.

176. Noth, *Deuteronomistic History*, 33–4; more recently Mayes, "Deuteronomy 4," 204.

177. E.g., Mayes, "Deuteronomy 4," 34–5.

with chs. 29–30,[178] particularly linked by the shared themes of disaster (29:22-28[23-29]) and restoration (30:1-10).[179] Even if Deuteronomy 4 and 29–30 derive from the same hand, this by itself does not constitute evidence for an exilic date, especially in light of the unreliability of the criteria noted above.

In short, whether Deuteronomy 4 precedes Ezekiel or is roughly contemporaneous with him, he may have known and alluded it. In fact, based on the parallels, a number of scholars have hypothesized as much. For example, Ganzel argued that Deuteronomy 4 specifically influenced Ezekiel's idol language.[180] David Halperin similarly argued that many features of Ezekiel 8 recall Deuteronomy 4, particularly the allusion to Deut. 4:17-18 in Ezek. 8:10.[181] Levitt Kohn suggested in passing that the scattering oath in Ezek. 20:23 alludes specifically to Deut. 4:26-27,[182] to which we will return in Chapter 6 of this study. The large number of parallels between Ezekiel and Deuteronomy 4 observed in this and subsequent chapters would be best explained not by coincidence but by Ezekiel's knowledge of Deuteronomy 4.

Idolatry and Defilement

Ezekiel's theology of idolatry exhibits a significant innovation due to the influence of Deuteronomy, namely, idolatry as a cause of defilement (טמא).[183] The Holiness Code and Ezekiel share a special interest in defilement.[184] But whereas the Priestly literature identifies several sources

---

178. Levenson, "Who Inserted the Book of the Torah?" 212–18; Weinfeld, *Deuteronomy 1–11*, 216; Friedman, "From Egypt to Egypt," 181–2.

179. Nelson, *Deuteronomy*, 63, 68. Many regard Deut. 30:1-10 as an expansion of 4:29-31 (see Driver, *Deuteronomy*, 328; Wolff, "Kerygma," 96–7; Robert Polzin, *Moses and the Deuteronomist: A Literary Study of the Deuteronomic History I: Deuteronomy, Joshua, Judges* [New York: Seabury, 1980], 70).

180. Ganzel, "Transformation," 36–40. In n. 22 she follows the view of Menahem Haran that chs. 1–4 of Deuteronomy are an integral part of the book (*The Biblical Collection: Its Consolidation to the End of the Second Temple Times and Changes of Form to the End of the Middle Ages*, vol. 2 [Jerusalem: Bialik/Magnes, 2003], 195–200 [Hebrew]).

181. Halperin, *Seeking Ezekiel*, 108–14, 119–20.

182. Levitt Kohn, *New Heart*, 100 n. 32.

183. See Ganzel, "Transformation," 44–6.

184. Jonathan Klawans, *Purity, Sacrifice, and the Temple: Symbolism and Supersessionism in the Study of Ancient Judaism* (Oxford: Oxford University Press,

of moral impurity, including sexual sins, the Molech cult, illicit divination, and bloodshed,[185] Ezekiel focuses on idolatry as the predominant cause.[186] Ka Leung Wong rightly observes:

> While sexual sin is mainly responsible for the defilement of the land…in the priestly texts (e.g. Lev 18), its importance in Ezekiel in the defilement of the land is of less significance, but not totally absent. Bloodshed does play a role in defiling the land (e.g. 21:1-14) in Ezekiel as in Nu 35:33-34, but the overwhelming concern of Ezekiel is idolatry… The defiling power of idolatry is immense. It can defile the sanctuary [5:11; 23:37-38], the land [36:18] and the idolaters themselves [14:11].[187]

Ganzel explains this unique feature of Ezekiel's theology in terms of the Priestly and Deuteronomic influences that underly it:

> The Priestly view of defilement undergoes a partial shift [in Ezekiel] from mainly physical causes to Ezekiel's unique conclusion, conceptually grounded in Deuteronomic notions, that the people's overwhelming engagement in idolatry was responsible for their defilement.[188]

Thus, Ezekiel offers a new, unique synthesis, combining the Holiness Code's special interest in defilement with Deuteronomy's concern for idolatry.

Summary

In this chapter, I argued for the strong influence of Deuteronomic language and theology on Ezekiel's conception of Israel's idolatry. To summarize, first, Ezekiel uses Deuteronomic terms for idolatry almost exclusively, even favoring them over Priestly alternatives (e.g., העביר בנים באש over נתן למולך). In some cases, he adopts the distinctively Deuteronomic association of a word (e.g., תועבה for idolatry) or uses a similar word in its Deuteronomic sense over its differing Priestly sense (e.g., שקץ). Second, in one instance he not only uses Deuteronomic terms

---

2005), 95: the book of Ezekiel exhibits "a sustained interest in the notion of moral defilement"; see further pp. 94–7 and idem, *Impurity and Sin in Ancient Judaism* (Oxford: Oxford University Press, 2000), 30–1.

185. Wong, *Idea of Retribution*, 154–5.
186. Ezek. 5:11; 20:7, 18, 26, 30-31; 22:3, 4; 23:7, 30, 39; 36:18; 37:23; 43:7 (cf. 20:39 with חלל).
187. Wong, *Idea of Retribution*, 154–5; cf. Mein, *Ethics of Exile*, 151.
188. Ganzel, "Transformation," 47.

for idols but interprets the situation in Babylonian exile using a distinctively Deuteronomic idea, namely, that Israel would worship עץ ואבן in exile. Third, Ezekiel not only supports the centralization of worship, but uses Deuteronomic language in his indictment against worship outside of Jerusalem. And fourth, the temple vision of Ezekiel 8 exhibits strong lexical links with Deuteronomy 4, suggesting the possibility that the prophet may have known and alluded to it.

The Rhetoric of Allusion

The rhetoric of Ezekiel's allusions to Deuteronomy's idol language rests in the status of Deuteronomy as authoritative instruction for Israel.[189] For Ezekiel, they are Yahweh's statutes and ordinances given to Israel in the wilderness (20:10-11, 18). As noted at the beginning of this chapter, for Ezekiel, idol worship was foremost a transgression against Yahweh's חקות and משפטים. By using the language of Deuteronomy's prohibitions of idolatry, he identifies these statutes and ordinances primarily with Deuteronomy. Furthermore, in Ezek. 20:18, Yahweh's exhortation to "their children in the wilderness" not to worship idols most closely aligns with Deuteronomy's prohibition of idolatry. In the cases of literary reference, Ezekiel's use of Deuteronomy's idol language constitutes a rhetorical technique Lyons calls "genre transformation": Ezekiel transforms Deuteronomy's laws into prophetic accusation.[190] The rhetoric of Ezekiel's use of Deuteronomic language in this case assumes Deuteronomy's status as divine torah: Israel has transgressed Yahweh's statutes and regulations, thereby bringing upon themselves the curses.[191] As I will argue in Chapter 6 of this study, Ezekiel understood the Babylonian exile as the fulfillment of Deuteronomy's threats of deportation for transgressing its statutes, when Yahweh "swore to them in the wilderness that he would scatter them among the nations" (Ezek. 20:23). Significantly, it is idolatry that is singled out in Deut. 4:25-28 as the offense that will provoke Yahweh to exile his people. Ezekiel viewed his people's sins as transgressions against the statutes contained in these documents and judged Israel according to their standard.

---

189. Cf. William M. Schniedewind, "Scripturalization in Ancient Judah," in Schmidt, ed., *Contextualizing Israel's Sacred Writings*, 305–21.

190. Lyons, "Persuasion and Allusion," 79.

191. Also Ganzel, "Transformation," 41: "By alluding to Deuteronomy, Ezekiel creates a cause-and-effect relationship between the current sins of the people and the punishments of destruction and exile cited in the Deuteronomic covenant."

Chapter 4

EZEKIEL 16 AND THE SONG OF MOSES*

Scholars have long recognized that in Ezekiel 16 the prophet draws on the harlotry metaphor of his prophetic predecessors to indict Jerusalem for its idolatry and foreign relations.[1] Moshe Greenberg, for example, described Ezekiel's expansion of this common motif when he noted, "By extending the metaphor in time, Ezekiel provides the adulterous wife of Hosea and Jeremiah with a biography."[2] However, commentators have thus far failed to notice that the building blocks of the oracle are found in the Song of Moses (Deut. 32:1-43).[3] In this chapter, I will argue that Ezekiel's depiction of Israel in ch. 16 (chiefly section A, vv. 1-43)[4] represents a

---

* An earlier version of this chapter was published as "Ezekiel 16 and the Song of Moses: A Prophetic Transformation?" *JBL* 130 (2011): 87–108.

1. See, e.g., Carley, *Ezekiel among the Prophets*, 49; Zimmerli, *Ezekiel*, 1:342; Greenberg, *Ezekiel 1–20*, 298; Leslie C. Allen, *Ezekiel 1–19*, WBC 28 (Dallas: Word, 1994), 247; Julie Galambush, *Jerusalem in the Book of Ezekiel: The City as Yahweh's Wife*, SBLDS 130 (Atlanta: Scholars Press, 1992), 61; Karl-Friedrich Pohlmann, *Das Buch des Propheten Hesekiel*, vol. 1, *Kapitel 1–19*, ATD 22/1 (Göttingen: Vandenhoeck & Ruprecht, 1996), 223; Block, *Ezekiel*, 1:466.

This is not to imply that the biblical prophets share a single, coherent "marriage metaphor" (see Sharon Moughtin-Mumby, *Sexual and Marital Metaphors in Hosea, Jeremiah, Isaiah, and Ezekiel*, OTM [Oxford: Oxford University Press, 2008], 6), but only that Ezekiel's harlot imagery has prophetic antecedents. On this, along with my position on the sexual and marital imagery that has dominated the discussion of Ezek. 16 in recent years, see my review of Moughtin-Mumby's monograph in *JHS* 9 (2009), online: http://www.jhsonline.org.

2. Greenberg, *Ezekiel 1–20*, 299.

3. The possibility of thematic links between Ezek. 16 and the Song of Moses was brought to my attention by Daniel Block in personal conversation.

4. On the tripartite arrangement of Ezek. 16 (vv. 1-43, 44-58, and 59-63, labeled sections A, B, and C), see Greenberg, *Ezekiel 1–20,* 292–6.

prophetic transformation of the rise and decline of Israel depicted in the Song, whereby he adopts the structure and themes of Deuteronomy 32 and infuses them with the prophetic motif of harlotry.[5]

I begin the investigation by outlining the thematic, lexical, and structural links between the two passages and then more explicitly discuss whether they meet the criteria for literary dependence. In the subsequent sections I address the following questions: Could Ezekiel have known and used the Song? Is it likely he would have known and used the Song? Did he in fact use the Song elsewhere in his prophetic book? And is it likely that he would have used the Song in the way proposed in this study? Finally, I mention numerous ways in which Ezekiel uniquely builds on and transforms his underlying text and then conclude by addressing the rhetorical import of Ezekiel's use of the Song.

Plot Structure and Thematic Links

Ezekiel 16 and Deuteronomy 32 display remarkable similarities of plot and themes, the full extent of which has not been fully noted. The two texts exhibit virtually identical plot structures, both depicting the rise and decline of Yahweh's people. In both, (a) Yahweh discovers destitute Israel in a barren location; (b) he delivers her and renders lavish care upon her so that (c) she prospers; (d) Israel in her prosperity forsakes Yahweh; (e) she pursues other gods and (f) forgets her origins, thereby (g) provoking Yahweh to anger; (h) Israel is punished for her sins; and finally, (i) Israel is restored. Several verbal parallels, synonyms, and rare motifs found in the two passages at the same point in the plot make it unlikely that these similarities are coincidental. The two texts also share similar formal features. Though Ezekiel 16 may be properly considered a *rîb* ("dispute")[6] and Deuteronomy 32 a *šîr* ("song, hymn"), the latter nevertheless contains strong *rîb* elements, including an indictment (vv. 15-18) and sentence (vv. 19-29).[7]

---

5. In this chapter I use "Deuteronomy 32" as a shorthand for the Song in Deut. 32:1-43.
6. See Block, *Ezekiel*, 1:459–62.
7. This is evidenced by many earlier scholars' identification of Deut. 32 as a *rîb* (see esp. G. Ernest Wright, "The Lawsuit of God: A Form-Critical Study of Deuteronomy 32," in *Israel's Prophetic Heritage: Essays in Honor of James Muilenburg*, ed. Bernhard W. Anderson and Walter Harrelson [New York: Harper & Brothers, 1962], 26–67).

Before considering the links in detail, a few comments are necessary by way of preface. First, the texts exhibit some fundamental differences in imagery, and Ezekiel's oracle is fuller and more detailed at certain points. Most of these differences are due to the liberty with which the prophet expands and transforms the Song. The particulars of Ezekiel's transformation will be taken up later, but in what follows I will focus on the thematic links and parallel plot structures, while recognizing, for example, that the harlot imagery is lacking in Deuteronomy 32. Second, the criteria for establishing literary dependence and its direction will be discussed below. It is to be noted in advance that the case for literary dependence across entire pericopes involves a cumulative argument. The persuasiveness of individual parallels would vary on a scale of possibility to probability when considered separately. When taken together, however, and in the close proximity of two well-defined passages, numerous distinctive parallels in combination can make a compelling case for literary dependence.

Yahweh's Discovery of Israel (Deut. 32:10 // Ezek. 16:6)

Both accounts of Israel's history with God begin with Yahweh finding destitute Israel in a barren location. In Ezekiel 16, the prophet depicts Jerusalem's origins with the image of an infant cast aside by her parents and later rescued from dire straits and cared for by Yahweh. In vv. 5-6, Yahweh passes by (עבר על) the infant and sees (ראה) her destitute in an open field (שדה). The Song similarly describes Yahweh's discovery of Israel in a barren location. In Deut. 32:10, he finds (מצא) Jacob in a desert land (מדבר) and encircles (סבב) him (in this case using masculine pronouns[8]). Though Ezekiel prefaces the discovery of the foundling with a "biography," to which we will return below, in both texts the discovery marks the start of Israel's relationship with her God Yahweh.

Though Ezekiel does not adopt the exact same language in this instance, the terms שדה and מדבר in the Bible have overlapping semantic domains, as evidenced by those passages where they occur together, as synonyms or in parallel poetic lines (Josh. 8:24; Job 24:5-6; Isa. 43:19-20;

---

8. Adjustment of person, number, and gender for both verbal subjects and objects is a common feature of inner-biblical literary borrowing, since later writers change the language to fit a new context (see Lyons, *From Law to Prophecy*, 79). In the present case, Ezek. 16 has Yahweh speak in the first person to Jerusalem, who is addressed in the second person. In the Song a narrator speaks of both Yahweh and Israel with third person pronouns.

Joel 1:19-20; 2:22).⁹ The verbs ראה and מצא are also conceptually similar, as is illustrated in Hos. 9:10 where the two verbs occur in parallel in a context nearly identical to our passages, namely, in reference to Yahweh finding Israel:

> Like grapes in the wilderness,
>   I found (מצא) Israel.
> Like the first fruit on the fig tree in its first season,
>   I saw (ראה) your ancestors. (Hos. 9:10)

Though it is unlikely that Ezekiel is dependent on Hosea here, since the imagery of the latter focuses on Yahweh finding Israel "like grapes" and "like the first fruit on the fig tree," instead of like a destitute foundling rescued and cared for as in Ezekiel and Deuteronomy,¹⁰ Hos. 9:10 wonderfully shows the semantic overlap of מצא and ראה in a similar context and thus demonstrates that both verbs can be used to refer to a discovery.

Since the foundling or discovery motif (*Fundmotiv*) for Israel's relationship to Yahweh appears only in Ezekiel 16 and Deuteronomy 32 in the Hebrew Bible,¹¹ one might reasonably propose influence from Deuteronomy 32 on Ezek. 16:6 alone. Thus, contra Hermann Gunkel's hypothesis that Ezekiel draws the motif from a common folktale type,¹² it is argued here—in conjunction with the prophet's wider dependence on Deuteronomy 32 noted next—that he appropriates it from the Song of Moses. A few scholars have noted the similar image in these two passages,¹³ but Millar Burrows came closest to the thesis presented here

---

9. Meir Malul, "Adoption of Foundlings in the Bible and Mesopotamian Documents: A Study of Some Legal Metaphors in Ezekiel 16:1-7," *JSOT* 46 (1990): 103.

10. It is more likely that Hosea is also dependent on Deut. 32:10, borrowing the notion of finding Israel in the wilderness, but he takes it in a different direction.

11. Ps. 27:10 speaks of Yahweh's adoption of the petitioner but not of a discovery.

12. Hermann Gunkel, *The Folktale in the Old Testament*, trans. M. D. Rutter, HTIBS 6 (Sheffield: Almond, 1987), 128–31; trans. of *Das Märchen im Alten Testament*, Religionsgeschichtliche Volksbücher 2 (Tübingen: J. C. B. Mohr, 1917). Greenberg earlier presented a persuasive critique of this hypothesis (*Ezekiel 1–20*, 300–301).

13. Greenberg, *Ezekiel 1–20*, 299; Zimmerli, *Ezekiel*, 1:336; idem, *Old Testament Theology in Outline*, trans. David E. Green (Edinburgh: T. & T. Clark, 1978), 23. Though scholars debate the exact referent of Ezekiel's foundling metaphor in Israel's history (see, e.g., Allen, *Ezekiel 1–19*, 236–7; Thomas Krüger, *Geschichtskonzepte im Ezechielbuch*, BZAW 180 [Berlin: de Gruyter, 1989], 184), the similarity in the metaphorical vehicle alone can suggest literary borrowing.

when he observed that "[Ezekiel] seems to combine the thought of [the foundling in] Dt 32 with [Hosea's] conception of Jerusalem as a girl tenderly reared by Yahweh."[14] However, uncertain of the priority of these two texts, Burrows refrained from conclusively deciding that Ezekiel is dependent on the Song and did not recognize parallels beyond the discovery and care of Israel. Greenberg intimated a further connection when he noted that the foundling motif functions in the same way in both the Song and Ezekiel 16, namely, "to start the account of God's relation to his people with a situation best designed to enhance his beneficence toward them and illustrate his providential and tender care of them,"[15] but scholars have not thus far recognized the full extent of the distinctive thematic and plot parallels that continue throughout the two passages.

Yahweh's Lavish Care (Deut. 32:10b-14 // Ezek. 16:7-13a)

In both passages, after discovering Israel, Yahweh rescues her and renders lavish care upon her. In Ezek. 16:7a, Yahweh recounts: "I made you flourish like a plant of the field, and you grew up and became tall and arrived at full adornment." And after Yahweh passed by a second time[16] and entered into a covenant with the young girl by passing his garment over her, he brought her from rags to riches:

> I bathed you with water and washed off your blood from you and anointed you with oil. I clothed you also with embroidered cloth and provided you with sandals of fine leather. I wrapped you in fine linen and covered you with fine fabric. And I adorned you with jewelry and put bracelets on your wrists and a chain on your neck. And I put a ring on your nose and earrings in your ears and a beautiful crown on your head. Thus you were adorned with gold and silver, and your clothing was of fine linen and fine fabric and embroidered cloth. You ate fine flour and honey and oil. (Ezek. 16:9-13a)

Similarly, in the Song of Moses, Yahweh tenderly cares for Jacob and provides him with the finest things.

---

14. Burrows, *Literary Relations of Ezekiel*, 23.
15. Greenberg, *Ezekiel 1–20*, 299–300.
16. Greenberg claims that this is an adjustment to the exodus tradition, whereby the intermediate period refers to Israel's time in Egypt, when it grew, waiting for Yahweh's redemption (ibid., 301). However, the second passing may be necessary for the metaphorical vehicle, since one cannot marry an infant (also contra the motive of Yahweh suggested by Linda Day, "Rhetoric and Domestic Violence in Ezekiel 16," *BibInt* 8 [2000]: 208–9).

...he cared for him;
he protected him as the apple of his eye.
Like an eagle that stirs up its nest,
that hovers over its young,
spreading out its wings, catching them,
bearing them on its pinions,
Yahweh alone guided him;
no foreign god was with him.
He enabled him to ride on the high places of the land,
and he ate of the produce of the field,
and he suckled him with honey out of the rock,
and oil out of the flinty rock.
Butter from the herd, and milk from the flock,
with the fat of lambs, rams of Bashan and goats,
with the finest of the wheat—
and from the juice of the grapes you drank wine. (Deut. 32:10b-14)

The most fascinating verbal parallel between these two passages is found at this point in the story in Deut. 32:11 and Ezek. 16:8, namely, the phrase פרש כנף. In Deuteronomy 32, Yahweh's care for Israel is portrayed as an eagle spreading (פרש) its wings (כנף) over its young; in Ezekiel 16, when Yahweh enters into a marriage covenant with Jerusalem, he spreads (פרש) his garment (כנף) over her. While spreading a garment over a woman undoubtedly refers to acquiring her in marriage (cf. Ruth 3:9),[17] if Ezekiel is drawing from Deuteronomy 32, then the phrase also represents an allusion to Deut. 32:11—a double entendre of sorts. Not only do the two פרש כנף statements appear in the same section of the plot, but both also occur immediately after the ראה/מצא and עבר על/סבב word pairs (Deut. 32:10a // Ezek. 16:8a) and are followed by the extended descriptions of Yahweh's lavish care (Deut. 32:12-14 // Ezek. 16:9-13).

This section of the plot contains another significant verbal parallel. As Georg Fohrer has pointed out, in the context of Yahweh's care, both passages speak of Israel eating honey and oil.[18]

---

17. Paul A. Kruger, "The Hem of the Garment in Marriage: The Meaning of the Symbolic Gesture in Ruth 3:9 and Ezek. 16:8," *JNSL* 12 (1984): 79–86. See Moughtin-Mumby, *Sexual and Marital Metaphors*, 172 n. 72, for further bibliography.

18. Georg Fohrer, *Die Hauptprobleme des Buches Ezechiel*, BZAW 72 (Berlin: Töpelmann, 1952), 144; followed by Rimon Kasher, *Ezekiel: Introduction and Commentary*, vol. 1, *Chapters 1–24*, Mikra le-Yiśrael (Tel Aviv: Am Oved, 2004), 55 (in Hebrew).

Deut. 32:13

He ate (אכל) the produce of the field,
and he suckled him with honey (דבש) out of the rock,
and oil (שמן) out of the flinty rock.

Ezek. 16:13 (also v. 19)

You ate (אכל) fine flour and honey (דבש) and oil (שמן).

Though שמן and דבש occur together a couple times in longer lists of commodities (Jer. 41:8; Ezek. 27:17),[19] only in these two texts does the Hebrew Bible speak of Israel (in extended metaphors) eating honey and oil—both in the context of Yahweh's care.

Israel Prospers (Deut. 32:15a // Ezek. 16:13b-14)

Because of Yahweh's care, Israel prospers. Deuteronomy 32:15a describes Israel's prosperity to the point of excess: "Jeshurun grew fat, and kicked; you grew fat, stout, and sleek." This compares with Ezek. 16:13b-14, where Ezekiel describes Jerusalem's rise to prominence and renown: "You grew exceedingly beautiful and advanced to royalty, and your fame went forth among the nations because of your beauty. Indeed, it was perfect through the splendor that I had bestowed on you, declares the Lord Yahweh."

Israel Forsakes Her God (Deut. 32:15b // Ezek. 16:15a)

Immediately after Israel increases, she forsakes Yahweh her God, who rescued her and made her thrive. Both texts ascribe the turning point to her self-confidence. In the Song, it was after Jeshurun grew fat from Yahweh's luxurious provision that he "forsook God who made him and scoffed at the Rock of his salvation" (32:15b). Ezekiel depicts Jerusalem's turn from Yahweh as the moment she trusts in her beauty (16:15a).

Israel's Idolatry (Deut. 32:16-17 // Ezek. 16:15b-22)

In the Song, Israel's idolatry takes up two verses:

---

19. The linguistic link to Lev. 2 is weaker. The word דבש only appears once there (Lev. 2:11-12) and not in immediate proximity to סלת and שמן (Lev. 2:7). On the other hand, if Ezekiel also has Lev. 2 in mind, he would appear to indict Israel for something that Lev. 2 forbids: offering דבש (for leavening) as a soothing aroma (ניחח ריח).

> They stirred him to jealousy with strange gods;
> with abominations they provoked him to anger.
> They sacrificed to demons that were no gods,
> to gods they had never known,
> to new gods that had come recently,
> whom your fathers had never dreaded. (32:16-17)

True to Ezekiel's intense detestation of idolatry,[20] the prophet expands the account of idolatry into a graphic display of harlotrous idolatry that encompasses eight verses, followed by a continuation of the metaphor to refer to Jerusalem's illegitimate foreign relations as well (16:23-34).[21] In this latter section, Jerusalem is said to take זרים ("strangers") instead of her husband (16:32), a possible allusion to Deut. 32:16, where זרים refers to the gods that Israel worshiped.

Israel Forgets Her Origins (Deut. 32:18 // Ezek. 16:22)

In her idolatry, Israel forgets her origins.[22] The exhortation to remember Yahweh and his providential care of Israel in the wilderness is a key theme in Deuteronomy, particularly ch. 8 (see especially vv. 14-16). The Song states that Jacob "forgot the God who gave [him] birth" (32:18), and in Ezek. 16:22 the prophet indicts Jerusalem for not remembering the "days of [her] youth when [she] was naked and bare." In both cases, after being blessed by Yahweh, Israel forgets that it was Yahweh who caused her to prosper.

Israel Angers Yahweh (Deut. 32:16, 21 // Ezek. 16:26)

In both passages, Israel angers Yahweh, which is signified by the verbal root כעס, "to provoke to anger." In the Song, Israel's idols are the source of Yahweh's anger.

---

20. Kutsko identifies idolatry as "the quintessential cause of the Babylonian exile" for Ezekiel (*Between Heaven and Earth*, 25; so also Jill Middlemas, "Transformation of the Image," in Tooman and Lyons, eds., *Transforming Visions*, 115–16.

21. Zimmerli considered this latter section on foreign relations to be secondarily added to the idolatry section (*Ezekiel*, 1:334–5, 347–8), but cf. Krüger, *Geschichtskonzepte*, 147–51. Even without these and the other verses that Zimmerli excises from the original Ezek. 16:1-43 (see *Ezekiel*, 1:347–8), the essential components outlined here remain.

22. It is reiterated as the justification for the punishment in 16:43.

Deut. 32:16

They stirred him to jealousy with strange gods (זרים);
with abominations (תועבות) they provoked him to anger (יכעיסהו).

Deut. 32:21a

They have made me jealous with what is no god (בלא־אל);
they have provoked me to anger (כעסוני) with their idols (הבלים).

In Ezekiel, the word occurs in the extended account of Jerusalem's harlotry. After the accounts of her idolatry and illegitimate foreign relations, it is stated that her actions have "provoked me to anger" (להכעיסני).

Israel's Indictment and Punishment (Deut. 32:19-25 // Ezek. 16:35-43)

Yahweh then punishes Israel. Both Ezekiel and the Song cite Israel's idolatry as the reason for her punishment. Thus, Deuteronomy 32 cites the provocation (כעס) of Yahweh caused by his people's idols (v. 21). Ezekiel as well indicts her for harlotry with idols in v. 36: "Because [יען] your lust was poured out and your nakedness uncovered in your whoring with your lovers and with all your abominable idols…" The difference between the modes of punishment will be noted in the final section.

Israel's Restoration (Deut. 32:35-36, 41-43 // Ezek. 16:53-55, 59-63)

One further correspondence remains to be considered: that of Israel's restoration after her punishment. Though the Song emphasizes Yahweh's vindication (32:35-36, 41-43), embodied in this is a clear restorative element. In v. 36 Yahweh "will have compassion on his servants when he sees that their power is gone," and in v. 43 he "avenges the blood of his servants" (LXX and 4QDeut^q: "sons") and "atones (כפר) for his people's land."[23] In Ezekiel, restoration is found in sections B (16:44-58, esp. vv. 53-55) and C (16:59-63). Though many see these sections as supplements by the prophet himself or his disciples,[24] the fact that the last sentence of Ezekiel 16 and the last sentence of the Song employ כפר,[25] a unique word in restoration oracles, to describe Yahweh's renewal of his

---

23. Taking the MT's אדמתו עמו in v. 43 as אדמת עמו (cf. LXX; Samaritan Pentateuch; 4QDeut^q). Alternatively, one may retain the MT's עמו אדמתו, "his land, his people," as the *lectio difficilior*.

24. E.g., Zimmerli, *Ezekiel*, 1:333–4. All agree that the parts of ch. 16 display an organic connection, in which section B (vv. 44-58) draws from and builds on the themes of vv. 1-43 and then section C (vv. 59-63) builds on both earlier sections (see Greenberg, *Ezekiel 1–20*, 295).

25. Ezek. 16:63: "…when I atone for you for all that you have done."

people suggests that the prophet's dependence on the Song may continue into sections B and C of ch. 16. If so, then in these latter sections, as in the section on idolatry above, Ezekiel takes the liberty to go well beyond the less developed elements of restoration in the Song, adding the characteristic restoration language "restore the fortunes" (v. 53), "return to the former state" (v. 55), and Ezekiel's distinctive theme of bearing shame (v. 54).

Literary Dependence?

Having outlined the links between Deuteronomy 32 and Ezekiel 16, we may now address more directly the question of literary dependence. The initial requirement is *availability*; that is, could Ezekiel have borrowed from the Song? In the next section, I will show that Ezekiel could have known and used Deuteronomy 32 by appealing to arguments for the recent scholarly consensus that the Song is an early composition and likely well known in the preexilic period. We turn now to whether the parallels meet the criteria for purposeful literary dependence, as outlined in the introduction.

As Miner pointed out, an allusion may consist of simply a shared word or concept.[26] What matters is that the parallel is sufficiently distinctive to direct the reader to the source text. Thus, the first criterion relevant for this discussion is *rare concept similarity*. In our texts the primary rare concept is the foundling motif, which occurs at the outset of the two accounts of Israel's history with Yahweh. As an image to describe the discovery and adoption of a destitute foundling, the motif occurs only in Ezekiel 16 and Deuteronomy 32 in the Hebrew Bible.[27] In both cases, it refers to Yahweh's discovery of Israel. We may also note here the distinctive motif of spreading a wing/garment (פרש כנף) and the word pair דבש and שמן, "honey and oil."

A related consideration at this point is the presence of what Jeffery Leonard calls nonshared language. In the discovery of the foundling at the outset of the two passages, Ezekiel appears to draw from the foundling motif in Deuteronomy 32, but not its exact terminology. However, Leonard is emphatic that the presence of such differences of expression "*in no way* undermines the possibility of a connection," since "unique or idiosyncratic language may be a reflection of the creativity or writing style of a given author."[28]

---

26. Miner, "Allusion," 38–9.
27. Hos. 9:10 (cited above) witnesses the verbs ראה and מצא, but it lacks a destitute foundling and her subsequent care by Yahweh.
28. Leonard, "Identifying Inner-Biblical Allusions," 249 (emphasis original).

Two further criteria for dependence are the *frequency* of parallels between two texts and their *distribution.* Together they build a cumulative argument for literary dependence. In the present case, the frequency and distribution of parallels between these two texts offer overwhelming evidence for dependence. The accumulation of thematic links in a nearly identical plot structure, corroborated by several lexical links at the same point in the plot, including the פרש כנף motif, the eating of דבש and שמן, the verbal root כעס to signify Israel's provocation of Yahweh, and כפר in Israel's restoration, makes it extremely unlikely that these parallels occur by chance. This phenomenon constitutes an example of what Leonard calls narrative tracking, "the process by which one text alludes to another by mimicking its narrative structure."[29] Admittedly, elements of this plot are scattered in other parts of the Hebrew Bible, but no other passage contains all the elements and none reproduces them in the same order as we find here.[30] Indeed, each element of the plot structure of Ezek. 16:1-43 is found in Deuteronomy 32 in essentially the same order, and the two passages are likewise unique in the extent of their story. Finally, the foundling motif and the other plot parallels mutually corroborate each other: the rare foundling motif gives a firm basis to propose wider dependence in these texts, and the subsequent plot similarities, marked by distinctive lexical links at the same point in the plot, confirm the hypothesis of dependence in the foundling motif.

A Synopsis of the Plot of Deuteronomy 32 and Ezekiel 16

Yahweh's Discovery of Israel	Yahweh's Discovery of Jerusalem
Deut. 32:10a	Ezek. 16:6
Setting: desert/wilderness (מדבר)	Setting: open field (שדה)
"He found (מצא) him"	"I saw (ראה) you"
"He encircled (סבב) him"	"I passed over (עבר על) you"
Yahweh's Lavish Care	Yahweh's Lavish Care
Deut. 32:10b-14	Ezek. 16:7a, 9-13a
"Like an eagle...spreading (פרש) its wings (כנף)...Yahweh..."	"I spread (פרש) my garment (כנף) over you"
"He suckled him with honey (דבש) out of the rock, and oil (שמן) out of the flinty rock"	"You ate fine flour and honey (דבש) and oil (שמן)"

29. Leonard, "Identifying Subtle Allusions."
30. The closest instance of these concentrated in one passage is Hos. 13:4-6, which over three verses mentions the wilderness, prosperity, and forgetting Yahweh.

Israel Prospers Deut. 32:15a	*Jerusalem Prospers* Ezek. 16:13b-14
Israel Forsakes God Deut. 32:15b	*Jerusalem Forsakes God* Ezek. 16:15a
Israel's Idolatry Deut. 32:16-17 "They stirred him to jealousy with זרים" (Deut. 32:16)	*Jerusalem's Idolatry (as Harlotry)* Ezek. 16:15b-34 "She takes זרים instead of her husband" (Ezek. 16:32)
Israel Forgets Its Origin Deut. 32:18 "You forgot the God who gave you birth"	*Jerusalem Forgets Its Origin* Ezek. 16:22 (also v. 43) "You did not remember the days of your youth, when you were naked and bare…"
Israel Angers Yahweh Deut. 32:16, 21 "They provoked him to anger (Hiphil, כעס)" "They provoked me to anger (Piel, כעס)"	*Jerusalem Angers Yahweh* Ezek. 16:26 "(You)…provoked me to anger (Hiphil, כעס)"
Israel's Punishment Deut. 32:23-25	*Jerusalem's Punishment* Ezek. 16:35-43
Israel's Restoration Deut. 32:36-43 Yahweh atones (כפר) for his people's land	*Jerusalem's Restoration* Ezek. 16:53-63 Yahweh atones (כפר) for his people's sins

In the following sections, I will address the *likelihood* that Ezekiel would allude to Deuteronomy 32 by arguing that the Song of Moses was well known to Ezekiel and his contemporaries and that it exerted a strong influence on subsequent biblical authors. In addition, I will show that Ezekiel alludes to Deuteronomy 32 outside of ch. 16, thus meeting the criterion of *recurrence*. Lastly, regarding the direction of dependence, Schultz's criterion of *interpretive reworking* suggests that Ezekiel drew from Deuteronomy 32 and not vice versa. I will argue below that Ezekiel 16 represents a reinterpretation of the Song or a reapplication of it to the time of Ezekiel and his contemporaries. Though in our case the preexilic provenance of Deuteronomy 32 rules out the possibility that the Song draws from Ezekiel 16, it would be difficult to imagine that the Song reworks Ezekiel 16 by stripping it of its harlotry imagery and offering a condensed version. Thus, Ezekiel 16 seems to represent a creative transformation of Deuteronomy 32, whereby the prophet uses the Song as the building blocks of his oracle.

In summary, the evidence for Ezekiel's use of Deuteronomy 32 displays the most important signs of literary dependence. The nearly identical plot structure and themes, corroborated by verbal parallels and rare concepts at the same points in the plot, confirm the presence of literary dependence.

Could Ezekiel Have Known and Used the Song?

To postulate Ezekiel's use of and allusion to the Song of Moses requires that Deut. 32:1-43 predate the book of Ezekiel. Though a wide range of dates have been proposed for the Song in the history of scholarship,[31] scholars since the 1930s have overwhelmingly supported an early date of composition.[32] This view has been substantiated in the comprehensive studies of Deuteronomy 32 by Paul Sanders and Solomon Nigosian, who considered multiple lines of evidence and both convincingly established the Song's early preexilic provenance.[33] In what follows, I will briefly outline the arguments for this conclusion.

Linguistic Considerations

Both Sanders and Nigosian built upon the linguistic study of David A. Robertson, who had established an early date for the Song based on its linguistic features.[34] Such features include the presence of early vocabulary

---

31. A comprehensive review of scholarship is found in Paul Sanders, *The Provenance of Deuteronomy 32*, OtSt 37 (Leiden: Brill, 1996), 1–98.

32. See ibid., 21–36, citing Otto Eissfeldt, *Das Lied Moses Deuteronomium 32:1-43 und Das Lehrgedicht Asaphs Psalm 78: samt einer Analyse der Umgebung des Mose-Liedes* (Berlin: Akademie-Verlag, 1958); William Foxwell Albright, "Some Remarks on the Song of Moses in Deuteronomy XXXII," *VT* 9 (1959): 339–46; Kaufmann, *Religion of Israel*; Wright, "Lawsuit of God"; G. E. Mendenhall, "Samuel's 'Broken *rîb*': Deuteronomy 32," in *No Famine in the Land: Studies in Honor of John L. McKenzie*, ed. James W. Flanagan and Anita Weisbrod Robinson, Homage Series 2 (Missoula, MT: Scholars Press, 1975), 63–74. See also Jeffrey H. Tigay, *Deuteronomy:* דברים. *The Traditional Hebrew Text with the New JPS Translation*, JPS Torah Commentary (Philadelphia: Jewish Publication Society, 1996), 512–13; Mark Leuchter, "Why Is the Song of Moses in the Book of Deuteronomy?" *VT* 57 (2007): 295–317.

33. Sanders, *Provenance*; Solomon A. Nigosian, "The Song of Moses (Deut. 32:1-43)" (Ph.D. diss., McMaster University, 1975); idem, "The Song of Moses (Dt 32): A Structural Analysis," *ETL* 72 (1996): 5–22; idem, "Linguistic Patterns of Deuteronomy 32," *Bib* 78 (1997): 206–24; idem, "Historical Allusions for Dating Deut 32," *BN* 119–20 (2003): 30–4.

34. David A. Robertson, *Linguistic Evidence in Dating Early Hebrew Poetry*, SBLDS 3 (Missoula, MT: Society of Biblical Literature, 1972), 155.

(especially the verbal root מחץ in v. 39), defective and plene spellings, the poetic suffix מו–, the appearance of the final *yod* in the perfective verb חָסָיוּ (v. 37), and the ubiquity of *yiqtol* forms expressing narrative (preterite) tense.[35] The 17 preterite *yiqtol* verbs are particularly noteworthy, since they rarely occur in exilic and postexilic biblical writings.[36] Moreover, many lexemes in the Song previously thought to be late have since been shown to have counterparts in the Ugaritic literature.[37] The presence of any single early feature is inconclusive for dating a text, since many of these phenomena occur as archaisms in standard Biblical Hebrew poetry. However, in his study on dating early Hebrew poetry, Robertson concluded that the accumulation of these features in a single poem represents the best evidence for establishing an early composition.[38]

Historical Context

Many scholars have attempted to date Deuteronomy 32 by correlating historical allusions in the Song with events in the history of Israel. Their assumption is that the Song was written after an enemy had delivered a crushing defeat to Israel. Consequently, the chief clue in the Song is the identity of this enemy, described as a "non-people" (לֹא־עָם) and a "foolish nation" (גוי נבל). Corresponding to different time periods, common designations have included Canaanite tribes, the Arameans, the Assyrians, and the Babylonians.[39] While Nigosian favored a particular historical referent,[40] and Sanders emphasized that the diversity of opinion suggests that the Song does not aim to identify clearly a historical context, both agree that nothing in the Song betrays a late date.[41] For example, if the Song were exilic or postexilic, we might expect some implicit or explicit reference to Babylon, deportation, or return to the land. Furthermore, nothing betrays

---

35. Sanders, *Provenance*, 296–333.

36. Ibid., 300, 313–15; Nigosian, "Linguistic Patterns," 211. For the preterite *yiqtol* form as the remnant of a short *yiqtol* form found in Byblian Canaanite, see Anson F. Rainey, "The Ancient Hebrew Prefix Conjugation in the Light of Amarnah Canaanite," *HS* 27 (1986): 4–19; and the response articles by Edward L. Greenstein, John Huehnergard, and Ziony Zevit, in *HS* 29 (1988): 7–42; also *IBHS*, 497.

37. Sanders, *Provenance*, 320.

38. Robertson, *Linguistic Evidence*, 135; so also Nigosian, "Linguistic Patterns," 211.

39. For bibliographical information on those who have espoused these theories, see Sanders, *Provenance*, 6–39.

40. Nigosian argued for the religious and political circumstances of the northern state near the second half of the ninth century BCE ("Historical Allusions").

41. Sanders, *Provenance*, 39; cf. Nigosian, "Structural Analysis," 22.

knowledge of the demise of the Northern Kingdom or even the presence of a united or divided monarchy. While this is an argument from silence, it is nevertheless noteworthy, since, as G. Ernest Wright reminds us, the threat of exile is a characteristic component of the exilic prophets and Deuteronomic historians, and thus its absence in Deuteronomy 32 is all the more striking.[42]

Intertextual Links

Further confirmation comes from the intertextual links between the Song of Moses and the prophetic books. Critical scholarship, represented as early as 1891 by C. H. Cornill,[43] viewed the Song as dependent on the prophets and thus exilic. Many scholars followed Cornill by citing strong links between the Song and Jeremiah, Ezekiel, and Isaiah 40–66. S. R. Driver, for example, cited approvingly Cornill's assertion that the Song was a "compendium of prophetic theology."[44] More recent studies, however, have reversed the traditional interpretation by arguing that the prophets made use of the Song and not vice versa. These include studies of Isaiah 40–66 by Thomas Keiser, Benjamin Sommer, and Hyun Chul Paul Kim, and Isaiah 1–39 by Ronald Bergey.[45] Studies of Jeremiah by William Holladay and Mark Leuchter and of Hosea by Umberto Cassuto affirm the same.[46]

---

42. G. Ernest Wright, "Deuteronomy: Introduction and Exegesis," in vol. 2 of *The Interpreter's Bible* (Nashville: Abingdon, 1953), 517.

43. C. H. Cornill, *Einleitung in das Alte Testament* (Freiburg: J. C. B. Mohr, 1891), 71.

44. S. R. Driver, *A Critical and Exegetical Commentary on Deuteronomy*, ICC (New York: Charles Scribner's Sons, 1895), 308.

45. Thomas Keiser, "The Song of Moses: A Basis for Isaiah's Prophecy," *VT* 55 (2005): 486–500; Sommer, *A Prophet Reads Scripture*, 134–6; Hyun Chul Paul Kim, "The Song of Moses (Deuteronomy 32.1-43) in Isaiah 40–55," in *God's Word for Our World*, vol. 1, *Biblical Studies in Honor of Simon John De Vries*, ed. J. H. Ellens et al., JSOTSup 388 (London: T&T Clark, 2004), 147–71; see also Fishbane, *Biblical Interpretation*, 478–9; Ronald Bergey, "The Song of Moses (Deuteronomy 32:1-43) and Isaianic Prophecies: A Case of Early Intertextuality?" *JSOT* 28 (2003): 33–54.

46. William Holladay, "Jeremiah and Moses: Further Observations," *JBL* 85 (1966): 17–27; Leuchter, "Why Is the Song?" 304–6; Umberto Cassuto, "The Prophet Hosea and the Books of the Pentateuch" (in Hebrew), in *Abhandlungen zur Erinnerung an Hirsch Perez Chajes*, ed. V. Aptowitzer and A. Z. Schwartz (Vienna: Alexander Kohut Memorial Foundation, 1933), 262–75; Eng. trans. "The Prophet Hosea and the Books of the Pentateuch," in Cassuto, *Biblical and Oriental Studies*, vol. 1, *Bible* (Jerusalem: Magnes, 1973), 79–100.

Is It Likely Ezekiel Would Have Known and Used the Song?

But how likely is it that Ezekiel would have borrowed from the Song? The influence of the Song on later biblical authors can be partially explained by considering the place of Deuteronomy 32 in ancient Israel. Matthew Thiessen's study of the formal and generic properties of Deuteronomy 32 determined that the Song of Moses functioned as a liturgical text in the public cultic sphere and thus was likely well known among Ezekiel's audience.[47] Though he speaks of a *rîb* embedded in the Song, several features suggest that the overall form of the work is a cultic hymn, including the numerous shifts in grammatical person, the imperatives of worship, and multiple speakers.[48] This suggests that Ezekiel would have known the Song and would have chosen it for rhetorical purposes because his contemporary audience or readers also knew the text.[49]

In addition, though not direct evidence for the status of the Song in the preexilic period, its liturgical function in Second Temple Judaism is attested by both the manuscript evidence and rabbinic tradition. We may first note the Qumran manuscript 4QDeut^q, about which Patrick Skehan and Eugene Ulrich write: "The limited height of the scroll, the arrangement of the lines, the small number of words per column, and the absence of the final verses of ch. 32 strongly suggest that 4QDeut^q probably contained only the Song of Moses (Deut. 32:1-43). It would thus join the category of 'special use' manuscripts."[50] This special use likely indicates a liturgical use of some sort for the Song,[51] and one wonders

---

47. Matthew Thiessen, "The Form and Function of the Song of Moses (Deuteronomy 32:1-43)," *JBL* 123 (2004): 401–24, esp. 422–3, where he cites Cassuto approvingly that the Song was widely known and the prophets frequently drew from it (*Biblical and Oriental Studies*, 1:44); cf. Daniel I. Block, "The Power of Song: Reflections on Ancient Israel's National Anthem (Deuteronomy 32)," in *How I Love Your Torah, O LORD! Studies in the Book of Deuteronomy* (Eugene, OR: Cascade, 2011), 162–88: the Song was "placed on the lips of all the people to go with them wherever they went and to be transmitted by the people to succeeding generations" (pp. 166–7).

48. Thiessen, "Form and Function," 407–10.

49. Thiessen himself recognized the implications of his study for the relationship of the Song to the prophetic literature (ibid., 423).

50. Patrick W. Skehan and Eugene Ulrich, "4QDeut^q," in *Qumran Cave 4.IX: Deuteronomy, Joshua, Judges, Kings*, ed. E. Ulrich et al., DJD 14 (Oxford: Clarendon, 1995), 138. *B. Meg.* 16b also notes that the Song was written stichographically.

51. See Emanuel Tov, "Excerpted and Abbreviated Biblical Texts from Qumran," *RevQ* 16 (1995): 581–600.

how far back this tradition reaches. Rabbinic traditions as well held that the poem was chanted by the Levites in the temple on the Sabbath (*b. Roš Haš.* 31a; *y. Meg.* 3.8, 74b).[52]

Did Ezekiel Know and Use the Song?

Support for the thesis that Ezekiel knew the Song may be found in other allusions to Deuteronomy 32 in the book of Ezekiel. The examples offered below show that the prophet does in fact know the Song of Moses and uses it for his prophetic message.[53]

רעב, חצים, "*Arrows, Famine*" (Ezek. 5:16-17 // Deut. 32:23-25, 42)

In Ezek. 5:16-17, the prophet appears to conflate Priestly and Deuteronomic traditions. Though this passage clearly draws from Lev. 26:22-26,[54] many commentators agree that Ezekiel borrows the terms "arrows" and "famine" from Deut. 32:23-25, 42.[55] In fact, the image of Yahweh using arrows as punishment on his people is unique to Deut. 32:23-25 and Ezek. 5:16-17 in the Hebrew Bible.[56] Regarding רעב, it is unlikely that Ezekiel derives it from the phrase "break the staff of bread" in Lev. 26:26, because of the close association of חצים and רעב in both Deuteronomy 32 and Ezekiel 16. As a final possible validation of this point, Ka Leung Wong suggests that in Ezek. 5:16 בהם, "against them," often emended to the expected בכם, is a literary remnant of the third person context of Deut. 32:23 in which בם appears.[57]

---

52. Ishmar Elbogen, *Jewish Liturgy: A Comprehensive History*, trans. Raymond P. Scheindlin (Philadelphia: Jewish Publication Society, 1993), 98, 139.

53. Of course, this evidence depends on the unity of Deut. 32:1-43. The major analyses of the structure of the Song of Moses have affirmed its unity, e.g., Wright, "Lawsuit of God," 26–67; Thiessen, "Form and Function," 417. Sanders writes: "My conclusion is that this version of the song can be regarded as a unity of composition dating to the pre-exilic period. There is nothing in the song which demonstrates that specific parts of it must be secondary. Most arguments that have been adduced against the unity of the song are extremely weak. Interpretation of vv. 30-31 as a secondary passage is possible but not necessary" (*Provenance*, 429–31).

54. Lyons, *From Law to Prophecy*, 94.

55. Fohrer, *Hauptprobleme*, 144; Greenberg, *Ezekiel 1–20*, 116–17; Block, *Ezekiel*, 1:213; Levitt Kohn, *New Heart*, 96–7; Ka Leung Wong, *The Idea of Retribution in the Book of Ezekiel*, VTSup 87 (Leiden: Brill, 2001), 94; Kasher, *Ezekiel*, 54; cf. Allen, *Ezekiel 1–19*, 77. Rabbinic interpreters as well drew a connection between these Ezek. 5:16-17 and Deut. 32:23-25, 42 texts in Sifre to Deut. 321:1.

56. Num. 24:8 refers to Yahweh using arrows against the nations.

57. Wong, *Idea of Retribution*, 94.

חרבי, *"My Sword" (Ezek. 21 // Deut. 32:41-42)*

Ezekiel borrows another of Yahweh's agents of death found in the Song: the sword.[58] The Song's distinctive חרבי, "my sword (i.e., Yahweh's)," mentioned twice in Deut. 32:41-42, occurs three times in Ezekiel 21 (21:8-10[3-5]), along with twelve other occurrences of חרב (also in Ezek. 30:25; 32:10). In the Song, the object of the sword's destruction is Yahweh's enemies, but Ezekiel appropriates the motif to describe God's judgment on his people (21:17[12]). Though the judgments of Leviticus 26 mention the sword,[59] these two passages share several common motifs: (1) the sword is sharpened; (2) the sword flashes; (3) the sword is in the hand; and (4) the sword consumes flesh. First, in Deut. 32:41, Yahweh states, "I sharpen my flashing sword" (שנותי ברק חרבי). Ezekiel 21 speaks repeatedly of a sharpened sword, as, for example, in Ezek. 21:14[9]: "a sword, a sword, sharpened and polished" (חרב חרב הוחדה וגם־מרוטה). While the two use synonyms (from the roots שנן and חדד), the common motif is nevertheless present. Second, Ezekiel 21 speaks of the flashing sword from Deut. 32:41 three times: "polished that it might flash (lit. have flashing)" (למען היה־לה ברק מרטה, 21:15[10]); "made to flash (lit. for lightning)" (עשויה לברק, 21:20[15]); "polished...to flash" (מרוטה...למען ברק, 21:33[28]); cf. Nah. 3:3. Third, Deut. 32:41 also states, "my hand takes hold [of the sword] in judgment" (תאחז במשפט ידי), and Ezek. 21:16[11] speaks of the sword grasped in the hand (בכף ביד,). Finally, just as Deut. 32:42 states that "my sword will devour flesh" (חרבי תאכל בשר), so Ezek. 21:9[4] states, "my sword shall be drawn from its sheath against all flesh" (תצא חרבי מתערה אל־כל־בשר; cf. Jer. 12:12; Hos. 11:6).

Ezekiel's reference to the sword in 7:15 may also have been influenced by the Song, specifically Deut. 32:25,[60] the same context from which Ezekiel borrowed רעב and חצים. Ezekiel's threat that "the sword shall be outside, and pestilence and famine inside" (החרב בחוץ והדבר והרעב מבית) closely resembles that of the Song: "outside the sword shall bereave, and inside terror" (מחוץ תשכל־חרב ומחדרים אימה).

---

58. See Fohrer, *Hauptprobleme*, 144.
59. Indeed, Ezekiel borrows from Lev. 26:33 the phrase הריק אחריכם חרב, "draw the sword after you," in Ezek. 5:2, 12; 12:14 (cf. 28:7; 30:11) (see Lyons, *From Law to Prophecy*, 63–4). However, in ch. 21 the prophet prefers the phrase הוצא חרבי מתערה, "remove my sword from its sheath" (vv. 3-5), which further suggests that Lev. 26 is not the basis for ch. 21.
60. Fohrer, *Hauptprobleme*, 144; Kasher, *Ezekiel*, 55; note Sifre to Deut. 321:6.

קנא, *"To Make Jealous" (Ezek. 8:3 // Deut. 32:16, 21)*

A less conclusive example is the occurrence of the verbal root קנא in Ezek. 8:3 and Deut. 32:16, 21, which is used to speak of idolatry provoking God to jealousy.[61] The verb is not used in this sense elsewhere in the Hebrew Bible except in 1 Kgs 14:22 and Ps. 78:58,[62] thus ruling out influence from the Priestly literature or another source.[63] Moreover, because the word does not occur often enough in the Deuteronomistic literature to be considered common Deuteronomistic language, it is possible that Ezekiel is influenced by this specific text.

Ezekiel's Programmatic Use of Scripture

Finally, is it likely that Ezekiel would have used Deuteronomy 32 in the way proposed in this essay? Here we may note that there are other examples of Ezekiel's programmatic use of earlier biblical texts. In particular, we note two types comparable to his use of the Song in Ezekiel 16: the creative reformulation of an earlier text and the use of an earlier text for the structure of a new oracle.[64] As an example of the former, Pancratius C. Beentjes and other scholars have shown that Jacob's blessing on Judah in Genesis 49 appears to be the basis for the language and imagery of Ezekiel 19.[65] In the first poem of ch. 19 (vv. 2-9) the prophet draws extensively from the description of Judah as a lion in Gen. 49:9:

---

61. Noted by Allen, *Ezekiel 1–19*, 142; Fohrer, *Hauptprobleme*, 144; Kasher, *Ezekiel*, 56. While Lutzky ("On the 'Image of Jealousy'") has hypothesized that originally a single word lay behind הקנאה המקנה in the phrase סמל המקנה הקנאה, which is derived from the root קנא, "to (pro)create," John Day has defended the traditional interpretation that the word reflects a III-א root written as a III-ה (*Yahweh and the Gods and Goddesses of Canaan*, JSOTSup 265 [Sheffield: Sheffield Academic, 2002], 62–3).

62. On the theme of Yahweh's jealousy more generally, see Brittany Kim, "Yhwh as Jealous Husband: Abusive Authoritarian or Passionate Protector? A Reexamination of a Prophetic Image," in *Daughter Zion: Her Portrait, Her Response*, ed. Mark J. Boda, Carol J. Dempsey, and LeAnn Snow Flesher, SBLAIL 13 (Atlanta: SBL, 2012), 127–47.

63. Though cf. the epithet אל קנא in Exod. 20:5; 34:14; etc.

64. Now summarized in Lyons, *Introduction to the Study of Ezekiel*, 102–10.

65. Pancratius C. Beentjes, "What a Lioness Was Your Mother: Reflections on Ezekiel 19," in *On Reading Prophetic Texts: Gender-Specific and Related Studies in Memory of Fokkelien van Dijk-Hemmes*, ed. B. Becking and M. Dijkstra, Biblical Interpretation Series 18 (Leiden: Brill, 1996), 26–31; Greenberg, "Notes on the Influence of Tradition on Ezekiel," 29–37; idem, *Ezekiel 1–20*, 357–8; Block, *Ezekiel*, 1:603, 608–10.

Judah is a lion's cub [גור אריה];
from the prey [טרף] you have gone up [עלית], my son.
Like a lion he lies down and crouches [רבץ];
As with a lioness [לביא], who dares to rouse him?

This is confirmed by his use of the vine language of Gen. 49:10-12 in the second poem (vv. 10-14), including "vine" (גפן) and "blood" (דם), but also "scepter" (שבט), a term denoting rulership.[66] If these links are purposeful, then Ezekiel 19 represents a creative play on the association of Judah with the lion, in which he subverts the noble lion image to portray brutality and exploitation on the part of Judah's monarchy.

An example of the prophet's structural use of Scripture is found in Ezek. 22:25-29, where he adopts the text of Zeph. 3:3-4 and transforms it freely.[67]

Her princes in the midst of her are roaring lions;
her judges are evening wolves;
   they leave nothing for the morning;
her prophets are wanton and treacherous people;
her priests have profaned that which is holy;
   they have violated the Torah. (Zeph. 3:3-4)

Ezekiel adds a fifth category to Zephaniah's fourfold list of objects of accusation (עם הארץ, "the people of the land") and alters the order, moving the priests to the second position. He changes שרים to נשיאים[68] and שפטים to שרים and expands the oracle in other ways so that the result is more than twice the length of the original.[69]

Ezekiel's Prophetic Transformation

Though Ezekiel adopts the plot and themes of Deuteronomy 32, he takes many liberties in reworking the earlier passage. The foremost among these, as we have noted, is his infusion of the prophetic harlotry motif.

---

66. On the possible influence of Nah. 2:12-14 and Zeph. 3:3, see Greenberg, *Ezekiel 1–20*, 357–8.

67. D. H. Müller, "Der Prophet Ezechiel entlehnt eine Stelle des Propheten Zephanja und glossiert sie," *WZKM* 10 (1905): 30–6; see also Block, *Ezekiel*, 1:724–7; Fishbane, *Biblical Interpretation*, 461–3; Schultz, *Search for Quotation*, 91–3.

68. Reading אשר נשיאיה with the LXX, against the MT's קשר נביאיה, "the conspiracy of her prophets" (see Zimmerli, *Ezekiel*, 1:465; Block, *Ezekiel*, 1:720).

69. For a fuller list of the changes, see Block, *Ezekiel*, 1:724 n. 26.

This entails the transformation of Israel into Yahweh's metaphorical wife, marked by the addition of a marriage after the discovery of Israel and the expansion of the two verses on Israel's idolatry into a detailed—and graphic[70]—account of her harlotries. The prophet develops the story further at other points as well. He includes an account of Israel's destitute state before her deliverance, including details about her parents (v. 3) and birth story (v. 4), which, along with the introduction of her "sisters," Samaria and Sodom, in section B (vv. 44-52), make up the "biography" that Ezekiel supplies for the infant. Michael Fishbane calls this type of creative reuse of an earlier text "transformative exegesis," whereby "a received oracle-format or its language is retained though its meaning is transformed by virtue of additions, specifications, or applications."[71]

The infusion of the harlotry motif may account for some distinctives of Ezekiel's oracle, which can be explained as adjustments to the metaphorical vehicle. For example, in Ezekiel's account of Israel's punishment (vv. 35-43), it is noteworthy that he does not draw from the language of Israel's punishment in the Song (Deut. 32:23-25), though he clearly does so in 5:16-17 and ch. 21. Why does he not do so in ch. 16, which otherwise has pervasive links with Deuteronomy 32? It seems that he adopts a different mode of punishment for Israel, one that corresponds to the nature of her transgression: Ezekiel has Israel's lovers stone her in accordance with the Mosaic prescription for adultery (Deut. 22:21, 24). Indeed, this is made explicit in Ezek. 16:38, where Yahweh declares, "I will sentence you with the sentences of adulteresses and murderers" (ושפטתיך משפטי נאפות ושפכת דם).[72] Though capital punishment is prescribed for murder in the legal corpora (Exod. 21:12; Lev. 24:17; Num. 35:16-34), stoning is explicitly specified for adultery. Regardless of whether Ezekiel has in mind or is drawing specifically from Deuteronomy 22,[73] he is surely familiar with the convention that adulterers are put to death by stoning. Similarly, Ezekiel's account of Jerusalem's prosperity, which speaks of her renowned beauty, being adorned with a necklace, earrings, and fine clothes, reflects an adjustment to the metaphorically female Israel.

---

70. Ezekiel makes a common metaphor shocking with sexual imagery. See Galambush, *Jerusalem*, 102; Thomas Renz, *The Rhetorical Function of the Book of Ezekiel*, VTSup 76 (Leiden: Brill, 1999), 144–8.

71. Fishbane, *Biblical Interpretation*, 465. As one of many examples, he cites the use of Deut. 32:9, 13 in Isa. 58:14 (pp. 478–9).

72. Ezekiel attributes the means of punishment to Jerusalem's metaphorical sin, harlotry, rather than idolatry, though Deut. 13:7-12[6-11] prescribes stoning as punishment for idolatry as well.

73. Ezekiel uses the verb רגם (cf. Lev. 20:2, 27), whereas Deuteronomy uses סקל.

Even as Ezekiel incorporates the harlot imagery from his prophetic predecessors, he modifies this tradition as well. First, as Julie Galambush points out, "Ezekiel…departs from the pattern of Hosea and Jeremiah in consistently distinguishing between idolatry and inappropriate foreign alliances in his depiction of Jerusalem's infidelity."[74] Jerusalem prostitutes herself with two groups—gods (vv. 15-22) and foreign powers (vv. 23-43)—thus reflecting both cultic and political infidelity. Second, the oracle reflects Ezekiel's own special concerns. For example, faithful to his concern for the purity of the Jerusalem temple, he "recasts the adultery metaphor to focus on the pollution that precipitates Yahweh's abandonment of the Jerusalem temple."[75] Other links to the temple in ch. 16 include the adornment of Yahweh's wife with the same materials that adorn Yahweh's sanctuary (made explicit by the Targum's rendering).[76] Third, Ezekiel incorporates other external elements into the metaphor. For example, after adding the marriage imagery to the foundling motif, he incorporates ancient Near Eastern legal terms and metaphors for the abandonment and adoption of the infant foundling.[77]

The Rhetoric of Transformation

To conclude, we reflect briefly on the purpose of Ezekiel's transformation of the Song of Moses, namely, to accuse and judge his fellow Israelites for their transgressions. By adopting the plot structure of the rise and fall of Israel in Deuteronomy 32, the prophet applies it to his contemporary context of idolatry and illegitimate foreign relations. As we have seen, this was accomplished by expanding the story of Israel's relationship with Yahweh and transforming it with the prophetic harlotry metaphor. Ezekiel's use of the Song of Moses, as well as the other two examples of Ezekiel's programmatic use of texts described above, attests to David Carr's assertion that, as educated professional scribes, Israel's authors were "trained from the outset to write by building on templates provided by earlier texts."[78]

---

74. Galambush, *Jerusalem*, 99–100.
75. Ibid., 78; see pp. 79–89 for details.
76. Ibid., 95.
77. Malul has argued that when parents abandoned a child in Mesopotamia, the use of the phrase "in her/the blood" represented a legal renunciation of their claim to her, and thus Yahweh's command to live "in her blood" signifies his formal adoption of the girl ("Adoption of Foundlings," 106, 110).
78. Carr, *Writing on the Tablet*, 159.

The rhetoric of Ezekiel's use of the Song lies in the recontextualization of Moses' depiction of Israel's decline. If Deuteronomy 32 was known among Ezekiel's audience, they would have recognized his allusions to it and felt the force of his application of the judgment in their treasured song to their current circumstances. Perhaps better than recontextualization is the term actualization, since Moses' Song foretells a coming fall into idolatry and Ezekiel declares that Moses' prediction of punishment has come to pass in the current generation.[79] The internal witness of Deuteronomy itself lends credence to this assertion. In the narrative framework of the Song, Moses predicts that "when many evils and troubles have come upon [the people], this Song shall confront them as a witness, for it will live unforgotten in the mouths of their offspring" (Deut. 31:21). Surely Ezekiel's generation remembered Moses' Song, and Ezekiel confronted them with it as a witness.

---

79. Cf. the Admonitions of Ipuwer: "What the ancestors foretold has now happened" (Miriam Lichtheim, *Ancient Egyptian Literature*, vol. 1, *The Old and Middle Kingdoms* [Berkeley: University of California Press, 1973], 150; *COS* 1:94).

Chapter 5

Ezekiel 20: Israel's History

In Ezekiel 20, the prophet presents a sweeping account of Israel's history reaching back to the period in Egypt. Responding to Yahweh's order to "declare to them the abominations of their ancestors" (v. 4), Ezekiel's account of history amounts to a record of consistent rebellion and apostasy.[1] The apparent divergences between Ezekiel 20 and the historical traditions reflected in the Pentateuch have long been the subject of scholarly discussion. This chapter focuses on the relationship of Ezekiel 20 and the Deuteronomic tradition, with particular attention to the prophet's use of Deuteronomic language and theology.

Commentators have commonly recognized a significant number of Deuteronomic locutions in Ezekiel 20. Johan Lust, for example, acknowledges that "le style et le vocabulaire du chapitre XX trahissent une forte influence deutéronomique."[2] The most extensive study on the subject is that of Risa Levitt Kohn, who concluded that the prophet in ch. 20 drew extensively from both Priestly and Deuteronomic traditions, producing his own unique synthesis.[3] Yet, some have argued that Ezekiel actually opposes Deuteronomic theology in ch. 20. In his 1986 article "Le vocabulaire d'Ézéchiel 20: le prophéte s'oppose á la vision deutéronomiste de l'histoire," Jacques Pons contended that Ezekiel uses Deuteronomic

---

1. Davis, *Swallowing the Scroll*, 106.
2. Johan Lust, "Ez., XX, 4-26: une parodie de l'histoire religieuse d'Israël," *ETL* 43 (1967): 521.
3. Risa Levitt Kohn, "'With a Mighty Hand and an Outstretched Arm': The Prophet and the Torah in Ezekiel 20," in Patton and Cook, eds., *Ezekiel's Hierarchical World*, 159–68; also idem, *New Heart*, 98–103; followed by Jacob Milgrom (Jacob Milgrom and Daniel I. Block, *Ezekiel's Hope: A Commentary on Ezekiel 38–48* [Eugene, OR: Cascade, 2012], 164–6).

language subversively as a polemic against the Deuteronomic theology allegedly espoused by his interlocutors, the elders of Israel.⁴ Scott Hahn and John Bergsma have proposed that the not-good laws of Ezek. 20:25-26 refer to the sacrificial laws of Deuteronomy, which for Ezekiel would have degraded the Priestly standards of worship.⁵

In what follows, I will examine the extent of Deuteronomic language in Ezekiel 20, at each point considering the possibility of Deuteronomy's influence on Ezekiel's conception of history. I then devote two excursuses one the evaluation of the theory of Pons and that of Hahn and Bergsma respectively, which in different ways posit that Ezekiel distances himself from or otherwise repudiates the Deuteronomic torah. In the final section, I offer more general conclusions about the nature of Ezekiel's historiography.

Deuteronomic Elements in Ezekiel 20

I begin with an in-depth analysis of the Deuteronomic language in Ezekiel 20. The present study builds upon Levitt Kohn's article, which presented a synopsis of the Priestly and Deuteronomic language in the chapter. She identified much of the Deuteronomic language but provided little commentary. Here I treat each of her Deuteronomic expressions in more detail, focusing particularly on Ezekiel's account of Israel's past (vv. 3-31) and its relationship to Deuteronomy.⁶ The discussion follows Block's division of vv. 5-26 into three panels: Israel in Egypt (vv. 5-9), the first desert generation (vv. 10-17), and the second desert generation (vv. 18-26).⁷ These links show that Ezekiel used many distinctively Deuteronomic terms and concepts in ch. 20 (indirect usage), even if not every case represents direct literary reference to a particular Deuteronomic text.

---

4. Jacques Pons, "Le vocabulaire d'Ézéchiel 20: le prophéte s'oppose á la vision deutéronomiste de l'histoire," in Lust, ed., *Ezekiel and His Book*, 214–33.

5. Hahn and Bergsma, "What Laws Were 'Not Good.'"

6. Four of Levitt Kohn's phrases I do *not* regard to be distinctively Deuteronomic: (1) inquiring of Yahweh (דרש), (2) "the seed of the house of Jacob," (3) "flowing with milk and honey," and (4) "by doing them you shall live." The last of these more likely draws from Lev. 18:5 than Deut. 30:15, 19 (Lyons, *From Law to Prophecy*, 115, 168).

7. Block, *Ezekiel*, 1:620–4. For a detailed review of possible divisions of the chapter, see Leslie Allen, "The Structuring of Ezekiel's Revisionist History Lesson (Ezekiel 20:3-31)," *CBQ* 54 (1992): 448–62.

The Election of Israel (vv. 5-6)

Ezekiel begins his national history with one of the most distinctively Deuteronomic concepts in the Hebrew Bible: Yahweh's election of Israel (ביום בחרי בישראל, "on the day I chose Israel"). The verb בחר plays a significant role in Deuteronomy's presentation of Israel's relationship with Yahweh (Deut. 4:37; 7:6, 7; 10:15; 14:2; cf. 1 Kgs 3:8), but never occurs with this sense in the other pentateuchal writings.[8] Most scholars therefore agree that Ezekiel must have been influenced by this important Deuteronomic theme.[9] An exception is Zimmerli, who questions a close connection with Deuteronomy, on grounds that "in Deuteronomy the oath [i.e., land promise] is always given to the patriarchs (Abraham, Isaac, and Jacob), whilst here it is given to the people coming out of Egypt."[10] However, a disparity is without basis, because Ezekiel's oath in 20:5 does not refer to the land promise, which in Deuteronomy is often given to the ancestors, but to Yahweh's self-revelation in Exod. 6:2-8. In reality, Ezekiel 20 and Deuteronomy display remarkable continuity in the application of בחר to the Egypt/wilderness generation, since in Deuteronomy the object of בחר is always the descendants (זרע), the addressees of Moses' speeches, never the patriarchs (see Deut. 4:37; 7:6, 7; 10:15; 14:2).

Ezekiel's use of this Deuteronomic concept and specific term raises the question whether he might allude to a particular Deuteronomic text. Block suggests Ezekiel's account of the nation's earliest history in 20:5-6 may allude to Deut. 7:6-8, which speaks of (1) Yahweh choosing (בחר) Israel, (2) keeping the oath to their ancestors, and (3) delivering them from Egypt.[11] Indeed, dependence on a passage such as Deut. 7:6-8 seems reasonable, since Ezekiel may have drawn from a short summary of the patriarchal promise and deliverance from Egypt instead of producing his own *ex nihilo*. The use of the verb בחר would naturally lead us to Deuteronomy and not to another pentateuchal source.

---

8. See Weinfeld, *Deuteronomy and the Deuteronomic School*, 327. On the election of Israel with בחר as a distinctive Deuteronomic concept, see Ronald E. Clements, *God's Chosen People: A Theological Interpretation of the Book of Deuteronomy* (London: SCM, 1968), 45–9. On the importance of election for Old Testament theology, see Horst Dietrich Preuss, *Old Testament Theology*, trans. Leo G. Perdue, 2 vols. (Louisville: Westminster John Knox, 1995), esp. 1:27–39.

9. Lust, "Ez., XX, 4-26: une parodie," 521; Greenberg, *Ezekiel 1–20*, 363; Block, *Ezekiel*, 1:625–6; Allen, *Ezekiel 20–48*, 9; Patton, "Ezekiel 20 and the Exodus Traditions," 82; Margaret S. Odell, *Ezekiel*, Smyth & Helwys Bible Commentary (Macon, GA: Smyth & Helwys, 2005), 249.

10. Zimmerli, *Ezekiel*, 1:407; Pons, "Le vocabulaire d'Ézéchiel 20," 219.

11. Block, *Ezekiel*, 1:626.

However, if Ezekiel draws from a Deuteronomic passage, an allusion to Deut. 4:37-38 seems more probable, since it displays closer links to Ezek. 20:5-6. First, Ezekiel closely links the election of Israel with the Egypt generation ("on the day when I chose Israel, I swore to the offspring of the house of Jacob"),[12] using the language of בחר and זרע, which, as noted above, parallels the Deuteronomic notion that Yahweh chose the ancestors' offspring. This idea is expressed explicitly in Deut. 4:37-38, where Moses states, "he choose their seed" (ויבחר בזרעו; also Deut. 10:15). Second, whereas Deut. 7:6-8 only mentioned Yahweh's resolve to deliver Israel from Egypt, both Deut. 4:37-38 and Ezek. 20:5-6 include the subsequent step of bringing them to the promised land.

Whether or not one can establish literary dependence on a single passage with confidence, the level of thematic and lexical similarity strongly suggests Deuteronomic influence on Ezek. 20:5-6.

Yahweh Scouting the Land (v. 6)

According to Ezekiel, Yahweh swore to bring his people "into a land that I had searched out for them" (אל־ארץ אשר־תרתי להם). Numbers 13–14 (traditionally, a Priestly passage) also uses the verb תור (Num. 13:2, 16, 17, 32; 14:7, 36, 38), but there men (אנשים) search out the land. The idea of Yahweh himself scouting the land is unique to Deuteronomy (1:33) and Ezekiel.[13] In both texts, he searches out the land "for Israel" (לכם / להם).

Detestable Things (v. 7)

As noted in Chapter 3 of this study, the term שקוצים, "detestable things," occurs frequently in the book of Ezekiel to refer to idols. The word is also used for idols in Deut. 29:16[17] and numerous times in DtrH and Jeremiah, but never in the Priestly literature. On this basis, we concluded that the use of שקוצים as a technical term for idols reflects Deuteronomic influence.

Rebellion (vv. 8, 13, 21)

One Deuteronomic element in Ezekiel 20 not included in Levitt Kohn's study is the description of Israel's apostasy as rebellion. Three times in the

---

12. Ezekiel does not mention the election of Abraham, but this does not mean he was unaware of or rejected the patriarchal covenant, since Ezek. 33:24 mentions Abraham's inheritance of the land (so also Levitt Kohn, *New Heart*, 103 n. 48). Nor is it necessary to say that in Ezekiel's theology, the promise was made to the Egypt generation, to the exclusion of the ancestors (contra Pons, "Le vocabulaire d'Ézéchiel 20," 219).

13. Levitt Kohn, "With a Mighty Hand," 161 n. 17.

chapter Ezekiel describes the people as rebellious (מרה בי), a theme that is almost exclusively Deuteronomic. The term is never used for Israel's disobedience in the Sinai and wilderness narratives of Exodus, Leviticus, and Numbers (except for the sin of Moses and Aaron in Num. 27:14). In contrast, Deuteronomy frequently uses two similar phrases to describe Israel's rebellion: מרה את פי יהוה (Deut. 1:26, 43; 9:23; cf. Josh. 1:18; 1 Sam. 12:14, 15; 1 Kgs 13:26) and ממרים הייתם עם־יהוה (Deut. 9:7, 24; 31:27). Therefore, as Patton notes, Ezekiel mirrors Deuteronomy in its use of the term to refer to the sin of the people as a whole.[14]

Yahweh's Anger (vv. 8, 13, 21)

In each of the three panels of Ezek. 20:5-26, Yahweh resolves to pour out his wrath upon his people. The first and third panels exhibit the same locution: "I committed to pour out my wrath upon them and spend my anger against them" (vv. 8, 21; ואמר לשפך חמתי עליהם לכלות אפי בהם).[15] The word pair אף וחמה is a favorite of Ezekiel.[16] Levitt Kohn notes that the use of אף and חמה to represent Yahweh's anger is characteristic of D/Dtr and Ezekiel, where the two words occur together numerous times in several varied contexts.[17] While אף is used for Yahweh's anger in the other pentateuchal literature, the combination of אף and חמה is distinctive to Deuteronomy in the Pentateuch (9:19; 29:22[23], 27[28]).[18] The pairing is frequent in Jeremiah as well (Jer. 7:20; 21:5; 32:31, 37; 33:5; 36:7; 42:18; 44:6).

While the two terms often appear in synonymous parallel lines in the poetic literature of the Hebrew Bible (Mic. 5:14; Nah. 1:6; Hab. 2:15; Pss. 6:1; 37:8; 78:38; Prov. 15:1, 18; 21:14; 22:24; 27:4; 29:22; Lam. 4:11), these certainly derive from the poetic convention of parallelism, which makes heavy use of synonyms, and are not generally about Israel's sins (except Mic. 5:15; Ps. 78:38). Thus, we must look to Deuteronomy and Jeremiah to find the closest parallel to Ezekiel's usage.

---

14. Patton, "Ezekiel 20 and the Exodus Traditions," 82–3. In an attempt to show that this link is likely not the product of Deuteronomistic redaction, Patton elsewhere cites other passages that use מרה in a similar way (idem, "Pan-Deuteronomism," 208). The closest examples are found in Pss. 78 and 106.

15. In the second panel, ואמר לשפך חמתי עליהם recurs, but in the subsequent clause Yahweh commits not to spend (כלה) his anger, but to eliminate (כלה) his people (v. 13).

16. Ezek. 5:13, 15; 7:8; 13:13; 22:20; 23:25; 25:14; 38:18.

17. Levitt Kohn, "With a Mighty Hand," 162 n. 20, who cites: Deut. 9:19; 29:27[28]; Jer. 7:20; 21:5; 32:31; 33:5; 36:7; 42:18; 44:6; Ezek. 5:13, 15; 7:8; 13:13; 20:8, 21; 22:20; 23:25; 25:14; 38:18.

18. Deut. 29:22[23] באף ובחמה; Deut. 29:27[28] באף ובחמה ובקצף גדול.

"My Eye Spared Them" (v. 17)

The expression עין + חוס is distinctive to Ezekiel and Deuteronomy. Thirteen of its fifteen occurrences are found in these two books (five in Deuteronomy and eight in Ezekiel). In Ezek. 20:17, the phrase ותחס עיני עליהם ("my eye spared them") describes Yahweh's mercy on Israel in the wilderness. Elsewhere in the book, the phrase is used in judgment oracles against the people of Ezekiel's time, in these instances denoting Yahweh's rejection of mercy: לא־תחוס עיני ולא אחמול ("my eye will not spare, nor will I have pity"; Ezek. 5:11; 7:4, 9; 8:18; 9:10; cf. 9:5; 16:5). In Deuteronomy, the subject of the verb is not Yahweh, but Israel, who are commanded not to spare their enemies (לא־תחס עינך עליהם; Deut. 7:16; 13:9; 19:13, 21; 25:12). The absence of the phrase in other biblical books suggests some degree of influence.[19] In fact, its function in Ezekiel may reflect an analogous relationship to its function in Deuteronomy. Just as Yahweh removed the wicked occupants of the land before, he would do the same again. Israel was to have no mercy (לא חוס עין) on the Canaanites, and now Yahweh and his executioners (פקדות) will have no mercy (לא חוס עין) on Israel (Ezek. 9:5).

The Scattering of Israel (v. 23)

As I will argue in detail in Chapter 6 of this study, the scattering motif in Ezekiel—represented with the verb הפיץ—uses Deuteronomy's exile language. At this point in the historical account of ch. 20, Ezekiel refers to an oath that Yahweh swore in the wilderness to scatter his people among the nations: "I lifted my hand to them in the wilderness to scatter them among the nations and disperse them among the lands." I will argue that the oath of Ezek. 20:23 is best explained as an allusion to the threat of exile in Deut. 4:25-28. Thus, the prophet does not simply speak of the current exile using Deuteronomic terms, but in this instance actually refers explicitly to a threat in Deuteronomy that Yahweh would expel his people from the land.

Worship on the High Places (vv. 27-29)

Verses 27-29 indict Israel for improper worship in the land:

> For when I had brought them into the land that I swore to give them, then wherever they saw any high hill or any leafy tree, there they offered their sacrifices and presented the provocation of their offering; there they sent up their pleasing odors, and there they poured out their drink offerings. (Ezek. 20:28)

---

19. Levitt Kohn, "With a Mighty Hand," 163 n. 30.

As I argued in Chapter 3 of this study, Ezekiel's references to worshiping "on every hill and under every green tree" in 6:13 and 20:28 resemble the language of Deuteronomy more closely than similar occurrences in DtrH and Jeremiah. Below I will argue that the prophetic indictment against high places in passages such as Ezek. 6:1-14; 18:6, 11, 15; 22:9, and 34:6 constitutes an authentic component of Ezekiel's proclamation. His polemic against high places demonstrates his support for the centralization of worship in Jerusalem, an idea closely associated with King Josiah's religious reform (2 Kgs 23) and based on the worship laws of Deuteronomy, particularly ch. 12.[20]

"Make Your Children Pass Through the Fire" (v. 31)

Toward the end of his account of Israel's history, Ezekiel charges Israel with sacrificing their own children (בהעביר בניכם באש), an accusation found also in Ezek. 16:21 and 23:37. The language for child sacrifice in Ezekiel and elsewhere in the Hebrew Bible was discussed in Chapter 3 of this study. There I showed that Ezekiel's use of בהעביר בניכם באש reflects the choice of a Deuteronomic phrase over the Holiness Code's נתן למולך (Lev. 20:2, 3, 4). The act of passing a child through the fire is expressly forbidden in Deut. 18:10 (cf. 12:31) and cited as one of Israel's sins in the Deuteronomistic literature (2 Kgs 16:3; 17:17; 21:6; 23:10).

Worshiping Wood and Stone (v. 32)

As I argued in Chapter 3 of this study, Ezekiel's reference to worshiping עץ ואבן ("wood and stone") in exile is an allusion to Deuteronomy's exile passages, which in three separate instances uniquely associate worshiping "wood and stone" with Israel's status in exile (Deut. 4:28; 28:36, 64). Its function here in ch. 20 is significant for Ezekiel's rhetoric against the elders. Ezekiel knows Deuteronomy's notion of worshiping עץ ואבן in exile and interprets the elders' determination to worship idols as the actualization of Deuteronomy's curse.

With a Strong Hand and Outstretched Arm (vv. 33-34)

We come now to Israel's restoration, described in vv. 33-44. In his account of the new exodus (vv. 33-39), Ezekiel uses a distinctive locution found in Deuteronomy to describe the first exodus: ביד חזקה ובזרוע נטויה ("with a mighty hand and an outstretched arm").[21] Though each expression occurs

---

20. Carley, *Ezekiel Among the Prophets*, 57–8; Greenberg, *Ezekiel 1–20*, 385.
21. Noted by Burrows, *Literary Relations*, 20; Carley, *Ezekiel among the Prophets*, 58; Patton, "Ezekiel 20 and the Exodus Traditions," 82.

by itself elsewhere in the pentateuchal traditions (ביד חזקה in Exod. 3:19; 6:1; 13:9; 32:11; Num. 20:20 and בזרוע נטויה in Exod. 6:6),[22] the full phrase cited by Ezekiel is unique to Deuteronomy, either with the ב preposition in Deut. 4:34; 5:15; 26:8 (also Jer. 32:31; Ps. 136:11-12) or without the ב preposition in Deut. 7:19; 11:2 (cf. 1 Kgs 8:42). In Deuteronomy the phrase always describes Yahweh's deliverance from Egypt, most often with the verb יצא (Hiphil), "to bring out." Thus Ezekiel draws upon this distinctive Deuteronomic association to describe the end of the exile as a new exodus when Yahweh will bring out (הציא) his people, "with a strong hand and an outstretched arm" (v. 34).

"Gather You Out of the Countries Where You Have Been Scattered" (v. 41)

As I will argue in Chapter 7 of this study, Ezekiel draws from the gathering language of Deut. 30:3-5 for his depiction of the end of the exile. An explicit return to the land is lacking in the Holiness Code, and no other tradition provides a likely basis for Ezekiel's language. The distinctive parallels between Ezekiel's gathering language and Deut. 30:3-5 make it unlikely that Ezekiel simply reverses the scattering motif for his restoration oracles.

A Polemic Against Deuteronomic Theology?

In his article "Le vocabulaire d'Ézéchiel 20: le prophéte s'oppose á la vision deutéronomiste de l'histoire," Jacques Pons argues that while Ezekiel uses Deuteronomic language in ch. 20, he does so for a polemical purpose.[23] Pons explicitly builds on the earlier work of Lust,[24] but concludes that Ezekiel 20 is a polemic against the elders of Israel, who were Dtr sympathizers. According to Pons, Ezekiel's three encounters with the elders of Israel mentioned in 8:1; 14:1; and 20:1 provided "the occasion to define his theological position in front of the elders, who could be supporters of the Dtr tradition."[25] His association of the elders with Deuteronomy and the Deuteronomistic movement relies on Leslie J. Hoppe's hypothesis that Israel's elders were responsible for composing the book of Deuteronomy, a view that is founded primarily on the favorable attention to the elders in the book (Deut. 1:9-15; 5:23; 19:12;

---

22. Also in Deuteronomy: יד חזקה in Deut. 3:24; 6:21; 7:8; 9:26; 34:12 and זרוע נטויה in Deut. 9:29.
  23. Pons, "Le vocabulaire d'Ézéchiel 20."
  24. Lust, "Ez., XX, 4-26: une parodie."
  25. Pons, "Le vocabulaire d'Ézéchiel 20," 216 (my translation).

21:1-9, 18-21; 22:13-21; 27:1; 29:9; 31:9).[26] If true, Pons reasons, the elders in Ezekiel would be Dtr sympathizers.

According to Pons, in Ezekiel's first encounter with the elders (chs 8–11), the prophet sought to show the elders that the Deuteronomic centralization of worship (Deut. 12) was inadequate, since even the temple could be a place of idolatry.[27] Pons asserts that Ezekiel took great pleasure in describing the seventy elders holding the censers in 8:11.[28] In the case of ch. 14, Pons makes only a vague contrast between prophets being judged by their words according to Deut. 18:20-22 and those who consult a prophet being judged in Ezek. 14:7. In this instance, it is unclear how Ezekiel challenged any aspect of Deuteronomic theology.

Pons uses Ezekiel 20 as an opportunity to study the prophet's relationship to the Deuteronom(ist)ic tradition. He contends that Ezekiel uses Deuteronomic terms in a polemical spirit,[29] often removing the positive connotations of the vocabulary and placing them in a darker landscape.[30] However, the argument for Ezekiel's polemic against Deuteronomy and the Deuteronomic vision of history is deeply flawed. Ezekiel's problem is not with the elders' theology, which is supposedly Deuteronomic, but with their idolatry (so Ezek. 14:3; 20:4). In what follows, I consider Pons' argumentation and evaluate his hypothesis.

Polemical Language in Ezekiel 20?

A detailed refutation of Pons' article is appropriate for a few reasons. First, Pons' thesis addresses the subject of this study directly—Ezekiel's relationship to Deuteronomy. Second, while some scholars cite it approvingly for the idea that Ezekiel subverts Deuteronomic tradition, few in English-speaking scholarship have engaged the article closely enough to see that it is deeply flawed.[31] Lastly, a critical engagement with Pons

26. Leslie J. Hoppe, "Elders and Deuteronomy: A Proposal," *Église et théologie* 14 (1983): 259–72. Bernard Levinson disputes Hoppe's "presupposition that the text's authors would in some direct way reflect themselves in their composition" (*Deuteronomy and the Hermeneutics of Legal Innovation* [New York: Oxford University Press, 1998], 111 n. 32). Furthermore, it is unclear the "elders" in Ezekiel should be closely associated with the preexilic elders of the land (cf. Stephen L. Cook, *The Social Roots of Biblical Yahwism*, SBLSBL 8 [Atlanta: Society of Biblical Literature, 2004], 214).

27. Later I will argue for the likely authenticity of 6:1-7, 13; 20:27-29, rendering this point moot. Ezekiel assumes and promotes centralization.

28. Pons, "Le vocabulaire d'Ézéchiel 20," 216.

29. Ibid., 217.

30. Ibid., 214.

31. For example, see Choi, *Traditions at Odds*, 137.

provides an opportunity to examine in more detail how Ezekiel's view of history relates to Deuteronomic ideas. The following evaluation follows the structure of Pons' article by adopting his headings.

The Abominations of the Fathers (v. 4)

In v. 4, Yahweh instructs Ezekiel to make known to the elders the abominations of their fathers (את־תועבת אבותם הודיעם). Pons understands this as a polemic against the positive portrayal of the אבות ("fathers") in Deuteronomy. In Deuteronomy idols are called תועבות ("abominations") always in the context of the idolatry of the nations, and so he regards it significant that by associating אבות with תועבות Ezekiel would substitute the Israelite ancestors for the nations. Pons then takes his conclusion a step further: "By linking תועבת and אבות Ezekiel breaks the link between the fathers and the land."[32] However, it is unclear why speaking of the תועבת אבותם diminishes the land promise that Yahweh swore to the ancestors, since the promise of land and progeny itself is neutral in terms of the merit of the fathers. Nowhere does Deuteronomy link the land promise to the ancestors' faithfulness.[33]

More importantly, the alleged conflict between the portrayal of the fathers in Ezekiel and Deuteronomy is mistaken. Pons appears to assume that אבות is a technical term, as if "the fathers" represent some sort of static concept. Yet, when Ezekiel speaks of "the abominations of the fathers," he enumerates a litany of sins spanning multiple generations. Thus, in Ezekiel, as in Deuteronomy,[34] אבות has a contextually derived referent. In Ezekiel 20, "fathers" are never the patriarchs Abraham, Isaac, and Jacob, as they are often in Deuteronomy (e.g., Deut. 1:8; 6:10; 9:5; 29:12[13]; 30:20). Therefore, Ezekiel does not in fact denigrate the ancestors of the promise.

The Election of Israel (v. 5)

Pons grants that Ezekiel's use of בחר reflects Deuteronomy's concept of election, but he draws attention to vocabulary in Deuteronomy's election passages that Ezekiel does *not* cite, including (1) language that gives

---

32. Pons, "Le vocabulaire d'Ézéchiel 20," 217.

33. In the pentateuchal narrative, some level of conditionality may be reflected in Gen. 18:19; 22:16-18. Deuteronomy only ties the fulfillment of the land promise to the faithfulness of the current generation (e.g., 8:1).

34. Jerry Hwang argues that Deuteronomy uses אבות to refer to both the patriarchs and the exodus generations for rhetorical purposes (*The Rhetoric of Remembrance: An Investigation of the "Fathers" in Deuteronomy*, Siphrut 8 [Winona Lake, IN: Eisenbrauns, 2012]).

election a "personal warmth" in Deuteronomy, such as God's love (אהב) and his desire for Israel to be his "holy" (עם קדוש) and "treasured people" (עם סגלה) in Deut. 7:6-8; (2) references to the patriarchs in Deut. 7:8; 9:5; (3) mention of the oppression in Egypt and therefore God's merciful response; and (4) the use of the verb ירש to describe the possession of the land in Deut. 9:4-6. Pons concludes that Ezekiel's decision not to cite certain words amounts to presenting Israel's election as "an arbitrary act, distant and cold."[35]

However, Pons' conclusion is dubious for several reasons. First, some of his observations are overstated. For example, the description of Israel as the "seed of the house of Jacob" represents a significant acknowledgement of the ancestor tradition.[36] The absence of the phrase "the land that Yahweh swore to Abraham, Isaac, and Jacob" in Ezekiel cannot be a purposeful avoidance of Deuteronomic language specifically, since that phrase is by no means exclusive to Deuteronomy (see, for example, Gen. 50:24; Exod. 6:8; 33:1; Num. 32:11). Second, the proposal that Ezekiel rejects the idea of Yahweh's gracious deliverance of his people from Egypt flies in the face of the prophet's metaphorical presentation of Israel's earliest history in ch. 16, where he presents Yahweh as the one who rescued and tenderly cared for his people. Third, Ezekiel uses the verb ירש in 36:12 to describe a future possession of the land.[37] Fourth, there may be a simpler explanation for Ezekiel not using terms such as אהב, , and עם סגלה. He may not be alluding to Deut. 7:7-8 and 9:4-6 at all, but, as I argued above, to Deut. 4:37-38, which does not include those terms. Regardless, not mentioning these terms hardly constitutes a subversion or polemic against Deuteronomy. Since all literary borrowing is selective, lack of borrowing does not automatically entail polemic. In the midst of divine punishment, the prophet may simply wish not to encourage over-confidence in the traditional promises of Israel's status with Yahweh.

The Oath and Promise (v. 6)

According to Pons, Ezekiel's use of נשא יד represents a deliberate movement away from Deuteronomy, which uses נשבע to describe oaths. However, נשבע is not exclusively Deuteronomic, nor is נשא יד exclusively Priestly (see Deut. 32:40). And more importantly, Ezekiel's preference for Priestly language does not mean he *rejects* the Deuteronomic equivalent.

---

35. Pons, "Le vocabulaire d'Ézéchiel 20," 218 (my translation).
36. So also Joyce, *Ezekiel*, 149.
37. Cf. the saying of the people and Ezekiel's response in 33:24-26.

The Description of the Land (v. 6)

Although Pons grants that the description of the land as זבת חלב ודבש ("flowing with milk and honey") follows the traditional use of the phrase in the pentateuchal literature, he argues Ezekiel uses the parallel phrase צבי היא לכל־הארצות ("the most glorious of all lands") ironically. He notes that in Isa. 28:1, 4; 13:19; 23:9, the word צבי, "glory," is used negatively, describing the pride of Babylon and Tyre. Since Ezekiel uses the word for the same purpose against Moab in 25:9, Pons reasons that the prophet uses it here in 20:6 in an ironic sense: "Si...צבי exprime le sentiment patriotique de l'epoque, il faut ajouter qu'Ézéchiel cherche à saper ce sentiment générateur de confiance en soi et de ruine."[38] The destruction that will befall the nations because of their pride will also befall Israel. However, the use of a term with a negative sense in one context does not mean that it is inherently negative, as passages such Isa. 4:2; 24:16 and Jer. 3:19 clearly demonstrate the positive use of צבי. Even if Pons were correct that צבי is used ironically, it is unclear how this has anything to do with a polemic against Deuteronomy and not rather a polemic against improper confidence in Israel's possession of the land.

In this and other cases, Pons fails to distinguish sufficiently between locutions that are distinctively Deuteronomic and those that are common to the other traditions. In so doing, he uses alleged instances of Ezekiel's creative historiography vis-à-vis "the general tradition" as evidence that Ezekiel issues a polemic *against Deuteronomic theology*.[39] Thus, we may first question whether Ezekiel's historiography is polemical at all, and second, whether alleged polemics are in fact aimed at Deuteronomy.

The Prohibition of Idolatry (v. 7)

Pons claims that Dtr reserves שקץ for the sins of Solomon (1 Kgs 11:5, 7; 2 Kgs 23:13) and uses גללים for the transgressions of other kings. He exploits this alleged distinction, concluding that Ezekiel's use of שקץ for the sins of the whole people means that "pour Éz le péché exceptionnel de Salomon est devenu celui de tous les Israélites."[40] However, Deut. 29:16[17] and 2 Kgs 23:24 contradict Pons' hypothesis, since שק[ו]ץ in these instances refers to the idols of the Canaanites and Israelites, respectively. Neither do its occurrences in Jeremiah (4:1; 7:30; 13:27; 16:18; 32:34) have any connection to Solomon's sins. So we must ask whether this distinction has any merit and whether the sixth-century prophet would have associated שקץ primarily with Solomon's idolatry.

---

38. Ibid., 220.
39. Ibid., esp. 219.
40. Ibid., 220.

At this point, Pons notes Ezekiel's accusation of idolatry in Egypt: "For Ezekiel, even before the series of laws are given (Ezekiel 20:10-11), there is already (v. 7) a condemnation of idolatry, even before God made anything (other than the election and promise) to justify such a claim to exclusivity."[41] Once again, Pons cites an alleged divergence with the general pentateuchal tradition in his argument for a polemic against Deuteronomy. Even so, while it is true that Ezekiel takes a degree of liberty in his historiography, the idea of idolatry in Egypt has some basis in Israelite tradition. Ezekiel is not alone in citing such an idea, since Josh. 24:14 similarly mentions "the gods that your fathers served beyond the river *and in Egypt*" (emphasis added).

The Rebellion of Israel (vv. 8, 13, 21)

While both Deuteronomy and Ezekiel 20 describe Israel's disobedience as rebellion, Pons highlights one difference. In Deuteronomy and the Deuteronomistic literature, the direct object marker את follows the verb מרה (Deut. 1:26, 43; 9:23; Josh. 1:18; 1 Sam. 12:14, 15; 1 Kgs 13:26; also Jer. 4:17; Pss. 78:56; 105:28). In its three occurrences in Ezekiel 20, on the other hand, the verb is followed by the preposition ב. According to Pons, Ezekiel's expression is more direct and indicative of Israel's refusal to enter the promised land.[42] Appealing to v. 21, Pons asserts that Yahweh denied entry to the land not only to the first generation, but the second generation as well. I will treat this aspect of his argument below.

First, concerning the alleged difference between מרה את and מרה ב, the מרה + ב construction is not unique to Ezekiel 20, but appears elsewhere in Hos. 14:1 and Ps. 5:11. Further, Ezekiel does not use מרה + ב exclusively, but in one instance outside of ch. 20 he uses the direct object marker (Ezek. 5:6). We may thus question whether the distinction between the two phrases is significant. In reality, the Hebrew Bible offers no basis for Pons' assertion that the use of the preposition ב denotes a stronger rebellion than the direct object marker את. In its various occurrences, no contextual evidence suggests a semantic difference. On linguistic grounds, the opposite may in fact be more likely, namely, that the direct object marker reflects a more direct rebellion than the preposition ב. The relevant linguistic category is affectedness, that is, the degree that the object of a verb is affected by the verbal action.[43] In his study

---

41. Ibid., 221 (my translation).
42. Ibid.
43. The seminal study by Hopper and Thompson argued that verbs are not simply transitive or intransitive, but display varying levels of transitivity (Paul J. Hopper and Sandra A. Thompson, "Transitivity in Grammar and Discourse," *Language* 56

of affectedness in Biblical Hebrew, W. Randall Garr concluded that in many linguistic contexts direct objects marked by את displayed a higher level of affectedness than oblique objects marked by prepositions.[44] On this basis, מרה את may in fact denote a more direct rebellion than מרה ב.

The Arrival at the Wilderness (vv. 10, 13, 15, 17, 18, 21, 23, 35, 36)

In contrast to Deuteronomy, which describes the wilderness as the place where Yahweh carried Israel (Deut. 1:31; 8:15; 11:5; 29:4[5]; 32:10), "pour Éz 20, le désert est une sorte de champ clos de la confrontation entre Israël et Dieu: révolte (v. 13), fureur de Dieu (v. 13b), refus de l'entrée en terre promise (v. 15), dernier avertissement (v. 18), annonce de la dispersion (v. 23); il y aura bien une nouvelle sortie (v. 35), mais pour affronter un nouveau jugement (v. 36)."[45] However, Deuteronomy does not simply depict the wilderness as a period of bliss. Although Yahweh's provision in "carrying" Israel is an important theme, the wilderness is associated with judgment in Deuteronomy as well. For example, the historical overview of Deuteronomy 1–3 narrates the episode when "Yahweh became angry and said, 'No one among this evil generation shall see the good land that I swore to give to your fathers'" (Deut. 1:34-35). In his first speech, Moses recounts the judgment at Baal-Peor, where Yahweh "destroyed from among you everyone who followed the Baal of Peor" (Deut. 4:3). Finally, Deut. 9:6-29 offers an extended account of Israel's sins in the wilderness and Yahweh's judgment. For Deuteronomy, it is important that Israel does not forget the transgressions of the wilderness period: "Remember and do not forget how you provoked Yahweh your God to wrath in the wilderness; you have been rebellious against Yahweh from the day you came out of the land of Egypt until you came to this place" (Deut. 9:7). In Deut. 9:24, Moses asserts that Israel "has been rebellious against Yahweh as long as

---

[1980]: 251–99). Semantic features that contribute to high transitivity include a high affectedness of the object, in addition to many others, including: having two or more participants, describing actions rather than states, affirmative rather than negative, having an agent with high potency, and comprises nouns which are highly individuated.

44. W. Randall Garr, "Affectedness, Aspect, and Biblical Hebrew *'et*," *ZAH* 4 (1991): 119–34.

45. Pons, "Le vocabulaire d'Ézéchiel 20," 222: "For Ezekiel 20, the desert is a kind of battleground in the confrontation between Israel and God: rebellion (v. 13), wrath of God (v. 13b), refusal of entry into the promised land (v. 15), last warning (v. 18), announcement of the dispersion (v. 23); there will be a new exodus (v. 35), but in order to face a new judgment (v. 36)" (my translation).

he has known [them]." Ezekiel's emphasis on the sins of Israel in the wilderness period agrees with Deuteronomy's outlook.[46] In contrast to Hos. 2:17 and Jer. 2:2, which depict the wilderness period as one of faithful devotion to Yahweh,[47] both Deuteronomy and Ezekiel highlight Israel's stubbornness and rebellion (Deut. 9:6-7, 24; 10:16; 29:3; 31:27; cf. 2 Kgs 21:15). Thus, Ezekiel is not subverting a cherished wilderness tradition, but proclaiming that just as God judged Israel in the wilderness period after delivering them from Egypt (to remove the wicked from among them), he would judge them again after delivering them from exile. In this respect, Ezekiel's judgment in "the wilderness of the peoples" is continuous with the earlier wilderness period.

God Spares Israel (v. 17)

Pons notes the different use of חוס + עין mentioned above, namely, that in Deuteronomy the verb is always an act of Israel and in Ezekiel an act of God.[48] Ezekiel twice uses the locution to depict Yahweh's mercy on Israel in the past. In Ezek. 16:5 no one had pity on Jerusalem except God. Similarly, in 20:17, Yahweh had compassion on Israel by choosing not to completely destroy them in the wilderness. However, in the majority of instances, the phrase denotes Yahweh's refusal to spare Israel in the current generation (Ezek. 5:11; 7:4, 9; 8:18; 9:5, 10; cf. 24:14). Its use in Ezekiel should not be understood as an example of the prophet's subversion of Deuteronomy. On the contrary, Ezekiel's adaptation of this Deuteronomic motif exhibits powerful rhetoric. As noted earlier, just as Yahweh destroyed the wicked occupants of the land before, he would do the same again. Israel was to have no mercy (לא חוס עין) on the Canaanites, and now Yahweh's executioners (פקדות) will have no mercy (לא חוס עין) on Israel (Ezek. 9:5). Thus, to adapt locutions creatively does not constitute subversion, a conclusion confirmed by Ezekiel's use of the Holiness Code, which use also displays creative adaptation.[49]

---

46. See Weinfeld, *Deuteronomy and the Deuteronomic School*, 31.

47. Lest these verses be misconstrued S. Talmon cautions: "Jeremiah, like Hosea, never develops the historical desert reminiscence into an ideal toward the attainment of which he wants to guide the nation... Jeremiah's divergence from the Pentateuchal presentation of the desert period therefore should be explained as a literary variation rather than as a case of a deliberate reassessment of history" ("The 'Desert Motif' in the Bible and in Qumran Literature," in *Biblical Motifs*, ed. A. Altmann [Cambridge, MA: Harvard University Press, 1966], section 7).

48. Pons, "Le vocabulaire d'Ézéchiel 20," 224.

49. See Lyons, *From Law to Prophecy*.

The Scattering of Israel (v. 23)

In place of the second generation's entrance into the land, Pons interprets Ezek. 20:23 as the announcement of an immediate scattering of the people in the wilderness. He writes: "For Ezekiel 20, the desert is the place of permanent rebellion: in place of the entrance into Canaan we have the dispersion."[50] In this matter he follows Johan Lust, who argued that Yahweh did not *swear* to exile Israel, but actually did scatter them in the wilderness period: "Exile is not presented as a threat for a future time, but as a *fait accompli*."[51] Thus, according to Ezekiel's theological interpretation of Israel's history, the residence in Canaan was not the possession of the promised land, but rather a continuation of the wilderness period.[52] Pons attempts to identify Ezekiel's motivation:

> Certainly, on a substantive nature, Ezekiel and Deuteronomy have the same idea of what constitutes idolatry. The difference relates to the valuation of the history of Israel in Canaan that Ezekiel finds too grand in Deut/Dtr. In the exceptional time of exile on the eve of the fall of Jerusalem, Ezekiel does not think that judging or rather evaluating the history of Israel, weighing the good and the bad, as did Dtr, would be an adequate therapeutic. One must deny this story, make it pass into the domain of death, then prepare a resurrection.[53]

However, the arguments for this theory are untenable. Lust based his argument on a novel interpretation of נשא יד in v. 23. In Chapter 6 of this study, I will argue for the common understanding of נשא יד as an oath formula, and therefore the conclusion that Ezek. 20:23 does not imply that Yahweh previously sent Israel into exile in the wilderness, but only that he threatened to do so.

Pons offers little direct evidence that according to Ezekiel, Yahweh scattered Israel in the wilderness. First, he holds that Ezekiel never mentions the entrance into the promised land, a claim dependent on the alleged secondary nature of vv. 27-29, which speak of Israel's sins in the land. The authenticity of these verses will be considered in more detail below. Pons essentially appeals to scholarly agreement, but also appears to let his particular idiosyncratic interpretation of Ezekiel 20 determine

---

50. Pons, "Le vocabulaire d'Ézéchiel 20," 222 (my translation).
51. Lust, "Ez., XX, 4-26: une parodie," 517 (my translation).
52. Ibid., 517: "Le séjour en Palestine ne fut pour lui que la continuation d'un séjour dans le désert, séjour prolongé à cause des péchés d'Israël."
53. Pons, "Le vocabulaire d'Ézéchiel 20," 226 (my translation).

the matter when he writes rather frankly: "Verses 27-29 must be an interpolation because they do not fit the development of Ezekiel's thought in this passage."[54] Second, according to Pons, the rhetoric of the chapter implies that Israel's sins precluded entry into the land. When the prophet addresses the elders after his review of history, he asks, "Will you defile yourselves after the manner of your ancestors and go astray after their detestable things?" (Ezek. 20:30). Following Reventlow,[55] Pons notes similarities with this question and Lev. 18:24, which speaks of the defiling practices of the Canaanites, and observes:

> Leviticus speaks of the peoples inhabiting Canaan before Israel, while Ezekiel speaks of the 'fathers'! But the difference is amazing: it is understood that the fathers have not been brought into the land of Canaan, in the Ezekielian scheme, because they would not have changed the ambient idolatry.[56]

However, Lev. 18:24 speaks of the Canaanites' sexual sins, not idolatry. Thus, while it may be that Israel succumbed to idolatry in the manner of the previous occupants of the land, the prophet does not use an allusion to Lev. 18:24 to make a connection between the idolatry of the Canaanites and the ancestors. Third, according to Pons, Israel's failure to keep "the laws that give life" (vv. 11, 13, 21) resulted in their failure to attain the land:

> It is Deuteronomy that insists on the link between life and entry into the land... In chapter 20, Ezekiel shows that this link is broken. In vv. 13-21, disobedience is mentioned in the same breath as the formula for the life-giving power of the law. Disobedient Israel will neither live nor enter the promised land... To reject the law was, following the deuteronomic schema itself, to close the door to the promised land.[57]

However, Deuteronomy does not link life and *entry* into the land, but rather life when dwelling in the land (so Deut. 4:40; 5:16, 33; 11:19; 30:16, 18; 32:47).

---

54. Ibid., 223 (my translation).
55. H. G. Reventlow, *Wächter über Israel: Ezechiel und seine Tradition*, BZAW 82 (Berlin: Töpelmann, 1962), 84.
56. Pons, "Le vocabulaire d'Ézéchiel 20," 226 (my translation).
57. Ibid., 223 (my translation).

Finally, perhaps the strongest argument against the theory that Yahweh refused entry of the second generation into the land comes from the preceding verse, which states that Yahweh relented from his anger: "I acted for the sake of my name, so that it should not be profaned in the sight of the nations, in whose sight I had brought them out" (v. 22). The notion that Yahweh spared Israel for the sake of his reputation among the nations recalls Num. 14:15-16, where Moses pleads that Yahweh not destroy Israel because "the nations who have heard about you will say, 'It is because Yahweh was not able to bring this people into the land he swore to give them that he has slaughtered them in the wilderness.'" The prophet appears to express the same rationale for concern over Yahweh's name. If Yahweh does not finish what he started by bringing Israel into the wilderness, his reputation will be tarnished. Thus, the idea that Yahweh would not destroy Israel but would bring them into the promised land is built into the theological history of Ezekiel 20 (vv. 9, 14, 22).

The Authenticity of vv. 27-29

As noted above, the theory that Ezekiel 20 denies Israel's entry into the promised land depends on the secondary nature of vv. 27-29, which speak of Israel's sins in the land. For Pons, this conclusion is a necessary corollary of his interpretation of the chapter. He explicitly reasons that since v. 23 signifies the dispersion of the people, vv. 27-29 must not be authentic: "Le contenu de ces vv. plaide donc suffisamment pour leur élimination."⁵⁸ He asserts that the polemic against Deuteronomy is no longer present in these verses,⁵⁹ although my critique of this alleged polemic in vv. 5-26 renders this point moot. Nevertheless, an evaluation of the authenticity of Ezek. 20:27-29 is in order.

Many scholars regard vv. 27-29 as secondary to the passage. According to Zimmerli, for example, the section constitutes "a clumsily introduced appendix to the narrative account of vv 5-26."⁶⁰ Here we will focus on arguments against vv. 27-28 only, leaving aside the authenticity of the parenthetical etiology in v. 29. Arguments for the secondary nature of these verses include the following. First, both vv. 27-29 and the concluding vv. 30-31 begin with לכן, followed by a command to speak. In addition to the seemingly abnormal repetition of לכן, in v. 27 the word introduces a

---

58. Ibid., 225.

59. Ibid.: "On penserait à un rédacteur influencé par la tradition sacerdotale n'ayant pas bien saisi la hardiesse de la pensée d'Ezechiel niant le séjour d'Israël en Canaan contre toute évidence historique."

60. Zimmerli, *Ezekiel*, 1:404.

further indictment, not a judgment, as it usually does in prophetic oracles.[61] Second, vv. 27-29 do not follow the consistent structure found in the earlier episodes in vv. 5-26. In particular, Lust points out that vv. 27-29 lack the repeated refrain found in the previous sections of the chapter: "Then I said I would pour out my wrath…but I acted for my name's sake."[62] Third, Zimmerli conjectured that the opening עוד זאת ("this also") signals a redactional element, citing Ezek. 36:37 as an apparent analogue. Fourth, v. 27 uses the verb גדף for "blaspheming" God in a context where, according to Zimmerli, we would expect the verb חלל ("to profane").[63]

However, these observations do not necessarily indicate that vv. 27-28 are secondary. As Krüger notes, the introductory formula לכן need not announce judgment or imminent divine intervention, but here may simply mark the transition from the long survey of the distant past (vv. 5b-26) to a new unit, in which the present audience is directly addressed.[64] Second, concerning the absence of Yahweh's decision to spare Israel for his name's sake, it is unlikely the prophet would express God's reprieve for Israel's most current sins, especially considering the imminent judgment he preached. Third, the claim that עוד זאת betrays an addition can hardly be substantiated. The phrase appears in 23:38 as well, where, regardless of the status of its larger context (23:36-49), it does not appear to mark an insertion. Further, עוד זאת is unique to Ezekiel in the Hebrew Bible (20:27; 23:38; 36:37) and therefore may have been an authentic Ezekielian locution. Fourth, though the root גדף does not occur as a verb elsewhere in the book, its nominal form גדופה is found in 5:15.[65] Finally, as Krüger has shown, vv. 27-29 exhibit many lexical links with the rest of ch. 20.[66]

What about the content of vv. 27-29? After vv. 5-26, Israel's time in the land, which is characterized by illegitimate worship and idolatry, is the obvious next stage in Israel's history. For Zimmerli, these verses constitute "the redactional rounding off of the whole chapter."[67] Yet it is unclear why the presentation of the next stage of Israel's history must be

---

61. Allen, *Ezekiel 20–48*, 13.
62. Lust, "Ez., XX, 4-26: une parodie," 502.
63. Zimmerli, *Ezekiel*, 1:412.
64. Krüger, *Geschichtskonzepte*, 210–11: "markiert es den Übergang von dem relativ langen erzählenden Abschnitt [5-26], in dem die Adressaten des Textes nicht direkt angesprochen wurden, zur Anrede in der 2.Pers." Cf. Block, *Ezekiel*, 1:641.
65. Block, *Ezekiel*, 1:641–2.
66. Krüger, *Geschichtskonzepte*, 211.
67. Zimmerli, *Ezekiel*, 1:191.

redactional rather than compositional.⁶⁸ Indeed, according to Greenberg, the content of these verses may explain some of their exceptional features:

> Since God's rejection of Israel has been completed by the end of the third stage [vv. 18-26], the pattern of God's address and the people's defiance cannot be repeated. After vss. 23-26 Israel can only act out its assigned role and defile itself through a perverse cult until it is desolated. Accordingly, vss. 27-29 show Israel practicing *bamot* worship, disdained by God. In that way *laken* (v. 27) suggests that Israel's cultic misconduct in its land was but a consequence of God's punitive measures described at the end of the third stage.⁶⁹

For Greenberg, vv. 27-29 represent a logical component in the narrative flow of Ezekiel 20. Indeed, it is reasonable to regard vv. 27-29 as a primary, climactic element in vv. 5-31.

There is no reason to doubt Ezekiel himself may be responsible for these verses since he elsewhere indicted Israel for violation of the Deuteronomic law of centralized worship, as discussed earlier in Chapter 3 of this study. First, illegitimate worship sites are not merely an appendix in the judgment oracle of 6:1-14 (which might appear to be the case in ch. 20), but instead constitute the main theme of the passage. After Yahweh instructs the prophet to direct his message to the hill country itself, Ezekiel pronounces judgment on the high places and their idolatrous altars in 6:3-7.⁷⁰ Second, in Ezekiel's list of virtues and vices in ch. 18, a righteous person "does not eat upon the mountains or lift up his eyes to the idols of the house of Israel" (18:6, 15). The abbreviated phrase "eat upon the mountains" appears in 18:11 and 22:9 as well. Third, the metaphorical actions of Jerusalem in ch. 16 display overtones of worship outside of the centralized sanctuary: (a) in v. 16 she makes במות טלאות, "colorful shrines," NRSV), (b) the words גב and רמה seem to recall the high places (vv. 24-25, 31), and (c) "in every square" and "at the head of every street" resembles the typical Deuteronomic language, "on every high hill and under every green tree."⁷¹

Yet, might the typically Deuteronomic language כל־גבעה רמה וכל־עץ עבת ("any high hill or any leafy tree") in 20:28 betray a secondary addition? Such language appears elsewhere in the book as well, in places that are not obviously secondary. At the end of the oracle against high

---

68. Davis, *Swallowing the Scroll*, 111.
69. Greenberg, *Ezekiel 1–20*, 378.
70. The portions in brackets are lacking in the LXX and may be secondary (see Lyons, *From Law to Prophecy*, 63; Zimmerli, *Ezekiel*, 1:179).
71. On references to high places in ch. 16, see Mein, *Ethics of Exile*, 115.

places in ch. 6, the prophet returns to the motif of the slain lying before their idols (vv. 13aβ-14). The verse then continues with characteristic Deuteronomic language similar to that found in 20:27:

Ezek. 6:13

On every high hill	אל כל־גבעה רמה
on the all the mountain tops,	בכל ראשי ההרים
and under every green tree,	ותחת כל־עץ רענן
and under every leafy oak.	ותחת כל־אלה עבתה

Few doubt the authenticity of this language in ch. 6. While some question whether the parallelistic structure is original,[72] arguments for the secondary nature of the entire phrase are arbitrary and based only on the fact that the language is Deuteronomic.[73] Further confirmation that such language need not be redactional comes from ch. 34, which uses the phrase בכל־ההרים ועל כל־גבעה רמה in a metaphorical context: "my sheep were scattered; they wandered over all the mountains and on every high hill" (v. 6).[74] In this instance, the phrase is used figuratively but nevertheless appears to allude to the illegitimate worship that took place in the hill country.[75]

Therefore, Ezek. 20:27-29 cannot be considered secondary simply because it mentions Israel's violation of the law of centralization, nor because it uses the Deuteronomic language, כל־גבעה רמה וכל־עץ עבת. Indeed, given the discernible presence of this theme in Ezekiel's oracles, it is reasonable that the indictment against high places in 20:27-28 and its Deuteronomic language derive from the prophet himself. If so, does Ezekiel's use of "Deuteronomic" language for worship in the hill country reflect influence from a particular biblical text? As I noted in Chapter 3 of this study, William Holladay has shown the close similarities of Ezek. 6:13 and 20:28 with Deut. 12:2, suggesting the possibility of literary appropriation.[76]

---

72. E.g., Zimmerli, *Ezekiel*, 1:181–2. As I will show in the next chapter, the words in brackets lacking in the LXX are closer to Hosea than Deuteronomy: [עבתה כל־אלה ותחת] רענן כל־עץ ותחת [ההרים ראשי בכל] רמה כל־גבעה אל.

73. See, e.g., ibid., 1:191.

74. Most scholars do not regard the phrase as secondary in 34:6. Anja Klein views vv. 1-10 as the original layer of ch. 34, of which vv. 3-4 and 7-8 are secondary (*Schriftauslegung im Ezechielbuch: Redaktionsgeschichtliche Untersuchungen zu Ez 34–39*, BZAW 391 [New York: de Gruyter, 2008], 32–42). Others have regarded vv. 7-8 as redactional (Zimmerli, *Ezekiel*, 2:212; Hossfeld, *Untersuchungen*, 237–8).

75. Zimmerli, *Ezekiel*, 2:215; Block, *Ezekiel*, 2:279 n. 42.

76. William Holladay, "On Every High Hill and Under Every Green Tree," *VT* 11 (1961): 175.

Even if the indictment against high places in vv. 27-29 were not an original component of the historical review of vv. 5-31, the evidence does not support the idea that Israel was actually scattered in the wilderness and therefore failed to possess the promised land. According to Pons, the rhetoric behind the prophet's revisionist historiography was "to fight better against the easy hope of the exiles."[77] While Ezekiel's historiography may reflect his attempt to minimize their over-confidence in the promises of old (especially the land promise), the prophet's rhetorical strategy did not include erasing Israel's possession of the promised land.

Serving Wood and Stone (v. 32b)

While Pons grants the presence of the "wood and stone" motif in both Deuteronomy and Ezekiel, he emphasizes that, whereas Deut. 4:28; 28:36, 64 use the verb עבד, Ezekiel uses שרת in 20:32. According to Pons, since the prophet associates שרת with idolatry as part of his Levite polemic in Ezek. 44:10-12, "Ezekiel would thus [appear to] challenge a sort of coalition of elders and Levites, whom he accuses of having promoted, and still wanting to promote in exile, idolatry. Ezekiel here reacts against a complacency about idolatry or at least a fatalism, of which Deut. 4:28 and 28:36, 64 reverberate."[78] In truth, the verb שרת, "to serve/minister," is neutral in the book of Ezekiel. While it describes the Levites' idol worship in 44:12, it is also used of proper Yahweh worship by both the Levites and Zadokites in 40:46; 43:19; and 44:11, 16.

The New Exodus and Judgment in the Wilderness (vv. 33-38)

Pons highlights the differing aspects of restoration in Deuteronomy and Ezekiel.[79] First, while Ezekiel uses the Deuteronomic phrase ביד חזקה ובזרוע נטויה ("with a strong hand and an outstretched arm") in vv. 33-34, he does so not in reference to the miraculous exodus from Egypt as Deuteronomy does, but rather in connection with the kingship of Yahweh and the new exodus.[80] Second, though Deuteronomy and Ezekiel share

77. Pons, "Le vocabulaire d'Ézéchiel 20," 232.
78. Ibid., 227.
79. Ibid., 228–31.
80. Pons draws attention to the association of ביד חזקה ובזרוע נטויה with Yahweh's kingship in Ezek. 20:32. He asserts that kingship is "synonymous with absolute power and arbitrariness" and therefore interprets the kingship of Yahweh negatively (ibid., 228). However, kingship for Ezekiel is not inherently tyrannical. In contrast to the oppression of Israel's recent kings (see 34:1-10), the new David (34:23-24; 37:24-25), for example, rules in justice and righteousness. There is therefore no basis to regard Yahweh's kingship as malevolent. On kingship in Ezekiel, see further Daniel

similar language for the return from exile, unlike Ezekiel, Deuteronomy presents a true conversion prior to deliverance (Deut. 30:1-2) and ascribes the gathering of Israel to Yahweh's mercy (רחם, Deut. 30:3). Third, after the gathering of Israel, Deuteronomy anticipates an immediate return to the land (Deut. 30:5), whereas in Ezekiel 20, Yahweh will deliver his people only to bring them into the wilderness for a new period of judgment and purging (vv. 35-38).

The following may be said in response. First, Ezekiel's use of language typically found in descriptions of the exodus from Egypt indicates he sought to describe the return from exile as a new exodus (see especially ביד חזקה ובזרוע נטויה and the verb הוצאתי).[81] To be sure, the prophet alters the positive connotations of the phrase ביד חזקה ובזרוע נטויה by adding בחמה שפוכה ("with wrath poured out"). Yet, there is no reason to conclude that Ezekiel's twist constitutes an intentional polemic against Deuteronomy rather than a polemic against Israel's rebellion. Second, as I will argue in Chapter 7 of this study, Ezekiel's perspective on the necessity of repentance before restoration does not demand a polemic against Deuteronomy specifically, since the Holiness Code also envisions repentance before restoration (Lev. 26:40-45). While Ezekiel draws from the language of both Deuteronomy and the Holiness Code, his vision of this aspect of restoration differs from both texts.[82] Third, while in Ezekiel 20 deliverance from exile involves further judgment, this view as well represents a difference not only with Deuteronomy, but with virtually all other restoration texts in the Hebrew Bible. This unique presentation of restoration may be explained as an intentional analogy between the earlier exodus and the new exodus: just as the exodus from Egypt involved a judgment and purification in the wilderness before entry into the promised land, so also with the new exodus from exile before entry into the land.

I. Block, "Transformation of Royal Ideology in Ezekiel," in Tooman and Lyons, eds., *Transforming Visions*, 208–46; repr. in Daniel I. Block, *Beyond the River Chebar: Studies in Kingship and Eschatology in the Book of Ezekiel* (Eugene, OR: Cascade, 2013), 10–44.

81. See Walther Zimmerli, "Le nouvel 'exode' dans le message des deux grands prophètes de l'Exil" in *Maqqél shâkedh: la branche d'amandier. Hommage à Wilhelm Fischer* (Montpellier: Cause, Graille, & Castelnau, 1960), 217. Repr. "Der 'Neue Exodus' in Der Verkündigung der Beiden Grossen Exilspropheten," in *Gottes Offenbarung: Gesammelte Aufsätze I*, 2nd ed., TB 19 (Munich: Kaiser, 1969), 192–204.

82. See Paul M. Joyce, "Ezekiel and Moral Transformation," in Tooman and Lyons, eds., *Transforming Visions*, 139–58.

Since other restoration oracles in the book describe a return to the land immediately after the gathering of Israel (והבאתי אותם אל־אדמתם in Ezek. 11:17-18; 34:13; 36:24; 37:21), the depiction of an intermediate period of judgment may derive from the rhetorical situation of ch. 20, namely, a response to the elders of Israel *before* the ultimate judgment of the destruction of Jerusalem.

Conclusion: Ezekiel and Deuteronomy/Dtr

A critical evaluation reveals that Pons' theory of a polemic against Deuteronomy in Ezekiel 20 is flawed on virtually all counts. The alleged subversion of Deuteronomic language is particularly unfounded for several reasons. First, Pons erroneously assumes that Ezekiel's occasional preference for Priestly language is indicative of a polemic against Deuteronomy. Second, he speciously cites differences between Ezekiel 20 and the general pentateuchal tradition as evidence for the prophet's polemic against Deuteronomy specifically. Third, Pons fails to recognize that Ezekiel's differing use of locutions may be the result of the prophet's creative rhetoric aimed at his audience, not Deuteronomic theology per se.[83] Finally, many of Pons' other arguments for subversion are simply overstated.

In fairness, it should be noted that Pons made his argument as an alternative to viewing the Deuteronomic elements of Ezekiel 20 as the result of redaction.[84] If the vocabulary is used in a subversive sense, Pons reasoned, then it would be more comprehensible that the prophet himself could be the creative force behind the Deuteronomic language in Ezekiel 20. Thus, Pons shares the assumption of those who ascribe the Deuteronomic language to redactors: that Ezekiel himself would not have been influenced by Deuteronomy. However, the arguments presented here demonstrate that this assumption is unjustified. There is no reason to assume he was not influenced by Deuteronomy, and Ezekiel 20 demonstrates that in fact he was.

---

83. As an analogue, Lyons has demonstrated that the prophet diverges from the Holiness Code in similar ways without a polemical motivation (see *From Law to Prophecy*, 85–8; discussed below in Chapter 7 of this study).

84. Pons' summary reflects this concern: (1) Ezek. 20 cannot be the work of a redactor; (2) the incontestable presence of Deut/dtr vocabulary came from a deliberate use by the prophet; and (3) Ezekiel utilizes this vocabulary to oppose Deuteronomic theology ("Le vocabulaire d'Ézéchiel 20," 232).

Do the Not-Good Laws (Ezekiel 20:25-26) Refer to Deuteronomy?

Verses 25-26 are the most enigmatic in Ezekiel 20, since the prophet appears to attribute bad laws to Yahweh. Scott Hahn and John Bergsma have argued that the "statutes that were not good and ordinances by which they could not live" refer to the laws of Deuteronomy.[85] The authors propose that Ezekiel describes Deuteronomy with such language on account of the alleged conflict between Priestly and Deuteronomic laws. Before responding to Hahn and Bergsma's thesis, a review of the traditional interpretation is necessary.[86]

The Traditional Interpretation

The traditional rendering of most translations is reflected in the NRSV (Ezek. 20:25-26):

Moreover I gave them statutes that were not good	וגם־אני נתתי להם חקים לא טובים
and ordinances by which they could not live.	ומשפטים לא יחיו בהם
I defiled them through their very gifts,	ואטמא אותם במתנותם
in their offering up all their firstborn,	בהעביר כל־פטר רחם
in order that I might horrify them,	למען אשמם
so that they might know that I am the LORD.	למען אשר ידעו אשר אני יהוה

Earlier in the chapter, Ezekiel spoke of Yahweh giving Israel statutes and ordinances by which the people *could have life* (v. 11). Then, in the following verses, he emphasizes repeatedly that Israel rebelled against those statutes and did not walk in them (e.g., 13, 16, 21, 24). Verse 25 therefore provides the antithesis to these life-giving statutes by proposing that Yahweh then gave them statutes and ordinances *that do not give life*. So to what do these bad laws refer?

---

85. Hahn and Bergsma, "What Laws?"
86. For a review of other theories, see Kelvin G. Friebel, "The Decrees of Yahweh that Are 'Not Good': Ezekiel 20:25-26," in *Seeking Out the Wisdom of the Ancients: Essays Offered to Honor Michael V. Fox on the Occasion of His Sixty-Fifth Birthday*, ed. Ronald L. Troxel, Kelvin G. Friebel, and Dennis R. Magary (Winona Lake, IN: Eisenbrauns, 2005), 22–8; Davis, *Swallowing the Scroll*, 113–14. On the earliest interpretations of this passage, see P. W. van der Horst, "'I Gave them Laws that Were Not Good': Ezekiel 20.25 in Ancient Judaism and Early Christianity," in *Sacred History and Sacred Texts in Early Judaism: A Symposium in Honour of A. S. van der Woude*, ed. J. N. Bremmer and F. Garcia Martinez (Kampen: Kok Pharos, 1992), 94–118.

According to the most common interpretation of this passage, vv. 25 and 26 are linked in such a way that the not-good laws in v. 25 relate to the gifts and offerings of firstborn in v. 26, which are understood to refer to child sacrifice. Thus, the not-good laws would refer to Yahweh's command to sacrifice children.[87] Ezekiel uses the phrase העביר כל־פטר רחם, literally "to cause every opener of the womb to pass," which exhibits the same language as the law of the firstborn in Exod. 13:12, where Yahweh commands Israel to "cause every opener of the womb to pass to Yahweh" (והעברת כל־פטר־רחם ליהוה). Although Exodus 13 does not in fact authorize child sacrifice, since the next verse specifies that *human* firstborn are not to be sacrificed but are to be redeemed (v. 13),[88] it is commonly argued that in Ezekiel's mind Yahweh either commanded child sacrifice or issued a law that would be widely (mis)interpreted as commanding child sacrifice.[89] If this interpretation is correct, in Ezekiel's mind, Yahweh gave his people not-good laws in order to defile them through the sacrifice of their firstborn (v. 26). In Patton's words, "the law itself was evil, given by Yahweh as punishment for their sinfulness in the wilderness, in order to guarantee their ultimate destruction."[90]

---

87. Patton, "Ezekiel 20 and the Exodus Traditions," 78–9; George C. Heider, "A Further Turn on Ezekiel's Baroque Twist in Ezek. 20:25-26," *JBL* 107 (1988): 722; idem, *The Cult of Molek: A Reassessment*, JSOTSup 43 (Sheffield: JSOT, 1985), 372; Jacob Milgrom, "Were the Firstborn Sacrificed to YHWH? To Molek? Popular Practice or Divine Demand?" in *Sacrifice in Religious Experience*, ed. Albert I. Baumgarten (Leiden: Brill, 2002), 52–3; Thomas Krüger, "Transformation of History in Ezekiel 20," in Tooman and Lyons, eds., *Transforming Visions*, 162–3; Greenberg, *Ezekiel 1–20*, 368–70; Allen, *Ezekiel 20–48*, 12; Mein, *Ethics of Exile*, 118; Joyce, *Ezekiel*, 151; Gili Kugler, "The Cruel Theology of Ezekiel," *ZAW* 129 (2017): 47–59.

88. One may point to Exod. 22:28-29[29-30], where Yahweh commands that the "firstborn of your sons" be "given" to him, though this also would presumably involve their redemption or may simply connote service or dedication to Yahweh. See Milgrom, "Were the Firstborn Sacrificed to YHWH?" 50–1, 54. On the latter option, see Rainer Albertz, *A History of Israelite Religion in the Old Testament Period*, trans. John Bowden (Louisville: Westminster John Knox, 1994), 1:192–3.

89. Indeed, Jacob Milgrom argues that among the general populace many believed that child sacrifice was approved and demanded by God (*Leviticus 17–22: A New Translation with Introduction and Commentary*, AB 3A [New York: Doubleday, 2000], 1551–65; idem, "Were the Firstborn Sacrificed to YHWH?" 49–56).

90. Patton, "Ezekiel 20 and the Exodus Traditions," 79.

Deuteronomy as the "Not-Good" Laws

Below I will support what I believe is a better interpretation of Ezek. 20:25-26. First, however, I will attend to the main burden of this section, namely, responding to the proposal that the not-good laws refer to the sacrificial laws of Deuteronomy.

Hahn and Bergsma propose that the prophet would describe Deuteronomy with such language because of the alleged conflict between Priestly and Deuteronomic laws. They begin by correctly locating v. 25 within Ezekiel's history: the time-frame for Yahweh giving not-good חקים and משפטים is the second wilderness generation. If this statement alludes to any pentateuchal legal material, the narrative flow of the chapter would align it with the second-generation instructions, namely, Deuteronomy.[91] Hahn and Bergsma come to the seemingly logical conclusion that the not-good laws must refer to the laws of Deuteronomy, or some law(s) therein. In their view, Ezekiel is speaking about something different than the divine statutes described earlier in the chapter, since the death-inducing statutes in v. 25 are described as חקים, the masculine plural form of חק, whereas the life-giving laws mentioned earlier in the chapter are presented as חקות, the feminine plural form.

Why would Ezekiel denounce the laws of Deuteronomy? Hahn and Bergsma argue that "Ezekiel writes from a Priestly perspective that views many of the distinctive laws of Deuteronomy as clearly inferior or even offensive."[92] Following Weinfeld, who regards Deuteronomy as a radical program of secularization,[93] they suggest that members of the Priestly guild would have found many of Deuteronomy's laws unacceptably lax.[94] According to Hahn and Bergsma, v. 26 provides a clue to the source of this conflict. Contra the traditional interpretation, which regards the "gifts" and "offerings of כל־פטר רחם" as a reference to child sacrifice, Hahn and Bergsma contend that the firstborn of v. 26 does not refer to human children but rather animal firstlings, since the phrase כל־פטר רחם may refer to humans or animals.[95] Thus, Ezekiel has in mind here not illegitimate human offerings but simply proper sacrificial practice.

---

91. Hahn and Bergsma, "What Laws?" 203–6.
92. Ibid., 208.
93. Weinfeld, *Deuteronomy and the Deuteronomic School*, 191–224.
94. Hahn and Bergsma, "What Laws?" 209–10.
95. Following Hartmut Gese, "Ezechiel 20,25f. und die Erstgeburtsopfer," in *Beitrage zur alttestamentlichen Theologie: Festschrift für Walther Zimmerli zum 70. Geburtstag*, ed. Herbert Donner, Robert Hanhart, and Rudolf Smend (Göttingen: Vandenhoeck & Ruprecht, 1977), 140–51.

Still, what is it about the Deuteronomic sacrificial instructions that Ezekiel would detest? They propose that some of Deuteronomy's laws would have been repulsive to Ezekiel's Priestly sensibilities. For example, whereas Leviticus requires the people to visit the sanctuary and sprinkle blood on the altar "for the slaughter of any and all animals (Lev 17:1-8)," Deuteronomy requires that only firstlings and voluntary sacrifices be brought to the sanctuary, thus allowing the profane slaughter of non-sacrificial animals (Deut. 12:6, 17; 15:19, 20). Consequently, for Ezekiel, the everyday slaughter of animals away from the temple would have been a grave transgression against the Priestly legislation. In addition, Leviticus 27 (vv. 9-10, 28) forbids the substitution or redemption of clean animals, which would seem to include firstlings. Deuteronomy 14 (vv. 22-26), on the other hand, appears to permit the redemption of firstlings for money in order that the worshiper may purchase an animal upon arrival at the temple. Ezekiel apparently would have been appalled by these practices and understandably condemned the instructions that ordained them.

According to Hahn and Bergsma, Ezekiel regarded both sets of laws as divine instruction and pitted them against each other. The prophet deemed Deuteronomy's laws not good "because, on the one hand, they degraded the pristine Priestly standards and, on the other, they were interwoven with predictions of human disobedience and inevitable divine judgment."[96] By giving his people these laws, Yahweh ensured their defilement.

Evaluation

No one has yet offered a full evaluation of Hahn and Bergsma's thesis. Here, I offer four counterpoints. First, Hahn and Bergsma's thesis rests on the argument that the gifts and offerings in v. 26 refer to animal rather than human sacrifices. However, their argument poses several problems. First, Hahn and Bergsma spuriously reason that since Exod. 13:13 explicitly excludes human firstborn from the כל־פטר־רחם that are to be set apart for Yahweh, the כל־פטר־רחם in Ezek. 20:26 would also refer to animals apart from humans.[97] Second, although Hahn and Bergsma attempt to discredit a connection between the gifts and offerings

---

96. Hahn and Bergsma, "What Laws?" 217.

97. Tuell disputes a strict distinction between בכור and כל־פטר־רחם, pointing out that both can equally refer to animals or humans (as in Exod. 13:12-13). He rejects Hahn and Bergsma's thesis, arguing that they are mistaken to view כל־פטר־רחם as

of v. 26 and the cult of Molech,⁹⁸ Ezekiel may speak of child sacrifice (to idols) without alluding specifically to Molech worship. Third, and most importantly, they overlook the numerous instances in the book of Ezekiel where the prophet speaks of child sacrifice, in some cases using similar language. Later in this very ch. 20, Ezekiel speaks of "causing children to pass through the fire" (20:31). In chs. 16 and 23, the prophet indicts Israel four times for "taking your sons and your daughters...and sacrificing them [to idols] to be eaten" (16:20; also 16:21; 23:37, 39). In most of these cases, the Hiphil of עבר is used (16:21; 20:31; 23:37), as it is in 20:26. Thus, the theory itself rests on a dubious foundation.

Second, many modern scholars minimize the differing literary contexts of the sacrificial laws in Leviticus 17 and Deuteronomy 12. The literary setting of the Leviticus instruction is the wilderness, and ch. 17 states that the law applies to animals slaughtered "outside the camp" (v. 3) or "in the open field" (v. 5). Repeatedly the law requires that the animal be brought to the Tabernacle ("Tent of Meeting"). Thus, Leviticus purports to offer sacrificial instructions for a community centered on a single camp. Deuteronomy 12, on the other hand, offers guidelines for life in the land, when many Israelites live "too far from the place that Yahweh chose to put his name" (cf. Deut. 12:21).

For the differing sacrificial laws mentioned by Hahn and Bergsma, Deuteronomy cites changed circumstances as the motivation for the instruction. When Deuteronomy allows profane slaughter in ch. 12, it offers not only a setting when the law is to be kept but also a rationale:

> *When Yahweh your God enlarges your territory*, as he has promised you, and you say, "I am going to eat some meat," because you wish to eat meat, you may eat meat whenever you have the desire. *If the place where Yahweh your God will choose to put his name is too far from you*, [then you may] slaughter as I have commanded you any of your herd or flock that Yahweh has given you, [and] you may eat within your towns whenever you desire. (Deut. 12:20-21)

---

referring exclusively to animal sacrifice (Steven Tuell, *Ezekiel*, NIBC [Peabody, MA: Hendrickson, 2009], 136–7). Actually, Hahn and Bergsma do not say this. They argue only that Exod. 13:13 intentionally excludes the human firstborn from כל־פטר־רחם.

98. Hahn and Bergsma, "What Laws?" 211–12.

This ordinance applies "when Yahweh your God enlarges your territory" and envisions circumstances when the worshiper lives far from the chosen place. The situation in the land is quite different than the wilderness camp, inasmuch as it is not practical for a worshiper to make a three-day journey to Jerusalem each time he kills an animal for food.

The law allowing substitution of animals for money in Deuteronomy 14 cites the same reason:

> *If...the distance is so great that you are unable to transport it, because the place where Yahweh your God will choose to set his name is too far away from you*, then you may turn it into money. With the money secure in hand, go to the place that Yahweh your God will choose; spend the money for whatever you wish—oxen, sheep, wine, strong drink, or whatever you desire. (Deut. 14:24-26)

Here also, Deuteronomy provides new guidelines for new circumstances, namely, the impracticality of regularly bringing animals to the distant temple.[99] Ultimately, whatever the provenance of these texts, the Priestly torah envisions a time in the wilderness when Israel dwelled within a single (transient) camp and sacrificed at a local tent. The Deuteronomic torah would ostensibly supersede this instruction when the people dwell in the land.[100]

While scholars commonly disregard Leviticus' own presentation of its historical context on grounds that the wilderness setting is an artificial construct created for much later Priestly legislation, we must ask, would the prophet of the sixth century BCE have ignored the literary settings of these two books? At issue is not simply the narrative frames of these law corpuses, but the laws themselves. Would not Ezekiel have recognized that the sacrificial instructions of Leviticus 17 explicitly prescribed laws for life centered in the wilderness camp, and, conversely, that

---

99. Peter Vogt argues that these changes may be seen, not as steps toward secularization, but rather an expansion of the sacred, since the entire land is now holy to Yahweh (*Deuteronomic Theology and the Significance of* Torah*: A Reappraisal* [Winona Lake, IN: Eisenbrauns, 2006], 164–92); so also the Holiness code (Israel Knohl, *The Sanctuary of Silence: The Priestly Torah and the Holiness Code* [Minneapolis: Augsburg Fortress, 1995; repr. Winona Lake, IN: Eisenbrauns, 2007], 185–6.

100. Cf. Fishbane, *Biblical Interpretation*, 252: "the profusion of slaughter sites is valid *only* up to the complete settlement of the land." Deut. 12:8-11 states that Israel's worship in the land should *not* be as it was in the wilderness. Nevertheless, the passage contrasts its instruction not with the Sinai instruction, but with "doing whatever is right in one's own eyes."

Deuteronomy 12 explicitly speaks of guidelines for settled life in the land? To ascribe to Ezekiel this alleged conflict is to make him either an adherent to the modern critical theory of Leviticus' provenance or a poor reader who has failed to notice *where* the sacrificial laws of Leviticus and Deuteronomy are to be carried out.

Third, if Ezekiel sought to condemn the practice of profane slaughter and the substitution of offerings, it is curious that he does not mention them anywhere else in the book. In several passages, he enumerates Israel's cultic sins in great detail, but nowhere does he indict Israel for their failure to bring all slaughtered animals to the temple or their failure to haul their firstlings on a three-day journey to Jerusalem. By contrast, he does indict Israel for child sacrifice multiple times.

Lastly, as argued in the previous section, the numerous instances of Deuteronomic language in Ezekiel 20 suggest the prophet was not broadly opposed to the Deuteronomic torah.[101] Pons' attempt to posit a subversion of Deuteronomic language and theology is misguided. Distinctively Deuteronomic locutions include the election of Israel with the verb בחר (v. 5), passing children through the fire (v. 31), worshiping wood and stone (v. 32), Yahweh gathering his people from the lands where they have been scattered (v. 33, 41), and Yahweh's deliverance with a mighty hand and an outstretched arm (v. 33, 34), among many others.

The Referent of the Not-Good Laws

So if the not-good laws do not refer to the laws of Deuteronomy, then to what do they refer? As stated earlier, the traditional interpretation has been that in Ezekiel's mind Yahweh ordered child sacrifice in order to defile his people. Kelvin Friebel has offered a better interpretation, namely, that the חקים and משפטים in 20:25-26 do not refer to divine instruction at all.[102] In what follows, I summarize Friebel's argument and then add two further points.

First, Friebel would agree with Hahn and Bergsma that by using the variant masculine form חקים, Ezekiel is no longer speaking of the same statutes (feminine חקות) from Yahweh mentioned earlier in the chapter. Furthermore, elsewhere in ch. 20, when the words חקות and משפטים refer to Yahweh's instructions, they always appear with a pronominal suffix (i.e., חקותי, "my statutes" [Ezek. 20:11, 13, 16, 19, 21, 24]).[103] Only here

---

101. So also Tuell, *Ezekiel*, 137.
102. Friebel, "The Decrees of Yahweh that Are 'Not Good.'"
103. Ibid., 28–9.

do the words occur in their absolute form. However, instead of referring to the laws of Deuteronomy, Friebel argues that the present verse speaks about something different than divine torah.

Friebel brilliantly proposes that the חקים and משפטים in v. 25 are not divine statutes and ordinances, but rather decrees and judgments, specifically the decrees and judgments of exile mentioned in the preceding v. 23.

Moreover, I swore to them in the wilderness that I would scatter them among the nations and disperse them through the countries. (v. 23)	גם־אני נשאתי את־ידי להם במדבר להפיץ אתם בגוים ולזרות אותם בארצות:
Moreover, I gave them *decrees* that were not good and *judgments* by which they could not have life. (v. 25)	וגם־אני נתתי להם חקים לא טובים ומשפטים לא יחיו בהם:

Friebel offers evidence for a connection between vv. 23 and 25. First, he notes the presence גם־אני at the beginning of both verses and describes two possibilities for understanding the function of the repetition. Either the second occurrence in v. 25 marks an additional, unrelated declaration of judgment, or it signals a resumption of v. 23, thus referring to that specific oath of judgment.[104] The latter option finds support from v. 12, where וגם occurs in a similar context. There the phrase וגם נתתי להם, "moreover, I gave to them," in v. 12 resumes and further elaborates on the preceding ואתן להם ("I gave to them") in v. 11. Therefore, according to Friebel, vv. 25-26 would resume the thought of the preceding vv. 23-24. Together they constitute a "two-part, parallel declaration of judgment, both beginning with גם־אני."[105] Verse 25 is commentary on v. 23, which may be summarized as follows: "[the] decree of judgment in v. 23 is not to the people's benefit—in other words, it is not good… It is essentially a declaration of death for the nation—in other words, it is not life-giving."[106]

---

104. Ibid., 29.
105. Ibid., 30. He further notes that v. 23 displays a "twofold declaration of judgment" ("to scatter and to disperse") followed by a fourfold list of reasons for their punishment in v. 24. Verses 25-26 similarly begin with a twofold declaration of judgment ("I gave them" and "I defiled them"), followed by a twofold list of reasons ("on account of their gifts" and "on account of passing their children through the fire").
106. Ibid., 29–30.

Friebel argues that משפטים in Ezek. 20:25 refers to divine judgments. Not only is it common for the term משפטים in the Hebrew Bible to refer to Yahweh's judgments, but we find another instance in Ezekiel where Yahweh executes משפטים (understood as "judgments") for failure to keep his משפטים (understood as "ordinances"). Lyons regards this as a pun used for rhetorical purposes.[107] In Ezek. 5:6-8 Israel is indicted for rebellion against Yahweh's covenant laws (חקות and משפטים), and immediately thereafter Yahweh declares his execution of judgments (משפטים):[108]

She has rebelled against <u>my ordinances</u>	ותמר את־משפטי
by doing wickedness more than the nations	לרשעה מן־הגוים
and against my statutes more than the countries	ואת־חקותי מן־הארצות
around her;	אשר סביבותיה
for they have rejected <u>my ordinances</u>	כי במשפטי מאסו
and have not walked in my statutes.	וחקותי לא־הלכו בהם:
Because you are more turbulent than the nations	יען המנכם מן־הגוים
that are all around you, and have not walked in	אשר סביבותיכם בחקותי לא
my statutes or obeyed <u>my ordinances</u>…	הלכתם ואת־משפטי
I will execute <u>judgments</u> in your midst	גם־אני ועשיתי בתוכך משפטים
in the sight of the nations	לעיני הגוים

This example provides an impressive parallel to Ezek. 20:23-26, showing that even in two adjacent verses משפטים may be used in two different senses—ordinances and judgments. In both cases, משפטים ("judgments") are invoked for failure to keep Yahweh's חקות and משפטים ("statutes and ordinances"). In addition, Ezek. 5:8 is the only other occurrence of משפטים in the book that is "not determined by a suffix or construct relationship," and thus, as we might expect, like 20:25 "bears the meaning 'judgments' in the sense of punishments for sin."[109]

Arriving at v. 26, the traditional understanding of these verses interprets the initial verb וָאֲטַמֵּא ("I defiled them") as a purpose for Yahweh giving his חקים and משפטים. Yahweh gave Israel not-good statutes and ordinances *in order that* he might defile them. However, as Friebel has shown, when Piel טמא occurs with a person as its object, the defilement always derives from the subject's impurity. That is, an impure subject makes another impure, on account of, for example, a sexually defiling act (e.g., Gen. 34:5) or the subject's exposure to a corpse (e.g., Num. 6:9).

---

107. Lyons, "Persuasion and Allusion," 81.
108. Ibid., 30.
109. Ibid.

Of course, in this instance it is clearly not *Yahweh's* impurity that defiles Israel, since the verse explicitly states that Israel's own gifts to idols were the cause of their defilement. The one exception to this use of Piel טמא is when a sanctified person *declares* an unclean person defiled, as the priest is instructed to do in Leviticus 13. Thus, based on its use in the Hebrew Bible, the verb טמא here is best understood as a declaration of Israel's status. Yahweh did not seek to defile his people, but simply declared them defiled based on what the people had done to defile themselves. In this reading of ואטמא, the *bet* prepositions in v. 26 would be understood not as "I defiled them *through* their gifts," but "I declared them defiled *on account of* their gifts."

Finally, concerning the last phrase, often rendered "in order that I might devastate them," Friebel points out that with a human object the verb שמם does not signify "to devastate them," but rather "to make them horrified," as it does in Ezek. 32:10. Thus, Yahweh did not intend to *devastate* his people, but rather to make them horrified at their transgressions. Friebel's interpretation of Ezek. 20:25-26 yields the following translation:

> And also I gave them decrees [regarding their dispersion and scattering] that were not good and judgments [of punishment] by which they would not have life. And I declared them defiled on account of their gifts [to their idols], on account of offering [by fire to idols] all [their] firstborn, so that I would cause them to be horrified, so that they would know that I am Yahweh.[110]

At this point I add two observations. First, a distinctive feature of this interpretation that Friebel has not highlighted is the nature of the wordplay between Ezek. 20:25 and the earlier description of Yahweh's life-giving instructions.[111] Ezekiel deliberately plays on the earlier theme of the life-giving power of Yahweh's statutes and ordinances in order to describe the death-inducing feature of his judgments and decrees.

> I gave them statutes and ordinances by which they could live. (20:11)

> I gave them decrees...and judgments by which they would not live. (20:25)

---

110. Ibid., 36.
111. Verse 18 shows that Ezekiel uses חקים and משפטים with diverse referents. There they refer to the (sinful) statutes and ordinances of the exodus generation.

Both are described as חקים/חקות and משפטים, and each sentence begins with "I gave them." According to Ezekiel, the people failed to keep the life-giving ordinances and thus brought upon themselves death-inducing judgments.

Second, Friebel's thesis becomes more compelling when it is seen that the חקים and משפטים in Ezek. 20:25 do in fact refer to something in Deuteronomy as Hahn and Bergsma's literary analysis of ch. 20 would suggest. However, these words do not refer to any of Deuteronomy's statutes and ordinances. Instead, the judgment of exile in Ezek. 20:23-26 represents an allusion to a particular judgment of exile in Deuteronomy. As I will argue in the next chapter, the oath to scatter Israel in v. 23 likely alludes to Deut. 4:25-28, which invokes an oath to scatter Israel if they transgress the covenant. Consequently, we have found a more likely referent of Ezek. 20:25 in Deuteronomy than the one proposed by Hahn and Bergsma.

Ezekiel 20 and Israelite Tradition

Scholars commonly assert that Ezekiel's historiography in ch. 20 is highly revisionistic. Ellen Davis, for example, describes Ezekiel's re-writing of history in this way: "No one ever recounted Israel's past as Ezekiel does; he presents the most radical revisioning of the tradition… What he achieves is a deliberate and thorough reconceptualization of Israel's past and present."[112] This kind of conclusion stems variously from (1) the notion that Israel's idolatry reached back to their sojourn in Egypt; (2) the theory of Lust and Pons that Ezekiel virtually erased the possession of the promised land from Israel's history; and (3) the interpretation of Ezek. 20:25-26 as Yahweh commanding child sacrifice in order to defile his people.

To be sure, Ezekiel's historiography is creative and highly selective. Like any ancient historiographer, he takes liberties to shape history in a way that serves his rhetorical goals. However, some alleged examples of Ezekiel's radical departure from his received traditions are overstated. As

---

112. Davis, *Swallowing the Scroll*, 105–6; cf. Block, *Ezekiel*, 1:462, 614. Conversely, Choi uses the supposed differences between Ezek. 20 and the pentateuchal traditions to conclude that Ezekiel, as well as other biblical writers, was simply unaware of pentateuchal historical traditions (*Traditions at Odds*, 136–43). However, Choi does not engage the scholarly consensus on Ezekiel's use of Israel's literary traditions, most conspicuously the Priestly literature.

this study has shown, two of the bases for Ezekiel's alleged revision of history are misconceived: Lust's theory that Yahweh actually scattered his people in the wilderness and denied them entry into the promised land reflects a flawed interpretation of Ezekiel 20, and Friebel's compelling interpretation of Ezek. 20:25-26 demonstrates that the not-good חקים and death-inducing משפטים are not divine laws at all but rather decrees and judgments in response to Israel's rebellion.

Other aspects of Ezekiel's history may have a basis in tradition as well. As noted earlier, the idea that Israel worshiped idols in Egypt has a conceptual basis in Israelite tradition, specifically Josh. 24:14, which speaks of "the gods that your ancestors served beyond the River *and in Egypt*."[113] Indeed, Josh. 24:14 names Israel's אבות and Ezekiel was charged with declaring the abominations of the אבות to the elders (Ezek. 20:4). In that instance, we cannot agree with S. R. Driver, who posited that "Ezekiel is not wholly just to the past" because he unconsciously projects present realities on the distant past.[114] Certainly, Ezekiel takes creative liberty in describing Yahweh's command in Egypt to abandon idols (20:7-8). Ezekiel may have been influenced by Lev. 18:3, where Yahweh orders Moses to tell the people, "you shall not do as they do in the land of Egypt, where you lived."[115] This command—given later in the wilderness—may have provided a sufficient impetus for Ezekiel to project Yahweh's commandment back to the period in Egypt.

Although stylized and selective, Ezekiel's historiography is not as radically inventive as some have claimed. For the most part, the narrative flow of Ezekiel 20 follows, not every detail, but the main points of the general tradition reflected in the pentateuchal narrative, leading Reventlow, for example, to conclude that "Ezekiel continually cites a well-defined tradition."[116] I do not take this to mean he must have been working from pentateuchal sources as texts necessarily, but only that he is

---

113. Lust, "Ez., XX, 4-26: une parodie," 516. Deut. 29:15-16[16-17] states that the Israelites saw Egypt's idols.

114. Driver, *Introduction*, 279.

115. John Day, "Inner Biblical Interpretation in the Prophets," in *The Place Is Too Small for Us: The Israelite Prophets in Recent Scholarship*, ed. Robert P. Gordon, SBTS 5 (Winona Lake, IN: Eisenbrauns, 1995), 237; repr. of "Prophecy," in *It Is Written: Scripture Citing Scripture: Essays in Honour of Barnabas Lindars*, ed. D. A. Carson and H. G. M. Williamson (Cambridge: Cambridge University Press, 1988), 39–55.

116. Reventlow, *Wächter über Israel*, 7: "Der Prophet Ezechiel zitiert in seiner Verkündigung fortwährend eine ganz bestimmte Tradition"; cited in Lust, "Ez., XX, 4-26: une parodie," 515.

aware of the general tradition that was reflected in those texts. Although Ezekiel's rhetoric included presenting Israel's history in such a way as to highlight persistent idolatry since its earliest days as a people, he mostly stays close to his received traditions. The creativity of his historiography lies not primarily in its departure from the tradition, but in its narrow focus on Israel's sins. As Patton puts it, Ezekiel 20 is not so much a "review of the mighty acts of Yahweh," but a review of the pervasive sin of Israel.[117] Reflecting on Israel's lack of faithfulness to Yahweh since its infancy as a nation, the prophet presents the story as *Unheilsgeschichte*, as it is often labeled, rather than *Heilsgeschichte*.[118]

Summary

In conclusion, the arguments advanced by Pons and by Hahn and Bergsma that the prophet distanced himself from Deuteronomy are misguided. Ezekiel did not use Deuteronomic language with a polemical purpose, nor did he repudiate Deuteronomy's worship laws by deeming them "not-good" (20:25). Instead, Ezekiel 20 demonstrates that the Deuteronomic tradition exerted a significant influence on the sixth-century prophet. At numerous points, the prophet uses Deuteronomic language and concepts to describe Israel's history. Notably, he begins his account with Yahweh's election (בחר) of Israel (v. 5). Many other elements are distinctively Deuteronomic: the idea that Yahweh himself scouted (תור) the promised land (v. 6), the characterization of Israel's apostasy in the wilderness as rebellion (vv. 8, 13, 21), the description of Yahweh's anger with the word pair אף and חמה (vv. 8, 13, 21), the presence of the expression עין + חוס (v. 17), the condemnation of high places with reference to "any high hill or any leafy tree" (v. 28), the accusation of child sacrifice with the phrase בהעביר בניכם באש (v. 31), the conception of worshiping "wood and stone" in exile (v. 32), the application of ביד חזקה ובזרוע נטויה to the new exodus (vv. 33-34), and the description of the end of the exile as Yahweh gathering Israel out of the countries from which they were scattered (v. 41). In addition, as I will argue in the next chapter, Yahweh's oath in the wilderness to scatter Israel in v. 23 likely constitutes a purposeful allusion to the threat of exile in Deut. 4:25-28.

117. Patton, "Ezekiel 20 and the Exodus Traditions," 75.
118. Lust, "Ez., XX, 4-26: une parodie," 488: "On n'y retrouve plus une histoire du salut, mais plutôt un exposé des malheurs provoqués par et survenus à Israël."

Chapter 6

THE SCATTERING OF ISRAEL

Exile and return occupy a fundamental place in Ezekiel's theology of judgment and restoration. For Ezekiel, Yahweh's expulsion of his people from their land represents divine punishment for their religious and social transgressions (36:19), which he saw as a failure to keep Yahweh's statutes (5:6-7; 11:12; 20:13, 16, 21, 24). Accordingly, the prophet cites specific injunctions in the Holiness Code and Deuteronomy in order to accuse and condemn his fellow Israelites. However, as a prophet whose ministry straddles the periods both before and after the judgment of 587 BCE, Ezekiel foresaw a renewed era when Yahweh would bring his people back to their land and display his gracious resolve to maintain his covenant with Israel by causing them to walk in his statutes (11:19-20; 36:27; 37:24).

One particular motif stands out as a dominant image for the prophet's warnings of exile and promises of return: the scattering and gathering of Israel among the nations. In this and the next chapter, I will examine these two related images. For each, I will outline the correspondences between Ezekiel's language and that of Deuteronomy, discuss the authenticity of the motif in Ezekiel, and explicitly treat the direction of influence by arguing for the priority of Deuteronomy's scattering and gathering passages and Ezekiel's purposeful allusion to them. At the end of each chapter, I will address the rhetorical function of Ezekiel's allusions to the pentateuchal language of exile and return.

We begin with an introduction to the motif of scattering and gathering. Ezekiel warns of exile or promises return more than twenty times using this distinctive motif.[1] The image of scattering or gathering Israel is

---

1. Ezek. 5:2, 10, 12; 6:8; 11:16-17; 12:14-15; 20:23, 34, 41; 22:15; 28:25; 34:13; 36:19, 24; 37:21; 39:27-28; in metaphorical contexts: 22:19; 34:5, 6, 12; of Egypt: 29:12-13; 30:23, 26; of Babylon: 22:19.

present to a lesser degree elsewhere in the Hebrew Bible, as we will survey below and in the next chapter, but nowhere is it more pronounced than in Ezekiel, where it occurs more often than any other book. In addition, as others have recognized, although the texts in Ezekiel display variations, they exhibit a remarkable consistency of expression not found in other books and thus warrant being called stereotyped formulae.[2]

The Holiness Code and Deuteronomy also contain the motif in variant forms, and the question naturally arises whether Ezekiel might draw from earlier traditions. Indeed, there is reason within the book itself to suspect Ezekiel may have known and drawn from traditional material for the scattering metaphor. In his depiction of the history of the wilderness period in ch. 20, the prophet cites Yahweh's threat to Israel: "I swore to them in the wilderness that I would scatter them among the nations and disperse them through the lands" (v. 23). Although Ezekiel takes some creative liberties in his historiography,[3] this text might suggest the prophet knew a prior tradition that Yahweh threatened to exile Israel in the wilderness period. Thus, we find in this passage a warrant to examine Ezekiel's relationship to the pentateuchal texts that speak of exile. The following investigation will consider whether Ezekiel knows and draws from any of these texts, and if so, which one(s).

Before treating the affinities of Ezekiel's language to that of Deuteronomy, here we will briefly note that Ezekiel does draw from the one passage in the Holiness Code that speaks of exile. In the punishments of Leviticus 26, Yahweh threatens to remove Israel from the land if they fail to keep his commandments. After an extended description of destruction, the threat turns to exile in v. 33: "I will scatter you among the nations and draw the sword after you" (ואתכם אזרה בגוים והריקתי אחריכם חרב). The following vv. 34-39 provide a picture of the state of exile for the land and its inhabitants.[4]

---

2. On the gathering formula, see, e.g., Geo Widengren, "Yahweh's Gathering of the Dispersed," in *In the Shelter of Elyon: Essays on Ancient Palestinian Life and Literature in Honor of G. W. Ahlström*, ed. W. Boyd Barrick and John R. Spencer, JSOTSup 31 (Sheffield: JSOT, 1984), 227–45; Johan Lust, "'Gathering and Return' in Jeremiah and Ezekiel," in *Le Livre de Jérémie*, ed. P. -M. Bogaert, BETL 54 (Leuven: Peeters, 1997), 120–1.

3. See the discussion in the previous chapter; Block, *Ezekiel*, 1:613–15.

4. For example, while the people are in the land of their enemies (בארץ איביכם), the land will have rest and enjoy the Sabbaths that were denied it (vv. 34-35). For those in exile the text speaks of utter destruction (vv. 36-39), e.g., "you will perish among the nations (בגוים) and the land of your enemies will consume you" (v. 38).

As Lyons has shown, Ezekiel clearly cites this single reference to scattering in the Holiness Code.⁵ In three separate instances the prophet cites the language of Lev. 26:33, which threatens exile with two phrases: ואתכם אזרה בגוים ("scatter you among the nations") and והריקתי אחריכם חרב ("draw the sword after you").

Lev. 26:33	ואתכם אזרה בגוים	**I will scatter** you among the nations,
	והריקתי אחריכם חרב	and **I will draw the sword after you**.
Ezek. 5:2	והשלשית תזרה לרוח	A third part **you shall scatter** to the wind,
	וחרב אריק אחריהם	and **I will draw the sword after them**.
Ezek. 5:12	והשלישית לכל־רוח אזרה	A third part **I will scatter** to all the winds
	וחרב אריק אחריהם	and **I will draw the sword after them**.
Ezek. 12:14	אזרה לכל־רוח	**I will scatter** (them) toward every wind,
	וחרב אריק אחריהם	and **I will draw the sword after them**.

The signs of literary dependence in this case are unmistakable due to the verbal and syntactic correspondence between these texts. Although Ezekiel does not use the full phrase אזרה בגוים, the verb זרה and the distinctive phrase חרב הריק אחריהם occur in parallel in both Lev. 26:33 and the three instances in Ezekiel. Furthermore, the criterion of recurrence is especially significant here. In addition to Ezekiel's widespread use of the Holiness Code (especially Lev. 26), Lev. 26:33 in particular—which also mentions the desolation of the land and its cities—is one of the three most frequently cited verses from the Holiness Code in Ezekiel.⁶ Similar language of drawing the sword occurs in threats against the prince of Tyre and Egypt in Ezek. 28:7 (והריקו חרבותם) and 30:11 (על־מצרים) as well.⁷

Scattering Language in Ezekiel and Deuteronomy

Ezekiel's Scattering Language

Though appealing to the Holiness Code as a basis for Ezekiel's language for exile explains these three unambiguous allusions to Lev. 26:33, in most cases Ezekiel uses a fixed formula for Yahweh's deportation of

---

5. Lyons, *From Law to Prophecy*, 118, 183.
6. Ibid., 78.
7. In ch. 21 Ezekiel makes special use of the sword as an agent of Yahweh's judgment. There, however, the three occurrences of yielding the sword in vv. 8-10[3-5] use different wording (הוצאתי חרבי מתערה) and, as I argued in Chapter 4 of this study, instead derive from Deut. 32.

Israel characterized by two parallel clauses: [אתם] בגוים וזרה [אתם] הפיץ בארצות, "to scatter [them] among the nations and disperse [them] among the lands."

Ezek. 12:15	בהפיצי אותם בגוים וזריתי אותם בארצות
Ezek. 20:23	להפיץ אתם בגוים ולזרות אותם בארצות
Ezek. 22:15	והפיצותי אותך בגוים וזריתיך בארצות
Ezek. 29:12	והפצתי את־מצרים בגוים וזריתים בארצות
Ezek. 30:23	והפצתי את־מצרים בגוים וזריתים בארצות
Ezek. 30:26	והפצתי את־מצרים בגוים וזריתים בארצות
Ezek. 36:19	ואפיץ אתם בגוים ויזרו בארצות

We may add a similar phrase that appears to be a modification of the formula. In Ezek. 11:16, Yahweh states, "I removed them far off among the nations and scattered them among the lands" (הרחקתים בגוים וכי הפיצותים בארצות). In this instance, the verb הרחיק appears in the first position and הפיץ drops to the second parallel line. The variation derives from the influence of the immediately preceding occurrence of the verbal root רחק in v. 15, where the inhabitants of Jerusalem declare, "Go far from Yahweh" (רחקו מעל יהוה). This modification is surely an intentional variant of the more typical scattering formula, since, as I will describe in the next chapter, we find the same technique in the gathering formula. In this literary modification, a contextually determined variant takes the place of the first verb, which then moves into the second position. Other references to scattering include Ezek. 6:8 (בגוים בהזרותיכם בארצות) and the numerous restoration passages where the Israelites are described as being gathered from the lands "where they have been scattered" (11:17; 20:34, 41; 28:25; 29:13).

Similarities with Deuteronomy

Before comparing the language of Deuteronomy and Ezekiel in more detail, we must first briefly survey the theme of exile in Deuteronomy. The threat of deportation is more prominent in Deuteronomy than in the Holiness Code, occurring in Deut. 4:27-28; 28:36-37, 41, 64; 29:24-27[25-28] (cf. 30:1, 18).[8] In ch. 4, Moses forbids all kinds of idolatry (vv. 15-24) and predicts that the failure to keep the prohibition will result

---

8. On the Deuteronomic conception of exile, see Dalit Rom-Shiloni, "Deuteronomic Concepts of Exile Interpreted in Jeremiah and Ezekiel," in *Birkat Shalom: Studies in the Bible, Ancient Near Eastern Literature, and Postbiblical Judaism Presented to Shalom M. Paul on the Occasion of His Seventieth Birthday*, ed. Chaim Cohen et al. (Winona Lake, IN: Eisenbrauns, 2008), 1:103–9.

in exile from the land (vv. 25-28): "you will soon utterly perish from the land that you are going over the Jordan to possess. You will not live long in it" (אבד תאבדון מהר מעל הארץ אשר אתם עברים את־הירדן שמה לרשתה לא־תאריכן ימים עליה, v. 26). The covenant curses of ch. 28 climax with the threat of deportation as the consequence of covenant unfaithfulness: "Yahweh will bring you and your king whom you set over you to a nation that neither you nor your fathers have known" (יולך יהוה אתך ואת־מלכך אשר תקים עליך אל־גוי אשר לא־ידעת אתה ואבתיך, v. 36). Deuteronomy 29:27[28] states that when the curse comes to pass people will say, "Yahweh uprooted them from their land in anger and fury and great wrath, and cast them into another land" (ויתשם יהוה מעל אדמתם באף ובחמה ובקצף גדול וישלכם אל־ארץ אחרת).

Among these varied statements about deportation, the motif of scattering occurs with the verb הפיץ in two of the three chapters that threaten exile. Deuteronomy 4:27 and 28:64 warn that "Yahweh will scatter you among [all] the peoples" (והפיצך יהוה בכל־העמים and והפיץ יהוה אתכם בעמים, respectively). Deuteronomy 30:3, which promises restoration, also uses the verb הפיץ to describe the places where Yahweh has sent his people. Thus, scattering is an important exile motif for Deuteronomy, occurring in all the passages that mention exile except ch. 29. Since Deuteronomy consistently uses the verb הפיץ, in contrast to Lev. 26:33's זרה, we may conclude that the use of הפיץ for exile is distinctively Deuteronomic among the pentateuchal sources.

In Ezekiel's formula הפיץ [אתם] בגוים וזרה [אתם] בארצות, the verb זרה always occurs in combination with הפיץ, the term that is characteristic of the Deuteronomic exile passages and never occurs in the Holiness Code. Minimally, we can label Ezekiel's use of הפיץ for exile as *indirect usage* of a distinctly Deuteronomic word.[9] At first glance, literary dependence on a Deuteronomic text would appear unlikely, because there is no syntactic correspondence, that is, no shared phrases, only a shared word. Ezekiel never uses the full Deuteronomic phrase הפיץ [אתם] בעמים ("scatter [them] among the peoples") for his pronouncement of exile but instead uses הפיץ בגוים ("scatter among *the nations*") coupled with זרה בארצות ("disperse among the lands"). However, there are reasons to conclude that Ezekiel was in fact drawing from Deuteronomy.

---

9. Others who recognize Ezekiel's use of a distinctively Deuteronomic term include Schwartz, "Ezekiel, P, and the Other Pentateuchal Sources," and Levitt Kohn, "With a Mighty Hand," 163 n. 32.

I will argue that Ezekiel's formula הפיץ בגוים וזרה בארצות is best explained as a combination of Deuteronomy's הפיץ [אתכם] בעמים (Deut. 4:27; 28:64) and the Holiness Code's זרה [אתכם] בגוים (Lev. 26:33) and that Ezekiel knows at least one of Deuteronomy's exile passages.[10] In what follows, I offer several lines of argumentation. Preliminarily, this hypothesis accords with Ezekiel's fusion of Priestly and Deuteronomic language and traditions elsewhere. Second, the way the prophet combines these phrases is consistent with his techniques of literary appropriation as outlined by Lyons in his study of Ezekiel's use of the Holiness Code. Third, Ezekiel's awareness of another distinctive idea found in Deuteronomy's exile passages supports the idea that he knows one of these texts. Finally, internal evidence strongly indicates Ezekiel's knowledge of one passage in particular.

The Fusion of Traditions in Ezekiel

To begin, Levitt Kohn has catalogued Ezekiel's use of language from Priestly and Deuteronomic traditions and found examples where he juxtaposes Priestly and Deuteronomic terms and concepts in the same passage.[11] Her premier example is the prophet's account of Israel's history in ch. 20, where he intersperses Priestly and Deuteronomic language throughout.[12] Other examples include his use of Leviticus 26 and Deuteronomy 32 for the agents of death in Ezek. 5:16-17[13] and the combination of the Priestly duties presented in Lev. 10:10-11 and Deut. 17:8, 9; 21:5 in Ezek. 44:23-25.

Ezekiel's Technique of Literary Appropriation

Second, we find a precedent for the specific way Ezekiel combines the terms. The argument here builds upon Lyon's study of Ezekiel's use of the Holiness Code. Lyons has shown convincingly that Ezekiel uses locutions from literary traditions and indeed creatively reformulates them by literary modification. When using the language of the Holiness Code, Ezekiel has a penchant for changing the exact form of expressions found

---

10. Cf. Rom-Shiloni, "Ezekiel and Jeremiah," 221; Hahn and Bergsma, "What Laws?" 206 n. 20; Burrows, *Literary Relations*, 21: "Perhaps Ez combines Dt and Lv."

11. Levitt Kohn, *New Heart*, 96–104.

12. Ibid., 98–103; idem, "With a Mighty Hand," 159–68; see further Chapter 5 of this study.

13. See Chapter 4 of this study.

in his source text and alters its language "in regular ways that allow us to speak of *techniques* of modification."[14] Lyons offers a typology of modifications based on an analysis of these techniques. In some cases, the result is a two-line parallel phrase characteristic of Ezekiel's style. Here we will deal with the two such techniques relevant to the present discussion.

Lyons interprets Ezekiel's scattering formula as an example of splitting a locution and recombining its parts into parallel lines, a technique of literary appropriation found widely in Ezekiel and, according to Benjamin Sommer, in Isaiah 40–66.[15] Lyons claims: "when Ezekiel uses H's locution ואתכם אזרה בגוים ('And you I will scatter among the nations,' Lev 26:33), he splits the clause and redistributes the elements to create a new two-line parallel expression והפיצותי אותך בגוים וזריתיך בארצות ('I will disperse you among the nations and scatter you among the lands')."[16] Thus, Lyons sees Lev. 26:33 as the sole influence on Ezekiel's scattering formula, and the introduction of הפיץ is simply the product of Ezekiel's creative recombination. He does not consider the possibility that Ezekiel might have combined H's ואתכם אזרה בגוים with another locution.

The scattering formula more likely belongs to another of Lyons' categories of literary appropriation: combination and conflation.[17] Lyons has shown the ubiquity of Ezekiel's combination of locutions, which sometimes come from the same source text but other times come from different sources. An example of the latter may be the combination and conflation of "high hill and leafy tree" language from Deut. 12:2 and Hos. 4:13 into parallel lines in Ezek. 6:13, described earlier in Chapter 3 of this study. In the technique of combination and conflation, the author does not split and reorder one clause but rather combines and conflates two separate clauses.

The proposed combination finds support in a virtually identical parallel elsewhere in Ezekiel. In Ezek. 25:7, we find a variation of Lev. 26:33 in which Lyons argues Ezekiel combines two locutions from elsewhere in Leviticus 26, vv. 22 and 38.[18] The pattern of the modification becomes apparent when the words are labeled.

---

14. Lyons, *From Law to Prophecy*, 88 (author's italics).
15. Thus ibid., 92–3; Sommer, *A Prophet Reads Scripture*, 68–9.
16. Lyons, *From Law to Prophecy*, 92.
17. Ibid., 95–7.
18. Lyons lists this case among examples of splitting and recombining (ibid., 92).

Lev. 26:22	והכריתה את־בהמתכם	A1 B1
	"I will cut off your livestock"	
Lev. 26:38	ואבדתם בגוים	A2 B2
	"I will destroy them among the nations"	
Ezek. 25:7	והכרתיך מן־העמים	A1 (B2)
	והאבדתיך מן־הארצות	A2 X
	"I will cut you off from the peoples, and make you perish from the lands"	

Like the scattering formula, Ezek. 25:7 exhibits parallel prepositional phrases with "peoples/lands/nations" in adjacent lines. The wording results from the combination and conflation of phrases, dropping one element from the sources and introducing a new element (designated "X" above).[19]

Ezekiel's use of Deuteronomy's הפיץ [אתכם] בעמים and the Holiness Code's זרה [אתכם] בגוים exhibits the same pattern of recombination.

Deut. 4:27; 28:64	והפיץ יהוה אתכם בעמים	A1 B1
Lev. 26:33	ואתכם אזרה בגוים	A2 B2
Ezekiel's Formula	והפיץ [אתכם] בגוים	A1 B2
	וזרה [אתכם] בארצות	A2 X

Like the first category mentioned, splitting and recombination, "Ezekiel does not simply juxtapose independent clauses from [his sources], but merges them together to create a new statement."[20] As in Ezek. 25:7,

---

19. Similarly, in Ezek. 44:20 the prophet draws upon the Priestly regulations found in Lev. 21 and combines elements from different parts of the chapter (ibid., 176).

Lev. 21:5	ופאת זקנם לא יגלחו	They shall not shave the edges of their beards.
Lev. 21:10	ראשו לא יפרע	He shall not let the hair of his head hang loose.
Ezek. 44:20	וראשם לא יגלחו ופרע לא ישלחו	They shall not shave their heads, and they shall not grow out loosely hanging hair.

The similarity becomes more apparent if the word order is adjusted:

Lev. 21:5	לא יגלחו פאת זקן	A1 B1
Lev. 21:10	לא יפרע ראש	A2 B2
Ezek. 44:20	לא יגלחו ראש ולא ישלחו פרע	A1 B2 A2 X

20. Ibid., 96.

the prophet combines and conflates two phrases, dropping one element (בעמים) and introducing another (בארצות). And, again, as in 25:7, the new element, בארצות, occurs here in the final position. Although the new element may simply be the result of Ezekiel's own creation, it could stem from the context of Lev. 26:36, 39, where ארצות describes the location of Israel's exile (בארצת איביכם, "in the lands of your enemies").

If this account of the scattering formula's literary background is correct, Ezekiel did not simply adopt the Deuteronomic keyword הפיץ, but appropriated and modified the entire Deuteronomic phrase הפיץ [אתכם] בעמים. The absence of Deuteronomy's בעמים in Ezekiel's formula is a result of the literary modification, which sets aside one element of its source. As Lyons observes, "literary borrowing involves a process of selection in which some words from the source text are not used."[21] In summary, Ezekiel's combination of Deuteronomy's הפיץ [אתכם] בעמים and the Holiness Code's זרה [אתכם] בגוים accords with his techniques of literary modification, and Ezek. 25:7 in particular provides an impressive parallel for the exact modification found in the scattering formula.

Ezekiel's Awareness of the Deuteronomic Exile Passages?

But does the prophet simply adopt a Deuteronomic phrase that is well known in contemporary religious parlance (*indirect usage*), or does he draw from a particular text (*literary borrowing* or *reference*)? This question is particularly significant given some scholars' tendency to regard the scattering passages in Deuteronomy as exilic additions (to which we will return below). First, based on the criterion of recurrence or contextual awareness, I will argue that Ezekiel knows (at least) one of the exile passages in Deuteronomy. His allusion to another distinctive idea in Deuteronomy's exile passages increases the probability he is drawing from one of these texts. Specifically, as noted in Chapter 3 of this study, Deuteronomy identifies one particular image of idolatry with Israel's state after the punishment of deportation: in exile, the Israelites will worship עץ ואבן, "wood and stone" (Deut. 4:25-28; 28:36, 64).

As I argued in Chapter 3 of this study, in their present situation of exile, Ezekiel and the elders discuss the idea of worshiping idols and he alludes to Deuteronomy's conception of worshiping עץ ואבן in exile. Can we conclude Ezekiel knows one of these Deuteronomic texts, either Deuteronomy 4 or 28? Significantly, Ezekiel is the one who mentions עץ ואבן to describe the alleged thought of the elders in exile rather than the elders themselves. The prophet appears to be familiar with

---

21. Ibid., 90.

Deuteronomy's association of worshiping the local gods in exile and interprets the elders' desire to worship idols in exile as the fulfillment of Deuteronomy's prediction. Therefore, Ezekiel's apparent allusion to one of Deuteronomy's distinctive ideas about exile increases the likelihood that he did in fact know one of Deuteronomy's exile passages.

Ezekiel's Knowledge of an Exile Tradition Reflected in Ezekiel 20:23?

As noted at the beginning of this chapter, internal evidence in the book of Ezekiel suggests the prophet may have known an earlier tradition. He does not simply speak of the Babylonian exile in terms similar to those of the Holiness Code and Deuteronomy, but in one instance actually refers explicitly to an earlier threat from Yahweh to expel his people from the land. According to Ezekiel, long ago in the wilderness period before entering the promised land, Yahweh "raised his hand to scatter them among the nations and disperse them among the countries" (Ezek. 20:23). Unless this statement is a case of historical revisionism—to which we will return below—it suggests Ezekiel knows and is influenced by a tradition that Yahweh swore long ago to expel Israel from the land.

* * *

Excursus: Does Ezekiel 20:23 Depict an Oath?

Before we investigate whether or not Ezek. 20:23 refers to one of the pentateuchal traditions, we must first address claims that the phrase "to lift one's hand" does not signify an oath, and therefore Ezek. 20:23 does not express a threat by Yahweh in the wilderness to exile Israel. Two scholars have argued against the majority opinion, which identifies נשא יד as an oath formula and therefore a synonym of נשבע. Johan Lust proposed that the phrase describes an active intervention on the part of Yahweh,[22] a theory that he first advanced in relation to Ezekiel 20.[23] In his survey of the data, Lust observes first that in some cases נשא יד clearly does not refer to an oath (e.g., Ps. 10:12; Isa. 49:22), and second that no other Semitic language attests the phrase as an oath formula. He concludes that those occurrences traditionally interpreted as oaths in the Bible need not refer to oaths at all. Instead, since יד is a common metaphor for power, when Yahweh lifts his hand to act, he is actively intervening, normally on behalf of his people.

---

22. Johan Lust, "For I Lift Up My Hand to Heaven and Swear: Deut 32:40," in *Studies in Deuteronomy: In Honour of C. J. Labuschagne on the Occasion of His 65th Birthday*, ed. Florentino García Martínez et al., VTSup 53 (Leiden: Brill, 1994), 155–64.

23. Lust, "Ez., XX, 4-26: une parodie," 488–527, esp. 517–24.

This interpretation of נשא יד led Lust to the idiosyncratic conclusion that in Ezek. 20:23 Yahweh did not make a threat, but in fact scattered Israel during the wilderness period.[24] According to Lust, "il en ressort...que Jahvé ne jura pas dans le désert, de disperser son peuple, mais plutôt qu'il le dispersa de fait à partir du desert, avant qu'il ne pût vraiment entrer dans la terre promise."[25] In his view, Ezekiel's theological interpretation of history includes the claim that Israel's residence in Canaan was simply an extension of their sojourn in the wilderness, and therefore the entry into the promised land was still unrealized in his day.[26] Lust concluded further that Ezekiel opposed the idea central to Deuteronomy, that Israel's imminent entry into Canaan constituted the possession of the land promised to their ancestors (Deut. 1:8 et passim). In his words:

> il s'ensuit également qu'Ézechiel réinterprète l'histoire d'Israël, surtout telle qu'elle est conçue par le Deutéronome, livre qui ne se lasse pas de désigner la première entrée en Palestine comme la vraie prise en possession de la terre promise... Nous en pouvons déduire que le prophète tint à se séparer de la tradition deutéronomique.[27]

However, Lust's proposal stands or falls on his interpretation of נשא יד.[28]

---

24. Ibid., 524; asserted also in idem, "Gathering and Return," 137; idem, "Ezekiel Salutes Isaiah: Ezekiel 20,32-44," in *Studies in the Book of Isaiah: Festschrift W. A. M. Beuken*, ed. J. Van Ruiten and M. Vervenne, BETL 132 (Leuven: Leuven University Press, 1997), 380.

25. Lust, "Ez., XX, 4-26: une parodie," 524: "It emerges...that Yahweh did not swear in the desert to scatter his people, but rather he actually scattered them from the desert before they could really enter the promised land."

26. Ibid., 517, 525–6.

27. Ibid., 524: "It also follows that Ezekiel reinterprets the history of Israel, especially as it is conceived by Deuteronomy, a book that does not grow tired of referring to the first entrance into Palestine as the true taking in possession of the promised land... We can deduct that the prophet was anxious to part from the deuteronomic tradition."

28. Even if Lust were correct that נשא יד signifies an act of power rather than an oath, it does not necessarily follow that Ezek. 20:23 denotes an actual scattering of the people in the wilderness and not a future event. Lust appears to reason that if Yahweh did not *swear* to scatter his people in 20:23, he must have actually done so back in the wilderness period. He assumes that elsewhere the formula always refers to a past event, contending that הארץ אשר נשאתי את־ידי לתת (or variant) is always used for Yahweh's act of giving the land to the ancestors, never their descendants. However, in Num. 14:30 the object is the wilderness generation, as is often the case with נשבע as well, e.g., Exod. 13:5; Deut. 6:10; 7:13; 26:3; 28:11; and Deut. 1:8; and 11:9, which mention both the ancestors and their descendants together as beneficiaries of Yahweh's land gift.

Despite the lack of evidence in other Semitic languages, the usage of the Hebrew Bible demands multiple meanings of נשא יד, one of them being an oath gesture. First, in Deut. 32:40, the lifted hand appears with the "as I live" oath formula. Although Lust disconnected נשא יד from חי אנכי לעלם by bifurcating the verse, his reconstruction seems contrived.[29] Second, the hand is associated with oaths elsewhere, even if the terms נשא and יד are not used. For example, in Isa. 62:8 Yahweh swears "by his right hand" (בימינו).[30] David Seely has drawn attention to Gen. 14:22 where Abraham's lifted (הרים) hand appears to signify an oath.[31] Third, נשא יד and נשבע appear to have been synonymous and interchangeable for both the biblical writers and later scribes. The use of נשא יד to speak of the land gift in Exod. 6:8 and Num. 14:30 has many nearly verbatim parallels using נשבע, especially in the Deuteronomic literature, but also in Num. 32:11. Later tradents also appear to have understood the two expressions as synonyms, as indicated by a Dead Sea Scroll manuscript that replaces נשא יד with נשבע in Exod. 6:8 (4Q Gen–Exod[a]). Lastly, as I will argue below, the mention of Yahweh lifting his hand להם (Ezek. 20:5, 6, 16, 23) cannot be understood as Yahweh taking action *for them*, but must mean lifting his hand *to them*. In conclusion, נשא יד is best interpreted as an oath gesture. Blane Conklin describes it as an authenticating element of an oath.[32] Consequently, Ezek. 20:23 does not suggest that Yahweh previously sent Israel into exile in the wilderness, but only that he threatened to do so. The prophet does not depart from the pervasive Deuteronomic idea that Israel's residence in Canaan was the fulfillment of the land promised to their ancestors.

C. A. Strine has argued that נשא יד does not signify an oath, but should be linked with an Akkadian formula for royal property transfers—the *našû-nadānu* ("take-give") formula.[33] In the *našû-nadānu* formula, "the monarch 'lifts up' or 'takes away' [*našû*] the house and land of A and 'gives' [*nadānu*] it to B, that is, he transfers

---

29. For a critique of Lust's interpretation of Deut. 32:40, see Eugene P. McGarry, "The Ambidextrous Angel (Daniel 12:7 and Deuteronomy 32:40): Inner-Biblical Exegesis and Textual Criticism in Counterpoint," *JBL* 124 (2005): 220–3. C. A. Strine supports Lust's bifurcation of the verse, but unnecessarily expects that each occurrence of יד must have the same meaning throughout Deut. 32, namely, a metaphor for power (*Sworn Enemies: The Divine Oath, the Book of Ezekiel, and the Polemics of Exile*, BZAW 436 [Berlin: de Gruyter, 2013], 75–81).

30. In Ezek. 17:18 "to give the hand" may signify an oath gesture. For other occurrences of נתן יד, see Block, *Ezekiel*, 1:535 n. 76.

31. See David Rolph Seely, "The Raised Hand of God as an Oath Gesture," in *Fortunate the Eyes That See: Essays in Honor of David Noel Freedman in Celebration of His Seventieth Birthday*, ed. Astrid B. Beck (Grand Rapids: Eerdmans, 1995), 411. Although Gen. 14:22 and Dan. 12:7 use רום instead of נשא, the two verbs clearly express the same idea (contra Strine, who suggests that רום יד and נשא יד are not directly related [*Sworn Enemies*, 9, cf. 81–2]).

32. Blane Conklin, *Oath Formulas in Biblical Hebrew*, Linguistic Studies in Ancient West Semitic 5 (Winona Lake, IN: Eisenbrauns, 2011), 14–17.

33. Strine, *Sworn Enemies*, 72–97.

property from one to the other."³⁴ Although scholars have generally identified לקח-נתן as the biblical equivalent of the *našû-nadānu* formula (see, e.g., Gen. 48:21; 2 Sam. 12:11; 1 Kgs 11:35),³⁵ Strine argues instead that נשא יד provides the closest parallel.³⁶ In light of the five times in the Hebrew Bible when נשא יד refers to Yahweh lifting his hand *to give Israel the land* (Exod. 6:8; Num. 14:30; Ezek. 20:28, 42; 47:14; Neh. 9:15), he concludes that Ezekiel uses the idiom as an adaptation of the *našû-nadānu* formula to describe Yahweh as "the royal authority who ultimately decides who will control the land."³⁷

However, the differences between the *našû-nadānu* and נשא יד formulae far outweigh the similarities. First, in the נשא יד formula, Yahweh does not lift (i.e., take) the land from another party and give it to Israel, but rather lifts his hand. In other words, the object of נשא is Yahweh's יד, unlike the *našû-nadānu* formula, in which the objects of *našû* and *nadānu* are always the items being transferred (land, property, etc.). Strine attempts to explain the discrepancy by proposing an adaptation of the Akkadian formula: whereas in the *našû-nadānu* formula "hand" is used to refer to the new party's possession of the property—it cannot be taken from his or her hand (*ištu qâti*)³⁸—in the נשא יד formula the hand is Yahweh's, the one who transfers the property. Strine proposes that the adaptation reflects the theological claim that the land ultimately belongs to Yahweh: "YHWH retains possession of the land even while transferring the right to dwell in it to one group or another."³⁹ But this is a significant discrepancy that diminishes the similarity between נשא יד and the *našû-nadānu* land-transfer formula and therefore undermines a connection between them.

Second, a close connection between נשא יד and the Akkadian formula would imply that נשא always refers to the taking of the land, as its cognate *našû* does. However, in Ezekiel נשא יד is used both for Yahweh's promise to give the land and his threat to revoke it (20:23). This usage compels Strine to concede that the נשא יד formula is tied to the land theme only loosely: it is used in Ezekiel 20 not solely to refer to Yahweh giving the land, but "to depict the series of decisions Yhwh made about who will dwell in the land."⁴⁰ This further diminishes the similarity between the two formulae.

Moreover, some instances of נשא יד have nothing to do with land and therefore do not fit the land-transfer interpretation. The possession of the land is not in view in 20:5b, where Yahweh lifts his hand, "saying, I am Yahweh your God." Outside

---

34. C. J. Labuschagne, "The *Našû-Nadānu* Formula and Its Biblical Equivalent," in *Travels in the World of the Old Testament: Studies Presented to Professor M. A. Beek on the Occasion of His 65th Birthday*, ed. G. Heerma van Voss et al., SSN 16 (Assen: Van Gorcum, 1974), 177.

35. Labuschagne, "The *Našû-Nadānu* Formula," 176–80; so also Jonas C. Greenfield, "*Našû-Nadānu* and Its Congeners," in *Essays on the Ancient Near East in Memory of Jacob Joel Finkelstein*, ed. Maria de Jong Ellis, MCAAS 19 (Hamden, CT: Archon, 1977), 87–91.

36. Strine, *Sworn Enemies*, 93–7.
37. Ibid., 123.
38. Ibid., 94–5.
39. Ibid., 95.
40. Ibid., 119.

of ch. 20, Ezek. 36:7 and 44:12 concern Yahweh's punishment of bearing shame or guilt. Although these two occurrences lead Strine to postulate two meanings of נשא יד ("two 'lifted hand' formulae"),[41] the interpretation of נשא יד as an oath accounts for all its occurrences in Ezekiel without positing a separate "'lifted hand' punishment formula."[42]

Third, this theory does not fit Ezek. 20:15, where Yahweh lifts his hand "*not* to bring them into the land." If the lifting of the hand denotes Yahweh's act of transferring possession of the land, how could Yahweh be said to lift his hand *not* to complete a land transfer?[43] In other words, why would Yahweh lift his hand in an instance where he has decided *not* to give Israel the land? The land-transfer interpretation of נשא יד would require the phrase "Yahweh *did not lift his hand* to bring them into the land" rather than "Yahweh lifted his hand not to bring them into the land." Significantly, then, this verse cannot be explained by the land-transfer interpretation. Neither does Lust's active-intervention theory fit this occurrence, since Yahweh lifts his hand *not* to act. It makes sense only as an oath.

Lastly, Strine never addresses the meaning of להם in the נשא יד formula in Ezekiel 20. Both the active-intervention and land-transfer interpretations would require that להם be understood as "for them": Yahweh lifts his hand to act *for them* (i.e., for their benefit). This understanding of להם could make sense in v. 6, but it does not in the other occurrences. For example, v. 15 cannot be understood as Yahweh acting *for* Israel when he "lifts his hand להם not to bring them into the land." Similarly, the scattering of Israel in v. 23 is not Yahweh acting *for* them. In v. 5b also, Yahweh's revelation of his name is not easily understood as taking action for Israel. In each of these cases, Yahweh more naturally seems to be lifting his hand *to them*, which coincides with the interpretation of נשא יד as an oath.

* * *

Ezekiel 20:23 and the Pentateuchal Traditions

Having argued for the presence of an oath in Ezek. 20:23, we may now return to the possibility that this statement in Ezekiel's account of Israel's history refers to a threat of exile that might be found in one of the pentateuchal traditions. The idea that Yahweh took an oath in the wilderness to scatter Israel is stated explicitly in the Hebrew Bible only here and in Ps. 106:26-27.[44] The two passages share virtually identical wording. However, instead of being an independent witness to a tradition that Yahweh swore

---

41. Ibid., 116–27 (quotation from p. 129).

42. Ibid., 126.

43. Strine claims that v. 15 denotes "the transfer of the land from the first, rebellious exodus generation to their children" (ibid., 119). However, it is difficult to see any land transfer in this verse, since Yahweh does *not* lift his hand.

44. On the basis of the allusion to Ezek. 20:23, it is likely that the second occurrence of להפיל in Ps. 106:26-27 should be read as להפיץ, which was influenced from the previous line (Fishbane, *Biblical Interpretation*, 471).

to scatter Israel in the wilderness, this postexilic psalm is influenced by Ezekiel's account of history, as evidenced by other distinctive parallels between the two chapters.[45]

Thus, scholars often assert that Yahweh's oath to scatter Israel in the wilderness finds no parallel in biblical tradition that could serve as a basis for Ezekiel's statement. Greenberg, for example, stated that the extant pentateuchal texts are silent about such an oath.[46] To be sure, it is possible this element of ch. 20 is simply the product of Ezekiel's theological (re)interpretation of Israel's history and not a reference to anything we might find in the biblical traditions. Therefore, the lack of an oath in the pentateuchal literature should be not considered a problem to be solved. On the other hand, as I argued in the previous chapter, despite the prophet's tendency to shape history to serve his rhetorical purposes, he appears to have a conceptual basis for many elements of his history that scholars have assumed were simply inventive. The idea that Yahweh swore to scatter Israel in the wilderness may be based on some tradition, even if the prophet adjusts the details.

There actually is evidence of a precedent in the pentateuchal literature for an oath to scatter Israel. To begin, as demonstrated in Chapter 5 of this study, when related to the pentateuchal account of Israel's exodus, sojourn at Sinai, and wilderness wandering, the narrative flow and literary structure of Ezekiel 20 suggest that Yahweh's oath to scatter Israel in v. 23 is addressed to the second wilderness generation.[47] This does not fit the threat of exile in Lev. 26:33, whose narrative context locates it in the first wilderness generation. If this statement alludes to any pentateuchal threat of exile, the narrative flow of the chapter aligns it with the second-generation legal material, namely, Deuteronomy. This thesis is reinforced by Ezekiel's constant use of the Deuteronomic term הפיץ and, as I will argue below, the likelihood of an allusion to a specific passage of Deuteronomy and the similarity in Ezekiel's and Deuteronomy's theology of exile.

To which text(s) in Deuteronomy might Ezekiel be alluding in 20:23? Hahn and Bergsma hypothesized that the oath to scatter Israel refers to Yahweh's oath in Deut. 32:40-41:[48]

---

45. George W. Coats, *Rebellion in the Wilderness: The Murmuring Motif in the Wilderness Traditions of the Old Testament* (Nashville: Abingdon, 1968), 224–31.
46. Greenberg, *Ezekiel 1–20*, 368; also Kugler, "Cruel Theology of Ezekiel," 50.
47. Hahn and Bergsma, "What Laws?" 203–6.
48. Ibid., 205.

For I lift up my hand to heaven and swear, "As I live forever, if I sharpen my flashing sword and my hand takes hold on judgment, I will take vengeance on my adversaries and will repay those who hate me."

They argue that the three נשא יד oaths in Ezekiel 20 (vv. 6, 15, 23) correspond to the only three occurrences of נשא יד in the pentateuchal literature.[49] They suggest v. 6 recounts Yahweh's oath to bring the Israelites out of Egypt in Exod. 6:8,[50] and v. 15 alludes to Num. 14:30 when it asserts that Yahweh lifted his hand that he would not allow the first generation to enter the promised land. Since vv. 6 and 15 allude to passages that also contain נשא יד, v. 23 might be expected to allude to a נשא יד formula as well. For them, Deut. 32:40 is the obvious candidate, especially given the context of the second wilderness generation in Ezekiel's history.

However, for a couple reasons, it is unlikely Ezek. 20:23 refers to Deut. 32:40. First, exile is not present in Deut. 32:30, 36d, as Hahn and Bergsma contend, or anywhere else in Deuteronomy 32.[51] Furthermore, apart from the canonical sequence of chapters, there is no evidence for their assertion that Yahweh's oath to take vengeance in Deut. 32:40-41 involves enacting *all* the preceding threats of judgment in Deuteronomy 27–31, including exile.[52] Second, contra Hahn and Bergsma, the two נשא יד formulae in vv. 6 and 15 do not actually correspond well to the נשא יד formulae in Exod. 6:8 and Num. 14:30. There, the נשא יד formulae are used to describe Yahweh's oaths to give the land (see below), not, as Ezekiel describes it, his oaths to bring the Israelites out of Egypt (20:6) or to let the first generation die in the wilderness (20:15).

Exod. 6:8	I will bring you into the land *that I lifted my hand to give to Abraham, to Isaac, and to Jacob.*
Num. 14:30	Not one of you shall come into the land *that I lifted my hand to make you dwell in.*

In the latter instance, Numbers 14, Yahweh swears the first generation will not enter the land in vv. 21 and 28, but the passage uses חי־אני rather than נשא יד. If Ezekiel knows this biblical text, he alludes to the חי־אני oath, but replaces it with the "lifted hand" formula. In the former instance, Ezek.

---

49. Ibid., 204.
50. Cf. Johan Lust, "Exodus 6,2-8 and Ezekiel," in *Studies in the Book of Exodus*, ed. Marc Vervenne, BETL 126 (Leuven: Peeters, 1996), 209–24.
51. Hahn and Bergsma, "What Laws?" 205 n. 16.
52. Ibid., 205.

20:6, the prophet appears to allude to Yahweh's promise in Exod. 6:2-8 to bring the Israelites out of Egypt, but he uses the נשא יד oath formula to refer to a tradition that was not explicitly an oath as it appears in the pentateuchal traditions. Significantly, then, if Ezekiel described Yahweh's promise in Exod. 6:6-8 as an oath, one need not find an *explicit oath statement* in the pentateuchal literature to provide the basis for Ezekiel's mention of scattering in v. 23.

Instead, among the pentateuchal exile texts, Deut. 4:25-28 in particular uses *language that strongly implies an oath* and therefore provides a likely basis for the prophet's claim in Ezek. 20:23.[53] Ancient Israelites would have understood Deut. 4:25-28 as a covenant oath. Moses says to the Israelites:

> If (when) you act corruptly by making a carved image in the form of anything...today I call heaven and earth to testify against you, that you will soon utterly perish from the land...and Yahweh will scatter you among the peoples. (Deut. 4:25-28)

Though this passage lacks an explicit oath statement (נשבע, חי־יהוה, etc.), the mention of calling witnesses in the context of a covenant would have naturally implied an oath to Ezekiel and other ancient readers. The act of calling witnesses is a common feature of ancient Near Eastern treaty oaths, functioning to ensure the terms agreed upon would be respected and observed.[54]

The connection between an oath and calling witnesses is clear in Moses' third address, which displays marked treaty features.[55] There his call for

---

53. Suggested in passing by Levitt Kohn (*New Heart*, 100 n. 32). Hahn and Bergsma mention it as another possibility ("What Laws?" 205 n. 18).

54. Donald L. Magnetti, "The Function of the Oath in the Ancient Near Eastern International Treaty," *AJIL* 72 (1978): 815; Hayim Tadmor, "Treaty and Oath in the Ancient Near East: A Historian's Approach," in *Humanizing America's Iconic Book: Society of Biblical Literature Centennial Addresses 1980*, ed. Gene M. Tucker and Douglas A. Knight, SBLBSNA 6 (Chico, CA: Scholars Press, 1982), 136; JoAnn Scurlock, "Oaths, ancient Near East," in *The Encyclopedia of Ancient History*, ed. Roger S. Bagnall et al. (Oxford: Wiley-Blackwell, 2013), 9:4848; Conklin, *Oath Formulas*, 17–18. For examples, see, Joseph A. Fitzmyer, *The Aramaic Inscriptions of Sefire*, BibOr 19A, rev ed. (Rome: Pontifical Biblical Institute, 1995); Simo Parpola and Kazuko Watanabe, eds., *Neo-Assyrian Treaties and Loyalty Oaths*, SAA 2 (Helsinki: Helsinki University Press, 1988).

55. On the treaty features of Deut. 29–30, see, for example, Alexander Rofé, "The Covenant in the Land of Moab (Deuteronomy 28:69-30:20): Historico-Literary,

heaven and earth to witness against Israel (Deut. 30:19) culminates what was earlier described as Israel entering into (עבר ב) a covenant and an oath (הברית הזאת והאלה הזאת, Deut. 29:11, 13[12, 14]). Here in Deuteronomy 4 also, the call for witnesses is found in the context of enacting a covenant. Even if vv. 25-28 were a later supplement to the passage,[56] they clearly build upon the preceding reference to "the covenant of Yahweh your God that he made with [Israel]" (4:23).[57]

In the ancient Near East, an oath ratified a covenant agreement and made it binding. According to Yigael Ziegler, "the oath's power emanates from the fact that every oath contains a conditional curse, even if it is not explicitly delineated in the oath's formula."[58] When an oath to a treaty or covenant is taken, the speaker declares his intent to keep its terms with the full understanding that failure to do so will incur severe consequences.[59] What role did witnesses play? Usually the gods were called as witnesses; according to Donald Magnetti, an appeal to divine beings was the only effective means of guaranteeing observance of the treaty, since the gods

---

Comparative, and Formcritical Considerations," in *Das Deuteronomium: Entstehung, Gestalt und Botschaft*, ed. Norbert Lohfink, BETL 68 (Leuven: Leuven University Press, 1985), 317.

56. As I argue later in this chapter, the mention of exile is not a sufficient criterion to identify an addition from the period of the Babylonian exile. With respect to the relationship between Deut. 4:25-28 to its context, many scholars recognize compositional unity in Deut. 4:1-40, even if postulating an exilic date for the entirety. See, e.g., Lohfink, *Höre, Israel!*, 87–120; idem, "Auslegung deuteronomischer Texte IV," *BibLeb* 4 (1964): 250–3; Levenson, "Who Inserted the Book of the Torah?" 203–7, 215; Dennis J. McCarthy, *Treaty and Covenant: A Study in Form in the Ancient Oriental Documents and in the Old Testament*, 2nd rewritten ed., AnBib 21a (Rome: Pontifical Biblical Institute, 1978), 190–4; Braulik, *Die Mittel*; idem, "Literarkritische und archaeologische Stratigraphie: Zu S. Mittmanns Analyse von Deuteronomium 4, 1-40," *Bib* 59 (1978): 351–83; Mayes, "Deuteronomy 4," 25–31; Weinfeld, *Deuteronomy 1–11*, 221–3, cited in Sanders, *Provenance*, 350 n. 290; although cf. the studies of Knapp and Nielsen, who divide the chapter into compositional layers (Dietrich Knapp, *Deuteronomium 4: Literarische Analyse und theologische Interpretation* [Göttingen: Vandenhoeck & Ruprecht, 1987]; Eduard Nielsen, *Deuteronomium*, HAT 1/6 [Tübingen: J. C. B. Mohr, 1995], 54–68).

57. Cf. Lohfink, "Auslegung deuteronomischer Texte IV," 250–3; Levenson, "Who Inserted the Book of the Torah?" 203–4.

58. Yael Ziegler, *Promises to Keep: The Oath in Biblical Narrative*, VTSup 120 (Leiden: Brill, 2008), 4; cf. Scurlock, "Oaths, ancient Near East," 4849.

59. Ziegler, *Promises to Keep*, 3. Cf. George E. Mendenhall, "Covenant Forms in Israelite Tradition," *BA* 17 (1954): 52: "the oath…is a conditional self-cursing, an appeal to the gods to punish the promiser if he defaults."

were called to bear witness to the terms of the agreement and punish those who transgressed it.⁶⁰ In Deut. 4:25-28, Moses does not call on deities to guarantee the covenant between Yahweh and Israel, but rather heaven and earth, as in Deut. 30:19 and 31:28 (העידתי בכם היום את־השמים ואת־הארץ).⁶¹ Verse 26 calls on the heavens and the earth to bear witness to the covenant and testify against Israel if she violates it by worshiping idols. As witnesses, all creation will testify that Israel has violated the covenant and that Yahweh will scatter them among the peoples as he warned (Deut. 4:26-28).

Thus, although no explicit "swearing" appears in this passage, ancient Israelites would have understood Deut. 4:25-28 as an oath. Since the narrative flow of Ezekiel 20 appears to align the oath in v. 23 with Deuteronomy's context of the second wilderness generation, it seems likely the prophet found in Deut. 4:25-28 a basis for the idea of an oath by Yahweh that he would scatter Israel among the peoples if they transgressed the covenant. In Chapter 3 of this study, I pointed out several unique connections between Ezekiel and Deuteronomy 4. I argued there for the plausibility of a date for the passage before Ezekiel. Ezekiel's dependence on Deut. 4:25-28 for Yahweh's oath to scatter Israel adds one more reason to suspect that he was influenced by Deuteronomy 4.

Ezekiel's Theology of Exile

The hypothesis of Deuteronomic influence on Ezekiel's exile language is corroborated by the distinctive theology of exile that Deuteronomy and Ezekiel share. Unlike Lev. 26:33, which only threatens exile after persistent rebellion,⁶² the exile passages in Deuteronomy speak of future

---

60. Magnetti, "The Function of the Oath," 815.

61. Though appealing to "the heavens and the earth," and natural elements such as mountains, rivers, and the sea, was not uncommon in oaths of the ancient Near East (see M. Delcor, "Les attaches littéraires, l'origine et la signification de l'expression biblique 'prende à témoin le ciel et la terre,'" *VT* 16 [1966]: 8–25; Herbert B. Huffmon, "The Covenant Lawsuit in the Prophets," *JBL* 78 [1959]: 291–4; Julien Harvey, *Le plaidoyer prophétique contre Israël après la rupture de l'alliance* [Paris: Desclée de Brouwer, 1967], 86–90), its presence in the Hebrew Bible likely stems from practical concerns. Since Yahweh was a party in the covenant, he could not serve as a witness, and, whether monolatrous or monotheistic, Israelite religion would not tolerate invoking other deities (Block, *Deuteronomy*, 132 n. 27).

62. As Lyons explains, "the judgments in Lev. 26 are presented as God's instruments to induce repentance. The author accomplishes this by listing the punishments in order of increasing intensity, and by separating them into groups with refrains that clearly state their restorative purpose," e.g., "if despite this you will not obey" in vv.

disobedience and subsequent dispossession of the land as inevitable. In chs. 4 and 29–31, the future apostasy of the people is described as a foregone conclusion. This idea is most explicit in Deuteronomy 31:

> The Lord said to Moses, "Soon you will lie down with your ancestors. Then this people will begin to prostitute themselves to the foreign gods in their midst, the gods of the land into which they are going; they will forsake me, breaking my covenant that I have made with them. My anger will be kindled against them in that day. I will forsake them and hide my face from them; they will become easy prey, and many terrible troubles will come upon them… On that day I will surely hide my face on account of all the evil they have done by turning to other gods… For when I have brought them into the land flowing with milk and honey, which I promised on oath to their ancestors, and they have eaten their fill and grown fat, they will turn to other gods and serve them, despising me and breaking my covenant." (Deut. 31:16-20, NRSV)

Later in the same chapter, Moses expresses the same attitude directly to the people and makes a dire prediction:

> I know well how rebellious and stubborn you are. If you already have been so rebellious toward the Lord while I am still alive among you, how much more after my death!… For I know that after my death you will surely act corruptly, turning aside from the way that I have commanded you. In time to come trouble will befall you, because you will do what is evil in the sight of the Lord, provoking him to anger through the work of your hands. (Deut. 31:27, 29, NRSV)

While this passage does not mention exile explicitly, Deuteronomy 29 describes a coming turn to idolatry that will result in exile:

> The next generation, your children who rise up after you, as well as the foreigner who comes from a distant country, will see the devastation of that land and the afflictions with which the Lord has afflicted it…they and indeed all the nations will wonder, "Why has the Lord done thus to this land? What caused this great display of anger?" They will conclude, "It is because they abandoned the covenant of the Lord, the God of their ancestors, which he made with them when he brought them out of the land of Egypt. They turned and served other gods, worshiping them, gods whom they had not known

18, 21, 23, 27 (*From Law to Prophecy*, 117–18; cf. Jože Krašovec, *Reward, Punishment, and Forgiveness: The Thinking and Beliefs of Ancient Israel in the Light of Greek and Modern Views*, VTSup 78 [Leiden: Brill, 1999], 164–5). Exile is listed in the last group of judgments.

and whom he had not allotted to them; so the anger of the Lord was kindled against that land, bringing on it every curse written in this book. The Lord uprooted them from their land in anger, fury, and great wrath, and cast them into another land, as is now the case." (Deut. 29:21-27[22-28], NRSV)

According to Gordon McConville, the end of the book "takes for granted that the people will indeed fail to be the true people of the covenant and that this will result in the full force of the curses of ch. 28 falling on them."[63]

Deuteronomy 4:25-28, to which the prophet alludes in Ezek. 20:23, may reflect a similar outlook.[64] The interpretive crux is the initial particle כי in 4:25, which may be understood conditionally or temporally. If כי is translated as "when," as many commentators understand it,[65] then this passage also speaks of Israel's future disobedience and exile as inevitable: "when…you have grown old in the land and you act corruptly by making a carved image…" Thus, the theology of exile reflected in Deuteronomy describes an unavoidable loss of the land due to Israel's idolatry.[66]

Whatever the provenance of these passages,[67] Ezekiel concurs with their sentiment concerning Israel's prospects for obedience. Greenberg hypothesized that the Deuteronomic theology of exile alone may have been the impetus for Ezekiel's oath in 20:23, observing that "it is but a step from Moses' prediction of apostasy and exile [in Deuteronomy] to Ezekiel's portrayal of God's oath to exile Israel…already taken in the wilderness."[68] Although we have identified a more concrete basis for Ezekiel's oath in Deut. 4:25-28, like Deuteronomy, Ezekiel presents an exceedingly bleak picture of Israel's prospects for faithful devotion to Yahweh. Chapter 20 in particular describes Israel's history as one of perpetual rebellion, reaching

---

63. J. Gordon McConville, *Grace in the End: A Study in Deuteronomic Theology*, Studies in Old Testament Biblical Theology (Grand Rapids: Zondervan, 1993), 135.

64. Hahn and Bergsma, "What Laws?" 205 and n. 19.

65. E.g., Kenneth J. Turner, *The Death of Deaths in the Death of Israel: Deuteronomy's Theology of Exile* (Eugene, OR: Wipf & Stock, 2011), 113–16; J. Gary Millar, *Now Choose Life: Theology and Ethics in Deuteronomy*, NSBT (Downers Grove, IL: InterVarsity, 1998), 164.

66. Turner observes that in Deuteronomy "the inevitability of exile is grounded in the pessimistic portrayal of Israel's heart and nature" (*Death of Deaths*, 248).

67. See, for example, Rofé, "Covenant in the Land of Moab," 313–14, who regards Deut. 29:21-27[22-28] as an interpolation. Even if these verses are "secondary," it does not automatically follow that they derive from the period of the Babylonian exile.

68. Greenberg, *Ezekiel 1–20*, 385.

all the way back to their residence in Egypt (20:8). The apostasy of Israel's first generations after the exodus (20:13, 16, 21) and in more recent times (e.g., 8:1-18) suggests that in Ezekiel's mind the nation was predisposed to rebellion. Ezekiel casts Israel's history expressing a negative view of Israel's capacity to obey. In Jacqueline Lapsley's words: "Because no generation ever did choose to obey Yahweh, the people simply were predisposed to wickedness, and did not possess the capacity to choose otherwise."[69] In order to rectify the situation, Ezekiel, like Deuteronomy, spoke of the need for a divine intervention to change Israel's heart (Deut. 30:6; Ezek. 11:19-20; 36:26-27).[70]

The oath to scatter Israel in Ezek. 20:23 suggests that for Ezekiel exile was a certain consequence of Israel's idolatry. Yahweh did not simply threaten or warn that he would exile his people, but rather swore to do so.[71] By alluding to Deut. 4:25-28 and emphasizing Israel's religious failures from its earliest days, Ezekiel agrees not simply with Deuteronomy's view of Israel's religious aptitude, but also with Deuteronomy's view that the seeds of Israel's loss of the land were present from the very beginning.

The Origin of the Scattering Motif in Ezekiel

We may now address whether these literary links represent allusions to Deuteronomy by the prophet himself or by a later hand. The scattering motif is normally uncontested as an authentic part of the prophet's message, likely because—unlike the gathering motif—it occurs in judgment rather than restoration passages.[72] Nevertheless, it appears in passages whose literary unity is sometimes questioned on other grounds (12:15; 20:23; 22:15; 29:12; 30:23, 26; 36:19). I have treated the redaction criticism of

---

69. Jacqueline E. Lapsley, *Can These Bones Live? The Problem of the Moral Self in the Book of Ezekiel*, BZAW 301 (Berlin: de Gruyter, 2000), 93.

70. See Joyce, *Divine Initiative*, 120–1. See further Chapter 7 of this study.

71. E.g., Zimmerli, *Ezekiel*, 1:411; Greenberg, *Ezekiel 1–20*, 368: "Since the people proved to be confirmed rebels, God sealed their fate even before they entered the promised land; it was only a question of time till that fate was realized."

72. Only a couple scholars delete the scattering motif simply on the grounds that the motif itself is late: Johan Lust, "Ez., XX, 4-26: une parodie"; cf. idem, *Traditie, redactie en kerygma bij Ezechiël: Een analyse van Ez. XX, 1-26*, Verhandelingen van de Koninklijke Vlaamse Academie, Klasse der Letteren 65 (Brussels: Paleis der Academiën, 1969); Karl-Friedrich Pohlmann, *Ezechielstudien: zur Redaktionsgeschichte des Buches und zur Frage nach den ältesten Texten*, BZAW 202 (Berlin: de Gruyter, 1992), 131–4; idem, *Hesekiel*, 1:31.

the seven passages elsewhere and concluded that, even if some of these passages are attributed to the school of Ezekiel, the motif originates with Ezekiel himself.[73]

Furthermore, there are positive reasons to regard the motif as an original component of the prophet's message. First, the uniformity of the scattering formula in its seven occurrences would support its authenticity. Although one could argue that the uniformity is the result of redaction, there is no convincing evidence to deny the motif to the sixth-century prophet. Second, in one instance, the formula appears with modified vocabulary dependent on context. As noted earlier, whereas normally it occurs with הפיץ as the first verb and זרה as the second, in 11:17 הרחיק has taken the first position and הפיץ has shifted into the second position (כי הרחקתים בגוים וכי הפיצותים בארצות). Significantly, it coincides with the same modification we find in the gathering motif outlined in the next chapter, which suggests the same author is at work in these texts and has embedded the formulae in their contexts in a consistent way.

The Direction of Influence

This study has argued on literary grounds that Ezekiel's scattering formula is best explained as a confluence of Priestly and Deuteronomic language. Now we must address more directly the dating of Deuteronomy's exile passages and whether they were available to Ezekiel.

Threats of Exile before 597/587 BCE?

In order for Deuteronomy's conception of exile to influence Ezekiel, the exile Deuteronomic exile passages must precede the prophet of the early sixth century. In the history of scholarship, the threat of exile has sometimes been seen as de facto evidence that a passage derives from the period of the Babylonian exile.[74] Writing on Deuteronomy 4 in 1899, Alfred Bertholet reasoned:

---

73. Jason Gile, "Deuteronomic Influence in the Book of Ezekiel" (Ph.D. diss., Wheaton College, 2013), 226–34.

74. See, for example, Wellhausen, *Prolegomena*, 383; Lohfink, "Auslegung deuteronomischer Texte IV," 250–3; H. D. Preuss, *Deuteronomium*, EdF 164 (Darmstadt: Wissenschaftliche Buchgesellschaft, 1982), 72–3, 156–7; Thomas Römer, "Book of Deuteronomy," in *The History of Israel's Traditions: The Heritage of Martin Noth*, ed. Steven L. McKenzie and M. Patrick Graham, JSOTSup 182 (Sheffield: Sheffield Academic, 1994), 186, 200; Nielsen, *Deuteronomium*, 11.

Dagegen sind beide Teile durch ein Stück auseinandergesprengt, das den Stempel exilischer Abfassung deutlich an der Stirn trägt: c) v. 25-31, selber zerfallend in a) v. 25-28, ein Wort zur Busse und b) v. 29-31, ein Wort zum Trost. Sobald man gelernt hatte, im Exil die Strafe zu sehen für die Sünden der Vergangenheit d.h. für die Übertretung des göttlichen Willens, lag es nahe, an die Übertretung einzelner Gebote anzuknüpfen, um zu zeigen, was ihre traurige Folge war, und dies paränetischer Absicht erst recht, wo die Exulanten sich fortwährend derselben Übertretung schuldig machten.[75]

Gerhard von Rad also reasoned: "the explanation that Israel was condemned to be scattered [in Deuteronomy 4]…gives a clue for dating the whole, since this preacher knows already of the exile of 587."[76] Similarly, Noth asserted that in the threat of exile in Deut. 4:25-28 "Dtr. puts into Moses' mouth the lessons learned from subsequent history with which he himself is familiar."[77]

This view is related to the more general tendency of some scholars to view the disasters mentioned in the curse lists of Leviticus 26 and Deuteronomy 28 as expressions of current circumstances. For example, in 1932, Adam Welch wrote concerning the curses in Deut. 28:27-37: "There is a note of pain and horror which can leave little doubt that the writer had lived through the conditions he described or had learned them from men who knew them at first hand."[78] More recently, Robert Kugler and Patrick Hartin state bluntly what is an unspoken assumption for others. Speaking of Deut. 28:47-68, they write that the section is "probably an editorial addition, since [it]…demonstrates an awareness of the circumstances of the exile."[79]

Exile in the Ancient Near Eastern Curse Literature

However, for several reasons, it is a mistake to presume that references to exile in the Hebrew Bible must come after the Babylonian exile of Judah. First, scholars such as Dennis McCarthy and Delbert Hillers concluded the biblical curses need not derive from the experiences of the Babylonian exile or any other period of disaster, since a comparison with the treaty curses of the Near East reveals that the author(s) of the biblical

---

75. Alfred Bertholet, *Deuteronomium* (Tübingen: J. C. B. Mohr, 1899), 14.
76. Von Rad, *Deuteronomy*, 50.
77. Noth, *Deuteronomistic History*, 34
78. Adam C. Welch, *Deuteronomy: The Framework to the Code* (London: Oxford University Press, 1932), 135. He takes vv. 27-37 to be from after the fall of Samaria.
79. Robert Kugler and Patrick Hartin, *An Introduction to the Bible* (Grand Rapids: Eerdmans, 2009), 105.

covenant curses drew upon a long and extensive tradition.[80] The quantity and distinctiveness of parallels between the biblical and non-biblical texts led Hillers to conclude "the existence of a tradition of curses over a thousand years old renders any attempt to relate individual curses [in the Hebrew Bible] to particular historical periods highly suspect."[81]

This observation applies specifically to references to exile. In ancient Near Eastern treaty documents, the threat of exile for failure to keep the terms of a treaty is well attested.[82] In the letters and treaties of Neo-Assyrian kings, the threat of deportation for disloyalty to the empire is well known.[83] The explicit threat of exile was not unique to the Assyrian

---

80. McCarthy, *Treaty and Covenant*, 172–87; Delbert R. Hillers, *Treaty-Curses and the Old Testament Prophets*, BibOr 16 (Rome: Pontifical Biblical Institute, 1964), 35; Weinfeld, *Deuteronomy and the Deuteronomic School*, 116–29; Laura Quick, *Deuteronomy 28 and the Aramaic Curse Tradition*, OTM (Oxford: Oxford University Press, 2018).

81. Hillers, *Treaty-Curses*, 35; also cited in Daniel Smith-Christopher, *A Biblical Theology of Exile* (Minneapolis: Augsburg Fortress, 2002), 99; cf. Daniel I. Block, *The Gods of the Nations: Studies in Ancient Near Eastern National Theology*, 2nd ed., ETS Studies (Grand Rapids: Baker, 2000), 104–6.

82. See B. Oded, *Mass Deportations and Deportees in the Neo-Assyrian Empire* (Wiesbaden: Reichert, 1979), 41–2; McCarthy, *Treaty and Covenant*, 173–4; Kenneth Kitchen, *On the Reliability of the Old Testament* (Grand Rapids: Eerdmans, 2003), 292–3; Kenneth A. Kitchen and Paul J. N. Lawrence, *Treaty, Law and Covenant in the Ancient Near East*, 3 vols. (Wiesbaden: Harrassowitz, 2012), 3:194–5. Only texts that mention deportation or forced migration, not simply destruction or captivity, should be included among the references to exile. Contra McCarthy, for example, the Sefire curses do not explicitly mention exile.

83. For example: (1) In a ninth-century treaty between Shamshi-Adad V and Marduk-zakir-shumi, king of Babylon, the treaty curses begin as follows: "[Whoever] sins [against this treaty *and does*] not [*carry out*] *his duty*, may Marduk, the great lord whose commands take precedence, [*by his unalterable word*] order his decay and the dispersion of his people" (Parpola and Watanabe, eds., *Neo-Assyrian Treaties*, 4–5 [SAA II, 1]; also Kitchen and Lawrence, *Treaty, Law and Covenant*, 1:936–7). (2) The eighth-century treaty between Ashur-Nerari V and Mati'-ilu, king of Arpad, warned that "if Mati'-ilu [sins] against th[is] sworn treaty… Mati'-ilu, together with his sons, daughters, [magnates] and the people of his land (will) [be ousted] from his country, (will) not return to his country, and (will) not behold his country again" (Parpola and Watanabe, eds., *Neo-Assyrian Treaties*, 8 [SAA II, 2]; also *ANET* Supp., 532–3; Kitchen and Lawrence, *Treaty, Law and Covenant*, 1:940–1). (3) Another text mentioning Ashur-Nerari expresses the same threat: "Ashur-nirari, king of Assyria, …should they not respect…Nineveh ditto…the people of his land…you shall go into exile" (A. R. Millard, "Fragments of Historical Texts from Nineveh: Middle Assyrian and Later Kings," *Iraq* 32 [1970]: 174, plate xxxvi). (4) Essarhaddon's treaty with Baal, king of Tyre, from the first half of the seventh century states: "May Melqarth

empire. Threats of exile are found in texts from the second millennium. For example, from as early as the eighteenth century BCE, the epilogue of the Code of Hammurabi threatened exile for violation of its laws:

> (But) should that man not heed my pronouncements, which I have inscribed upon my stela... May the god Enlil...declare with his venerable speech the obliteration of his city, *the dispersion of his people*, the supplanting of his dynasty, and the blotting out of his name and his memory from the land.[84]

In addition, Oded cites two treaties that deal with the treatment of deportees to show that the Egyptian and Hittite empires likewise punished rebellious states by deporting their inhabitants.[85]

Thus, we find in ancient Near Eastern texts a long tradition of curses that threaten exile from which the biblical writers could draw. Regarding the implications of these data for dating of biblical texts, McCarthy writes:

and Eshmun deliver your land to destruction and your people to deportation; may they [uproot] you from your land" (iv 14-15) (Parpola and Watanabe, eds., *Neo-Assyrian Treaties*, 8 [SAA II, 5]; also *ANET* Supp., 534; Kitchen and Lawrence, *Treaty, Law and Covenant*, 1:960–1). (5) In a letter to a vassal who had fled to Elam, Ashurbanipal threatened to deport his people: "Because you have not sent (back) these people, I am coming to destroy your cities. I will carry off (the people) of Susa, Madaktu and Hidalu" (*ARAB* II, §878 [p. 341]). (6) In a letter to Esarhaddon, mention is made of deportation for disloyalty to the king: "Istar of N[ineveh] (and) Istar of Arbela have said: 'We shall root out from Assyria those who are not loyal to the king, our lord!'" (Simo Parpola, *Letters from Assyrian Scholars to the Kings Esarhaddon and Assurbanipal, Part I: Texts*, AOAT 5/1 [Kevelaer: Butzon & Bercker, 1970], 158–9, text no. 213; cited in Oded, *Mass Deportations*, 41).

The vassal treaties of Esarhaddon contain no explicit references to exile. One line depends on the translation of the phrase *ana salali* ("carry away/ravage/plunder"). Wiseman translates it in one instance as "to be carried off": "Do not transgress your treaty, (or)...you will be turning over your dwellings to be shattered, your people to be carried off" (lines 292-95) (D. J. Wiseman, "The Vassal-Treaties of Esarhaddon," *Iraq* 20 [1958]: 52). Kitchen finds one reference to exile, although it lacks a verb denoting deportation. He claims exile is implied in the following lines: "may your avengers overtake (and) kill you, your brothers (and) your sons...may you to your women, your sons, your daughters and to your houses, not return" (Kitchen and Lawrence, *Treaty, Law and Covenant*, 1:994–7 [§78-79], 3:225).

84. *COS* 2.131, p. 352; also Kitchen and Lawrence, *Treaty, Law and Covenant*, 1:180–1.

85. See *ANET* 204; *ANET* Supp. 530; cited in Oded, *Mass Deportation*, 42. Other texts mention that citizens in the Hittite empire and Ugarit were banished for lawbreaking or disloyalty to the king (see the Hittite instruction in *ANET* 211 and the Ugaritic text RS 17.352).

> The element of military disaster and its consequences, hunger, slavery, exile…is common in the curse literature [of the ancient Near East]. Hence we cannot reject out of hand any reference to exile as a secondary addition. Why must Deuteronomy be denied the right to use it as a threat as did the composer of Esarhaddon's treaty and of the Sefire text, cases where there is no question of *vaticinium ex eventu*, but only knowledge of the probable result of ancient warfare? Hence a simple reference to exile like that of [Deut.] 28:36-37 is hardly a sign that the passage is a later addition.[86]

Therefore, as some scholars acknowledge, the biblical writers could have threatened Israel with exile for religious transgressions before experiencing an exile of their own.[87] Rom-Shiloni has offered a positive argument that Deuteronomy's threats of exile precede 587 BCE: they conceive of exile as total, in contrast to the books of Jeremiah and Ezekiel, which reflect the historical situation of the Babylonian exile, namely, the partial exile of the people.[88]

Still, some have argued that the multiple conclusions and introductions in Deuteronomy 28 (vv. 15, 47, 58) reflect redactional seams that point to later, presumably exilic, supplements. However, Hillers points to other curse lists that display the same phenomenon.[89] Following Hillers, Weinfeld gives particular attention to a vassal treaty of Esarhaddon, which contains multiple "conclusions."[90] In this instance, secondary redaction is

---

86. Dennis J. McCarthy, *Treaty and Covenant: A Study in Form in the Ancient Oriental Documents and in the Old Testament*, AnBib 21 (Rome: Pontifical Biblical Institute, 1963), 124, quoted in Smith-Christopher, *Biblical Theology*, 99–100. Cf. the revised edition in McCarthy, *Treaty and Covenant* (2nd ed.), 180.

87. E.g., Cross, *Canaanite Myth*, 287; Christensen, *Deuteronomy 1–11*, 93; Friedman, "From Egypt to Egypt," 176 n. 23; Levenson, "Who Inserted the Book of the Torah?" 208 n. 18: "The mere threat and description of exile cannot be taken as a sure reflection of the events of 587. Exile was a threat before it was an historical reality [for Israel]"; Nelson, *Double Redaction*, 23. Nelson regards Deut. 4:25-28 and its threat of deportation as preexilic (pp. 93–4).

88. Rom-Shiloni, "Deuteronomic Concepts of Exile," 113.

89. Hillers, *Treaty-Curses*, 32. McCarthy finds this and other criteria unconvincing as well, but ultimately interprets vv. 47 and following to be exilic since in this last section the curses are no longer conditional but rather assured fact (*Treaty and Covenant*, 180–1). However, while it is true that v. 47 forgoes the conditional framework of the preceding curses, the introduction in v. 58 returns to the conditional begun in v. 15. Since abrupt changes in such features as the person and number of the addressee, the topic of curses, and literary style are common in curse lists (Hillers, *Treaty-Curses*, 32–4; Weinfeld, *Deuteronomy and the Deuteronomic School*, 128–9), this variation should not be unexpected.

90. Weinfeld, *Deuteronomy and the Deuteronomic School*, 128–9.

impossible, since the original copy has survived and bears an exact date. Rather than indicating later supplementation, such formulae simply denote section breaks in the curse lists. As Hillers concluded, both Deuteronomy 28 and the lists of curses in the treaties of Esarhaddon, Sefire, and Ashur-Nerari "give the impression of being composite, not because of late redactional activity, but because the scribes have combined a variety of traditional curses."[91] Thus, this feature of Deuteronomy 28 does not necessarily indicate that vv. 47-68 or any other section of the list derives from the period of the Babylonian exile.

Exile as Historical Reality in the Ancient Near East
Second, the biblical writers would have been aware that exile was a real possibility in light of the actual practice of deportation carried out by suzerain states against disloyal vassals. Bustenay Oded has collected extensive evidence for deportations by Assyrian kings, from Ashur-dan II in the tenth century to Ashurbanipal in the seventh century. In particular, Tiglath-pileser III, Sargon II, and Sennacherib practiced the most deportations, with the extant records attributing to them 37, 38, and 20 deportations, respectively.[92] In addition, Kenneth Kitchen has called attention to Assyrian examples as early as the thirteenth century.[93] The

---

91. Hillers, *Treaty-Curses*, 40; followed by Weinfeld, *Deuteronomy and the Deuteronomic School*, 129.

92. Oded, *Mass Deportations*, 19–20. To cite a couple of examples among many, an inscription of Sargon II records the deportation of a people on account of the disloyalty of its king: "Because Urzana, the king, their prince, had not been afraid of the word (or name) of Assur, and had cast off the yoke of my sovereignty, and forgot to serve me, I decided to carry off the people of that city, and gave the order that the god Haldia, the protector of Urartu, should be led forth" (*ARAB* II, §172 [p. 95]). Another text speaks of the punishment rendered against Samerina for rebellion against Assyria: "[The inhabitants of Sa]merina, who agreed [and plotted] with a king [hostile to] me, not to do service and not to bring tribute [to Aššur] and who did battle, I fought against them with the power of the great gods, my lords. I counted as spoil 27,280 people... I settled [some] of them in the midst of Assyria. I repopulated Samerina more than before" (*COS* 2.118D [pp. 295–6]).

For numerous other records, one may consult Oded's impressive survey (*Mass Deportations*, esp. 1–40).

93. Kenneth Kitchen, "Ancient Orient, 'Deuteronism' [sic], and the Old Testament," in *New Perspectives on the Old Testament*, ed. J. Barton Payne (Waco, TA: Word, 1970), 6–7. For example: (1) Before Ashur-dan II in the tenth century, Tiglath-pileser I, ca. 1100 BCE, declared: "4,000 of the Urumai and Abeshlai,—Hittite people who were not submissive, [I carried off] and reckoned them [as people of my land]" (*ARAB* I, §318 [p. 101]; see also §321). (2) In the thirteenth century, after conquering

practice of deportation was by no means exclusive to the Assyrians, but, as Oded notes, was common to all the peoples of the ancient Near East, spanning different periods in history.⁹⁴ Kitchen has compiled numerous examples from the broader Near East.⁹⁵

The presence of deportations and threats of deportation in the ancient Near East shows that the phenomenon was widely known, spanning a long period of history. The ancient historical records indicate that, as Kitchen put it, "the concept and practice of exile was a potential threat to the Hebrews and other politically 'small' groups for most of the second and first millennium B.C."⁹⁶ Nelson similarly observed that Deuteronomy's

the land of Uruadri (Urartu), Shalmaneser I carried away select young men for service in the Assyrian empire (*ARAB* I, §114). (3) In another text he boasted of capturing the land Hanigalbat: "I cut down their hordes, 14,400 of them I overthrew and took as living captives" (*ARAB* I, §116). (4) His successor, Tukulti-Ninurta I, claimed to have carried away 28,000 Hittite warriors at his accession to the throne (*ARAB* I, §164, 171).

94. Oded, *Mass Deportations*, 41.

95. Kitchen, "Ancient Orient," 5–7. For example: (1) From the Mari archives of the early second millennium he cites seven references to deportations or deportees. In one letter the prince of Mari declares the capture of the town of Bakram and the deportation of its people to Mari (Georges Dossin, *Archives Royales de Mari, V: Correspondance de lasmah-Addu* [Paris: Imprimerie Nationale, 1952], Letter 2). (2) In the Hittite kingdom in the sixteenth century BCE, King Hattusili I mentions relocating the populations of two towns for service to a Hittite temple (H. Otten, "Keilschrifttexte," *MDOG* 91 [1958]: 83, rs. 11–17). (3) In fifteenth-century Egypt, the annals of Thutmose III's military campaigns state that he brought back to Egypt 2,503 persons from Syria (*ANET*, 237). (4) His successor, Amenhotep II, returned from campaigns in Syria with over 100,000 men (and women?) (*ANET*, 247 and n. 48). (5) A stela of the next king, Thutmose IV, refers to a location in Thebes as a colony of Syrian captives (*ANET*, 248). (6) In the late fourteenth century, the annals of the Hittite king Mursil II describe transplanting whole population groups after military conquests. Kitchen cites an "innumerable" group of deportees in the king's third year, of which 15,500 people were assigned to the royal palace, 15,[?]00 in his fourth year, and 66,000 in his fifth year (Albrecht Götze, *Die Annalen des Muršiliš* [Leipzig: Hinrichs, 1933], 56–7, 64–5, 76–7, 170–1). (7) In the thirteenth century, an Egyptian text describes Ramesses II as "he who has removed Nubia to the Northland, and the Syrians to Nubia; who has placed the Shasu-Asiatics in the Westland (= Libya), and established the Libyans on the (E.) hills..." (Kitchen, "Ancient Orient," 6). Similarly, Ramesses III in the twelfth century brought deportees from campaigns in Libya to be settled in Egypt.

96. Kitchen, "Ancient Orient," 5. Despite regarding some texts as exilic, Frank Moore Cross makes the same point, acknowledging that in principle the threat of

threats of exile "do not necessarily presuppose an exilic date, but only an audience familiar with deportation as a feature of Assyrian imperial policy."[97] The ancient Israelites did not need an exile of their own before they could speak of such a phenomenon. Exile would naturally have been mentioned with other catastrophes simply because it was well known from ancient Near Eastern warfare.

Exile in Eighth-Century Israel

Nevertheless, if one still requires a historical event in ancient Israel to provide an impetus for such threats in the biblical literature, one need not look to the Babylonian exile of 597/587. The eighth-century Assyrian dispersion of the Northern Kingdom at the hand of Shalmaneser V (followed by Sargon II) provided a precedent for deportation and thus an impetus to warn Judah of a possible exile of its own,[98] especially given the theological interpretation of the fall of Samaria as divine judgment reflected in 2 Kgs 17:7-18.[99] Second Kings 17:6 describes Israelites carried away to Assyria and placed "in Halah, and on the river Habor, the river of Gozan, and in the cities of the Medes."[100] Records from Mesopotamia

---

exile "need not necessarily stem from an exilic editor. Captivity and exile were all too familiar fates in the Neo-Assyrian age. More important, the threat of exile or captivity was common in the curses of the Ancient Near Eastern treaties and came naturally into the curses attached to Israel's covenant" (*Canaanite Myth*, 287).

97. Nelson, *Deuteronomy*, 68.

98. So also Hillers, *Treaty-Curses*, 33–4; George Adam Smith, *The Book of Deuteronomy*, Cambridge Bible for Schools and Colleges (Cambridge: Cambridge University Press, 1918), 69, 307; Hans Wildberger, *Isaiah 1–12*, CC (Minneapolis: Augsburg Fortress, 1991), 274; Halperin, *Seeking Ezekiel*, 111; Rom-Shiloni, "Deuteronomic Concepts of Exile," 109, who cites Stephen Stohlmann, "The Judaean Exile after 701 BCE," in *Scripture in Context II*, ed. W. W. Hallo, J. C. Moyer, and L. G. Perdue (Winona Lake, IN: Eisenbrauns, 1983), 147–75. Cf. Welch, *Framework*, 136, who cites the siege of Samaria in relation to the curses in Deuteronomy 28 generally.

99. The double-redaction theory of the DtrH attributes 2 Kgs 17:1-23 to Dtr1 (Cross, *Canaanite Myth*, 281). Even if the Deuteronomistic interpretation of the fall of the Northern Kingdom in 2 Kgs 17:7-18 was recorded and incorporated into the Deuteronomistic History after 587 we may expect the sentiment to have earlier precedents.

100. For a synthesis of the biblical and Assyrian sources, see Bob Becking, *The Fall of Samaria: An Historical and Archaeological Study*, SHANE 2 (Leiden: Brill, 1992); Bustanay Oded, "II Kings 17: Between History and Polemic," *Jewish History* 2 (1987): 37–50.

mention the capture of Samaria as well (Babylonian Chronicle 1:28).[101] Thus, it would be valid to locate the threat of exile at least as early as the late eighth century in Israel.[102]

Exile in Biblical Literature

Finally, the threat of exile is particularly at home in the biblical tradition where expulsion from the land for religious infidelity functions as a fitting counterpart to the giving of the land (*Landgabe*) tradition. Von Rad has argued that the promise of the land was deep-seated in Israel's religious consciousness from the earliest period.[103] In the biblical literature, it permeates the Genesis–Joshua narrative, being common to all possible underlying traditions.[104] In Genesis 12, the land is promised to Abraham (Gen. 12:7),[105] a tradition reflected in Ezekiel's time (Ezek. 33:24). It was extended to Isaac (Gen. 26:3-4), Jacob (Gen. 28:4, 13; 35:12), and all his descendants (Gen. 48:4). In Egypt, Yahweh revisited his promise to the Israelites (Exod. 6:4, 8).[106] In Deuteronomy, the promise of the land and the expectation of Israel's imminent entrance is at the forefront.[107] At the beginning of the book of Joshua, Yahweh commissions Joshua to lead the people into the land promised to their ancestors (Josh. 1:6), and at the end the narrator declares the promise realized (Josh. 21:43). Regardless of

---

101. A. Kirk Grayson, *Assyrian and Babylonian Chronicles*, TCS 5 (Locust Valley, NY: Augustin, 1975), 73.

102. Cf. Nelson, *Deuteronomy*, 68: "What Moses foresees as a possible future (idolatry, national destruction, exile into pagan lands) would have been a concrete reality for even the earliest of Deuteronomy's readers, in the shape of the calamity suffered by the northern kingdom."

103. Gerhard von Rad, "The Promised Land and Yahweh's Land in the Hexateuch," in *The Problem of the Hexateuch and Other Essays* (Philadelphia: Fortress, 1966), 79–93. See further Christopher J. H. Wright, *God's People in God's Land: Family, Land, and Property in the Old Testament* (Grand Rapids: Eerdmans, 1990), 3–43; Norman C. Habel, *The Land is Mine: Six Biblical Land Ideologies*, OBT (Minneapolis: Fortress, 1995), 36–53, esp. 45; Walter Brueggemann, *The Land: Place as Gift, Promise, and Challenge in Biblical Faith*, 2nd ed., OBT (Minneapolis: Fortress, 2002).

104. Peter Diepold, *Israels Land*, BWANT 95 (Stuttgart: Kohlhammer, 1972), 187–8.

105. Gen. 13:15, 17; 15:7, 18; 17:8; 24:7; 26:3; 50:24.

106. Exod. 12:25; 13:5, 11; Lev. 14:34; 20:24; 25:2, 38; Num. 11:12; 14:8, 16; 32:11.

107. Deut. 1:8, 21, 35, 39; 4:1; 6:3, 10, 18, 23; 7:13; 8:1; 9:5, 28; 10:11; 11:9, 21; 12:1; 19:8; 26:3, 15; 27:3; 28:11; 30:20; 31:7, 20, 21, 23; 34:4. See Patrick D. Miller, "The Gift of God: The Deuteronomic Theology of the Land," *Int* 23 (1969): 451–69.

how the ancestor, *Landgabe*, and Sinai traditions developed historically,[108] the gift of the land was connected to the demands of Israel's relationship with Yahweh well before Ezekiel.[109]

Given the centrality of the land as divine gift and the requirements for Israel's fidelity to Yahweh, the threat of exile in the biblical literature is not unexpected. As Rom-Shiloni puts it, in Deuteronomy exile "is a counterconcept to the concept of the land as a gift."[110] Indeed, the conditionality of Israel's possession of the land is explicit in Deut. 4:25-26, where Moses declares that if Israel forgets the covenant they "will not live long in [the land]."[111] It is reasonable to suppose that before the Babylonian exile Israel's covenant traditions reflected the view that Israel's relationship with Yahweh and her status in the land depended on religious fidelity. If Israel would not keep Yahweh's commands, the gift of the land would be revoked.

Ezekiel's Literary Appropriation

If the pentateuchal threats of exile originated before the Babylonian exile, Ezekiel could have alluded to them in his judgment oracles. While someone could propose that Ezekiel drew not from Deuteronomy but from the broader ancient Near Eastern curse traditions, the arguments presented earlier reinforce the theory that Ezekiel drew from Deuteronomy's language specifically. To summarize, first, Ezekiel's combination of the Deuteronomic and Priestly expressions הפיץ בעמים and זרה בארצות to create the formula הפיץ בגוים וזרה בארצות conforms to one of his known methods of literary appropriation, combination and conflation. Indeed,

---

108. Gerhard von Rad, "The Form-Critical Problem of the Hexateuch," in *The Problem of the Hexateuch and Other Essays*, 1–78; Martin Noth, *A History of Pentateuchal Traditions*, trans. B. W. Anderson (Englewood Cliffs, NJ: Prentice-Hall, 1972), 54–8, 79–115, 147–56.

109. Walther Zimmerli, "Promise and Fulfillment," in *Essays in Old Testament Interpretation*, ed. Claus Westermann (London: SCM, 1963), 89–122; Hans Walter Wolff, "The Kerygma of the Yahwist," in Brueggemann and Wolff, eds., *The Vitality of Old Testament Traditions*, 49; Wright, *God's People in God's Land*, 13–15, 24–43. See also J. Philip Hyatt, "Was There an Ancient Historical Credo in Israel and an Independent Sinai Tradition?" in *Translating and Understanding the Old Testament*, ed. Harry Thomas Frank and William L. Reed (Nashville: Abingdon, 1970), 152–70; E. W. Nicholson, *Exodus and Sinai in History and Tradition* (Richmond: John Knox, 1973).

110. Rom-Shiloni, "Deuteronomic Concepts of Exile," 108.

111. Habel, *The Land is Mine*, 45. Rom-Shiloni describes the land as a "conditional gift" ("Deuteronomic Concepts of Exile," 104).

his combination of sources in Ezek. 25:7 provides a virtually exact parallel. Second, Ezekiel's reference to Deuteronomy's association of worshiping "wood and stone" in exile suggests he knows at least one of the Deuteronomic exile passages. Third, and most importantly, in 20:23 Ezekiel explicitly refers to an earlier tradition that Yahweh swore to scatter Israel among the nations. The plot structure and narrative flow of ch. 20 indicate a setting for this oath during the second wilderness generation, which naturally points to Deuteronomy. One text in particular appears to be the basis for the allusion. In Deut. 4:25-28, the call for witnesses to testify to Yahweh's promise to scatter Israel in the context of an explicit covenant would have been understood as a treaty oath to Ezekiel and other ancient readers. For these reasons, it seems most likely Ezekiel purposely draws from the Deuteronomic language of exile and at least once refers specifically to one of Deuteronomy's exile passages.

The Rhetoric of Allusion

This chapter has shown that Ezekiel's message was shaped by the pentateuchal threats that Yahweh would remove his people from their land if they failed to keep his statutes and ordinances. In the years before the fall of Jerusalem, Ezekiel transformed Deuteronomy's threats of exile, just as he did the remedial punishments of Leviticus 26, from covenant threats into "oracles of imminent or present judgment."[112] While in Babylon, Ezekiel interpreted the current situation of exile in light of these pentateuchal threats. For Ezekiel, the Babylonian exile was the fulfillment of what Yahweh had sworn long ago in the wilderness (20:23). Indeed, in ch. 20, Ezekiel interprets the exile as the realization of Deuteronomy's prediction that the Israelites would be scattered among the nations—where they would worship "wood and stone." His literary appropriation of these threats reveals that his interpretation of the exile as Yahweh's punishment on his unfaithful people was shaped significantly by Deuteronomic language and ideas.

112. Lyons, "Persuasion and Allusion," 83.

Chapter 7

THE GATHERING OF ISRAEL

In the aftermath of the fall of Jerusalem, Ezekiel's restoration oracles provided hope for Israel's return to their land. The book mentions the gathering of Yahweh's scattered people in several restoration passages. We may now investigate whether Ezekiel's use of this common motif, like the scattering motif, is influenced by an earlier tradition, or is simply the result of Ezekiel's own reversal of the scattering motif. Whereas Ezekiel drew from both the Holiness Code and Deuteronomy for the language of scattering, the Holiness Code never explicitly refers to a return from exile.[1] To be sure, Leviticus 26 promises restoration after exile if the people repent: "I will remember my covenant with Jacob, and I will remember my covenant with Isaac and my covenant with Abraham, and I will remember the land" (v. 42). Although the phrase והארץ אזכר, "I will remember the land," in v. 42 is highly suggestive of a future return,[2] it remains implicit at best. Restoration language occurs again in vv. 44-45, but it also lacks an explicit reference to Yahweh bringing his people back to their land.

Therefore, while Ezekiel draws heavily from the Holiness Code for a variety of themes, the Holiness Code does not provide a linguistic or conceptual background for the gathering and return of Israel to their land. Deuteronomy 30, on the other hand, presents a clear regathering of Israel as a result of repentance in exile:[3]

---

1. So also Peter R. Ackroyd, *Exile and Restoration: A Study of Hebrew Thought of the Sixth Century B.C.* (Philadelphia: Westminster, 1968), 90.
2. Milgrom, *Leviticus 23–27*, 2329–42.
3. Deut. 4:29-31 describes the renewal of the broken covenant when Israel returns to Yahweh in exile, but it does not explicitly mention a return to the land.

> When all these things have happened to you, the blessings and the curses that I have set before you, if you call them to mind among all the nations where the Lord your God has driven you, and return to the Lord your God, and you and your children obey him with all your heart and with all your soul, just as I am commanding you today, then the Lord your God will restore your fortunes and have compassion on you, gathering you again from all the peoples among whom the Lord your God has scattered you. Even if you are exiled to the ends of the world, from there the Lord your God will gather you, and from there he will bring you back. The Lord your God will bring you into the land that your ancestors possessed, and you will possess it; he will make you more prosperous and numerous than your ancestors. (Deut. 30:1-5, NRSV)

The similarities between Ezekiel's restoration oracles and Deut. 30:1-5 warrants an investigation into their relationship.[4] We begin with a comparison of their language before addressing the possibility and the direction of influence.

As in the previous chapter, this discussion will comprise three main parts. The first section compares the language of return in Deuteronomy and Ezekiel and argues that the verbal parallels are best explained by the prophet's use of Deuteronomic language. Section two argues more explicitly for the direction of dependence. Section three argues that the gathering motif originated with the prophet himself. In the final section, I will address the rhetoric of Ezekiel's allusion to Deuteronomy's promise of return.

Gathering Language in Ezekiel and Deuteronomy

The language of gathering and return to the land in Ezekiel and Deuteronomy bear remarkable similarities.

Ezekiel's Gathering Language

A cursory reading of the nine references to gathering in Ezekiel reveals that the motif occurs as a stereotypical formula, though more variable than the scattering motif.[5] Like Ezekiel's scattering formula, the references to gathering most often appear in two syntactically congruent parallel lines. Ezekiel 20:41-42 is a representative example:

---

4. Below, I will assess one significant difference between them.
5. So also Lust, "Gathering and Return," 121.

בהוציאי אתכם מן־העמים	When I bring you out from the peoples
וקבצתי אתכם מן־הארצות	and gather you from the countries
אשר נפצתם בם	where you have been scattered
...	...
בהביאי אתכם אל־אדמת ישראל	when I bring you into the land of Israel.

Ezekiel's gathering formula contains three distinguishing elements:

1. *Statement of Gathering from the Nations*: Yahweh gathers his people from the places where they were scattered. Every occurrence contains the verb קבץ, "to gather," with Yahweh as subject and a (normally pronominal) object denoting the people, followed by a prepositional phrase with מן denoting the location from which the people will be gathered.[6]
2. *Relative Clause*: A relative clause with the verb פוץ often explains that Israel will be gathered from the places to which they were previously scattered.
3. *Statement of Return to the Land:* Yahweh brings (usually הביא) his people back to (אל) their land—or, in the case of 20:34, first to the wilderness of the peoples.

Following Frank-Lothar Hossfeld's classification, we may profitably distinguish three basic variations of the motif.[7] The first group, which comprises 11:17; 20:34-35 and 20:41-42, contains all three elements of the formula.[8]

Group 1

Ezek. 11:17

וקבצתי אתכם מן־העמים	I will gather you from the peoples
ואספתי אתכם מן־הארצות	and assemble you from the countries
אשר נפצותם בהם	where you have been scattered.
ונתתי לכם את־אדמת ישראל	And I will give you the land of Israel,
ובאו־שמה	and they will come there.

---

6. Cf. Hossfeld, *Untersuchungen*, 310.

7. Ibid., 309–14. See also the discussion in Stefan Ohnesorge, *Jahwe gestaltet sein Volk neu: Zur Sicht der Zukunft Israels nach Ez 11,14-21; 20,1-44; 36,16-38; 37,1-14.15-28*, FzB 64 (Würzburg: Echter, 1991), 21–9.

8. According to Hossfeld, the formula contains four elements that he identifies as: bringing out, gathering, relative clause, and leading into the land. However, the concept of "bringing out" (הוצא) is only present in ch. 20, undoubtedly due to its exodus theme.

Ezek. 20:34-35

והוצאתי אתכם מן־העמים	I will bring you out from the peoples
וקבצתי אתכם מן־הארצות	and gather you from the countries
אשר נפוצתם בם	where you have been scattered
...	...
והבאתי אתכם אל־מדבר העמים	And I will bring you into the wilderness of the peoples.

Ezek. 20:41-42

בהוציאי אתכם מן־העמים	When I bring you out from the peoples
וקבצתי אתכם מן־הארצות	and gather you from the countries
אשר נפצתם בם	where you have been scattered
...	...
בהביאי אתכם אל־אדמת ישראל	when I bring you into the land of Israel.

The second group, which includes 34:13; 37:21; 36:24 and 36:12, resembles the first but lacks the relative clause אשר נפוצתם בם ("where you have been scattered").

Group 2

Ezek. 34:13

והוצאתים מן־העמים	And I will bring them out from the peoples and
וקבצתים מן־הארצות	gather them from the countries,
והביאתים אל־אדמתם	and will bring them into their own land.

Ezek. 36:24

ולקחתי אתכם מן־הגוים	I will take you from the nations
וקבצתי אתכם מכל־הארצות	and gather you from all the countries
והבאתי אתכם אל־אדמתכם	and bring you into your own land.

Ezek. 37:21

אני לקח את־בני ישראל מבין הגוים	I will take the children[9] of Israel from the nations
אשר הלכו־שם	among which they have gone,
וקבצתי אתם מסביב	and will gather them from all around,
והבאתי אותם אל־אדמתם	and bring them to their own land.

The third group consists of shorter variants. Ezekiel 39:27 retains two parallel gathering lines but lacks the relative clause and the return statement, and Ezek. 28:25 and 29:13 employ a single gathering line but add the relative clause.

---

9. Cf. LXX οικον.

Group 3

Ezek. 39:27

| בשובבי אותם מן־העמים | When I return them from the peoples |
| וקבצתי אתם מארצות איביהם | and gather them from the lands of their enemies. |

Ezek. 28:25

| בקבצי את־בית ישראל מן־העמים | When I gather the house of Israel from the |
| אשר נפצו בם | peoples among whom they are scattered… |

Ezek. 29:13

| אקבץ את־מצרים מן־העמים | I will gather the Egyptians from the peoples |
| אשר־נפצו שמה | where they were scattered… |

Hossfeld also proposed a hypothetical relative chronology to explain their variation. He argues that the "New Exodus" of 20:34-35, which continued the exodus imagery of vv. 1-31, reflects the original form of the gathering motif, and the other occurrences of the motif are variations which he attributed to redactors.[10] However, without presenting arguments for this development of the formula, the hypothesis of extensive redaction remains speculative and uncompelling. We should not expect Ezekiel to use the same verbatim language in every instance. Indeed, as I will argue below, the variation has a certain logic that suggests a single writer.

Similarities with Deuteronomy 30

Ezekiel's gathering language bears striking similarities to the language of restoration in Deuteronomy 30.[11]

Deut. 30:3-5

ושב יהוה אלהיך את־שבותך	Yahweh your God will restore your fortunes
ורחמך	and have compassion on you,
ושב וקבצך מכל־העמים	and he will gather you from all the peoples
אשר הפיצך יהוה אלהיך שמה	where Yahweh your God has scattered you.
אם־יהיה נדחך בקצה השמים	If your outcasts are in the uttermost parts of heaven,
משם יקבצך יהוה אלהיך	from there Yahweh your God will gather you,
ומשם יקחך	and from there he will take you.
והביאך יהוה אלהיך אל־הארץ	Yahweh your God will bring you into the land
אשר־ירשו אבתיך וירשתה	that your ancestors possessed, that you may possess it.

---

10. Hossfeld, *Untersuchungen*, 314: "Hinter den nach Verwandtschaftsgraden zum Original gestaffelten Gruppen kann eine redaktionelle Schichtung nur vermutet werden."

11. Also noted by Rom-Shiloni, "Deuteronomic Concepts of Exile," 120.

The density and distribution of verbal parallels between Deut. 30:3-5 and Ezekiel are unmistakable. In fact, Deuteronomy 30 contains all three elements of Ezekiel's formula in the same order—(1) statement of gathering from the nations, (2) relative clause, and (3) statement of return to the land—in many instances using the same language. First, the most common word for gathering in Ezekiel, קבץ, which occurs in every instance of the gathering motif in Ezekiel, is the single Deuteronomic word for gathering, occurring twice in Deut. 30:3-5. As in Ezekiel's formula, in Deut. 30:3, the gathering verb is followed with an object denoting the people and the location of gathering with the preposition מן. Second, just as it is typical for Ezekiel's formula to qualify the gathering line with the relative clause אשר נפוץ בם / שמה ("where you have been scattered"), so Deuteronomy 30 follows its gathering clause with the relative clause אשר הפיצך יהוה אלהיך שמה ("where Yahweh your God has scattered you")—both with the verb פוץ. While Ezekiel uses the passive verb נפוץ and Deuteronomy specifies "Yahweh your God" as the subject, the passive verb in Ezekiel fittingly reflects the exiles' present situation, that is, in the lands where the people are *currently* scattered.[12] Third, just as almost every occurrence in Ezekiel includes Yahweh bringing (הביא) the people to (אל) the land (אדמה), so Deuteronomy uses nearly the same language: והביאך יהוה אלהיך אל־הארץ ("Yahweh your God will bring you back to the land"). Finally, two of Ezekiel's gathering formulas use the verb לקח ("take"). Like Deut. 30:3-5, Ezek. 36:24 and 37:21 utilize the following three verbs in conjunction: לקח ("take"), קבץ ("gather"), and הביא ("bring").

Is Ezekiel Instead Influenced by Jeremiah or Another Prophet?

Some might wonder whether the linguistic and conceptual similarities between Ezekiel and Deut. 30:3-5 can be explained in some other way, perhaps by appealing to a common source, for example, Jeremiah or another prophet. However, the connection becomes more pronounced when one observes that these formulaic phrases are uncommon elsewhere

---

12. One nearly verbatim quotation of Deut. 30 appears in MT Ezek. 4:13, where the phrase "among the nations where I will drive them" (בגוים אשר אדיחם שם) resembles "among all the nations where Yahweh your God has driven you" (בכל־הגוים אשר הדיחך יהוה אלהיך שמה) in Deut. 30:1. However, the phrase אדיחם אשר שם is lacking in LXX Ezekiel and probably a late insertion influenced by either Deut. 30 or passages in Jeremiah (Jer. 8:3; 16:15; 23:3, 8; 24:9; 29:14, 18; 46:28; cf. Jer. 27:10, 15; 40:12; 43:5).

in the literary traditions of the Hebrew Bible. Isaiah 40–55, whose central theme is the return from exile, displays all sorts of unique and metaphorical images, including the highway (מסלה) and new exodus motifs, but never follows the formulaic expression that is found in Deut. 30:3 and is characteristic of Ezekiel.[13] Generally, Isaiah favors figurative, and often terse, representations of exile and return (e.g., 27:12). The terseness of his language is exemplified in instances when he simply writes, "go out," "depart," and other similar phrases without the further specification of "to the land" or "among the nations" that are found in the pentateuchal traditions and in Ezekiel. It appears that Isaiah's language is inspired more by the narrative traditions of the exodus—expressed in the highway and new exodus motifs[14]—than the language found in Deuteronomy 30.

The gathering metaphor occurs occasionally in the eighth- and seventh-century prophetic books: Mic. 2:12; 4:6; Isa. 11:12; and Zeph. 3:19.

---

13. For example, Isa. 52:7-12 presents a remarkable picture of return to the land, beginning with the messenger's announcement of peace, happiness, and salvation. In v. 8, the watchmen and the entire city look up to see the return of Yahweh to Zion. With Yahweh as their rear guard, the people are commanded to depart (סורו) and go out (צאו) from there (vv. 11-12). Isa. 48:20 also commands Israel, "Go out (צאו) from Babylon, flee (ברחו) from Chaldea... Yahweh has redeemed his servant Jacob." Chapters 40–55 end with return to the land as well. In 55:11-13, Yahweh promises that his word will not fail, that Israel shall "go out (תצאו) in joy and be led forth (תובלון) in peace." In the second servant song (49:1-13), the servant is given the task of "bringing back (לשובב) Jacob to [Yahweh], that Israel would be gathered (אסף) to him." The rest of the section employs a variety of phrases to express the return to the land: "to raise up (להקים) the tribes of Jacob," "to bring back (להשיב) the preserved of Israel," "to establish the land (להקים ארץ)," "to apportion the desolate \ inheritances (להנחיל נחלות שממות)," "to lead (ינהגם) them," "to guide them (ינהלם) by springs of water," "to make the mountains a road (דרך)," "to raise up my highways (מסלתי)," and finally, in v. 12, "those from afar shall come (יבאו)." We find the verb נהג in v. 10, but not in the sense of "to drive out" of the land as in Deuteronomy, but rather "to lead" back to the land. Isa. 43:5-6 employs both קבץ and הביא, but not with the prepositional phrase מן plus גוים, עמים, or ארצות, as in Deut. 30 and Ezekiel. Since these verbs are not uncommon by themselves, the text reveals no clear influence from Deut. 30.

14. See Bernard W. Anderson, "Exodus Typology in Second Isaiah," in Anderson and Harrelson, eds., *Israel's Prophetic Heritage*, 177–95; Carroll Stuhlmueller, *Creative Redemption in Deutero-Isaiah*, AnBib 43 (Rome: Pontifical Biblical Institute, 1970), 59–98.

Mic. 2:12	אסף אאסף יעקב כלך	I will surely assemble all of you, O Jacob;
	קבץ אקבץ שארית ישראל	I will gather the remnant of Israel;
	יחד אשימנו כצאן בצרה	I will set them together like sheep in a pen,
	כעדר בתוך הדברו תהימנה מאדם	like a flock in its pasture, a noisy multitude of men.
Mic. 4:6	אספה הצלעה	I will assemble the lame
	והנדחה אקבצה	and gather those who have been driven away
	ואשר הרעתי	and those whom I have afflicted.
Isa. 11:12	ואסף נדחי ישראל	He will assemble the banished of Israel,
	ונפצות יהודה יקבץ	and gather the dispersed of Judah
	מארבע כנפות הארץ	from the four corners of the earth.
Zeph. 3:19	והושעתי את־הצלעה	And I will save the lame
	והנדחה אקבץ	and gather the banished.

Even these occurrences of the gathering metaphor differ from the more formulaic language of Deuteronomy and Ezekiel. Isaiah 11:12 is closest to Deuteronomy 30, with its use of the verb "gather" (קבץ), the banished (נדחים), the dispersed (פוץ), and the nations (גוים in v. 11).[15] However, this verse lacks the syntactic correspondence displayed in the formulaic string of a gathering verb, an object denoting Israel, the preposition מן, and the specification of location, as in Deuteronomy and Ezekiel.

Since the gathering motif also occurs in Jeremiah, some might wonder whether Ezekiel was influenced by Jeremiah and not by Deuteronomy

---

15. The restoration oracle in Isa. 14:1-2, often dated to the Babylonian exile (e.g., Marvin A. Sweeney, *Isaiah 1–39: With an Introduction to Prophetic Literature*, FOTL 16 [Grand Rapids: Eerdmans, 1996], 231–2), is a better candidate for having a literary connection to Deut. 30: "Yahweh will have compassion (ירחם) on Jacob and will choose Israel again, and will set them (הניחם) again in their own land (אדמתם)." Unlike the pentateuchal texts, here the sojourner and "peoples" (עמים) will assist in the return by "taking (לקחום) them and bringing (הביאום) them to their place (מקומם)." This text bears remarkable similarities to the restoration of Deut. 30, which predicts that when the people return to Yahweh in exile he "will restore your fortunes and have compassion on you (רחמך), and he will gather you again from all the peoples (עמים) where [he] has scattered you…from there [he] will gather you, and from there he will take you (יקחך), and [he] will bring you (הביא) into the land that your fathers possessed" (30:3-5). Both texts speak of Yahweh having compassion (רחם) on his people, and both use הביא and לקח in succession to refer to the return to the land (ומשם יקחך והביאך יהוה אלהיך אל־הארץ in Deut. 30:4-5, and ולקחום עמים והביאום אל־מקומם in Isa. 14:2).

directly. Among Jeremiah's varied references to return to the land, the concept of gathering occurs a few times.[16] In Jer. 23:3, gathering appears in conjunction with the shepherd metaphor, just as it does in Ezekiel 34. Other occurrences include Jer. 31:8-10 and 32:37. In general, the motif is less stereotyped in Jeremiah than in Ezekiel.[17] Most notably, the place of dispersion varies much more in Jeremiah. The form it takes in Jer. 29:14 most closely resembles the language of Ezekiel.

ושבתי את־[שביתכם כ]	I will restore your fortunes
(שבותכם ק)	
וקבצתי אתכם מכל־הגוים	and gather you from all the nations
ומכל־המקומות אשר הדחתי אתכם	and from all the places where I have driven you,
שם נאם־יהוה	declares Yahweh,
והשבתי אתכם אל־המקום	and I will bring you back to the place
אשר־הגליתי אתכם משם	from which I sent you into exile.

Still, Jer. 29:14 differs from Ezekiel's formula in several ways. Although this verse resembles the Ezekielian parallel line structure with its dual prepositional phrases, it lacks a verb in the second position. Also, unlike Ezekiel, who consistently follows Deuteronomy 30 by expressing the return to the land with הביא, Jeremiah uses השיב (as also in Jer. 23:3; 32:37).

Rosalie Kuyvenhoven contends that Jeremiah borrows the theme of gathering from Ezekiel.[18] Whether or not this is the case, we can see that Jeremiah's language sometimes recalls Deuteronomy 30 rather than Ezekiel. Though שוב שבות occurs in Ezekiel (39:25), its presence in Jer. 29:14 with the gathering motif may suggest that Jeremiah also is dependent on Deuteronomy 30. Similarly, Jeremiah seems to have a proclivity for the root נדח, which is found in Deut. 30:4 but not in Ezekiel. This hypothesis is reinforced by Jer. 33:26, which quotes both of the first two clauses of Deut. 30:3: כי־אשוב את־שבותם ורחמתים ("for I will restore their fortunes and will have mercy on them"). This conclusion accords with Rom-Shiloni's observation that:

---

16. E.g., Jer. 30:10-11: "Fear not, O Jacob my servant, declares Yahweh, nor be dismayed, O Israel. For behold, I will save you from far away, and your offspring from the land of their captivity. Jacob will return and have quiet and ease, and none will make him afraid. For I am with you to save you, declares Yahweh. I will make a full end of all the nations among whom I scattered you, but of you I will not make a full end." Lust notes other return language in Jer. 12:15; 16:14-15; 24:6; 29:10; 30:3, 10-11; 40:12; 42:12 ("Gathering and Return," 123).

17. For a comparison, see Kuyvenhoven, "Jeremiah 23:1-8," 17–21.

18. Ibid.

both prophets are familiar with a corpus of pentateuchal traditions and find them to be powerful anchors with which they can ground their own messages. Yet each prophet's usage of those traditions seems to be independent of the other… [Consequently,] similarities between Ezekiel and Jeremiah are not necessarily the result of implicit or indirect connections between the two books, but may stem from the prophets' independent use of the same biblical sources.[19]

In some instances, then, there is good reason to conclude that both Ezekiel and Jeremiah drew directly from Deuteronomy.

Ezekiel and Yahweh's Compassion

The language of Ezek. 39:25 closely mirrors that of Deut. 30:3. The syntactic correspondence between these two passages is striking:

Ezek. 39:25	אשיב את־[שבית כ] (שבות ק) יעקב ורחמתי כל־בית ישראל	I will restore the fortunes of Jacob and have mercy on the entire house of Israel.
Deut. 30:3	ושב יהוה אלהיך את־שבותך ורחמך	Yahweh your God will restore your fortunes and have mercy on you.

Both verses use the words שוב שבות and רחם together to describe Yahweh's restoration of his people. Since Ezekiel alludes to Deuteronomy 30 for the gathering motif, it seems plausible he would allude to the passage's broader restoration message as well by using its language of שוב שבות and רחם.

The reference to Yahweh's compassion (רחם) on Israel in 39:25 is exceptional in Ezekiel. Indeed, the book never explicitly mentions Yahweh's love (אהב), forgiveness (סלח), comfort (נחם), grace (חן), and, apart from this verse, compassion (רחמים).[20] In accordance with

---

19. Rom-Shiloni, "Ezekiel and Jeremiah," 219; see also Henk Leene, who argues that Jeremiah drew from Ezekiel for the concept of the inward transformation that Yahweh would do in his people ("Blowing the Same Shofar: An Intertextual Comparison of Representations of the Prophetic Role in Jeremiah and Ezekiel," in de Moor, ed., *The Elusive Prophet*, 175–98; idem, *Newness in Old Testament Prophecy*, OtSt 64 [Leiden: Brill, 2014], 334–44).

20. See, e.g., Baruch J. Schwartz, "Ezekiel's Dim View of Israel's Restoration," in *The Book of Ezekiel: Theological and Anthropological Perspectives*, ed. Margaret S. Odell and John T. Strong, SBLSymS 9 (Atlanta: Society of Biblical Literature, 2000), 53–5, and the various essays in Paul M. Joyce and Dalit Rom-Shiloni, eds., *The God Ezekiel Creates*, LHBOTS 607 (New York: Bloomsbury T&T Clark, 2015).

the limited role of repentance in the book (see below), this was due to Ezekiel's heavy emphasis on judgment and the people's unworthiness for mercy in the period following the exile and fall of Jerusalem.[21] Prior to the time of the fall of Jerusalem, Ezekiel was consumed by his people's consistent religious infidelity and the weight of the impending judgment, and, as argued below, the gravity of the judgment continued into the restoration. However, it seems plausible Ezekiel foresaw a time after the full judgment of the nations and return of Israel to its land when he could speak of Yahweh having compassion on his people.[22] Since shame has a constructive and restorative function for God's people in Ezekiel (16:54, 61; 36:32; 43:10-11; 44:13),[23] compassion need not be incompatible with their continued shame described in the next verse (39:26;[24] cf. also in 16:52, 54, 61, 63; 43:10-11).

Daniel Block and Michael Lyons have outlined several passages that balance the harsh depictions of Yahweh with the compassionate side of his character.[25] According to Lyons, "a close reading of the book reveals something more complex than harshness alone. It is actually possible to observe how the prophet moves between the twin poles of Yhwh's harsh judgment and his compassion."[26] Lyons further explains that, just as Ezekiel's harsh descriptions of Yahweh have a rhetorical function, so also the depictions of Yahweh's kindness:

> First, the statements about Yhwh's kindness in the past [e.g., Ezekiel 16] create an argument about the enormity of Israel's guilt: Yhwh cared for them, and they should have responded in gratitude and obedience, but instead rebelled against him. Thus their punishment is deserved. Second, the statements about Yhwh's restoration of Israel in the future [e.g., 39:25-26 or ch. 37] are attempts to prevent despair and hope.[27]

---

21. Contra Schwartz, who asserts that Yahweh acts only out of self-interest and a narcissistic concern for his reputation ("Ezekiel's Dim View," 64–7).

22. Cf. Lyons, *Introduction to the Study of Ezekiel*, 144.

23. Cook, *Ezekiel 38–48*, 106, who cites, e.g., Lapsley, "Shame and Self Knowledge," 145–8; Ruth Poser, *Das Ezechielbuch als Trauma-Literatur*, VTSup 154 (Leiden: Brill, 2012); Daniel Y. Wu, *Honor, Shame, and Guilt: Social-Scientific Approaches to the Book of Ezekiel*, BBRS 14 (Winona Lake, IN: Eisenbrauns, 2016).

24. Reading MT's נָשָׂא, "bear," not נָשָׁה, "forget" (see Cook, *Ezekiel 38–48*, 106).

25. Ibid., 143–6, and Daniel I. Block, "The God Ezekiel Wants Us to Meet: Theological Perspectives on the Book of Ezekiel," in Joyce and Rom-Shiloni, eds., *The God Ezekiel Creates*, 162–92.

26. Lyons, *Introduction to the Study of Ezekiel*, 143.

27. Ibid., 146.

Therefore, depictions of Yahweh's harshness and his kindness can both have a place in Ezekiel's prophetic message.

The Direction of Influence

Ezekiel's and Deuteronomy's language is too similar to be coincidental, particularly because, as seen above, the shared phrases are so distinct compared to the language of return in other biblical texts. But which text influenced the other? This question requires closer attention, given the tendency among scholars to date Deut. 30:1-10 to a period after or concurrent with the prophet Ezekiel's ministry and indeed the possibility that Deut. 30:1-10 instead draws from the language of Ezekiel and Jeremiah. In this section, I will argue that the similarities are best explained by Ezekiel's use of Deuteronomy, not vice versa. Before discussing the date of Deut. 30:1-10 and its availability to Ezekiel, I begin with positive arguments for Ezekiel's use of Deuteronomy 30.

Ezekiel's Literary Appropriation

First, the priority of Deuteronomy 30 in relationship to Ezekiel is validated by the criterion of literary modification. The form of the gathering motif as parallel lines in Ezekiel suggests the similarity of language between Deuteronomy and Ezekiel is best explained by the prophet's use of the gathering language of Deut. 30:3-5. As in the scattering motif, Ezekiel has a penchant for creating parallel lines when drawing on literary sources, and the particular pattern displayed in the gathering motif may be classified as a classic example of what Lyons calls "splitting and recombination."[28] This modification involves splitting apart a locution—in this case Deuteronomy's קבץ מן־העמים—and recombining the parts in parallel lines. This technique, which corresponds to other instances of Ezekiel's use of earlier texts, makes it doubtful that Deut. 30:3-5 relies on the language of Ezekiel and Jeremiah. Thus, it seems more likely that Ezekiel drew from Deuteronomy.

When compared with Deut. 30:3-5, the form of Ezekiel's gathering sayings exhibit a certain logic. If Ezekiel is drawing from Deuteronomy 30, why does he not consistently quote verbatim the full Deuteronomic phrase מן־[כל־]העמים + קבץ? In forming two parallel lines, Ezekiel modifies the source text. This is clear because in the few instances when the gathering motif appears in Ezekiel in a single line, we find Deuteronomy's full phrase קבץ מן־העמים.

---

28. Lyons, *From Law to Prophecy*, 95–7.

Deut. 30:3	וקבצך מכל־העמים	
Ezek. 28:25	בקבצי את־בית ישראל מן־העמים	
Ezek. 29:13	אקבץ את־מצרים מן־העמים	

But when the gathering motif appears in parallel lines, as it most often does, Ezekiel alters it in a consistent way: he introduces a variant verb in the first line, often derived from the immediate context, and the verb קבץ shifts to the second line.[29]

Ezek. 20:34	והוצאתי אתכם מן־העמים
	וקבצתי אתכם מן־הארצות
Ezek. 20:41	בהוציאי אתכם מן־העמים
	וקבצתי אתכם מן־הארצות
Ezek. 34:13	והוצאתים מן־העמים
	וקבצתים מן־הארצות
Ezek. 36:24	ולקחתי אתכם מן־הגוים
	וקבצתי אתכם מכל־הארצות
Ezek. 37:21	אני לקח את־בני ישראל מבין הגוים
	אשר הלכו־שם
	וקבצתי אתם מסביב
Ezek. 39:27	בשובבי אותם מן־העמים
	וקבצתי אתם מארצות איביהם

In each of these examples, the phrase מן־העמים remains in the first line (or the alternative הגוים in 36:24 and 37:21) and קבץ drops to the second line. This pattern represents a classic example of the literary modification called "splitting and recombination,"[30] that is, splitting apart a locution—in this case קבץ מן־העמים—and recombining the parts in parallel lines. This proposed literary modification also explains why עמים—drawn from Deuteronomy 30—typically parallels ארצות in the gathering formula (rather than גוים, which is most common in the scattering formula).[31]

Two allegedly peculiar forms of the gathering metaphor are found in Ezek. 39:27 and 28. The former actually follows the Ezekielian pattern.

| Ezek. 39:27 | בשובבי אותם מן־העמים | …when I have brought them back |
| | וקבצתי אתם מארצות איביהם | from the peoples and gathered them from their enemies' lands… |

---

29. Only Ezek. 11:17 lacks parallel lines.
30. Lyons, *From Law to Prophecy*, 95–7.
31. Cf. Block, *Ezekiel*, 1:352 n. 38.

Although this is the only occurrence of שוב in conjunction with the gathering metaphor in Ezekiel,[32] the verse follows Ezekiel's typical formula of parallel lines with קבץ in the second position. Since the first verb is generally variable, one should give little weight to the presence of שוב as a basis for inauthenticity.

By contrast, Ezek. 39:28 is likely a late expansion. The vocabulary and style of the gathering saying are altogether different from the other occurrences in the book of Ezekiel.

Ezek. 39:28	וכנסתים על־אדמתם	I gather them to their land
	ולא־אותיר עוד מהם שם	and will not leave any of them there any longer.

The verb כנס occurs elsewhere only in late compositions and appears to be a Late Biblical Hebrew root.[33] While Hurvitz and Rooker may be correct that such language is not impossible in Ezekiel's lexicon,[34] the absence of the entire phrase quoted above in the LXX suggests it is a late expansion.[35]

Other Allusions to Deuteronomy 30:3-5

Second, Ezekiel's literary appropriation of קבץ מן־העמים is supported by the criterion of recurrence, that is, his use of other elements of Deuteronomy 30's return language. To review the similarities noted above, in most occurrences of the motif in Ezekiel the gathering is followed by a relative clause and a statement describing Yahweh bringing his people back to the land (והביאתים אל־אדמתם or slight variation).[36] This mirrors

---

32. William A. Tooman, *Gog of Magog: Reuse of Scripture and Compositional Technique in Ezekiel 38–39*, FAT 2/52 (Tübingen: Mohr-Siebeck, 2011), 67.

33. Pss. 3:7; 147:2; Eccl. 2:8; 3:5; Est. 4:16; Neh. 12:44; 1 Chron. 22:2.

34. Avi Hurvitz deems the presence of the verb "a reliable indicator of lateness," but nevertheless judges its appearance in Ezekiel as a forerunner of Late Biblical Hebrew (*A Linguistic Study of the Relationship between the Priestly Source and the Book of Ezekiel: A New Approach to an Old Problem*, CahRB 20 [Paris: Gabalda, 1982], 123–5). Similarly, Mark F. Rooker asserts that the term occurs first in the book of Ezekiel (*Biblical Hebrew in Transition: The Language of the Book of Ezekiel*, JSOTSup 90 [Sheffield: Sheffield Academic, 1990], 156–8).

35. See Mackie, *Expanding Ezekiel*, 118–19; Johan Lust, "The Final Text and Textual Criticism: Ez 39,28," in Lust, ed., *Ezekiel and His Book*, 49–50. Lust himself understands v. 28b to be an insertion into an already late summary of Ezekiel's teachings (p. 49).

36. Contra Rosalie Kuyvenhoven ("Jeremiah 23:1-8: Shepherds in Diachronic Perspective," in *Paratext and Megatext as Channels of Jewish and Christian Traditions: The Textual Markers of Contextualization*, ed. A. A. den Hollander,

the order of Deut. 30:3-5, which exhibits a relative clause and the nearly identical phrase והביאך יהוה אלהיך אל־הארץ after the gathering statement.[37] In one instance, Ezekiel uses נתן, "give you the land of Israel," rather than הביא, "bring" (Ezek. 11:17), but this variation is the result of a purposeful change based on the context of the passage, since the ownership of the land is under discussion in ch. 11.[38] Finally, Ezek. 36:24 and 37:21 use the verb לקח in the first position of the scattering formula, a verb found in Deut. 30:4. Thus, like Deut. 30:3-5, these two passages utilize the following three verbs in conjunction: לקח ("take"), קבץ ("gather"), and הביא ("bring").

Therefore, the abundance of lexical links, in some cases with a high degree of syntactic correspondence, and the distinctive motif of "gathering from the nations/peoples" shared by Deut. 30:3-5 and Ezekiel suggest literary dependence on Deuteronomy 30, not simply the appropriation of Deuteronomic language used in common parlance (indirect usage). In both Deut. 30:3-5 and most instances of Ezekiel's formula, we find a distinct progression: the gathering motif (קבץ) with the preposition מן plus עמים or ארצות, followed by a relative clause with פוץ specifying the places from which the people will be gathered, and finally, the return of the people described as Yahweh bringing them to their land (הביאתים אל־אדמתם). As with the scattering motif, Ezekiel appears to draw upon a distinct pentateuchal tradition, suggesting the gathering motif cannot simply be explained as a creative reversal of the scattering motif.[39] The proposed literary modification, along with Ezekiel's variants derived from his own literary context, suggest that Ezekiel draws from Deuteronomy 30, not vice versa.

The Theology of Restoration

Despite the clear verbal parallels between Deuteronomy 30 and Ezekiel, one might object that Deuteronomy and Ezekiel display opposing theologies of restoration. Whereas Deuteronomy 30 specifies repentance as a prerequisite for the return to the land,[40] the focus of restoration in

---

U. B. Schmid, and W. F. Smelik, Jewish and Christian Perspectives 6 [Leiden: Brill, 2003], 19), Ezekiel's primary use of הביא rather than השיב is not because Ezekiel does not speak of a "return," but because he is dependent on the language of Deut. 30.

37. Lust, "Gathering and Return," 124.
38. Cf. Kuyvenhoven, "Jeremiah 23:1-8," 18 n. 62.
39. Contra Lyons, *From Law to Prophecy*, 93, 101.
40. Marc Zvi Brettler understands only v. 1a as the protasis of the conditional clause rather than all of vv. 1-2. Accordingly, the repentance in vv. 1b-2 is part of the apodosis and would not be conditional for the following restoration in vv. 3-6

Ezekiel is Yahweh's unilateral action.[41] Is it likely that Ezekiel would adopt the language of Deuteronomy in this instance but not its intrinsic theology? First, Deuteronomy is not alone in envisioning repentance preceding restoration; this is found in the Holiness Code as well (Lev. 26:40-42). Therefore, it is not simply that Ezekiel's theology differs from Deuteronomy's, but rather that his view differs from *both* pentateuchal traditions.[42] This difference between Ezekiel and the Holiness Code is particularly striking, since the Holiness Code is Ezekiel's foremost theological influence and Ezekiel so often alludes to the very passage that mentions repentance before restoration, that is, Leviticus 26. Therefore, divergence in theology does not preclude Ezekiel's allusion to Deuteronomy 30, since it is clear he also alluded to Leviticus 26 without espousing its view of repentance. Literary dependence does not require complete theological congruity with Ezekiel's source traditions.[43]

Michael Lyons has convincingly explained this apparent inconsistency in Ezekiel's relationship to the Holiness Code. The same principle informs Ezekiel's relationship to Deuteronomy 30. According to Lyons, the difference in outlook has to do with Ezekiel's interpretation of Israel's capacity to repent in their exilic situation and his view that the restoration is strictly God's initiative.[44] He elaborates:

> Ezekiel depicts the people as incorrigible. He selectively describes Israel's past history in order to show that they are unable and unwilling to depart from the negative practices of their ancestors (Ezek 16, esp. vv. 44-55;

("Predestination in Deuteronomy 30:1-10," in Schearing and McKenzie, eds., *Those Elusive Deuteronomists*, 174–7). However, even if the restoration is not conditioned upon repentance in Deut. 30, in contrast to Ezekiel the passage explicitly notes that repentance precedes the restoration (cf. Mark J. Boda, "Renewal in Heart, Word, and Deed: Repentance in the Torah," in *Repentance in Christian Theology*, ed. Mark J. Boda and Gordon T. Smith [Collegeville, MN: Liturgical, 2006], 12 n. 24).

41. See Mein, *Ethics of Exile*, 211–12, 239, 262: "Yahweh restores Israel for his own sake alone, and irrespective of the repentance of the people" (p. 239); Schwartz, "Ezekiel's Dim View," 49; Thomas Raitt, *A Theology of Exile: Judgment/Deliverance in Jeremiah and Ezekiel* (Philadelphia: Fortress, 1977), 188; Joyce, "Ezekiel and Moral Transformation." C. A. Strine has qualified this view ("The Role of Repentance in the Book of Ezekiel: A Second Chance for the Second Generation," *JTS* 63 [2012]: 467–91, esp. 487–90).

42. Rom-Shiloni, "Ezekiel as the Voice of the Exiles," 18.

43. Cf. Leonard, "Identifying Inner-Biblical Allusions," 246: "Shared language need not be accompanied by shared ideology to establish a connection."

44. Lyons, *From Law to Prophecy*, 85–8.

ch. 20, esp. v. 30). The idea that the people are incorrigible is brought out most vividly in his statement of their need for a "new heart": the people are spiritually abnormal, and must therefore undergo some kind of ontological change in order to follow God's commands (Ezek 11:19-20). It [is] significant that appeals to repent are extremely rare in Ezekiel (only Ezek 14:6; 18:30-32; 33:11), suggesting that the prophet was pessimistic about the possibility of a positive response to his message. Even more significant is the fact that Ezekiel never ties his descriptions of restoration to these appeals to repent.[45]

While Ezekiel does indeed call the people to repentance (14:6; 18:21-32), the prophet makes no direct connection between their response and Yahweh's action to restore his people.[46]

Because Ezekiel is "extremely pessimistic about the possibility that his contemporaries are either willing or able to repent,"[47] Israel's hope for restoration depends only on Yahweh's unilateral intervention to transform his people and cause them to walk in his statutes (11:19-20; 36:27). Ezekiel's imagery is close to Deuteronomy. As noted in the previous chapter, Deuteronomy speaks of future disobedience and subsequent dispossession of the land as inevitable, because Israel had proven themselves to be rebellious. Moses called Israel to circumcise their heart (Deut. 10:16), but for Deuteronomy, in the end, Yahweh would have to do it (Deut. 30:6). Yahweh himself would circumcise their heart so that they can love him fully. Block observes an interesting similarity: both Ezekiel and Deuteronomy exhibit the same ambivalence, in one moment calling Israel to change their heart (Ezek. 18:31; Deut. 10:16) and in the next acknowledging that Yahweh would have to change their heart (Ezek. 11:19; 36:24-34; Deut. 30:6).[48] Since Ezekiel and Deuteronomy use different language for a similar concept (new heart vs. circumcised heart), we would not conclude based on verbal similarity alone that Deuteronomy's conception of inward transformation influenced Ezekiel. However, if the other arguments in this chapter are accurate, and indeed Ezekiel knew and used Deuteronomy 30 in other instances, this would provide cumulative evidence—based on the criterion of recurrence—that Deuteronomy's conception of inward transformation influenced him.

---

45. Ibid., 86.
46. Mein, *Ethics of Exile*, 211–12.
47. Lyons, *Introduction to the Study of Ezekiel*, 133; see further the discussion of Ezek. 20 in the previous chapter.
48. Daniel I. Block, *Triumph of Grace: Literary and Theological Studies in Deuteronomy and Deuteronomic Themes* (Eugene, OR: Cascade, 2017), 328 n. 63.

Dating Deuteronomy 30:3-5

We may now more directly address the date of Deuteronomy 30 and its availability to Ezekiel, since many scholars assign Deut. 30:1-10 to a (late) exilic redactor.[49] While I will argue below for the plausibility that Deut. 30:1-10 originated before Ezekiel, let me acknowledge at the outset that, in principle, the passage could have been known to Ezekiel in oral form even if it was roughly contemporaneous with him, originating in the early part of the Babylonian exile.

Discussions of the provenance of the passage generally fall under the purview of Deuteronomistic studies. In his seminal *Überlieferungsgeschichtliche Studien*, Noth viewed the Deuteronomistic historical work as a proclamation of irreversible doom that was completely negative about the prospect of renewal.[50] However, subsequent scholarship has with near uniformity modified this view. In 1961, Hans Walter Wolff highlighted the hopeful sections of Deut. 4:25-31; 30:1-10 and 1 Kgs 8:46-53 and argued that, rather than being part of the preexilic Deuteronomy received by the Deuteronomist, Deut. 30:1-10 (as well as 4:29-31) was likely penned by "a *second* writer from the deuteronomistic circle, who carried the theme of the history work specifically back into Moses' time in order to insure that the entire work would be read and taken to heart in his own day."[51] Frank Moore Cross followed Wolff by placing Deut. 30:1-10 in the exilic period, ascribing the passage to his Dtr2 editor.[52] Nelson differed from Cross by attributing Deut. 4:29-31 and 30:1-20 not to Dtr2, but to a still later Deuteronomist, whom he identified with Wolff's "second hand."[53]

Below I will make positive arguments for the plausibility that Deut. 30:1-10 was available to Ezekiel. But first I will respond to Wolff's and other scholars' arguments for an exilic date.[54] First, he argues that Deut.

---

49. E.g., Wolff, "Kerygma," 96; Cross, *Canaanite Myth*, 278; von Rad, *Deuteronomy*, 50; Nelson, *Deuteronomy*, 4; Nicholson, *Deuteronomy and Tradition*, 35–6.

50. See especially Noth, *Deuteronomistic History*, 97–8: "Clearly [Dtr] saw the divine judgement which was acted out in his account of the external collapse of Israel as a nation as something final and definitive and he expressed no hope for the future, not even in the very modest and simple form of an expectation that the deported and dispersed people would be gathered together."

51. Wolff, "Kerygma," 96 (italics original).

52. Cross, *Canaanite Myth*, 278; so also Richard Elliott Friedman, *The Exile and Biblical Narrative: The Formation of the Deuteronomistic and Priestly Works*, HSM 22 (Chico, CA: Scholars Press, 1981), 19.

53. Nelson, *Double Redaction*, 94.

54. Wolff, "Kerygma," 93–5.

30:1-10 presupposes and alludes to the entirety of ch. 28, part of which he regarded as exilic. However, as I argued in the previous chapter, arguments for dividing Deuteronomy 28 into redactional layers carry significant methodological problems and raise serious doubts about dating any part to the Babylonian exile.[55] Second, both Deut. 28:45-68 and 30:1-10 refer to the Deuteronomic law code as a "book of instruction" (ספר התורה) in 28:58, 61; 30:10, a phrase that to Wolff suggests a level of historical distance from the code itself. Even though this argument would not necessarily point to an exilic provenance, Hillers points out that in Near Eastern treaty documents, the reference to stipulations in a "book" is normal treaty terminology. This should not be unexpected since, according to Hillers, "preparation and preservation of written copies of a treaty was an essential element in treaty-making."[56] Third, Deut. 30:1-10 has resonances with some Deuteronomistic passages, most notably 1 Kgs 8:46-53, which also anticipates exile and is widely attributed to an exilic hand. However, Gordon McConville has reasonably argued for the opposite direction of dependence—that 1 Kings 8 draws from Deuteronomy 30.[57] Finally, Wolff cited language uncharacteristic of the Deuteronomistic History and more typical of Jeremiah to postulate that Deut. 30:1-10 was post-Dtr, from a deutero-Deuteronomist. However, the rarity of a theme in Deuteronomy does not necessarily mean that it was inserted in the exilic period; Jeremiah may have drawn from its single occurrence in Deuteronomy.

---

55. Additionally, Jože Krašovec finds this unconvincing because exile also occurs in the first section in vv. 36-37 and because "some legal texts and treaties of the ancient Near East contain features that match those found throughout the biblical text" ("The Distinctive Hebrew Testimony to Renewal Based on Forgiveness," *ZABR* 5 [1999]: 230).

56. Hillers, *Treaty-Curses*, 32, see also 45–7. For example, stipulations in Sefire I B repeatedly refer to "the treaty which is in this inscription" (lines 23, 28, 33), where the word "inscription" is *spr'*, cognate to ספר in Deuteronomy. (On the use of *spr'* to refer to a stone inscription, see Joseph A. Fitzmyer, "The Aramaic Suzerainty Treaty from Sefire in the Museum of Beirut," *CBQ* 20 [1958]: 456; Hillers, *Treaty-Curses*, 46). In light of this convention, passages in Deuteronomy that refer to the book of instruction need not imply a late date. Such references do reflect a time in which the law code was seen as part of a larger treaty document, but there is no reason to view this as a development in the exilic period.

57. J. Gordon McConville, "1 Kings 8:46-53 and the Deuteronomic Hope," *VT* 42 (1992): 67–79.

In scholarship since Wolff, the dating of Deut. 30:1-10 to the Babylonian exile is often assumed rather than argued. Many simply assert the exilic date of the passage, presupposing a sentiment similar to that of von Rad, who wrote:

> It is surely beyond question that the speaker of this section is himself living in the period of the exile, and that he is therefore addressing a word of immediate importance to his hard-pressed contemporaries who were likely to be somewhat far removed from taking the punishment quite personally.[58]

Others have argued that Deut. 29:29 would flow directly into 30:11 without the intervening 30:1-10.[59] However, even if 30:1-10 is a later insertion into the book, one must provide further evidence that the passage was inserted during the Babylonian exile and not earlier.

A Compendium of Prophetic Language?

Some scholars have proposed that the restoration passage of Deut. 30:3-5 is a late compendium of prophetic language. In a short note, Norbert Mendecki recorded verbal parallels between Deut. 30:3-4 and restoration passages in Jeremiah, Ezekiel, and Isaiah 40–66 and suggested that Deuteronomy 30 draws from these prophetic books.[60] However, Mendecki did not provide arguments for the direction of dependence. Similarly, Lust proposed that Deut. 30:3-5 "has combined the terminology of Jeremiah with that of Ezekiel in such a way that one has to conclude that it was inspired by these prophetic writings."[61] Lust offers little defense of this assertion. He argues that since the gathering motif and content of Deut. 30:3-5 are not characteristically Deuteronom(ist)ic[62] and

---

58. Von Rad, *Deuteronomy*, 183. Writing in 1964, von Rad noted Wolff's 1961 article, "Das Kerygma des deuteronomistischen Geschichtswerk," and cited parallels with Jeremiah.

59. E.g., Friedman, "From Egypt to Egypt," 183, who cites Wright, "Deuteronomy," 507.

60. Norbert Mendecki, "Dtn 30,3-4: nachexilisch?" *BZ* 29 (1985): 267–71.

61. Lust, "Gathering and Return," 125.

62. So also Marc Zvi Brettler, who asserted that the mention of Yahweh circumcising the people's hearts in Deut. 30:6 reflects a late non-Deuteronomic idea. In his view, Deut. 30:1-10 therefore is one of the latest sections within the book, a "pseudo-deuteronomic" text influenced by Jeremiah that attempts to speak in Deuteronomic style but nevertheless betrays a non-Deuteronomic idea ("Predestination in Deuteronomy 30:1-10," 185–6). In contrast, according to E. W. Nicholson, the Deuteronomists are responsible for the Jeremianic prose tradition and thus not distinct from the circle that created Deut. 30:1-10 (*Preaching to the Exiles: A Study of the Prose Tradition in the Book of Jeremiah* [New York: Schocken, 1971], 119).

therefore not likely to be inserted in the (alleged) Deuteronomistic redactions of Ezekiel and Jeremiah,⁶³ the direction of influence must instead go the other way. That is, Ezekiel and Jeremiah popularized the motif, and Deut. 30:3-5 later conflated the language from these prophets. Assuming the common dating of Deut. 30:1-10 to the (post)exilic period, Lust rejects (or fails to consider) the possibility that the passage was available to Ezekiel. Like Wolff, he assumes that if gathering and restoration are rare in Deuteronomy and the Deuteronomistic History, it would be more likely that Deut. 30:3-5 was inspired by the prophetic material at a very late date than vice versa. However, as noted above, the rarity of a theme or theology in a corpus is not a reliable criterion for stratifying biblical texts.

Gathering Language before 597/587 BCE?

Is it possible that biblical writers would speak of return from exile before 597/587 BCE? The restoration language of Deut. 30:3-5 may reasonably have been available to Ezekiel for several reasons. First, some scholars assume the mention of Israel gathered from exile must betray a provenance during the Babylonian exile.⁶⁴ However, like the scattering motif, the gathering motif could be used before 587 to describe the return of the dispersed Northern Kingdom, whose inhabitants may be described as scattered throughout the nations.⁶⁵ Ezekiel 37:15-22 demonstrates that Ezekiel for one envisioned the regathering of the exiles from the Northern Kingdom as well as the Southern Kingdom. Some have theorized that Deuteronomy originated in the Northern Kingdom,⁶⁶ including Albrecht

---

63. Lust, "Gathering and Return," 123–6; also Ohnesorge, *Jahwe gestaltet*, 24; contra Herrmann, *Die prophetischen Heilserwartungen*, 186, 247, 264; Winfried Thiel, *Die deuteronomistische Redaktion von Jeremia 1–25*, WMANT 41 (Neukirchen-Vluyn: Neukirchener, 1973), 273–4.

64. E.g., David M. Carr, *Introduction to the Old Testament: Sacred Texts and Imperial Contexts of the Hebrew Bible* (Oxford: Wiley-Blackwell, 2010), 173.

65. In addition to 2 Kgs 17:6, which states that "Hoshea carried Israelites away to Assyria and placed them in Halah, and on the Habor, the river of Gozan, and in the cities of the Medes," Assyrian royal records describe the deportation of peoples as a common practice (see Oded, *Mass Deportations*). Elsewhere Oded points out that the Neo-Babylonians continued the practice of mass deportation, though unlike the Assyrians the Babylonians did not resettle the exiled land with foreign occupants ("Judah and the Exile," in *Israelite and Judaean History*, ed. J. H. Hayes and J. M. Miller, 3rd ed. [Philadelphia: Westminster, 1977], 475).

66. See, for example, Adam Welch, *Code of Deuteronomy: A New Theory of Its Origin* (London: James Clark, 1924), 38–9, 75–6, 113, 128–9; Nicholson, *Deuteronomy and Tradition*, 58–82, and the sources cited on page 58 n. 1. For a more recent treatment, see the articles in *HeBAI* 4/2 (2015), including Cynthia Edenburg and

Alt, who argued that *Urdeuteronomium* originated as a program of restoration drawn up in northern Israel in the wake of the fall of Samaria.[67] Whether or not one accepts the hypothesis of a "northern" Deuteronomy, the references to scattering and gathering fit well in the wake of the dispersion of the inhabitants of the Northern Kingdom. Consequently, if one requires an exile before speaking of a return, then the exile of 722 provides a sensible context. Certainly those who remained after that disaster, whether in the Northern or Southern Kingdom, expressed hopes for their restoration.

Considering the date of restoration texts such as Lev. 26:40-45; Deut. 4:29-31; and 30:1-10, Weinfeld spoke of the plausibility of their preexilic provenance, since "the idea of conversion in exile started to crystallize in northern Israel and is reflected in Hosea."[68] Indeed, references to Yahweh's gathering of his people occur in preexilic books, in particular Mic. 2:12; 4:6; Isa. 11:12; and Zeph. 3:19. Although the gathering language has been used to argue that those passages are secondary,[69] Geo Widengren found this to be an artificial criterion.[70] Without denying the possibility that some have an exilic origin, depending to a great extent on other criteria, to deny categorically this language to the eighth-century prophets betrays an *a priori* assumption about the nature and content of preexilic prophecy.[71] Indeed, a passage such as Ezek. 37:15-22, which

---

Reinhard Müller, "A Northern Provenance for Deuteronomy? A Critical Review," *HeBAI* 4 (2015): 148–61, and Gary N. Knoppers, "The Northern Context of the Law-Code in Deuteronomy," *HeBAI* 4 (2015): 162–83.

67. Alt, "Die Heimat des Deuteronomiums," 2:250–1. Cf. later Gerhard von Rad, *Studies in Deuteronomy*, SBT 9 (London: SCM, 1953), 40–1, 60–2.

68. Weinfeld, *Deuteronomy 1–11*, 209 (see further p. 218).

69. James Luther Mays, for example, asserts that Mic. 4:6-7 "assumes the existence of the diaspora created by the fall of Jerusalem…[and thus] belongs to the late exilic or post-exilic salvation prophecies concerned with the recovery of the scattered exiles" (*Micah: A Commentary*, OTL [London: SCM, 1976], 100). With near unanimity, redaction critics view Isa 11:12 as a later interpolation because of the reference to the exile of Judah in v. 12, e.g., B. Duhm, *Das Buch Jesaia*, 2nd ed., HAT 3/1 (Göttingen: Vandenhoeck & Ruprecht, 1902), 82; G. Hölscher, *Die Propheten* (Leipzig: J. C. Hinrichs, 1914), 316; Otto Eissfeldt, *Einleitung in das Alte Testament*, 3rd ed. (Tübingen: J. C. B. Mohr, 1964), 426; Wildberger, *Isaiah 1–12*, 489–90.

70. Widengren, "Yahweh's Gathering," 230.

71. Thus Francis I. Andersen and David Noel Freedman, *Micah: A New Translation with Introduction and Commentary*, AB 24E (New York: Doubleday, 2000), 333–4: "The language of [Mic. 2:12-13] is vague enough to fit any situation in which a scattered people are gathered together again; but there is no specific detail that

speaks of the restoration of the Northern Kingdom, shows that restoration prophecies could be declared before their fulfillment. Thus, there is no reason to deny that the motif of Yahweh gathering Israel—whether in the eighth-century prophets, Deuteronomy, or Ezekiel—could have preceded the Babylonian exile.

Second, the motif of scattering and gathering has a rich history in ancient Mesopotamian literature that reaches much earlier than the eighth century, as far back as the early second millennium, and therefore provides a literary and thematic background for the biblical literature, even in the earliest of periods. Specifically, Widengren has shown that the scattering and gathering of peoples occupied a prominent place in Mesopotamian royal ideology.[72] Important for comparison with the biblical literature,

---

fits only the Babylonian Exile. The background could equally well be the crisis of 701 B.C.E and its aftermath, or even one of the earlier disasters in which the whole population were displaced by Israel's more immediate neighbors (Amos 1)... On general grounds it is hard to believe that eight-century prophets, making predictions like those in Mic 1:6 and 3:12 against the background of the well-known, centuries-long history of Yahweh and his people, never asked what Yahweh would do after that. Since the worst they predicted...is exile for at least a remnant and possible survival of some others in the homeland, there must always have been the chance and the hope of a revival and a renewal... We do not believe that these ideas came to Israelites only after they had been removed to Babylon."

72. Widengren, "Yahweh's Gathering," 234–40; cf. Block, *Ezekiel*, 2:290–1. For example: (1) In the prologue of the Code of Hammurabi, the king calls himself "the gatherer of the scattered people of Isin." In another text he declares, "the scattered population of Sumer and Akkad I gathered" (Lorenz Dürr, *Ursprung und Ausbau der israelitisch-jüdischen Heilserwartung: Ein Beitrag zur Theologie des Alten Testamentes* [Berlin: Schwetschke & Sohn, 1925], 120, cited in Block, *Ezekiel*, 2:290). (2) In an early second-millennium Sumerian inscription, Nur-Adad, the king of Larsa, boasts among other things that he had "regathered [Ur's] scattered people" (*COS* 2:249). (3) Similarly, in an inscription of Assurbanipal, the king says of Babylon: "Its scattered people I gathered and then restored to their place." The Marduk Prophecy declares that the prince "will gather the scattered... He will gather together the scattered land" (Tremper Longman III, *Fictional Akkadian Autobiography: A Generic and Comparative Study* [Winona Lake, IN: Eisenbrauns, 1991], 234–5). (4) The ritual of the New Year Festival at Babylon includes the proclamation that the king has not commanded the scattering of Babylon, which nevertheless affirms the association of the king as scatterer. Cyrus the Great would later claim to stand in this tradition in order to legitimize his kingship. After boasting, "I am Cyrus, king of the world, great king, legitimate king, king of Babylon, king of Sumer and Akkad, king of the four rims (of the earth)," he declares of various peoples: "I...gathered all their (former) inhabitants and returned (to them) their habitations" (*ANET* 316).

Widengren notes that in some cases the role of scatterer and gatherer is applied to a deity. As one example, a Mesopotamian psalmist expresses to his god: "the house of the scattered you gather."[73]

Widengren concluded that the biblical image of Yahweh scattering and gathering his people derives from this broader tradition.[74] Without justifying a concrete date for these pentateuchal sources, a preexilic provenance for the Holiness Code and Deuteronomy does not require that the concepts of scattering and gathering were created *ex nihilo* in the pentateuchal texts (contra von Rad).[75] Rather, the motif was well known in the ancient milieu before the pentateuchal literature. The early Mesopotamian portrayal of kings and deities who scatter and gather the people provides a background for such language, even before the events of 722 and 597/587.

Third, with respect to the date of Deut. 30:1-10, Leviticus 26 provides a preexilic precedent for the sequence of blessings, curses, and renewal that is found in Deuteronomy 28 + 30:1-10. Ezekiel alludes to each part of Leviticus 26, including the restoration verses in vv. 40-45, suggesting its preexilic provenance.[76] Some have argued that the promise of restoration after judgment would "blunt the rhetorical force of the threats,"[77] but Lyons rightly observes that Leviticus 26 "depicts the punishments as instruments to induce repentance."[78] Therefore, he concludes, "the hope of restoration does not 'contradict' the threat; restoration is simply the desired outcome that the punishments are designed to prompt. The reference to restoration does not deny that the promised threat will materialize, nor does it lessen the foreseen suffering and death."[79] Jože Krašovec has shown that Deut. 30:1-10 mirrors the function of Lev. 26:40-45. Just

---

73. For bibliography and more examples, see Widengren, "Yahweh's Gathering," 234–40 and Block, *Ezekiel*, 2:290–1.

74. Widengren, "Yahweh's Gathering," 240.

75. Gerhard von Rad, *Das fünfte Buch Mose: Deuteronomium* (Göttingen: Vandenhoeck & Ruprecht, 1964), 131; Friedman, *Exile and Biblical Narrative*, 19.

76. See Lyons, *From Law to Prophecy*, 31–2.

77. See ibid., 31, who quotes H. L. Ginsberg, *Israelian Heritage*, 80–1: "a religious writer who wished to deter Israel from going the limit would be defeating his own ends if he assured Israel that Yhwh was incurably indulgent after all."

78. Lyons, *From Law to Prophecy*, 31: "The author [of Lev. 26] accomplishes this strategy by listing the punishments in order of increasing intensity, and by separating them into groups with refrains that clearly state the restorative purpose of the punishments: 'if despite this you will not obey…' (26:18, 27); 'if you continue hostile to me, and are not willing to listen…' (26:21); 'if in spite of these you are not disciplined back to me…' (26:23)."

79. Ibid., 32.

as Lev. 26:40-45 introduces the possibility of renewal after punishment (Lev. 26:14-39), Deut. 30:1-10 functions the same way in relation to Deuteronomy 28.[80] Thus, Deut. 30:1-10 may have functioned as a natural counterpart to Deuteronomy 28 before 587 BCE.

The Origin of the Gathering Motif in Ezekiel

Given the striking lexical links between Ezekiel's gathering sayings and the allegedly (post)exilic date of Deut. 30:1-10, some judge these passages to be secondary in Ezekiel. Instead of arguing that Deuteronomy 30 drew from Ezekiel (the "compendium of prophetic language" approach), these scholars conclude that a later redactor of the book of Ezekiel drew from the restoration passage of Deut. 30:1-10.[81] In this section, I will assess more directly whether these literary links represent allusions to Deuteronomy originate with the prophet himself.

As noted in the Introduction, it is difficult to know whether the appearance of redaction should be attributed to Ezekiel or to his followers, since what is often assumed to be later scribal insertions may in some cases be either from the prophet's own hand at a later time *or* the compiler(s)' process of grouping—and sometimes simply juxtaposing—Ezekiel's material in the process of forming a prophetic book.[82] Thus, any structural dissonance might derive from the editorial placement of Ezekiel's oracles. I do not deny the presence of material crafted by Ezekiel's followers and later tradents. However, as reviewed in Chapter 1 of this study, the "Ezekielian" nature and style of much that appears secondary has led some scholars to postulate a major role for the prophet in the composition of his oracles and even the production of his book.

A Sensible Context for the Gathering Motif

Johan Lust and Karl-Friedrich Pohlmann have rejected the authenticity of the gathering motif in Ezekiel. On redaction-critical grounds, Lust contended the motif was not present in the original layer of the book of Ezekiel.[83] In a subsequent article, he argued more explicitly that the motif must derive from the Hellenistic period, when Jews were

---

80. Krašovec, *Reward, Punishment, and Forgiveness*, 160–84.
81. E.g., Liwak, "Überlieferungsgeschichtliche Probleme."
82. In van der Toorn's words, the design of prophetic books often involves "juxtaposition, often without any apparent transition, of oracles about different subjects and from different periods" (*Scribal Culture*, 177).
83. Lust, "'Gathering and Return,'" 119–42.

dispersed "throughout the nations."[84] Lust reasons that the situation of the Babylonian deportation, along with the Judean settlement in Egypt (Jer. 24:8; 44:1), "can hardly have been described as a 'gathering from all the countries into which they were dispersed.'"[85] According to Lust, "if the author was alluding to the [Babylonian] exile, one would expect him to mention a deportation to one particular country."[86]

Karl-Friedrich Pohlmann similarly assumes that the theme of the gathering of those dispersed among the nations reflects the situation of the Hellenistic diaspora. He posits two main redactional stages in the book of Ezekiel, an early *golah*-oriented redaction that spoke favorably of those exiled in 597, and a later diaspora redaction that reflected the situation and concerns of the Jewish diaspora. Pohlmann attributes the scattering and gathering motifs to this second redaction, which he dates to the fourth century.[87]

However, one need not look to the Hellenistic period to find a suitable provenance for these passages. Despite Lust's unnecessarily rigid expectation that בגוים means "*throughout [all]* the nations," rather than simply "*among* the nations," he is mistaken when he asserts that the Babylonian exile consisted only of Judahites in Mesopotamia and to a lesser extent Egypt. Though that alone could account for בגוים, he overlooks Jer. 40:11-12, which speaks of "Judeans who were in Moab and among the Ammonites and in Edom and in other lands...the places to which they had been driven."

Restoration in Ezekiel

The authenticity of the gathering motif is bound up with broader discussions of the authenticity of restoration oracles in the book of Ezekiel. The presence of both judgment and restoration in a single prophetic book has

---

84. Idem, "Exile and Diaspora: Gathering from Dispersion in Ezekiel," in *Lectures et relectures de la Bible: Festschrift P.-M. Bogaert*, ed. Jean-Marie Auwers and André Wénin, BETL 144 (Leuven: Peeters, 1999), 115: "This phrasing does not appear to imply an adequate description of the exile in Babylon by the Chebar. It rather evokes the dispersion of the Jews all over the world in the Greek period."

85. Ibid., 113–14. Stated differently, "the repeated reference to the 'gathering' of the 'dispersed' seems to postulate a diaspora situation rather than an exilic one. The liberation from exile is not normally described as a gathering of the dispersed. The expressions in question most likely betray a post-exilic situation in the Persian and Greek periods" (idem, "Ezekiel Salutes Isaiah," 380).

86. Lust, "Exile and Diaspora," 121.

87. Pohlmann, *Ezechielstudien*, 131–4; idem, *Hesekiel*, 1:31. Note the critique of Pohlmann in Albertz, *Israel in Exile*, 349–50.

yielded varied interpretations in modern scholarship. The most extreme positions view judgment and restoration to be incompatible in the ministry of a prophet or in a prophetic book.[88] It is not surprising, then, that oracles promising salvation have been prime targets in the history of redaction criticism.[89]

Thomas Raitt has persuasively demonstrated that restoration plays a fundamental role alongside judgment in Ezekiel and Jeremiah. Raitt speaks of a dramatic shift from doom to salvation in the ministries of these prophets that corresponds roughly to the pre- and post-judgment periods.[90] As Zimmerli observed, "Das Jahr 587 hat für Ezechiels Verkündigung eine einschneidende Wende gebracht."[91] In general, we may surmise that before 587 Ezekiel's message was primarily one of judgment and thereafter one of hope.[92] Raitt cites a pivotal change that "made possible and justified the shift from a radicalized judgment message to an unqualified salvation message[:]…the people's accountability for sin was transformed once the Exile, interpreted as God's punishment, was in full force."[93] With the exile, the judgment had been meted out,[94] resulting in a shift from judgment oracles to salvation oracles.

Several features of the restoration oracles in Ezekiel suggest they come from the same prophet who preached judgment. Raitt has shown that in the book of Ezekiel salvation is affirmed in tension with the earlier judgment, which is neither nullified nor forgotten.[95] As he elaborates, "the

---

88. See, e.g., Pohlmann, *Ezechielstudien*, 253.

89. Note especially S. Herrmann, who denied all restoration in the book of Ezekiel to the prophet (*Die prophetischen Heilserwartungen*, 290).

90. Raitt, *Theology of Exile*, 106–27.

91. Walther Zimmerli, "Das Phänomen der 'Fortschreibung' im Buch Ezechiel," in *Prophecy: Essays Presented to Georg Fohrer on his Sixty-Fifth Birthday*, ed. J. A. Emerton, BZAW 150 (Berlin: de Gruyter, 1980), 186.

92. So also Allen, *Ezekiel 20–48*, xxii; Joyce, *Ezekiel*, 110. I do not go so far as to consider this a rule as Raitt implies: "The deliverance is never spoken at a time… before the threats of judgment would have become a historical fact" (*Theology of Exile*, 114). Raitt viewed 11:16-21 as the only restoration oracle before 587 (p. 113).

93. Raitt, *Theology of Exile*, 108.

94. Ibid., 114; cf. Zimmerli, "Das Phänomen der 'Fortschreibung,'" 187: "Infolgedessen ändert sich des Propheten Amt in der Situation nach 587. Er hat nicht mehr apodiktisch das kommende Unheil anzukündigen… Er hat in des Volkes Heute hinein zu sprechen, wenn dieses fragt, was es denn nun im Heute angesichts der bestehenden Möglichkeit von Zukunft zu tun hat."

95. Raitt, *Theology of Exile*, 115. Cf. pp. 174–5: "By a logic which is difficult to grasp, Jeremiah and Ezekiel combined in their sayings an uncompromising message of judgment and an unconditional message of deliverance… In their view judgment

early deliverance message was brought into a kind of organic connection with the judgment message, and it was made clear that the mercy of the deliverance did not ignore the integrity of the judgment.'"[96] He observes that the oracles of restoration in Ezekiel often explicitly recall the transgressions charged against Israel in Ezekiel's judgment messages. To name a few examples, in 11:18 when the exiles return to the land, they will remove all its שקוצים and תועבות. Similarly, in 37:23, they will no longer defile themselves with their idols. In 36:33, restoration involves Yahweh cleansing his people from all their iniquities.[97] In what follows, I offer additional examples to show the organic connection between judgment and restoration in Ezekiel.

First, in many cases, the deliverance involves or results in further reflection on the judgment. Thus, for example, in the midst of messages of restoration, the Israelites are variously called to remember their transgressions, be ashamed, and loathe themselves (e.g., 20:43; 36:31-32). The tension between judgment and deliverance in Ezek. 16:53-63 is particularly striking. There Yahweh declares that he will restore their fortunes *in order that* (למען) they might bear their disgrace and be ashamed (vv. 53-54). Similarly, the last section of the chapter, vv. 59-63, presents a particularly tortuous path back and forth between restoration and recollection of judgment:

> For thus says the Lord Yahweh: I will deal with you as you have done, you who have despised the oath in breaking the covenant. Yet I will remember my covenant with you in the days of your youth, and I will establish for you an everlasting covenant. Then you will remember your ways and be ashamed…I will establish my covenant with you…in order that (למען) you may remember and be confounded, and never open your mouth again because of your shame, when I atone for you for all that you have done, declares Yahweh.

The oracle begins with an initial statement of judgment in v. 59 and then alternates between promises of restoration and injunctions to feel shame. And like vv. 53-54, these verses emphasize that the purpose of restoration is not simply to bless Israel but rather to bring her to shame

---

and deliverance neither negate one another, nor contradict one another, nor provide in the case of the one the framework to understand the other, nor mollify the impact of the other in the time in which it is proclaimed." On the authenticity of Ezekiel's oracles of deliverance, cf. pp. 108–10.

96. Ibid., 125 (original was italicized).
97. Ibid., 124. In Diagram B he also lists 20:43-44; 36:22-23, 32.

for her transgressions (v. 63).⁹⁸ These examples clearly demonstrate that the restoration oracles in Ezekiel display a "clear remembrance of the judgment and the implication that the deliverance is in tension with it."⁹⁹ With respect to the authenticity of these oracles, Raitt surmises that "only prophets who [also] preached judgment included within their promises of...deliverance the otherwise anomalous and extraneous element of a vivid remembrance of some component of the judgment message."¹⁰⁰ It would be unlikely for a scribe in the post-judgment period to maintain a strict remembrance of the judgment itself.

Second, not only do the oracles of restoration recall elements of the earlier judgment message, in ch. 20 the deliverance entails or results in *new* judgment.¹⁰¹ Here the restoration does not include an immediate return to the land. Instead, vv. 35-38 outline a period in the wilderness when Yahweh will further purge the rebels from his people. As Allen describes it, "the positive message of proclamation is interwoven with an announcement of (partial) judgment (vv 33-38)."¹⁰² Greenberg inquires whether characterizing this passage as later words of hope "does justice to the angry tone of vv. 32-44, [and] whether the forecast of a compulsory exile, a purge 'in the wilderness of the peoples,' and the future self-loathing of the redeemed really depart from the condemnations of the first part of the oracle."¹⁰³

Third, in his restoration oracles, Ezekiel takes great pains to justify the restoration while also maintaining the validity of the judgment. Thus, for example, restoration is never for Israel's sake, as if the people deserve it. As Ezek. 36:22 declares, "it is not for your sake, O house of Israel, that I am about to act, but for the sake of my holy name, which you have profaned among the nations." Variations of this theme pervade the book. Thus, instead of dealing with Israel according to their evil ways

---

98. On the role of shame in Ezekiel, see the excellent essay by Jacqueline E. Lapsley, "Shame and Self Knowledge: The Positive Role of Shame in Ezekiel's View of the Moral Self," in Odell and Strong, eds., *The Book of Ezekiel*, 143–73. On shame more broadly, see John K. Chance, "The Anthropology of Honor and Shame: Culture, Values, and Practice," *Semeia* 68 (1994): 139–51; Saul Olyan, "Honor, Shame and Covenant Relations in Ancient Israel and Its Environment," *JBL* 115 (1996): 201–18; Johanna Stiebert, "Shame and Prophecy: Approaches Past and Present," *BibInt* 8 (2000): 255–75.
99. Raitt, *Theology of Exile*, 123.
100. Ibid.
101. Cf. Schwartz, "Ezekiel's Dim View," 55–6.
102. Allen, *Ezekiel 20–48*, 7.
103. Greenberg, *Ezekiel 1–20*, 377.

or corrupt deeds, Yahweh restores them for the sake of his reputation (20:44), especially in the eyes of the nations (20:41; 36:22-32; cf. 37:28). According to Ezekiel, both punishment and restoration serve to instill the knowledge of Yahweh. While this theme is pervasive in oracles of judgment,[104] we find it in oracles of deliverance as well.[105] Concerning the return from exile, for example, Ezek. 20:42 states: "You shall know that I am Yahweh when I bring you into the land of Israel, the land that I swore to give to your ancestors."

Thus, Ezekiel's oracles of restoration do not depict unbridled salvation. Instead, the salvation is intended to make Israel reflect further on her transgressions and punishment. According to Raitt, "Nothing outside of Jeremiah and Ezekiel can attest the remarkable combination of unconditional promises of deliverance together with a vivid awareness of the validity and profoundly serious implications of judgment."[106] This phenomenon in the oracles of salvation suggests they came from the same prophet of judgment.

The shift from judgment to restoration parallels another shift in the prophet's ministry brought about by the fall of Jerusalem. The dumbness imposed on Ezekiel at his prophetic calling (3:26) is lifted in 587 when he hears the news that the city has fallen (33:22; cf. 24:27). Like the shift from judgment to restoration, the end of the dumbness amounts to a fundamental shift in the nature of Ezekiel's ministry. Robert Wilson has shown that Ezekiel's dumbness before 587 represented the prohibition that Ezekiel act as an intermediary between Yahweh and the people.[107] The prophet may still deliver oracles (3:27), but he is not permitted to intercede for the people or allow them to inquire of Yahweh. According to Block, the punishment is inevitable at this point, and no intercession will avert

---

104. The recognition formula appears as a result of punishment in Ezek. 5:13; 6:7, 10, 13, 14; 7:4; 9; 11:10, 12; 12:15, 20; 13:9, 14, 21, 23; 14:8; 15:7; 17:21, 24; 21:5; 22:16; 22:22; 23:49; 25:5, 7, 11, 17; 26:6, 14; 28:22, 23, 24; 29:6, 9, 16; 30:8, 19, 25, 26; 32:15, 29; 35:4, 9, 12, 15; 38:23; 39:7.

105. Ezek. 16:62; 20:42, 44; 28:26; 34:27, 30; 36:11; 36:23, 36, 38; 37:6, 13, 14, 28.

106. Raitt, *Theology of Exile*, 126.

107. This interpretation of Ezekiel's dumbness relies on the proper understanding that איש מוכיח in legal contexts signifies a mediator or arbiter, rather than a judge or reprover (Robert R. Wilson, "An Interpretation of Ezekiel's Dumbness," *VT* 22 [1973]: 98–100; idem, *Prophecy and Society*, 284; followed by Block, *Ezekiel*, 1:155–8; Joyce, *Ezekiel*, 82–3). Allen simply dismisses Wilson's proposal before advocating a more literal interpretation in which Ezekiel's speechlessness is absolute with intermittent oracles of judgment (*Ezekiel 1–19*, 61–4).

the fall of the city.[108] Wilson's proposal explains the two instances when the elders come to "seek" Yahweh by the prophet, and Yahweh refuses. Instead, he commands Ezekiel to judge them (14:1-3; 20:1-4). After the punishment, Israel's requests to inquire are granted (e.g., 36:37-38).[109] It seems that the events of 587—the culmination of Yahweh's judgment on Israel—issued a similar change in the prophet's ministry with respect to the content of his message.

This fundamental shift from judgment to salvation does not preclude the possibility of salvation oracles before 587 or further elements of judgment after 587. Interestingly, Zimmerli and others have argued that 11:14-21—the restoration oracle most commonly seen as out of place among the judgment oracles of chs. 1–24—in fact reflects a provenance before 587.[110] Nevertheless, it is possible that restoration oracles after 587 may have been editorially placed among—or indeed immediately after—earlier judgment oracles. No passages are more germane to this discussion than the restoration endings of 16:40-63 and 20:33-44. Chapter 20 in particular includes a date formula that assigns the oracle to the period before 587.[111] However, some have questioned whether vv. 33-44 are integral components of the original pre-587 oracle or were added after 587. We will consider these passages in more detail below, in particular considering the possibility that the prophet later supplemented his oracles with restoration endings.

Modified Vocabulary

One of the most compelling arguments for the authenticity of the gathering motif in Ezekiel is found internally. As we noted earlier, when the motif occurs in a single line, we find the entire phrase קבץ מן־העמים from Deut. 30:3. However, when it occurs in two parallel lines, we find a consistent alteration with the introduction of a new verb in the first position, often with מן־העמים, and the shift of the verb קבץ to the second line. The consistency with which the motif is employed in Ezekiel—including the unique alteration of the phrase by splitting and recombination—suggests the likelihood of a common author.

---

108. Block, *Ezekiel*, 1:158. Cf. Wilson, "Interpretation," 101: "The time for a fair trial has past [*sic*]."

109. Wilson, "Interpretation," 103–4.

110. Zimmerli, *Ezekiel*, 1:263; Greenberg, *Ezekiel 1–20*, 203–4; Joyce, *Ezekiel*, 110.

111. The seventh year, fifth month, and tenth day (of the exile of Jehoiachin), or approximately 591 BCE.

Perhaps more important is the fact that the newly introduced word in the first position is generally determined by the context.[112] The motif does not have the appearance of a secondary insertion, since it is otherwise adapted to and embedded in its context. For example, in ch. 20, Ezekiel presents the departure from the nations as a New Exodus. In vv. 33-44, the prophet clearly alludes to the exodus tradition to describe the gathering of the people, and in both instances he uses the variant form "to bring forth from the peoples" (הוציא מן־העמים), employing the exodus key word הוציא.[113] Ezekiel then follows these two exodus allusions in the second line with the alternative קבץ מן־הארצות, in accordance with the splitting and recombining technique noted above.

Gathering in Oracles against the Nations

The presence of the gathering motif in an oracle concerning a foreign nation reinforces the likelihood of the authenticity of the gathering motif in Ezekiel. In ch. 29, after a series of oracles against Egypt and immediately following the judgment of scattering, v. 13 contains a prediction of restoration for Egypt. Though the result of this "restoration" is a "lowly kingdom," that "will never again exalt itself above the nations" (v. 15), the oracle nevertheless includes the return of the people to their land and the typical restoration language שוב שבות (v. 15). This "limited" restoration parallels the qualified restoration of Israel in Ezekiel's salvation oracles. The restoration of Egypt would be an unlikely late insertion into the book, suggesting that the gathering metaphor is an authentic component of Ezekiel's message, not simply a late restoration motif inserted into the book to speak of Israel's reclaiming of its land.

A Counterpart to the Scattering Motif

Finally, gathering is a natural counterpart to scattering. Although Lust generally treats the gathering motif as a self-standing motif apart from its parallel, the two are best interpreted as complementary sides of a single motif. While it would be possible that a later redactor "reversed" Ezekiel's scattering metaphor, the presence of modified vocabulary, its application to a foreign nation, and the following discussions on each passage make a redactional origin for every occurrence of the motif unlikely

---

112. Lust recognized that the first verb of the return formula is variable and related to context ("Gathering and Return," 121).

113. Also noted by Lust (ibid., 121 n. 11).

* * *

Excursus: Contested Restoration Passages

In contrast to Siegfried Herrmann, who understands the scattering and gathering motif in Ezekiel to derive from a Deuteronomistic redactor, and Johan Lust, who argues for a Hellenistic origin for these passages, I will argue that the motif is an integral component of Ezekiel's restoration message. While Lust contends that the gathering motif was never employed in the original layers of the book, he does not offer a thorough defense of this view.[114] The substantial evidence for the authenticity of the motif in many passages suggests any redactional occurrences are recapitulations of an authentic Ezekielian motif.

This excursus constitutes a brief look at some of the contested restoration passages that contain the gathering motif. Elsewhere I have treated these passages more fully, including engagement with the scholarly literature.[115]

Ezekiel 11:14-21

Ezekiel 11:14-21 is the most conspicuous restoration oracle in the predominantly judgment-concentrated chs. 1–24. Scholars generally attribute vv. 14-21 to the prophet,[116] but disagree about whether they were originally part of a pre-587 restoration oracle[117] or instead were delivered by Ezekiel after the fall of Jerusalem and later placed in the first half of the book.[118] The scattering and gathering motifs occur in vv. 16 and 17, respectively. Some critics argue that v. 17 is secondary due to the change from third person addressee to second person and the double occurrence of לכן אמר ("therefore, speak") in vv. 16 and 17.[119] However, Greenberg and

---

114. Ibid., 140–1.

115. Gile, "Deuteronomic Influence in the Book of Ezekiel."

116. Exceptions include Cooke, *Ezekiel*, 124; Herrmann, *Die prophetischen Heilserwartungen*, 246; Liwak, "Überlieferungsgeschichtliche Probleme," 110–43.

117. Zimmerli, *Ezekiel*, 1:263; Greenberg, *Ezekiel 1–20*, 203–4; Block, *Ezekiel*, 1:342–3. Raitt and Joyce concur, explicitly naming 11:14-21 as the *only* restoration oracle delivered before 587 (Raitt, *Theology of Exile*, 113; Joyce, *Ezekiel*, 109–10).

118. Those who argue for a date after 587 appeal to the similar form of 33:23-25 (which is dated after 587) and to the notion that restoration oracles are typically products of the post-judgment period (e.g., Eichrodt, *Ezekiel*, 142–3; William H. Brownlee, *Ezekiel 1–19*, WBC 28 [Waco: Word, 1986], 163; Eichrodt, *Ezekiel*, 142; Zimmerli, *Ezekiel*, 1:256; Liwak, "Überlieferungsgeschichtliche Probleme," 110; Greenberg, *Ezekiel 1–20*, 204; Block, *Ezekiel*, 1:342; Allen, *Ezekiel 1–19*, 131; Joyce, *Ezekiel*, 109).

119. Herrmann, *Die prophetischen Heilserwartungen*, 244; Liwak, "Überlieferungsgeschichtliche Probleme," 112; Hossfeld, *Untersuchungen*, 406–7; Lust, "Gathering and Return," 140; Ohnesorge, *Jahwe gestaltet*, 29. Whereas most assert a later editor, Zimmerli entertained the possibility that Ezekiel himself may have secondarily added it (Zimmerli, *Ezekiel*, 1:263); Wevers, *Ezekiel*, 31.

Block argue that the change in grammatical person reflects a change in the rhetorical addressee. According to Block, "the alternation of person is necessitated by the fact that Ezekiel is dealing with two audiences, one rhetorical (Jerusalem), the other real (the exiles), those far away and those near at hand, respectively."[120] We find another example of this phenomenon in 33:24-29.[121] Moreover, alternations of person occur elsewhere in contexts that are not otherwise considered intrusive (e.g., 20:40-41; 28:20-23). In the case of 28:20-23, for example, Zimmerli regards these verses as a unity and admits that "one must simply accept the change in style."[122]

Moreover, the most serious problem with deleting v. 17 is that the gathering of the people is necessary for the logic of the passage, since the following verses assume the return to the land introduced in v. 17. Verse 18, which begins with ובאו שמה ("and they will come there"), makes no sense without v. 17, since שמה would have no contextual referent. Although Zimmerli eliminates the problem by deleting both vv. 17 and 18,[123] vv. 19-20 are problematic without v. 17 as well. As Graffy points out, if v. 17 is removed, the resulting text "implies that the new heart would be bestowed in the exile, a point which would contradict the tradition found again in Ezek 36, and also in Jer 32,37-41."[124] Therefore, excising the gathering motif in v. 17 creates more problems than it solves.

Ezekiel 20:32-44

Ezekiel 20 mentions the gathering of Israel in vv. 34 and 41. These verses are located in the restoration section of the chapter (vv. 32-44), which builds upon the historical retrospect of vv. 1-31. While the date formula in 20:1 places the oracle in 591 BCE, the relationship of vv. 32-44 to vv. 1-31 is a matter of debate. Certainly, the writer of vv. 32-44 meant for the restoration oracle to be a continuation of the preceding account of Israel's history. First, the beginning of the second section at v. 32 exhibits no new introductory formula that would suggest it is an independent

---

120. Block, *Ezekiel*, 1:345; Liwak, "Überlieferungsgeschichtliche Probleme," 112–13. Greenberg, *Ezekiel 1–20*, 190: "The sudden change…reflects awareness of the exile audience, the real addressees of the prophet."

121. On Ezek. 33:24-29, see Adrian Graffy, *A Prophet Confronts His People: Disputation Speech in the Prophets*, AnBib 104 (Rome: Biblical Institute Press, 1984), 48, who writes: "Although the whole speech, like Ezek 11,14-17, is to be understood as actually delivered to the exiles, the grammatical addressee after the introductory formulae changes from those in Jerusalem in the first refutation in vv. 25-26 to those in the exile in the second refutation in vv. 27-29. A similar process is seen in Ezek 11,16-17."

122. Zimmerli, *Ezekiel*, 2:97, who regards the conclusion of redaction advocated by Cooke and Wevers as arbitrary.

123. Zimmerli, *Ezekiel*, 1:263.

124. Graffy, *Prophet Confronts His People*, 48 n. 71.

oracle.[125] Second, the two sections display marked thematic continuity.[126] Most notably, both share the broad themes of exodus, judgment in the desert, and the abandonment of idols. In addition, numerous lexical links ground these themes and tie the two sections together.[127]

Zimmerli sees "no compelling ground for denying to the prophet Ezekiel this well-defined...oracle [i.e., vv. 32-44]."[128] I believe 20:32-44 is best understood as an example of the shift from judgment to restoration that occurred after 587 BCE, as noted by Raitt and others.[129] In Chapter 1 of this study, in the section entitled "Ezekiel's Role in Producing the Book," we noted several scholars who believe Ezekiel may have been the editor or (re)shaper of his own oracles. If Ezekiel himself supplemented his earlier oracle by drawing from and continuing its themes, I propose calling such a prophetic act "resumptive composition."[130] The phenomenon corresponds to one manifestation of what Zimmerli calls *Fortschreibung*, or "literary development."[131] In his 1980 essay, Zimmerli distinguished two types of development, one characterized by the internal development of oracles and the other by the extension of an oracle that leaves the basic text intact.[132] What I call "resumptive composition" is synonymous

---

125. Block, *Ezekiel*, 1:612. Cf. Allen, *Ezekiel 20–48*, 8: "The brevity of the introduction and the linking with the conjunction *waw* (cf. Isa 49:14) may suggest that Ezekiel himself meant it as a sequel to the earlier oracle."

126. See Block, *Ezekiel*, 1:612 n. 5; Allen, *Ezekiel 20–48*, 8.

127. These include: "I will bring them into the desert" (הביא אל־המדבר, vv. 10, 35), "rebels" (מרד, מרה, vv. 8, 38), Yahweh's oath by raised hand (נשא יד, vv. 5, 15, 23, 28, 42), "as I live" (חי־אני, vv. 3, 31, 33), Israel's "gifts" (מתנות, vv. 31, 39), Yahweh's "out-poured wrath" (בחמה שפוכה / שפך חמה, vv. 8, 13, 21, 33, 34), Yahweh's motivation for his name's sake (עשה למען שמי, vv. 9, 14, 22, 44), and the second person plural accusations of self-defilement (נטמאים / נטמאתם, vv. 31, 43).

128. For Zimmerli this depends on there being "a genuine kernel of Ezekiel material" in chs. 40–48 (*Ezekiel*, 1:414).

129. In contrast, Tova Ganzel understands 11:14-21; 16:59-63; and 20:33-44 to be restoration oracles from the pre-destruction period ("The Descriptions of the Restoration of Israel in Ezekiel," *VT* 60 [2010]: 197–211).

130. This phenomenon overlaps with but should not be confused with Block's category of "resumptive exposition," which primarily refers to the tendency "to reuse in later contexts motifs that have been introduced in early chapters" (*Ezekiel*, 1:24–5). Block lists as examples the vision of the divine glory and throne-chariot (1:1-28; 8:1–11:25; 43:1-9), the watchman motif (3:16-21; 33:1-9), Ezekiel's muteness (3:26-27; 33:22), and security in Jerusalem portrayed as a pot (11:1-12; 24:1-14).

131. Zimmerli, "Das Phänomen der 'Fortschreibung.'"

132. Ibid., 177: "Man kann dabei formal zwei verschiedene Typen der Weiterführung unterscheiden. Es kann sich auf der einen Seite um eine tief in den zunächst vorliegenden Text eingreifende, diesen umgestaltende Form der Fortschreibung handeln, die der Rekonstruktion der Erstfassung desselben Schwierigkeiten bereitet.

with this second form of literary development. As examples, Zimmerli cites the attachment of an *Erweiterung* to 16:1-43 that builds on the base text but takes it in a new direction.[133] In the case of ch. 20, Zimmerli sees vv. 32-44 as an update to the older oracle that proclaims a new development in Israel's story.[134]

Ezekiel 28:25-26

Ezekiel 28:25-26 comprises a seemingly out-of-place note of restoration for Israel in the midst of Ezekiel's oracles against foreign nations. The small oracle builds on the preceding verse, which, like 29:21, declares the significance of the judgment on the nations for Ezekiel's audience.[135] Scholars agree the placement of these verses among the oracles against the nations reflects an editorial decision at some stage of the composition or transmission of the book.[136] The extensive links between the language of vv. 25-26 and other passages in the book indicate that these verses model Ezekielian theology and style. While these verses could have originated as "a fragment of [authentic] Ezekielian proclamation editorially inserted here to expand on the good news for his people,"[137] it may be a later scribal insertion that emulates Ezekiel's style.[138]

Ezekiel 36:23c-38

The Greek Papyrus 967 and the Old Latin Codex Wirceburgensis omit 36:23c-38 and place ch. 37 after chs. 38–39.[139] Many scholars have defended the authenticity of the passage in the Hebrew text of Ezekiel by arguing for an omission based on scribal parablepsis caused by homoioteleuton, since the last words present in Pap. 967 at v. 23b and the last words of v. 38 constitute the recognition formula in nearly identical form.[140] Today, a number of scholars argue the textual evidence is best explained not by an omission in Pap. 967 but by an insertion into the proto-MT.

Daneben ist aber auch die andere Form einfacher Erweitung zu finden, in der die Erweiterung in der Art, wie es schon in Ez 16 zu sehen war, das Vorgefundene einfach durch einen weiterführenden Zusatz ergänzt und den Grundtext unberührt läßt."

133. Ibid., 176; cf. idem, *Ezekiel*, 1:69.

134. Zimmerli, "Das Phänomen der 'Fortschreibung,'" 187.

135. Block, *Ezekiel*, 2:151 n. 29.

136. Cf. ibid., 2:123: "probably reflects the editorial process more than the nature of prophetic preaching."

137. Ibid., 2:127.

138. Eichrodt, for example, dates verses vv. 25-26 "at least half a century" after the prophet's time (*Ezekiel*, 398). Similarly, Zimmerli asserts that "vv. 25f belong to a very late phase in the formation of the book, one which certainly is no longer from the hand of the prophet himself" (*Ezekiel*, 2:100).

139. Allan Chester Johnson, Henry Snyder Gehman, and Edmund Harris Kase, Jr., *The John H. Scheide Biblical Papyri: Ezekiel*, Princeton University Studies in Papyrology 3 (Princeton: Princeton University Press, 1938).

140. Floyd V. Filson, "The Omission of Ezek. 12:26-28 and 36:23b-28 in Codex 967," *JBL* 62 (1943): 31–2; followed by Wevers, *Ezekiel*, 192.

By this interpretation, Ezek. 36:23c-38 was not present in the earliest form of the Hebrew text but was added at one of the latest stages of the book's textual growth. This view was proposed as early as 1943 by William A. Irwin and developed further by Johan Lust,[141] who argued that (1) 36:23c-38 would be an exceptionally large block of text to skip over by parablepsis and (2) parablepsis alone does not explain the variant chapter order of Pap. 967.[142] According to Lust, "if the omission had been caused by a single *homoioteleuton*, the MS should then have continued with the next verse, which is 37:1 in the traditional order of the book."[143] Instead, Lust posited that the passage was composed to provide a transition between 36:16-23b and ch. 37. The late date of the passage is allegedly corroborated by Late Biblical Hebrew vocabulary and un-Ezekielian style.[144]

141. William Irwin, *The Problem of Ezekiel: An Inductive Study* (Chicago: University of Chicago Press, 1943), 62–4; Johan Lust, "Ezekiel 36–40 in the Oldest Greek Manuscript," *CBQ* 43 (1981): 517–33; idem, "Gathering and Return," 140–1. See also Pierre Maurice Bogaert, "Le témoignage de la Vetus Latina dans l'étude de la tradition des Septante: Ézéchiel et Daniel dans le Papyrus 967," *Bib* 59 (1978): 384–95.

142. Irwin, *Problem of Ezekiel*, 62 n. 3; Lust, "Ezekiel 36–40," 519–20.

143. Lust, "Ezekiel 36–40," 520. María Victoria Spottorno has suggested a different theory of parablepsis that explains both the omission of 36:23c-38 and the altered order of chapter ("La omisión de Ez. 36:23b-38 y la transposición de capítulos en el papiro 967," *Emerita* 50 [1982]: 93–8). She recognizes that parablepsis of such a long passage as 36:23c-38 would be unusual (p. 95), but nevertheless attempts to explain Pap. 967 with an even longer parablepsis. She proposes that the scribe of some predecessor to Pap. 967 jumped from the recognition formula in 36:23b to the recognition formula in 37:28, thereby skipping 36:23c-38 and all of ch. 37. Upon realizing the mistake, he then inserted ch. 37 after completing chs. 38–39 (p. 97). Spottorno contends that if 36:23c-38, which constitutes 1451 letters in Codex Vaticanus, occupied a single page in a parent text of Pap. 967, the relative size of ch. 37 would (potentially exactly) occupy two pages, and chs. 38–39, four pages (pp. 95–7). This hypothetical page distribution would have produced an even more likely situation for the scribe to skip over 36:23c–37:28, since the homoioteleuton of the two recognition formulae would have been found at the exact end of their respective pages. Unlike the standard theory of parablepsis proposed by Filson, this account answers Lust's claim that accidental omission cannot explain why 38:1 follows 36:23b in Pap. 967. Nevertheless, Spottorno's theory relies on a conjecture that, as she herself recognized, finds no support in the textual evidence: in order for the scribe's eye to jump directly from 36:23b to 38:1, she presumes the omission of the phrase immediately following the recognition formula of 37:28 in the predecessor to Pap. 967: מקדש את־ישראל בהיות מקדשי בתוכם לעולם / ο αγιαζων αυτους εν τω ειναι τα αγια μου εν μεσω αυτων εις τον αιωνα.

144. Lust, "Ezekiel 36–40," 521–4. Utilizing the linguistic study of Mark Rooker (*Biblical Hebrew in Transition*), Michaël van der Meer argues, contra Lust, that none of the alleged Late Biblical Hebrew expressions conclusively demonstrate a

Two recent books represent the most extensive studies of Pap. 967 to date. First, Ashley Crane has built upon the work of Lust and presented plausible circumstances that would explain 36:23c-38 as a late insertion.[145] Crane's study led Block, who had earlier mounted a sustained critique of Lust's theory,[146] to accept that Pap. 967 may represent a Hebrew text that antedates the text tradition underlying the MT.[147] Second, Ingrid Lilly's comprehensive study applies text-critical, literary, and codicological analyses to Pap. 967.[148] She argues that Pap. 967 and the MT represent two different, viable text-types ("variant literary editions"). Although she challenges arguments that 36:23c-38 was omitted due to an error, she resists the conclusion that Pap. 967's text on the whole is earlier than the MT's.[149]

Engaging this issue in any more detail is beyond the scope of this study. Although I continue to wonder if the loss of a page in one of the predecessors to Pap. 967 has been sufficiently ruled out,[150] Crane and Lilly have presented cogent arguments that 36:23c-38 is a secondary addition to the book. For the purposes of this study, we may

post-Ezekiel date for the passage ("A New Spirit in an Old Corpus? Text-Critical, Literary-Critical and Linguistic Observations regarding Ezekiel 36:16-38," in *The New Things: Eschatology in Old Testament Prophecy, Festschrift for Henk Leene*, ed. F. Postma, K. Spronk, and E. Talstra, ACEBTSup 3 [Maastricht: Shaker, 2002], 147–58).

145. Ashley S. Crane, *Israel's Restoration: A Textual-Comparative Exploration of Ezekiel 36–39*, VTSup 122 (Leiden: Brill, 2008), 230–45, who summarizes Lust, "Ezekiel 36–40"; Block, *Ezekiel*, 1:337–42; and Lust, "Textual Criticism of the Old and New Testaments: Stepbrothers?" in *New Testament Textual Criticism and Exegesis: Festschrift J. Delobel*, ed. Adelbert Denaux, BETL 161 (Leuven: Leuven University Press, 2002), 28–31.

146. Block, *Ezekiel*, 1:337–43.

147. Block, "Transformation of Royal Ideology," 238.

148. Ingrid E. Lilly, *Two Books of Ezekiel: Papyrus 967 and the Masoretic Text as Variant Literary Editions*, VTSup 150 (Leiden: Brill, 2012). On 36:23c-38 see especially pp. 11–25, 57–60, 122–7, 194–212.

149. Ibid., 21–5, 302.

150. See Johnson, Gehman, and Kase, *John H. Scheide Biblical Papyri*, 8–9; Filson, "Omission," 31; Allen, *Ezekiel 20–48*, 177–8; cf. Joyce, *Ezekiel*, 205–6. Following the calculations of Johnson and Irwin, Crane protests that 36:23c-38 would not likely have occupied one leaf (*Israel's Restoration*, 213). Spottorno, on the other hand, has offered a possible reconstruction of a predecessor to Pap. 967 that could have had 36:23c-38 on a single page with approximately 1500 letters ("La omisión de Ez. 36:23b-38"). Even if this proves impossible for Pap. 967 itself, contra Crane this section may have occupied a single page at some point in the transmission history of the text, since different codices would have been formatted in different ways and therefore yielded various page sizes. The plausibility of the accidental loss of a folio may be supported by Thackeray's proposal that this passage was

conclude that even if 36:23c-38 is a late, anthological insertion that draws from the themes, vocabulary, and style of Ezekiel, its inclusion of the gathering motif echoes an authentically Ezekielian motif.

Ezekiel 38–39

The unity of the Gog oracles in chs. 38–39 has stimulated much discussion in the history of scholarship.[151] The gathering metaphor appears in 39:21-29, a section whose relationship to the preceding oracles in 38:1–39:20 has been much disputed.[152] It is true 39:21-29 shift the focus from the eschatological conflicts between Yahweh and Gog to the more domestic situation of Israel's exile. In addition, the section exhibits some words and phrases that are unique in Ezekiel.[153] As Block argues, the numerous points of contact between vv. 21-29 and the earlier oracles in the book betray some connection with the prophet, even if they were composed in order to integrate the Gog oracles with the rest of the book.[154]

William Tooman argues the entirety of chs. 38–39 are not from Ezekiel but instead are a late, Hellenistic pastiche of Ezekielian style.[155] After documenting the pervasive stylistic links between chs. 38–39 and the rest of the book, his argument for the date of the Gog oracles rests on the passage's apparently unique language.[156] According to Tooman, the author of chs. 38–39 attempted to copy Ezekielian style, but did so imperfectly. The alleged non-Ezekielian words and phrases include: כסף וזהב instead of זהב וכסף, the use of גלה to speak of Israel going into exile (39:23, 28), the phrase

frequently used as a lectionary in the synagogue (cf. ibid., 214, 225–30). Moreover, Lilly has compiled a strong case that Pap. 967 had a public reading function (*Two Books*, 261–4, 300). After the omission, the placement of ch. 37 may have been easily confounded in an unbound codex, especially if ch. 37 occupied two distinct pages, as Spottorno suggests. Pap. 967 also exhibits the transposition of chs. 5–6 and 7–8 of Daniel, suggesting that Pap. 967 (or one of its predecessors) may have been unbound.

151. For surveys, see Margaret Odell, "'Are You He of Whom I Spoke by My Servants the Prophets?' Ezekiel 38–39 and the Problem of History in the Neobabylonian Context" (Ph.D. diss., University of Pittsburgh, 1988), 1–42; Paul Fitzpatrick, *The Disarmament of God: Ezekiel 38–39 in its Mythic Context*, CBQMS 37 (Washington, DC: Catholic Biblical Association of America, 2004), 1–48.

152. For a review, see Daniel I. Block, "Gog and the Pouring Out of the Spirit: Reflections on Ezekiel xxxix 21-29," *VT* 37 (1987): 258–61; repr. in Block, *Beyond the River Chebar*, 95–125.

153. Block mentions מן־היום ההוא והלאה (v. 22), אסתר פני מהם (vv. 23, 24, 29), צריהם (v. 23), and רחם (v. 25), the last of which we will return to below (ibid., 261–2).

154. See ibid., 262; idem, *Ezekiel* 2:427 n. 10.

155. Tooman, *Gog of Magog*; idem, "Transformation of Israel's Hope: The Reuse of Scripture in the Gog Oracles," in Tooman and Lyons, eds., *Transforming Visions*, 50–105.

156. Tooman, *Gog of Magog*, 39–64 and 65–72, respectively.

ואת־ידי אשר־שמתי בהם ("my hand that I laid upon them," 39:21), the root רחם ("compassion," 39:25), and the distinct forms of the gathering motif in Ezek. 39:27, 28.[157] In other instances, Tooman claims the author of chs. 38–39 uses Ezekielian locutions differently than elsewhere in the book.[158] Further studies of Ezekiel 38–39 will have to evaluate Tooman's thesis, particularly whether this level of unique language in chs. 38–39 points to divergent authorship or whether Ezekiel himself may have used such locutions in diverse ways and with varied referents. Lastly, if it is a pastiche, C. A. Strine has argued that the compositional technique of pastiche is not exclusively a phenomenon of the late Second Temple Period.[159]

To conclude this section, we have shown it is unlikely every instance of gathering language comes from late redaction. On the contrary, for many of the passages in which gathering occurs, there is considerable evidence it originated with the prophet himself, and possible interpolations (for example 28:25-26 and 39:28) continue Ezekiel's use of the gathering motif.

* * *

The Rhetoric of Allusion

In conclusion, this chapter has outlined the striking verbal links between Ezekiel's gathering formula and Deuteronomy 30 and argued for the plausibility that Ezekiel drew upon Deuteronomy's language for his prophetic promises of return to the land.[160] First, the criteria of density and distribution suggest a direct literary connection between Deuteronomy 30 and Ezekiel. Specifically, both Deuteronomy and Ezekiel describe the gathering of Israel and return to their land with a similar formula containing three elements in the same order: the gathering motif (קבץ) with the preposition מן plus עמים or ארצות, followed by a relative clause with פוץ specifying the places from which the people will be gathered, and finally, the return of the people described as Yahweh bringing them to their land (הביאתים אל־אדמתם). Second, even if Deuteronomy 30 were roughly contemporaneous with Ezekiel, there are indications that Ezekiel drew from Deuteronomy 30 and not vice versa. Ezekiel's formula is best explained as a literary modification of Deut. 30:3-5, specifically the splitting of קבץ מן־העמים and recombination into parallel lines. Indeed, as shown above, this literary modification explains many of the variations of

---

157. Ibid., 65–8; cf. idem, "Transformation of Israel's Hope," 53–7.

158. Tooman, *Gog of Magog*, 68–72.

159. C. A. Strine, "On the Compositional Models for Ezekiel 38–39: A Response to William Tooman," *VT* 67 (2017): 589–601.

160. So also Widengren, "Yahweh's Gathering," 233.

Ezekiel's formula, which are often determined by their immediate literary context.

If Ezekiel drew from the tradition of Deuteronomy 30 for his conception of Israel's restoration, then he rooted his own prophetic promises in the promises of the Deuteronomic tradition. Thus, his message of hope was not entirely new, but a proclamation of what he knew to be the assurance of Yahweh's continued faithfulness to his people in the wake of judgment and disaster. To the extent that the language of Deuteronomy 30 was known to Ezekiel's audience and associated with Mosaic tradition, they would have heard his prophetic promises as a prophetic renewal of Deuteronomy's promises of restoration after judgment.

Chapter 8

Conclusion

This study has identified the influence of Deuteronomy on Ezekiel in areas that are significant for his prophetic message. In various ways, it shaped how he saw Israel's past history of rebellion against Yahweh, the present situation of divine judgment, and the future hope of restoration. The prophet used Deuteronomy's distinctive language and concepts and in some cases seems to have known and alluded to specific texts. To conclude, I offer a summary of the findings of this study, as well as final reflections on Ezekiel's view of Deuteronomy and his use of Scripture.

Summary

Chapter 3 investigated Ezekiel's language and his conception of idolatry, which for him was the principal sin that led to the Babylonian exile. Ezekiel shares Deuteronomy's special concern for idolatry and indeed uses its language almost exclusively to describe Israel's idols and idolatrous practices. In one instance, he cites Deuteronomy's unique association of worshiping עץ ואבן in exile to interpret the elders' determination to worship idols (20:32). Ezekiel also uses Deuteronomic language in his condemnation of (idolatrous) worship sites outside of Jerusalem. The temple vision of Ezekiel 8 displays strong lexical links to Deuteronomy, particularly Deut. 4:16-19, suggesting that Ezekiel's vision deliberately depicts a fundamental transgression of the torah of Deuteronomy 4. For Ezekiel, idol worship is foremost a transgression against Yahweh's חקות and משפטים (e.g., 20:16). By using Deuteronomy's language, he identifies these statutes and ordinances primarily with Deuteronomy's prohibitions of idolatry.

8. Conclusion

In Chapter 4, I argued that Ezekiel 16 represents a prophetic transformation of the rise and decline of Israel depicted in the well-known Song of Moses in Deuteronomy 32, whereby he adopts its structure and themes and infuses them with the prophetic motif of harlotry. The frequency and distribution of parallels between these two texts offers overwhelming evidence for dependence. The two texts exhibit many thematic links in a nearly identical plot structure: (a) Yahweh discovers destitute Israel in a barren location; (b) he delivers her and renders lavish care upon her so that (c) she prospers; (d) Israel in her prosperity forsakes Yahweh; (e) she pursues other gods and (f) forgets her origins, thereby (g) provoking Yahweh to anger; (h) Israel is punished for her sins; and finally, (i) Israel is restored. It is highly improbable that these similarities are coincidental, since they are corroborated by several lexical links at the same point in the plot, including the פרש כנף motif, eating (אכל) דבש and שמן, the verbal root כעס to signify Israel's provocation of Yahweh, and כפר in Israel's restoration. By adopting the plot structure of the rise and fall of Israel in the Song of Moses, the prophet applies it to his contemporary context of idolatry and illegitimate foreign relations, declaring that Moses' prediction of punishment has come to pass in the current generation.

Chapter 5 showed that Ezekiel's view of Israel's history in ch. 20 displays strong influence from Deuteronomy. At numerous points, the prophet uses Deuteronomic language and concepts to describe Israel's history. He did not do so with a polemical purpose, nor did he repudiate Deuteronomy's worship laws by deeming them "not-good" (v. 25), as some have asserted. He begins his account with Yahweh's election (בחר) of Israel in v. 5, a distinctively Deuteronomic concept, and adopts numerous other terms unique to Deuteronomy as well. Ezekiel 20 also includes many of the significant allusions to Deuteronomy noted in other chapters of this study, notably the reference to Yahweh's threat to scatter the people in Deut. 4:25-28 (v. 23) and the association of worshiping "wood and stone" in exile (v. 32).

In Chapter 6, I argued that Ezekiel's typical formula for expressing Yahweh's scattering of Israel, הפיץ [אתם] בגוים וזרה [אתם] בארצות, constitutes a combination and conflation of the Deuteronomic and Priestly locutions, הפיץ בעמים and זרה בארצות, respectively. Such a combination conforms to one of his known methods of literary appropriation and indeed finds a virtually exact parallel in his use of sources in Ezek. 25:7. Ezekiel's reference to Deuteronomy's conception of worshiping "wood and stone" in exile suggests he knows at least one of the Deuteronomic exile passages. In 20:23, Ezekiel explicitly alludes to an earlier tradition that Yahweh swore to scatter Israel among the nations. The plot structure and narrative flow of ch. 20 indicate a setting for this oath during the second wilderness generation, which naturally points to Deuteronomy. One text in particular appears to be the basis for the allusion. In Deut. 4:25-28, the call for witnesses to testify to Yahweh's promise to scatter Israel—in the context of an explicit covenant—would have been understood as a treaty oath to Ezekiel and other ancient readers. Therefore, the oath to scatter Israel described in Ezek. 20:23 most likely alludes to Deut. 4:25-28. Thus, Ezekiel purposely draws from the Deuteronomic language of exile and at least once clearly alludes to an exile passage in Deuteronomy.

Chapter 7 argued that Ezekiel also draws from Deuteronomy for his message that Yahweh would gather his people and return them to their land. Ezekiel's gathering formula contains three distinguishing elements that mirror Deut. 30:3-5: (a) a statement of God gathering (קבץ) Israel from the nations, which is best explained as a literary modification of Deuteronomy 30, specifically splitting קבץ מן־העמים and recombining its parts into parallel lines, (b) a relative clause with the verb פוץ that explains Israel will be gathered from the places to which they were previously scattered, and (c) a statement of Yahweh bringing (הביא) Israel back to their land. Although Deut. 30:3-5 is commonly dated to the exilic or postexilic period, Ezekiel could still have used Deuteronomy 30 if it was roughly contemporaneous with him. But the deportation of the Northern Kingdom in 722 BCE and the presence of the scattering and gathering motifs in the broader ancient Near East provide a historical and literary context from which to speak about gathering before 587 BCE. The direction of influence finds further support by the criterion of literary modification, since the variations of Ezekiel's gathering formula are best explained as modifications of Deuteronomy 30.

Ezekiel and Scribal Expansion

Based on the literary and theological coherence of the book, as well as Ezekiel's apparent expertise in literary traditions, this study has concluded that much of the Deuteronomic influence evident in the book of Ezekiel is attributable to the prophet himself. At the same time, we might expect Deuteronomy's influence on Ezekiel to motivate "additional coordination between the books by later redactors," since textual referencing seems to beget more referencing.[1] Timothy Mackie has observed this phenomenon

---

1. Credit to the anonymous reviewer of this monograph series.

in the relationship between Ezekiel and the Holiness Code: "the presence of so many expansions based on [the Holiness Code] demonstrates not only an awareness of [the] pre-existing relationship [between Ezekiel and the Holiness Code], but also an attempt to further solidify the bond between these two texts."[2] In a similar way, since Ezekiel's followers continued his distinctive theology and literary style, it should not be surprising if the expansions in the book reflect his text-borrowing practices and indebtedness to Deuteronomy. Possible examples discussed earlier include: תבנית רמש ובהמה in Ezek. 8:10 and וישבו להכעיסני in Ezek. 8:17 (both treated in Chapter 3), as well as Ezek. 28:25-26, בגוים אשר אדיחם שם in Ezek. 4:13, and וכנסתים על־אדמתם ולא־אותיר עוד מהם שם in 39:28 (cited in Chapter 7).

Deuteronomy as Divine Torah for Ezekiel

This study has shown that, along with the Holiness Code, Ezekiel regarded Deuteronomy's laws as divine torah for Israel, given by Yahweh in the wilderness (20:11). These two literary traditions served as the primary basis for Ezekiel's indictment against the people for failure to keep Yahweh's חקות and משפטים. While Ezekiel routinely cites injunctions from the Holiness Code to indict Israel for their transgressions—most notably in the cultic and social spheres—he also draws from Deuteronomic language and concepts, particularly for his polemic against idolatry. In so doing, he transforms divine laws into prophetic accusations that underline the seriousness of Israel's sins.

Furthermore, Deuteronomy significantly influenced Ezekiel's response to the crisis of the early sixth century, shaping the way he saw Israel's *past*, *present*, and *future*. First, Ezekiel interprets and describes Israel's past largely in Deuteronomic terms. In ch. 20, he adopts Deuteronomic vocabulary for his overview of Israel's history and indeed, like Deuteronomy, sees their rebellion reaching back to the earliest period of their history as a people. Israel transgressed the divine instructions, beginning in the wilderness and continuing in the land (20:5-29) even unto the current generation (14:6; cf. 20:30-31). It was Ezekiel's task to declare to them their abominations (20:4). Deuteronomy was formative for Ezekiel's other historical review as well. In his metaphorical description of Israel's history in ch. 16, he interprets Israel's sins in light of the unfolding drama of Israel's rise and fall in the Song of Moses (Deut. 32:1-43). Like the Song, Ezekiel recounts how, in spite of Yahweh's gracious deliverance

---

2. Mackie, *Expanding Ezekiel*, 214–15.

and care for his people (16:4-14), Israel rebelled against Yahweh by their idolatry and foreign relations (16:15-43).

Second, Ezekiel finds in both the Holiness Code and Deuteronomy the basis for interpreting the present situation of Babylonian exile as Yahweh's judgment on his people. Both pentateuchal traditions predicted that Israel would lose the land for covenant unfaithfulness. Now in exile, Ezekiel concluded that Yahweh had scattered Israel from their land just as he threatened long ago. Although he alludes to the language of Lev. 26:33, Ezekiel combines it with Deuteronomy's scattering language and indeed refers to Deut. 4:25-28 when he mentions an oath given "in the wilderness" at the time of the second wilderness generation (20:23). In addition, Ezekiel alludes to one of Deuteronomy's distinctive ideas about exile, namely, that in exile Israel would worship עץ ואבן, "wood and stone" (20:32). In his confrontation with the elders, the prophet interprets the elders' desire to worship idols as the realization of Deuteronomy's prediction.

Third, Ezekiel saw in the tradition of Deuteronomy 30 the divine promise of hope that Israel still had a future. His message that Yahweh would gather his people and bring them back to their land is not new, but rather an idea rooted in Deuteronomy. By alluding to the language of Deut. 30:3-5, he asserts that Yahweh's promises of restoration in Deuteronomy offer hope to the present context of disaster and exile.

In addition to assessing Ezekiel's relation to Deuteronomy and its influence on his prophetic message, this study has contributed to the interpretation of the book of Ezekiel, most notably by identifying probable literary references. According to Schultz and Ben-Porat, a semantic loss occurs when readers do not recognize a quotation or allusion. Thus, the rhetorical impact of Ezekiel's allusions is lost when interpreters miss them. For example, by alluding to Deut. 4:25-28, Ezekiel asserted that the present circumstance of exile was the fulfillment of an oath Yahweh had sworn long ago in the wilderness. Similarly, the allusions to the Song of Moses in ch. 16 communicated that the Song's prediction of Israel's fall had come to pass in the current generation. In these and other cases, identifying allusions to Deuteronomy provides a fuller understanding of the prophet's message.

Ezekiel's Use of Scripture

This study adds one more voice to the growing chorus that recognizes Ezekiel as a prophet who creatively used Israel's texts and traditions for his prophetic message. Indeed, we have seen that Ezekiel was influenced by one of the textual traditions that many have regarded as having negligible influence on him. His use of Deuteronomy as a literary tradition provides further evidence Ezekiel had "ingested" Israel's literary traditions in the process of his education-enculturation, and, like other scribes and orators, he used memorization to create "new works that…echo those works in which the scribal author was trained."[3]

To say that Ezekiel used Deuteronomic language and in some cases alluded to specific texts need not imply he knew the book of Deuteronomy in its entirety, nor, as discussed in the Introduction, that he had access to a written copy of Deuteronomy. Ezekiel could have known parts of Deuteronomy from memory, either because he memorized (portions of) it in his scribal training or because he heard it recited orally.

His use of Deuteronomy's language and ideas has many similarities to what scholars have observed about his use of other traditions. First, Ezekiel's allusions to Deuteronomy do not generally constitute "inner-biblical exegesis" in the strict sense,[4] since his goal is not principally to interpret the meaning of his source texts.[5] Instead, he uses Deuteronomy mostly for rhetorical purposes. Second, Ezekiel uses Deuteronomy in much the same rhetorical way as he uses the Holiness Code, by adapting its language for his messages of indictment, judgment, and restoration.[6] Third, in some cases Ezekiel's literary use of Deuteronomy corresponds to his techniques of literary modification identified by Lyons, particularly "combination and conflation" and "splitting and recombination into parallel lines."[7]

Ezekiel's Relation to the Holiness and Deuteronomic Traditions

If the Priestly-Holiness School and Deuteronomy represent distinct streams of tradition in ancient Israel, Ezekiel bears witness to crossover and overlap. While this study has highlighted Deuteronomy's influence on Ezekiel, this should not diminish the fact that Ezekiel was a Priestly

---

3. Carr, *Writing on the Tablet*, 159.

4. See Fishbane, *Biblical Interpretation*, e.g., 282. On methodological clarity in the use of "inner-biblical exegesis" and related terms, see Meek, "Intertextuality, Inner-Biblical Exegesis, and Inner-Biblical Allusion."

5. Lyons, *From Law to Prophecy*, 159; cf. Sommer, *A Prophet Reads Scripture*, 172–3.

6. Cf. Lyons, *From Law to Prophecy*, 114–27.

7. Ibid., 88–109.

prophet firmly planted in the Holiness School.[8] The strong Priestly influence on Ezekiel, particularly in the cultic and social spheres, is well known. In some cases, we have seen Ezekiel appropriate Deuteronomic language and concepts through his Priestly-Holiness lens. For example, while Ezekiel's focus on idolatry and his use of Deuteronomy's vocabulary suggest its influence on the prophet, his conception of idolatry as the source of defilement reflects his Priestly worldview. Similarly, while Ezekiel speaks of centralized worship using Deuteronomic language, for him the central sanctuary is closely tied to his Priestly conception of temple-centered stratified holiness.[9]

Ezekiel as Theologian and Rhetorician

While Ezekiel uses literary sources and inherits varied religious traditions, his theology cannot be reduced to an amalgamation of them. Ezekiel used Deuteronomy's language and concepts in creative ways, much as he did other literary traditions. As von Rad observed regarding Ezekiel's relationship to the Priestly tradition, "he was dependent on it, and yet free from it."[10] For example, while Ezekiel drew from both the Holiness Code and Deuteronomy, he did not propound their notion of repentance as a precondition for restoration. Similarly, while using Deuteronomy's language for gathering and even compassion, his conception of restoration was unique in its focus on continued judgment and shame. Ezekiel was not slavishly bound to his inherited traditions—and certainly not to any single tradition.

Ezekiel was, above all, a master theologian and rhetorician, who creatively adapted Israel's traditions in order to speak Yahweh's word at a critical moment in Israel's history. The result is a prophetic message that reflects influence not only from the Priestly-Holiness tradition but from Deuteronomy as well. As described in this study, Deuteronomy's language and ideas fundamentally shaped the way Ezekiel interpreted Israel's past violation of Yahweh's statutes and regulations, their present circumstances having borne his judgment, and the hope for a renewed future.

---

8. Cf. Joyce, *Ezekiel*, 38: "A better expression of the interrelation of priestly and deuteronomistic elements in Ezekiel would be to say that he is first and foremost a priest, but one not altogether immune from the deuteronomistic influences that eddied around him both in Jerusalem and in Babylonia."

9. Credit to the anonymous reviewer of this monograph series.

10. Gerhard von Rad, *Old Testament Theology*, vol. 2, *The Theology of Israel's Prophetic Traditions* (Louisville, KY: Westminster John Knox, 2001), 225.

Bibliography

Ackerman, Susan. *Under Every Green Tree: Popular Religion in Sixth-Century Judah.* HSM 46. Atlanta: Scholars Press, 1992.
Ackerman, Susan. "A *MARZĒAḤ* in Ezekiel 8:7-13?" *HTR* 82 (1989): 267–81.
Ackroyd, Peter R. *Exile and Restoration: A Study of Hebrew Thought of the Sixth Century B.C.* Philadelphia: Westminster, 1968.
Albertz, Rainer. *A History of Israelite Religion in the Old Testament Period.* Translated by John Bowden. 2 vols. Louisville: Westminster John Knox, 1994.
Albertz, Rainer. *Israel in Exile: The History and Literature of the Sixth Century BCE.* Translated by David Green. SBLSBL 3. Atlanta: Society of Biblical Literature, 2003.
Albright, W. F. "The High Place in Ancient Palestine." In *Volume du Congrès: Strasbourg 1956*, edited by G. W. Anderson, 242–58. VTSup 4. Leiden: Brill, 1957.
Albright, W. F. "Some Remarks on the Song of Moses in Deuteronomy XXXII." *VT* 9 (1959): 339–46.
Allen, Leslie C. *Ezekiel 1–19.* WBC 28. Dallas: Word, 1994.
Allen, Leslie C. *Ezekiel 20–48.* WBC 29. Dallas: Word, 1990.
Allen, Leslie C. "The Structuring of Ezekiel's Revisionist History Lesson (Ezekiel 20:3-31)." *CBQ* 54 (1992): 448–62.
Alster, Bendt. "Tammuz." *DDD*, 828–34.
Alt, Albrecht. "Die Heimat des Deuteronomiums." In *Kleine Schriften zur Geschichte des Volkes Israel*, 2:250–75. Munich: Beck, 1953.
Altick, Richard. *The Art of Literary Research.* New York: W. W. Norton, 1963. (4th ed. New York: W. W. Norton, 1993.)
Andersen, Francis I., and David Noel Freedman. *Micah: A New Translation with Introduction and Commentary.* AB 24E. New York: Doubleday, 2000.
Anderson, Bernard W. "Exodus Typology in Second Isaiah." In *Israel's Prophetic Heritage: Essays in Honor of James Muilenburg*, edited by Bernard W. Anderson and W. Harrelson, 177–95. New York: Harper & Brothers, 1962.
Bakhtin, Mikhail. *Problems of Dostoevsky's Poetics.* Translated by R. W. Rotsel. Ann Arbor, MI: Ardis, 1973.
Bakhtin, Mikhail. *Rabelais and His World.* Translated by Helene Iswolsky. Cambridge, MA: MIT, 1965.
Barr, James. *The Typology of Literalism in Ancient Biblical Translations.* MSU 15. Göttingen: Vandenhoeck & Ruprecht, 1979.
Barrick, W. Boyd. "High Place." *ABD* 3:196–200.
Barrick, W. Boyd. "The Word BMH in the Old Testament." Ph.D. diss., University of Chicago Divinity School, 1977.
Baxandall, Michael. *Patterns of Intention: On the Historical Explanation of Pictures.* New Haven: Yale University Press, 1985.

Becking, Bob. *The Fall of Samaria: An Historical and Archaeological Study*. SHANE 2. Leiden: Brill, 1992.

Begg, C. "The Literary Criticism of Deut 4,1-40: Contributions to a Continuing Discussion." *EThL* 56 (1980): 10–55.

Beentjes, Pancratius C. "What a Lioness Was Your Mother: Reflections on Ezekiel 19." In *On Reading Prophetic Texts: Gender-Specific and Related Studies in Memory of Fokkelien van Dijk-Hemmes*, edited by B. Becking and M. Dijkstra, 21–35. Biblical Interpretation Series 18. Leiden: Brill, 1996.

Beetham, Christopher A. *Echoes of Scripture in the Letter of Paul to the Colossians*. BIS 96. Leiden: Brill, 2008.

Ben-Porat, Ziva. "The Poetics of Literary Allusion." *PTL* 1 (1976): 105–28.

Bergey, Ronald. "The Song of Moses (Deuteronomy 32:1-43) and Isaianic Prophecies: A Case of Early Intertextuality?" *JSOT* 28 (2003): 33–54.

Bertholet, Alfred. *Deuteronomium*. Tübingen: J. C. B. Mohr, 1899.

Binger, T. *Asherah, Goddess in Ugarit, Israel and the Old Testament*. JSOTSup 232. Sheffield: Sheffield Academic, 1997.

Block, Daniel I. *The Book of Ezekiel*. 2 vols. NICOT. Grand Rapids: Eerdmans, 1997, 1998.

Block, Daniel I. "The God Ezekiel Wants Us to Meet: Theological Perspectives on the Book of Ezekiel." In *The God Ezekiel Creates*, edited by Paul M. Joyce and Dalit Rom-Shiloni, 162–92. LHBOTS 607. New York: Bloomsbury T&T Clark, 2015.

Block, Daniel I. *The Gods of the Nations: Studies in Ancient Near Eastern National Theology*. ETS Studies. 2nd ed. Grand Rapids: Baker, 2000.

Block, Daniel I. "Gog and the Pouring Out of the Spirit: Reflections on Ezekiel xxxix 21-29." *VT* 37 (1987): 257–70. Repr. in *Beyond the River Chebar: Studies in Kingship and Eschatology in the Book of Ezekiel*, 95–125. Eugene, OR: Cascade, 2013.

Block, Daniel I. "The Power of Song: Reflections on Ancient Israel's National Anthem (Deuteronomy 32)." In *How I Love Your Torah, O LORD! Studies in the Book of Deuteronomy*, 162–88. Eugene, OR: Cascade, 2011.

Block, Daniel I. "Transformation of Royal Ideology in Ezekiel." In *Transforming Visions: Transformations of Text, Tradition, and Theology in Ezekiel*, edited by William A. Tooman and Michael A. Lyons, 208–46. PTMS 127. Eugene, OR: Pickwick, 2010. Repr. in *Beyond the River Chebar: Studies in Kingship and Eschatology in the Book of Ezekiel*, 10–44. Eugene, OR: Cascade, 2013.

Block, Daniel I. *Triumph of Grace: Literary and Theological Studies in Deuteronomy and Deuteronomic Themes*. Eugene, OR: Cascade, 2017.

Block, Haskell M. "The Concept of Influence in Comparative Literature." In *Influx: Essays on Literary Influence*, edited by Ronald Primeau, 74–81. Port Washington, NY: Kennikat, 1977.

Bloom, Harold. *The Anatomy of Influence: Literature as a Way of Life*. New Haven: Yale University Press, 2011.

Bloom, Harold. *The Anxiety of Influence: A Theory of Poetry*. New York: Oxford University Press, 1973.

Boda, Mark J. "Renewal in Heart, Word, and Deed: Repentance in the Torah." In *Repentance in Christian Theology*, edited by Mark J. Boda and Gordon T. Smith, 3–24. Collegeville, MN: Liturgical, 2006.

Bodi, Daniel. "Les *gillûlîm* chez Ézéchiel et dans l'Ancien Testament, et les différentes pratiques cultuelles associées à ce terme." *RB* 100 (1993): 481–510.

Bogaert, Pierre Maurice. "Le témoignage de la Vetus Latina dans l'étude de la tradition des Septante: Ézéchiel et Daniel dans le Papyrus 967." *Bib* 59 (1978): 384–95.

Braulik, Georg. "Die Ausdrücke für 'Gesetz' im Buch Deuteronomium." *Bib* 51 (1970): 40–66.

Braulik, Georg. "Literarkritische und archaeologische Stratigraphie: Zu S. Mittmanns Analyse von Deuteronomium 4, 1-40." *Bib* 59 (1978): 351–83.

Braulik, Georg. *Die Mittel deuteronomistischer Rhetorik erhoben aus Deuteronomium 4,1-40*. AnBib 68. Rome: Pontifical Biblical Institute, 1978.

Brettler, Marc Zvi. "Predestination in Deuteronomy 30:1-10." In *Those Elusive Deuteronomists: The Phenomenon of Pan-Deuteronomism*, edited by L. S. Schearing and S. L. McKenzie, 174–7. JSOT 268. Sheffield: Sheffield Academic, 1999.

Bright, John. "The Date of the Prose Sermons of Jeremiah." *JBL* 70 (1951): 15–35.

Brownlee, William H. *Ezekiel 1–19*. WBC 28. Waco: Word, 1986.

Brueggemann, Walter. *The Land: Place as Gift, Promise, and Challenge in Biblical Faith*. 2nd ed. OBT. Minneapolis: Fortress, 2002.

Burrows, Millar. *The Literary Relations of Ezekiel*. Philadelphia: Jewish Publication Society, 1925.

Carley, Keith W. *Ezekiel Among the Prophets: A Study of Ezekiel's Place in Prophetic Tradition*. SBT 2/31. London: SCM, 1975.

Carr, David M. *The Formation of the Hebrew Bible: A New Reconstruction*. Oxford: Oxford University Press, 2011.

Carr, David M. *Introduction to the Old Testament: Sacred Texts and Imperial Contexts of the Hebrew Bible*. Oxford: Wiley-Blackwell, 2010.

Carr, David M. "The Many Uses of Intertextuality in Biblical Studies: Actual and Potential." In *Congress Volume Helsinki 2010*, edited by Marti Nissinen, 505–35. VTSup 148. Leiden: Brill, 2012.

Carr, David M. "Method in Determination of Dependence: An Empirical Test of Criteria Applied to Exodus 34:11-26 and Its Parallels." In *Gottes Volk am Sinai. Untersuchungen zu Ex 32–34 und Dtn 9–10*, edited by Matthias Köckert and Erhard Blum, 107–40. Gütersloh: Kaiser Gütersloher, 2001.

Carr, David M. "Orality, Textuality, and Memory: The State of Biblical Studies." In *Contextualizing Israel's Sacred Writings: Ancient Literacy, Orality, and Literary Production*, edited by Brian B. Schmidt, 161–73. SBLAIL 22. Atlanta: SBL, 2015.

Carr, David M. *Writing on the Tablet of the Heart: Origins of Scripture and Literature*. Oxford: Oxford University Press, 2005.

Cassuto, Umberto. "The Prophet Hosea and the Books of the Pentateuch" (Hebrew). In *Abhandlungen zur Erinnerung an Hirsch Perez Chajes*, edited by V. Aptowitzer and A. Z. Schwartz, 262–75. Vienna: Alexander Kohut Memorial Foundation, 1933. Eng. trans. "The Prophet Hosea and the Books of the Pentateuch." In Cassuto, *Biblical and Oriental Studies*, vol. 1, *Bible*, 79–100. Jerusalem: Magnes, 1973.

Chance, John K. "The Anthropology of Honor and Shame: Culture, Values, and Practice." *Semeia* 68 (1994): 139–51.

Cheney, P. "Influence." In *The Princeton Encyclopedia of Poetry and Poetics*, edited by Roland Greene et al., 703–5. 4th ed. Princeton: Princeton University Press, 2012.

Childs, Brevard. *Introduction to the Old Testament as Scripture*. Philadelphia: Fortress, 1979.

Choi, John H. *Traditions at Odds: The Reception of the Pentateuch in Biblical and Second Temple Period Literature*. LHBOTS 518. New York: T&T Clark, 2010.

Christensen, Duane. *Deuteronomy 1–11*. WBC 6A. Dallas: Word, 1991.
Clayton, Jay, and Eric Rothstein. "Figures in the Corpus: Theories of Influence and Intertextuality." In *Influence and Intertextuality in Literary History*, edited by Jay Clayton and Eric Rothstein, 3–36. Madison: University of Wisconsin Press, 1991.
Clements, R. E. "The Ezekiel Tradition: Prophecy in a Time of Crisis." In *Israel's Prophetic Tradition: Essays in Honor of Peter R. Ackroyd*, edited by Richard J. Coggins, Anthony Phillips, and Michael Knibb, 119–36. Cambridge: Cambridge University Press, 1982.
Clements, R. E. *God's Chosen People: A Theological Interpretation of the Book of Deuteronomy*. London: SCM, 1968.
Coats, George W. *Rebellion in the Wilderness: The Murmuring Motif in the Wilderness Traditions of the Old Testament*. Nashville: Abingdon, 1968.
Coggins, Richard J. "What Does 'Deuteronomistic' Mean?" In *Words Remembered, Texts Renewed: Essays in Honour of John F. A. Sawyer*, edited by Jon Davies, Graham Harvey, and Wilfred G. E. Watson, 135–48. JSOTSup 195. Sheffield: Sheffield Academic, 1995. Repr. in *Those Elusive Deuteronomists: The Phenomenon of Pan-Deuteronomism*, edited by L. S. Schearing and S. L. McKenzie, 22–35. JSOTSup 268. Sheffield: Sheffield Academic, 1999.
Collins, Terrence. *The Mantle of Elijah: The Redaction Criticism of the Prophetical Books*. Biblical Seminar 20. Sheffield: JSOT, 1993.
Conklin, Blane. *Oath Formulas in Biblical Hebrew*. Linguistic Studies in Ancient West Semitic 5. Winona Lake, IN: Eisenbrauns, 2011.
Cook, Stephen L. *The Apocalyptic Literature*. Interpreting Biblical Texts. Nashville: Abingdon, 2003.
Cook, Stephen L. *Ezekiel 38–48: A New Translation with Introduction and Commentary*. AYB 22B. New Haven: Yale University Press, 2018.
Cook, Stephen L. "God's Real Absence and Real Presence in Deuteronomy and Deuteronomism." In *Divine Presence and Absence in Exilic and Post-Exilic Judaism*, edited by I. J. de Hulster and N. MacDonald, 121–50. FAT II/61. Tübingen: Mohr Siebeck, 2013.
Cook, Stephen L. *The Social Roots of Biblical Yahwism*. SBLSBL 8. Atlanta: Society of Biblical Literature, 2004.
Cook, Stephen L., and Corrine L. Patton, eds. *Ezekiel's Hierarchical World: Wrestling with a Tiered Reality*. SBLSymS 31. Atlanta: Society of Biblical Literature, 2004.
Cooke, G. A. *A Critical and Exegetical Commentary on the Book of Ezekiel*. ICC. Edinburgh: T. & T. Clark, 1936.
Cornill, C. H. *Das Buch des Propheten Ezechiel*. Leipzig: Hinrichs, 1886.
Cornill, C. H. *Einleitung in das Alte Testament*. Freiburg: J. C. B. Mohr, 1891.
Crane, Ashley S. *Israel's Restoration: A Textual-Comparative Exploration of Ezekiel 36–39*. VTSup 122. Leiden: Brill, 2008.
Cross, Frank Moore. *Canaanite Myth and Hebrew Epic: Essays in the History of the Religion of Israel*. Cambridge, MA: Harvard University Press, 1973.
Crouch, C. L. "What Makes a Thing Abominable? Observations on the Language of Boundaries and Identity Formation from a Social Scientific Perspective." *VT* 65 (2015): 516–41.
Davis, Ellen F. *Swallowing the Scroll: Textuality and the Dynamics of Discourse in Ezekiel's Prophecy*. JSOTSup 78. Bible and Literature 21. Sheffield: Sheffield Academic, 1989.

Day, John. "Inner Biblical Interpretation in the Prophets." In *The Place Is Too Small for Us: The Israelite Prophets in Recent Scholarship*, 230–46, edited by Robert P. Gordon. Winona Lake, IN: Eisenbrauns, 1995. Repr. of "Prophecy." In *It Is Written: Scripture Citing Scripture*, edited by D. A. Carson and H. G. M. Williamson, 39–55. Cambridge: Cambridge University Press, 1988.

Day, John. *Molech: A God of Human Sacrifice in the Old Testament*. Cambridge: Cambridge University Press, 1989.

Day, John. *Yahweh and the Gods and Goddesses of Canaan*. JSOTSup 265. Sheffield: Sheffield Academic, 2002.

Day, Linda. "Rhetoric and Domestic Violence in Ezekiel 16." *BibInt* 8 (2000): 205–30.

Delcor, M. "Les attaches littéraires, l'origine et la signification de l'expression biblique 'prende à témoin le ciel et la terre.'" *VT* 16 (1966): 8–25.

Demsky, A. "Education, Jewish." *Encyclopaedia Judaica* 6 (1971): 381–98.

Diepold, Peter. *Israels Land*. BWANT 95. Stuttgart: Kohlhammer, 1972.

Dohmen, Christoph. "Heißt סמל 'Bild, Statue'?" *ZAW* 96 (1984): 263–6.

Dossin, Georges. *Archives Royales de Mari, V: Correspondance de Iasmah-Addu*. Paris: Imprimerie Nationale, 1952.

Driver, S. R. *A Critical and Exegetical Commentary on Deuteronomy*. ICC. New York: Charles Scribner's Sons, 1895.

Driver, S. R. *Introduction to the Literature of the Old Testament*. New York: Charles Scribner's Sons, 1913.

Duhm, B. *Das Buch Jesaia*. 2nd ed. HAT 3/1. Göttingen: Vandenhoeck & Ruprecht, 1902.

Dürr, Lorenz. *Ursprung und Ausbau der israelitisch-jüdischen Heilserwartung: Ein Beitrag zur Theologie des Alten Testamentes*. Berlin: Schwetschke & Sohn, 1925.

Edenburg, Cynthia. "How (Not) to Murder a King: Variations on a Theme in 1 Sam 24; 26." *SJOT* 12 (1998): 64–85.

Edenburg, Cynthia, and Reinhard Müller. "A Northern Provenance for Deuteronomy? A Critical Review." *HeBAI* 4 (2015): 148–61.

Eichrodt, Walther. *Ezekiel: A Commentary*. Translated by Cosslett Quin. OTL. Philadelphia: Westminster, 1970. Translation of *Der Prophet Hesekiel*. 3rd ed. ATD 22. Göttingen: Vandenhoeck & Ruprecht, 1968.

Eissfeldt, Otto. *Das Lied Moses Deuteronomium 32:1-43 und Das Lehrgedicht Asaphs Psalm 78: samt einer Analyse der Umgebung des Mose-Liedes*. Berlin: Akademie-Verlag, 1958.

Eissfeldt, Otto. *Einleitung in das Alte Testament*. 3rd ed. Tübingen: J. C. B. Mohr, 1964.

Eissfeldt, Otto. *Molk als Opferbegriff im Punischen und Hebräischen und das Ende des Gottes Moloch*. Halle: Niemeyer, 1935.

Elbogen, Ishmar. *Jewish Liturgy: A Comprehensive History*. Translated by Raymond P. Scheindlin. Philadelphia: Jewish Publication Society, 1993.

Eliot, T. S. "Tradition and the Individual Talent." In *The Sacred Wood: Essays on Poetry and Criticism*, 42–54. London: Methuen, 1920. Repr. in *Influx: Essays on Literary Influence*, edited by Ronald Primeau, 15–21. Port Washington, NY: Kennikat, 1977.

Faur, José. "The Biblical Idea of Idolatry." *JQR* 69 (1978): 1–15.

Fechter, Friedrich. *Bewältigung der Katastrophe: Untersuchungen zu ausgewählten Fremd-völkersprüchen im Ezechielbuch*. BZAW 208. Berlin: de Gruyter, 1992.

Filson, Floyd V. "The Omission of Ezek. 12:26-28 and 36:23b-28 in Codex 967." *JBL* 62 (1943): 27–32.

Finnegan, Ruth. *Literacy and Orality*. Oxford: Basil Blackwell, 1988.

Fishbane, Michael. *Biblical Interpretation in Ancient Israel*. Oxford: Clarendon, 1985.
Fitzmyer, Joseph A. *The Aramaic Inscriptions of Sefire*. BibOr 19A. Rev ed. Rome: Pontifical Biblical Institute, 1995.
Fitzmyer, Joseph A. "The Aramaic Suzerainty Treaty from Sefire in the Museum of Beirut." *CBQ* 20 (1958): 444–76.
Fitzpatrick, Paul. *The Disarmament of God: Ezekiel 38–39 in its Mythic Context*. CBQMS 37. Washington, DC: Catholic Biblical Association of America, 2004.
Fohrer, Georg. *Die Hauptprobleme des Buches Ezechiel*. BZAW 72. Berlin: Töpelmann, 1952.
Freedy, Kenneth S. "The Glosses in Ezekiel i–xxiv." *VT* 20 (1970): 129–52.
Friebel, Kelvin G. "The Decrees of Yahweh that Are 'Not Good': Ezekiel 20:25-26." In *Seeking Out the Wisdom of the Ancients: Essays Offered to Honor Michael V. Fox on the Occasion of His Sixty-Fifth Birthday*, edited by Ronald L. Troxel, Kelvin G. Friebel, and Dennis R. Magary, 21–36. Winona Lake, IN: Eisenbrauns, 2005.
Friedman, Richard Elliott. *The Exile and Biblical Narrative: The Formation of the Deuteronomistic and Priestly Works*. HSM 22. Chico, CA: Scholars Press, 1981.
Friedman, Richard Elliott. "From Egypt to Egypt: Dtr1 and Dtr2." In *Traditions in Transformation: Turning Points in Biblical Faith*, edited by Baruch Halpern and Jon D. Levenson, 167–92. Winona Lake, IN: Eisenbrauns, 1981.
Furniss, Graham. *Orality: The Power of the Spoken Word*. New York: Palgrave Macmillan, 2004.
Galambush, Julie. *Jerusalem in the Book of Ezekiel: The City as Yahweh's Wife*. SBLDS 130. Atlanta: Scholars Press, 1992.
Ganzel, Tova. "The Descriptions of the Restoration of Israel in Ezekiel." *VT* 60 (2010): 197–211.
Ganzel, Tova. "The Transformation of Pentateuchal Descriptions of Idolatry in Ezekiel." In *Transforming Visions: Transformations of Text, Tradition, and Theology in Ezekiel*, edited by William A. Tooman and Michael A. Lyons, 33–49. PTMS 127. Eugene, OR: Pickwick, 2010.
Garr, W. Randall. "Affectedness, Aspect, and Biblical Hebrew *'et*." *ZAH* 4 (1991): 119–34.
Gese, Hartmut. "Ezechiel 20,25f. und die Erstgeburtsopfer." In *Beitrage zur alttestamentlichen Theologie: Festschrift für Walther Zimmerli zum 70. Geburtstag*, edited by Herbert Donner, Robert Hanhart, and Rudolf Smend, 140–51. Göttingen: Vandenhoeck & Ruprecht, 1977.
Gibson, Jonathan. *Covenant Continuity and Fidelity: A Study of Inner-Biblical Allusion and Exegesis in Malachi*. LHBOTS 625. London: Bloomsbury T&T Clark, 2019.
Gile, Jason. "Deuteronomic Influence in the Book of Ezekiel." Ph.D. Diss., Wheaton College, 2013.
Gile, Jason. "Ezekiel 16 and the Song of Moses: A Prophetic Transformation?" *JBL* 130 (2011): 87–108.
Gile, Jason. Review of Joyce, *Ezekiel*. *BibInt* 18 (2010): 178–9.
Gile, Jason. Review of Lyons, *From Law to Prophecy*. *BBR* 21 (2011): 111–12.
Gile, Jason. Review of Moughtin-Mumby, *Sexual and Marital Metaphors*. *JHS* 9 (2009), http://www.jhsonline.org.
Gile, Jason. Review of Tooman and Lyons, eds., *Transforming Visions*. *JHS* 11 (2011), http://www.jhsonline.org.
Gleis, Matthias. *Die Bamah*. BZAW 251. Berlin: de Gruyter, 1997.
Goody, Jack. *The Interface between the Written and the Oral*. Cambridge: Cambridge University Press, 1987.

Götze, Albrecht. *Die Annalen des Muršiliš*. Leipzig: Hinrichs, 1933.
Graffy, Adrian. *A Prophet Confronts His People: Disputation Speech in the Prophets*. AnBib 104. Rome: Biblical Institute, 1984.
Grayson, A. Kirk. *Assyrian and Babylonian Chronicles*. TCS 5. Locust Valley, NY: Augustin, 1975.
Greenberg, Moshe. *Ezekiel 1–20: A New Translation with Introduction and Commentary*. AB 22. Garden City, NY: Doubleday, 1983.
Greenberg, Moshe. *Ezekiel 21–37: A New Translation with Introduction and Commentary*. AB 22A. Garden City, NY: Doubleday, 1997.
Greenberg, Moshe. "Notes on the Influence of Tradition on Ezekiel." *JANESCU* 22 (1993): 29–37.
Greenberg, Moshe. "What Are Valid Criteria for Determining Inauthentic Matter in Ezekiel?" In *Ezekiel and His Book: Textual and Literary Criticism and Their Interrelation*, edited by J. Lust, 123–35. BETL 74. Leuven: Leuven University Press, 1986.
Greene, Roland et al., eds. *The Princeton Encyclopedia of Poetry and Poetics*. 4th ed. Princeton: Princeton University Press, 2012.
Greenfield, Jonas C. "*Našû-Nadānu* and Its Congeners." In *Essays on the Ancient Near East in Memory of Jacob Joel Finkelstein*, edited by Maria de Jong Ellis, 87–91. MCAAS 19. Hamden, CT: Archon, 1977.
Greenspahn, Frederick E. "Syncretism and Idolatry in the Bible." *VT* 54 (2004): 480–94.
Guillén, Claudio. "The Aesthetics of Influence." In *Influx: Essays on Literary Influence*, edited by Ronald Primeau, 49–73. Port Washington, NY: Kennikat, 1977.
Gunkel, Hermann. *The Folktale in the Old Testament*. Translated by M. D. Rutter. HTIBS 6. Sheffield: Almond, 1987. German original *Das Märchen im Alten Testament*. Religionsgeschichtliche Volksbücher 2. Tübingen: J. C. B. Mohr, 1917.
Gurney, O. R. "Tammuz Reconsidered: Some Recent Developments." *JSS* 7 (1962): 147–60.
Habel, Norman C. *The Land is Mine: Six Biblical Land Ideologies*. OBT. Minneapolis: Fortress, 1995.
Hahn, Scott Walker, and John Sietze Bergsma. "What Laws Were 'Not Good'? A Canonical Approach to the Theological Problem of Ezekiel 20:25-26." *JBL* 123 (2004): 201–18.
Halbertal, Moshe, and Avishai Margalit. *Idolatry*. Translated by Naomi Goldblum. Cambridge, MA: Harvard University Press, 1992.
Halperin, David J. *Seeking Ezekiel: Text and Psychology*. University Park, PA: Pennsylvania State University Press, 1993.
Haran, Menahem. *The Biblical Collection: Its Consolidation to the End of the Second Temple Times and Changes of Form to the End of the Middle Ages*, vol. 2. Jerusalem: Bialik/Magnes, 2003 (Hebrew).
Haran, Menahem. "Ezekiel, P, and the Priestly School." *VT* 58 (2008): 211–18.
Harvey, Julien. *Le plaidoyer prophétique contre Israël après la rupture de l'alliance*. Paris: Desclée de Brouwer, 1967.
Hassan, Ihab H. "The Problem of Influence in Literary History: Notes towards a Definition." *JAAC* 14 (1955): 66–76. Repr. in *Influx: Essays on Literary Influence*, edited by Ronald Primeau, 34–46. Port Washington, NY: Kennikat, 1977.
Hays, Richard. *Echoes of Scripture in the Letters of Paul*. New Haven: Yale University Press, 1989.

Hays, Christopher B. "Echoes of the Ancient Near East? Intertextuality and the Comparative Study of the Old Testament." In *The Word Leaps the Gap: Essays on Scripture and Theology in Honor of Richard B. Hays*, edited by J. Ross Wagner, C. Kavin Rowe, and A. Katherine Grieb, 20–43. Grand Rapids: Eerdmans, 2008.

Heider, George C. *The Cult of Molek: A Reassessment*. JSOTSup 43. Sheffield: JSOT, 1985.

Heider, George C. "A Further Turn on Ezekiel's Baroque Twist in Ezek 20:25-26." *JBL* 107 (1988): 721–8.

Heiser, Michael. "Monotheism, Polytheism, Monolatry, or Henotheism? Toward an Assessment of Divine Plurality in the Hebrew Bible." *BBR* 18 (2008): 1–30.

Hendel, Ronald S. "The Social Origins of the Aniconic Tradition in Early Israel." *CBQ* 50 (1988): 365–83.

Hermerén, Göran. *Influence in Art and Literature*. Princeton: Princeton University Press, 1975.

Herrmann, Siegfried. *Die prophetischen Heilserwartungen im Alten Testament*. BWANT 85. Stuttgart: W. Kohlhammer, 1965.

Hillers, Delbert R. *Treaty-Curses and the Old Testament Prophets*. BibOr 16. Rome: Pontifical Biblical Institute, 1964.

Holladay, William H. "Jeremiah and Moses: Further Observations." *JBL* 85 (1966): 17–27.

Holladay, William H. "On Every High Hill and Under Every Green Tree." *VT* 11 (1961): 170–6.

Hollander, John. *The Figure of Echo: A Mode of Allusion in Milton and After*. Berkeley: University of California Press, 1984.

Hölscher, Gustav. *Hesekiel: Der Dichter und das Buch*. BZAW 39. Giessen: Alfred Töpelmann, 1924.

Hölscher, Gustav. *Die Propheten*. Leipzig: J. C. Hinrichs, 1914.

Hoppe, Leslie J. "Elders and Deuteronomy: A Proposal." *Église et théologie* 14 (1983): 259–72.

Hopper, Paul J., and Sandra A. Thompson. "Transitivity in Grammar and Discourse." *Language* 56 (1980): 251–99.

Horst, P. W. van der. "'I Gave them Laws that Were Not Good': Ezekiel 20.25 in Ancient Judaism and Early Christianity." In *Sacred History and Sacred Texts in Early Judaism: A Symposium in Honour of A. S. van der Woude*, edited by J. N. Bremmer and F. Garcia Martinez, 94–118. Kampen: Kok Pharos, 1992.

Hossfeld, Frank-Lothar. "Ezechiel und die deuteronomisch-deuteronomistische Bewegung." In *Jeremia und die deuteronomistische Bewegung*, edited by Walter Gross, 271–95. BBB 98. Weinheim: Beltz Athenäum, 1995.

Hossfeld, Frank-Lothar. *Untersuchungen zu Komposition und Theologie des Ezechielbuches*. FzB 20. Würzburg: Echter, 1977. 2nd ed., 1983.

Huffmon, Herbert B. "The Covenant Lawsuit in the Prophets." *JBL* 78 (1959): 285–95.

Humbert, P. "Le substantif *tôʿebâ* et le verbe *tʿb* dans l'Ancien Testament." *ZAW* 72 (1960): 227–31.

Hurvitz, Avi. *A Linguistic Study of the Relationship between the Priestly Source and the Book of Ezekiel: A New Approach to an Old Problem*. CahRB 20. Paris: Gabalda, 1982.

Hwang, Jerry. *The Rhetoric of Remembrance: An Investigation of the "Fathers" in Deuteronomy*. Siphrut 8. Winona Lake, IN: Eisenbrauns, 2012.

Hyatt, J. Philip. "Was There an Ancient Historical Credo in Israel and an Independent Sinai Tradition?" In *Translating and Understanding the Old Testament*, edited by Harry Thomas Frank and William L. Reed, 152–70. Nashville: Abingdon, 1970.

Irwin, William. *The Problem of Ezekiel: An Inductive Study*. Chicago: University of Chicago Press, 1943.

Jacobsen, Thorkild. "Toward the Image of Tammuz." *HR* 1 (1961): 189–213. Repr. in *Toward the Image of Tammuz and Other Essays on Mesopotamian History and Culture*, edited by William L. Moran, 73–103. HSS 21. Cambridge, MA: Harvard University Press, 1970.

Johnson, Allan Chester, Henry Snyder Gehman, and Edmund Harris Kase, Jr. *The John H. Scheide Biblical Papyri: Ezekiel*. Princeton University Studies in Papyrology 3. Princeton: Princeton University Press, 1938.

Joyce, Paul M. *Divine Initiative and Human Response in Ezekiel*. JSOTSup 51. Sheffield: Sheffield Academic, 1989.

Joyce, Paul M. *Ezekiel: A Commentary.* LHBOTS 482. T&T Clark, 2007.

Joyce, Paul M. "Ezekiel and Moral Transformation." In *Transforming Visions: Transformations of Text, Tradition, and Theology in Ezekiel*, edited by William A. Tooman and Michael A. Lyons, 139–58. PTMS 127. Eugene, OR: Pickwick, 2010.

Joyce, Paul M., and Dalit Rom-Shiloni, eds. *The God Ezekiel Creates*. LHBOTS 607. New York: Bloomsbury T&T Clark, 2015.

Judge, Thomas A. *Other Gods and Idols: The Relationship between the Worship of Other Gods and the Worship of Idols within the Old Testament*. LHBOTS 674. New York: Bloomsbury T&T Clark, 2019.

Kasher, Rimon. *Ezekiel: Introduction and Commentary*, vol. 1, *Chapters 1–24*. Mikra le-Yiśrael. Tel Aviv: Am Oved, 2004 (Hebrew).

Kaufmann, Yehezkel. *The Religion of Israel: From Its Beginnings to the Babylonian Exile*. Translated and abridged by Moshe Greenberg. Chicago: University of Chicago Press, 1960.

Keck, Elizabeth. "Glory of Yahweh, Name Theology, and Ezekiel's Understanding of Divine Presence." Ph.D. diss., Boston College, 2011.

Keiser, Thomas. "The Song of Moses: A Basis for Isaiah's Prophecy." *VT* 55 (2005): 486–500.

Kelly, Joseph Ryan. "Identifying Literary Allusions: Theory and the Criterion of Shared Language." In *Subtle Citation, Allusion, and Translation in the Hebrew Bible*, edited by Ziony Zevit, 22–40. Sheffield: Equinox, 2017.

Kim, Brittany. "Yhwh as Jealous Husband: Abusive Authoritarian or Passionate Protector? A Reexamination of a Prophetic Image." In *Daughter Zion: Her Portrait, Her Response*, edited by Mark J. Boda, Carol J. Dempsey, and LeAnn Snow Flesher, 127–47. SBLAIL 13. Atlanta: SBL, 2012.

Kim, Hyun Chul Paul. "The Song of Moses (Deuteronomy 32.1-43) in Isaiah 40–55." In *God's Word for Our World*, vol. 1, *Biblical Studies in Honor of Simon John De Vries*, edited by J. H. Ellens et al., 147–71. JSOTSup 388. London: T&T Clark, 2004.

Kitchen, Kenneth. "Ancient Orient, 'Deuteronism' [sic], and the Old Testament." In *New Perspectives on the Old Testament*, edited by J. Barton Payne, 1–24. Waco: Word, 1970.

Kitchen, Kenneth. *On the Reliability of the Old Testament*. Grand Rapids: Eerdmans, 2003.

Kitchen, Kenneth A., and Paul J. N. Lawrence. *Treaty, Law and Covenant in the Ancient Near East*. 3 vols. Wiesbaden: Harrassowitz, 2012.

Klawans, Jonathan. *Impurity and Sin in Ancient Judaism*. Oxford: Oxford University Press, 2000.

Klawans, Jonathan. *Purity, Sacrifice, and the Temple: Symbolism and Supersessionism in the Study of Ancient Judaism*. Oxford: Oxford University Press, 2005.

Klein, Anja. *Schriftauslegung im Ezechielbuch: Redaktionsgeschichtliche Untersuchungen zu Ez 34–39*. BZAW 391. New York: de Gruyter, 2008.
Knapp, Dietrich. *Deuteronomium 4: Literarische Analyse und theologische Interpretation*. Göttingen: Vandenhoeck & Ruprecht, 1987.
Knohl, Israel. *The Sanctuary of Silence: The Priestly Torah and the Holiness Code*. Minneapolis: Augsburg Fortress, 1995. Repr. Winona Lake, IN: Eisenbrauns, 2007.
Knoppers, Gary N. "The Northern Context of the Law-Code in Deuteronomy." *HeBAI* 4 (2015): 162–83.
Konkel, Michael. Review of Stephen L. Cook and Corrine L. Patton, eds., *Ezekiel's Hierarchical World: Wrestling with a Tiered Reality. RBL* 2005, online: http://www.bookreviews.org.
Krašovec, Jože. "The Distinctive Hebrew Testimony to Renewal Based on Forgiveness." *ZABR* 5 (1999): 223–35.
Krašovec, Jože. *Reward, Punishment, and Forgiveness: The Thinking and Beliefs of Ancient Israel in the Light of Greek and Modern Views*. VTSup 78. Leiden: Brill, 1999.
Kristeva, Julia. "Word, Dialogue, and Novel." In *Desire in Language: A Semiotic Approach to Literature and Art*, edited by Leon S. Roudiez, 64–91. Translated by Thomas Gora, Alice Jardine, and Leon S. Roudiez. New York: Columbia University Press, 1980. First published in Σημειωτικη: *Recherches pour une sémanalyse*, 143–73. Paris: Seuil, 1969.
Kruger, Paul A. "The Hem of the Garment in Marriage: The Meaning of the Symbolic Gesture in Ruth 3:9 and Ezek 16:8." *JNSL* 12 (1984): 79–86.
Krüger, Thomas. *Geschichtskonzepte im Ezechielbuch*. BZAW 180. Berlin: de Gruyter, 1989.
Krüger, Thomas. "Transformation of History in Ezekiel 20." In *Transforming Visions: Transformations of Text, Tradition, and Theology in Ezekiel*, edited by William A. Tooman and Michael A. Lyons, 159–86. PTMS 127. Eugene, OR: Pickwick, 2010.
Kugler, Gili. "The Cruel Theology of Ezekiel." *ZAW* 129 (2017): 47–58.
Kugler, Robert, and Patrick Hartin. *An Introduction to the Bible*. Grand Rapids: Eerdmans, 2009.
Kutscher, Raphael. "The Cult of Dumuzi/Tammuz." In *Bar-Ilan Studies in Assyriology Dedicated to Pinhas Artzi*, edited by Jacob Klein and Aaron Skaist, 29–44. Ramat-Gan: Bar Ilan University Press, 1990.
Kutsko, John F. *Between Heaven and Earth: Divine Presence and Absence in the Book of Ezekiel*. Biblical and Judaic Studies from the University of California, San Diego 7. Winona Lake, IN: Eisenbrauns, 2000.
Kuyvenhoven, Rosalie. "Jeremiah 23:1-8: Shepherds in Diachronic Perspective." In *Paratext and Megatext as Channels of Jewish and Christian Traditions: The Textual Markers of Contextualization*, edited by A. A. den Hollander, U. B. Schmid, and W. F. Smelik, 1–36. Jewish and Christian Perspectives 6. Leiden: Brill, 2003.
Labuschagne, C. J. "The *Našû-Nadānu* Formula and Its Biblical Equivalent." In *Travels in the World of the Old Testament: Studies Presented to Professor M. A. Beek on the Occasion of His 65th Birthday*, edited by G. Heerma van Voss et al., 176–80. SSN 16. Assen: Van Gorcum, 1974.
Lapsley, Jacqueline E. *Can These Bones Live? The Problem of the Moral Self in the Book of Ezekiel*. BZAW 301. Berlin: de Gruyter, 2000.
Lapsley, Jacqueline E. "Shame and Self-Knowledge: The Positive Role of Shame in Ezekiel's View of the Moral Self." In *The Book of Ezekiel: Theological and Anthropological Perspectives*, edited by Margaret S. Odell and John T. Strong, 143–73. SBLSymS 9. Atlanta: Society of Biblical Literature, 2000.

LaRocca-Pitts, Elizabeth C. *"Of Wood and Stone": The Significance of Israelite Cultic Items in the Bible and Its Early Interpreters*. Winona Lake, IN: Eisenbrauns, 2001.

Leene, Henk. "Blowing the Same Shofar: An Intertextual Comparison of Representations of the Prophetic Role in Jeremiah and Ezekiel." In *The Elusive Prophet: The Prophet as a Historical Person, Literary Character and Anonymous Artist*, edited by J. C. de Moor, 175–98. OtSt 45. Leiden: Brill, 2001.

Leene, Henk. *Newness in Old Testament Prophecy: An Intertextual Study*. OtSt 64. Leiden: Brill, 2014.

Leonard, Jeffery M. "Identifying Inner-Biblical Allusions: Psalm 78 as a Test Case." *JBL* 127 (2008): 241–65.

Leonard, Jeffery M. "Identifying Subtle Allusions: The Promise of Narrative Tracking." In *Subtle Citation, Allusion, and Translation in the Hebrew Bible*, edited by Ziony Zevit, 91–113. Sheffield: Equinox, 2017.

Leuchter, Mark. "Why Is the Song of Moses in the Book of Deuteronomy?" *VT* 57 (2007): 295–317.

Levenson, Jon D. "Who Inserted the Book of the Torah?" *HTR* 68 (1975): 203–33.

Levinson, Bernard M. *Deuteronomy and the Hermeneutics of Legal Innovation*. New York: Oxford University Press, 1998.

Levinson, Bernard M., and Jeffrey Stackert. "Between the Covenant Code and Esarhaddon's Succession Treaty: Deuteronomy 13 and the Composition of Deuteronomy." *JAJ* 3 (2012): 123–40.

Levitt Kohn, Risa. "Ezekiel at the Turn of the Century." *CBR* 2 (2003): 9–31.

Levitt Kohn, Risa. *A New Heart and a New Soul: Ezekiel, the Exile and the Torah*. JSOTSup 358. Sheffield: Sheffield Academic, 2002.

Levitt Kohn, Risa. "With a Mighty Hand and an Outstretched Arm: The Prophet and the Torah in Ezekiel 20." In *Ezekiel's Hierarchical World: Wrestling with a Tiered Reality*, edited by C. Patton and S. Cook, 159–68. SBLSymS 31. Atlanta: Society of Biblical Literature, 2004.

Lichtheim, Miriam. *Ancient Egyptian Literature*, vol. 1, *The Old and Middle Kingdoms*. Berkeley: University of California Press, 1973.

Lilly, Ingrid E. *Two Books of Ezekiel: Papyrus 967 and the Masoretic Text as Variant Literary Editions*. VTSup 150. Leiden: Brill, 2012.

Liwak, Rudiger. "Überlieferungsgeschichtliche Probleme des Ezechielbuches: eine Studie zu post-ezechielischen Interpretationen und Kompositionen." Ph.D. diss., Bochum, 1976.

Lohfink, Norbert F. "Auslegung deuteronomischer Texte IV." *BibLeb* 4 (1964): 250–3.

Lohfink, Norbert F. *Das Hauptgebot: Eine Untersuchungliterarischer Einleitungsfragen zu Dtn 5–11*. AnBib 20. Rome: Pontifical Biblical Institute, 1963.

Lohfink, Norbert F. *Höre, Israel! Auslegung von Texten aus dem Buch Deuteronomium*. Die Welt der Bibel 18. Düsseldorf: Patmos, 1965.

Longman, Tremper, III. *Fictional Akkadian Autobiography: A Generic and Comparative Study*. Winona Lake, IN: Eisenbrauns, 1991.

Luckenbill, Daniel David. *Ancient Records of Assyria and Babylonia*. 2 vols. Chicago: University of Chicago Press, 1926–27.

Lundbom, Jack R. *Deuteronomy: A Commentary*. Grand Rapids: Eerdmans, 2013.

Lust, Johan. "Exile and Diaspora: Gathering from Dispersion in Ezekiel." In *Lectures et relectures de la Bible: Festschrift P.-M. Bogaert*, edited by Jean-Marie Auwers and André Wénin, 99–122. BETL 144. Leuven: Peeters, 1999.

Lust, Johan. "Exodus 6,2-8 and Ezekiel." In *Studies in the Book of Exodus*, edited by Marc Vervenne, 209–24. BETL 126. Leuven: Peeters, 1996.

Lust, Johan. "Ez., XX, 4-26: une parodie de l'histoire religieuse d'Israël." *ETL* 43 (1967): 488–527.

Lust, Johan. "Ezekiel 36–40 in the Oldest Greek Manuscript." *CBQ* 43 (1981): 517–33.

Lust, Johan. "Ezekiel Salutes Isaiah: Ezekiel 20,32-44." In *Studies in the Book of Isaiah: Festschrift W. A. M. Beuken*, edited by J. Van Ruiten and M. Vervenne, 367–82. BETL 132. Leuven: Leuven University Press, 1997.

Lust, Johan. "The Final Text and Textual Criticism: Ez 39,28." In *Ezekiel and His Book: Textual and Literary Criticism and Their Interrelation*, edited by J. Lust, 48–54. BETL 74. Leuven: Leuven University Press, 1986.

Lust, Johan. "For I Lift Up My Hand to Heaven and Swear: Deut 32:40." In *Studies in Deuteronomy: In Honour of C. J. Labuschagne on the Occasion of His 65th Birthday*, edited by Florentino García Martínez et al., 155–64. VTSup 53. Leiden: Brill, 1994.

Lust, Johan. "'Gathering and Return' in Jeremiah and Ezekiel." In *Le Livre de Jérémie*, edited by P.-M. Bogaert, 119–42. BETL 54. Leuven: Peeters, 1997.

Lust, Johan. "Idols? גלולים and εἴδωλα in Ezekiel." In *Florilegium Lovaniense: Studies in Septuagint and Textual Criticism in Honour of Florentino García Martínez*, edited by H. Ausloos, B. Lemmelijn, and M. Vervenne, 317–33. BETL 224. Leuven: Peeters, 2008.

Lust, Johan. "Textual Criticism of the Old and New Testaments: Stepbrothers?" In *New Testament Textual Criticism and Exegesis: Festschrift J. Delobel*, edited by Adelbert Denaux, 15–32. BETL 161. Leuven: Leuven University Press, 2002.

Lust, Johan. *Traditie, redactie en kerygma bij Ezechiël: Een analyse van Ez. XX, 1-26*. Verhandelingen van de Koninklijke Vlaamse Academie, Klasse der Letteren 65. Brussels: Paleis der Academiën, 1969.

Lust, Johan. "The Use of Textual Witnesses for the Establishment of the Text: The Shorter and Longer Texts of Ezekiel." In *Ezekiel and His Book: Textual and Literary Criticism and Their Interrelation*, edited by J. Lust, 7–20. BETL 74. Leuven: Leuven University Press, 1986.

Lutzky, H. C. "On the 'Image of Jealousy' (Ezekiel viii 3, 5)." *VT* 46 (1996): 121–4.

Lyons, Michael A. *An Introduction to the Study of Ezekiel*. New York: Bloomsbury T&T Clark, 2015.

Lyons, Michael A. *From Law to Prophecy: Ezekiel's Use of the Holiness Code*. LHBOTS 507. New York: T&T Clark, 2009.

Lyons, Michael A. "Marking Innerbiblical Allusion in the Book of Ezekiel." *Bib* 88 (2007): 245–50.

Lyons, Michael A. "Persuasion and Allusion: The Rhetoric of Text-Referencing in Ezekiel." In *Text and Canon: Essays in Honor of John H. Sailhamer*, edited by Robert L. Cole and Paul J. Kissling, 76–89. Eugene, OR: Pickwick, 2017.

Lyons, Michael A. "Transformation of Law: Ezekiel's Use of the Holiness Code (Leviticus 17–26)." In *Transforming Visions: Transformations of Text, Tradition, and Theology in Ezekiel*, edited by William A. Tooman and Michael A. Lyons, 1–32. PTMS 127. Eugene, OR: Pickwick, 2010.

MacDonald, Dennis R., ed. *Mimesis and Intertextuality in Antiquity and Christianity.* Harrisburg, PA: Trinity Press International, 2001.

MacDonald, Nathan. *Deuteronomy and the Meaning of "Monotheism."* FAT II/46. 2nd ed. Tübingen: Mohr Siebeck, 2012.

MacDonald, Nathan. "The God that the Scholarship on Ezekiel Creates." In *The God Ezekiel Creates*, edited by Paul M. Joyce and Dalit Rom-Shiloni, 193–202. LHBOTS 607. New York: Bloomsbury T&T Clark, 2015.

Machacek, Gregory. "Allusion." *PMLA* 122 (2007): 522–36.

Mackie, Timothy P. *Expanding Ezekiel: The Hermeneutics of Scribal Addition in the Ancient Text Witnesses of the Book of Ezekiel*. FRLANT 257. Göttingen: Vandenhoeck & Ruprecht, 2015.

Mackie, Timothy P. "Transformation in Ezekiel's Textual History: Ezekiel 7 in the Masoretic Text and the Septuagint." In *Transforming Visions: Transformations of Text, Tradition, and Theology in Ezekiel*, edited by William A. Tooman and Michael A. Lyons, 249–78. PTMS 127. Eugene, OR: Pickwick, 2010.

Magnetti, Donald L. "The Function of the Oath in the Ancient Near Eastern International Treaty." *AJIL* 72 (1978): 815–29.

Malul, Meir. "Adoption of Foundlings in the Bible and Mesopotamian Documents: A Study of Some Legal Metaphors in Ezekiel 16:1-7." *JSOT* 46 (1990): 97–126.

Mason, Rex. "Zechariah 9–14." In *Bringing Out the Treasure: Inner Biblical Allusion in Zechariah 9–14*, edited by Mark J. Boda and Michael H. Floyd, with a major contribution by Rex Mason, 3–209. JSOTSup 370. Sheffield: Sheffield Academic, 2003.

Matties, Gordon H. *Ezekiel 18 and the Rhetoric of Moral Discourse*. SBLDS 126. Atlanta: Scholars Press, 1990.

Mayes, A. D. H. "Deuteronomy 4 and the Literary Criticism of Deuteronomy." *JBL* 100 (1981): 23–51.

Mays, James Luther. *Micah: A Commentary*. OTL. London: SCM, 1976.

McCarthy, Dennis J. *Treaty and Covenant: A Study in Form in the Ancient Oriental Documents and in the Old Testament*. AnBib 21. Rome: Pontifical Biblical Institute, 1963.

McCarthy, Dennis J. *Treaty and Covenant: A Study in Form in the Ancient Oriental Documents and in the Old Testament*. 2nd ed. AnBib 21a. Rome: Pontifical Biblical Institute, 1978.

McConville, J. Gordon. "1 Kings 8:46-53 and the Deuteronomic Hope." *VT* 42 (1992): 67–79.

McConville, J. Gordon. *Deuteronomy*. AOTC 5. Downers Grove, IL: InterVarsity, 2002.

McConville, J. Gordon. *Grace in the End: A Study in Deuteronomic Theology*. Studies in Old Testament Biblical Theology. Grand Rapids: Zondervan, 1993.

McGarry, Eugene P. "The Ambidextrous Angel (Daniel 12:7 and Deuteronomy 32:40): Inner-Biblical Exegesis and Textual Criticism in Counterpoint." *JBL* 124 (2005): 211–28.

McLaughlin, John L. *The Marzēaḥ in the Prophetic Literature: References and Allusions in Light of the Extra-Biblical Evidence*. Leiden: Brill, 2001.

Meek, Russell L. "Intertextuality, Inner-Biblical Exegesis, and Inner-Biblical Allusion: The Ethics of a Methodology." *Biblica* 95 (2014): 280–91.

Meer, Michaël N. van der. "A New Spirit in an Old Corpus? Text-Critical, Literary-Critical and Linguistic Observations regarding Ezekiel 36:16-38." In *The New Things: Eschatology in Old Testament Prophecy, Festschrift for Henk Leene*, edited by F. Postma, K. Spronk, and E. Talstra, 147–58. ACEBTSup 3. Maastricht: Shaker, 2002.

Mein, Andrew. *Ezekiel and the Ethics of Exile*. OTM. Oxford: Oxford University Press, 2001.

Mein, Andrew. "Ezekiel as a Priest in Exile." In *The Elusive Prophet: The Prophet as Historical Person, Literary Character and Anonymous Artist*, edited by Johannes C. de Moor, 199–213. OtSt 45. Leiden: Brill, 2001.

Mein, Andrew. "Ezekiel: Structure, Themes, and Contested Issues." In *The Oxford Handbook of the Prophets*, edited by Carolyn J. Sharp, 190–206. Oxford: Oxford University Press, 2016.

Mendecki, Norbert. "Dtn 30,3-4: nachexilisch?" *BZ* 29 (1985): 267–71.

Mendenhall, G. E. "Covenant Forms in Israelite Tradition." *BA* 17 (1954): 50–76.

Mendenhall, G. E. "Samuel's 'Broken *rîb*': Deuteronomy 32." In *No Famine in the Land: Studies in Honor of John L. McKenzie*, edited by James W. Flanagan and Anita Weisbrod Robinson, 63–74. Homage Series 2. Missoula, MT: Scholars Press, 1975.

Meyer, Hermann. *Das Zitat in der Erzählkunst: Zur Geschichte und Poetik des europäischen Romans*. Stuttgart: J. B. Metzlersche Verlagsbuchhandlung, 1961.

Middlemas, Jill. "Exclusively Yahweh: Aniconism and Anthropomorphism in Ezekiel." In *Prophecy and the Prophets in Ancient Israel*, edited by John Day, 309–24. London: T&T Clark, 2010.

Middlemas, Jill. "Transformation of the Image." In *Transforming Visions: Transformations of Text, Tradition, and Theology in Ezekiel*, edited by William A. Tooman and Michael A. Lyons, 113–38. PTMS 127. Eugene, OR: Pickwick, 2010.

Middlemas, Jill. *The Troubles of Templeless Judah*. OTM. Oxford: Oxford University Press, 2005.

Milgrom, Jacob. "Does H Advocate the Centralization of Worship?" *JSOT* 88 (2000): 59–76.

Milgrom, Jacob. *Leviticus 17–22: A New Translation with Introduction and Commentary*. AB 3A. New York: Doubleday, 2000.

Milgrom, Jacob. *Leviticus 23–27: A New Translation with Introduction and Commentary*. AB 3B. New York: Doubleday, 2001.

Milgrom, Jacob. "The Nature and Extent of Idolatry in Eighth–Seventh Century Judah." *HUCA* 69 (1998): 1–13.

Milgrom, Jacob. "Were the Firstborn Sacrificed to YHWH? To Molek? Popular Practice or Divine Demand?" In *Sacrifice in Religious Experience*, edited by Albert I. Baumgarten, 49–55. Leiden: Brill, 2002.

Milgrom, Jacob, and Daniel I. Block. *Ezekiel's Hope: A Commentary on Ezekiel 38–48*. Eugene, OR: Cascade, 2012.

Millar, J. Gary. *Now Choose Life: Theology and Ethics in Deuteronomy*. NSBT. Downers Grove, IL: InterVarsity, 1998.

Millard, A. R. "Fragments of Historical Texts from Nineveh: Middle Assyrian and Later Kings." *Iraq* 32 (1970): 167–76.

Miller, Geoffrey D. "Intertextuality in Old Testament Research." *CBR* 9 (2011): 283–309.

Miller, Patrick D. "The Gift of God: The Deuteronomic Theology of the Land." *Int* 23 (1969): 451–69.

Miller, Robert S., II. *Oral Tradition in Ancient Israel*. BPC 4. Eugene, OR: Cascade, 2011.

Miller, Robert S., II. "The Performance of Oral Tradition in Ancient Israel." In *Contextualizing Israel's Sacred Writings: Ancient Literacy, Orality, and Literary Production*, edited by Brian B. Schmidt, 161–74. SBLAIL 22. Atlanta: SBL, 2015.

Miner, Earl. "Allusion." In *Encyclopedia of Poetry and Poetics*, edited by Alex Preminger, 18. Princeton, NJ: Princeton University Press, 1965. Rewritten in *The New Princeton Encyclopedia of Poetry and Poetics*, edited by Alex Preminger and T. V. F. Brogan, 38–9. Princeton, NJ: Princeton University Press, 1993.

Moughtin-Mumby, Sharon. *Sexual and Marital Metaphors in Hosea, Jeremiah, Isaiah, and Ezekiel*. OTM. Oxford: Oxford University Press, 2008.

Müller, D. H. "Der Prophet Ezechiel entlehnt eine Stelle des Propheten Zephanja und glossiert sie." *WZKM* 10 (1905): 30–6.

Nelson, Richard D. *Deuteronomy: A Commentary*. OTL. Louisville: Westminster John Knox, 2002.

Nelson, Richard D. *The Double Redaction of the Deuteronomistic History*. JSOTSup 18. Sheffield: JSOT, 1981.

Newsom, Carol A. "Moral 'Recipes' in Deuteronomy and Ezekiel: Divine Authority and Human Agency." *HeBAI* 6 (2017): 488–509.

Nicholson, E. W. *Deuteronomy and the Judaean Diaspora*. Oxford: Oxford University Press, 2014.

Nicholson, E. W. *Deuteronomy and Tradition: Literary and Historical Problems in the Book of Deuteronomy*. Philadelphia: Fortress, 1967.

Nicholson, E. W. *Exodus and Sinai in History and Tradition*. Richmond: John Knox, 1973.

Nicholson, E. W. *Preaching to the Exiles: A Study of the Prose Tradition in the Book of Jeremiah*. New York: Schocken, 1971.

Niditch, Susan. *Oral World and Written Word: Ancient Israelite Literature*. Louisville: Westminster John Knox, 1996.

Nielsen, Eduard. *Deuteronomium*. HAT 1/6. Tübingen: J. C. B. Mohr, 1995.

Nigosian, Solomon A. "Historical Allusions for Dating Deut 32." *BN* 119–20 (2003): 30–4.

Nigosian, Solomon A. "Linguistic Patterns of Deuteronomy 32." *Bib* 78 (1997): 206–24.

Nigosian, Solomon A. "The Song of Moses (Dt 32): A Structural Analysis." *ETL* 72 (1996): 5–22.

Nigosian, Solomon A. "The Song of Moses (Deut. 32:1-43)." Ph.D. diss., McMaster University, 1975.

Nihan, Christophe. *From Priestly Torah to Pentateuch: A Study in the Composition of Leviticus*. FAT 2/25. Tübingen: Mohr Siebeck, 2007.

Noble, Paul R. "Esau, Tamar, and Joseph: Criteria for Identifying Inner-Biblical Allusions." *VT* 52 (2002): 219–52.

Nogi, Ken-ichi. "The Main Theological Concepts of the Book of Deuteronomy and Their Influence on Jeremiah and Ezekiel." MA thesis, Columbia Theological Seminary, 1971.

Noort, Ed. "Child Sacrifice in Ancient Israel: The *Status Quaestionis*." In *The Strange World of Human Sacrifice*, edited by Jan N. Bremmer, 103–25. Studies in the History and Anthropology of Religion 1. Leuven: Peeters, 2007.

Noort, Ed. "Genesis 22: Human Sacrifice and Theology in the Hebrew Bible." In *The Sacrifice of Isaac: The Aqedah (Genesis 22) and Its Interpretations*, edited by Ed Noort and Eibert Tigchelaar, 1–20. Leiden: Brill, 2002.

North, C. R. "The Essence of Idolatry." In *Von Ugarit nach Qumran: Festschrift für Otto Eissfeldt*, edited by Johannes Hempel and Leonhard Rost, 151–60. BZAW 77. Berlin: Töpelmann, 1958.

Noth, Martin. *The Deuteronomistic History*. JSOTSup 15. Sheffield: Sheffield Academic, 1981. Translation of *Überlieferungsgeschichtliche Studien: Die sammelnden und bearbeitenden Geschichtswerke im Alten Testament*. Schriften der Königsberger Gelehrten Gesellschaft Geisteswissenschaftliche Klasse 18. Jh. H. 2 Bd. 1. Tübingen: Niemeyer, 1943.

Noth, Martin. *A History of Pentateuchal Traditions*. Translated by B. W. Anderson. Englewood Cliffs, NJ: Prentice-Hall, 1972.

O'Brien, Kelli S. *The Use of Scripture in the Markan Passion Narrative*. LNTS 384. New York: T&T Clark, 2010.
O'Hare, Daniel. *"Have You Seen, Son of Man?": A Study of the Translation and Vorlage of LXX Ezekiel 40–48*. SBLSCS 57. Atlanta: Society of Biblical Literature, 2010.
Oded, Bustenay. "II Kings 17: Between History and Polemic." *Jewish History* 2 (1987): 37–50.
Oded, Bustenay. "Judah and the Exile." In *Israelite and Judaean History*, edited by J. H. Hayes and J. M. Miller, 435–88. 3rd ed. Philadelphia: Westminster, 1977.
Oded, Bustenay. *Mass Deportations and Deportees in the Neo-Assyrian Empire*. Wiesbaden: Reichert, 1979.
Odell, Margaret S. "'Are You He of Whom I Spoke by My Servants the Prophets?' Ezekiel 38–39 and the Problem of History in the Neobabylonian Context." Ph.D. diss., University of Pittsburgh, 1988.
Odell, Margaret S. "Creeping Things and Singing Stones: The Iconography of Ezek 8:7-13 in Light of Syro-Palestinian Seals and *The Songs of the Sabbath Sacrifice*." In *Images and Prophecy in the Ancient Eastern Mediterranean*, edited by Martti Nissinen and Charles E. Carter, 195–210. Vandenhoeck & Ruprecht, 2009.
Odell, Margaret S. *Ezekiel*. Smyth & Helwys Bible Commentary. Macon, GA: Smyth & Helwys, 2005.
Odell, Margaret S. "What was the Image of Jealousy in Ezekiel 8?" In *The Priests in the Prophets: The Portrayal of Priests, Prophets, and Other Religious Specialists in the Latter Prophets*, edited by Lester L. Grabbe and Alice Ogden Bellis, 134–48. JSOTSup 408. New York: T&T Clark, 2004.
Ohnesorge, Stefan. *Jahwe gestaltet sein Volk neu: Zur Sicht der Zukunft Israels nach Ez 11,14-21; 20,1-44; 36,16-38; 37,1-14.15-28*. FzB 64. Würzburg: Echter, 1991.
Olson, Dennis. *The Death of the Old and the Birth of the New: The Framework of the Book of Numbers and the Pentateuch*. BJS 71. Chico, CA: Scholars Press, 1985.
Olyan, Saul M. *Asherah and the Cult of Yahweh in Israel*. Atlanta: Scholars Press, 1988.
Olyan, Saul M. "Honor, Shame and Covenant Relations in Ancient Israel and Its Environment." *JBL* 115 (1996): 201–18.
Ong, Walter. *Oral World and Literacy*. 2nd ed. London: Routledge, 2002.
Otten, H. "Keilschrifttexte." *MDOG* 91 (1958): 73–84.
Otto, Eckart. "The Pre-Exilic Deuteronomy as a Revision of the Covenant Code." In *Kontinuum und Proprium: Studien zur Sozial- und Rechtsgeschichte des Alten Orients und des Alten Testaments*, 112–22. Wiesbaden: Harrassowitz, 1996.
Pakkala, Juha. "The Date of the Oldest Edition of Deuteronomy." *ZAW* 121 (2009): 388–401.
Pardee, Dennis. "*Marziḥu, Kispu*, and the Ugaritic Funerary Cult: A Minimalist View." In *Ugarit, Religion and Culture: Proceedings of the International Colloquium on Ugarit, Religion and Culture; Edinburgh, July 1994. Essays in Honour of Professor John C. L. Gibson*, edited by N. Wyatt, W. G. E. Watson, and J. B. Lloyd, 273–87. UBL 12. Münster: Ugarit-Verlag, 1996.
Parpola, Simo. *Letters from Assyrian Scholars to the Kings Esarhaddon and Assurbanipal, Part I: Texts*. AOAT 5/1. Kevelaer: Butzon & Bercker, 1970.
Parpola, Simo, and Kazuko Watanabe, eds. *Neo-Assyrian Treaties and Loyalty Oaths*. SAA 2. Helsinki: Helsinki University Press, 1988.
Patton, Corrine L. "'I Myself Gave Them Laws that Were Not Good': Ezekiel 20 and the Exodus Traditions." *JSOT* 69 (1996): 73–90.

Patton, Corrine L. "Pan-Deuteronomism and the Book of Ezekiel." In *Those Elusive Deuteronomists: The Phenomenon of Pan-Deuteronomism*, edited by L. S. Schearing and S. L. McKenzie, 200–215. JSOTSup 268. Sheffield: Sheffield Academic, 1999.

Patton, Corrine L. "Priest, Prophet, and Exile: Ezekiel as a Literary Construct." In *Ezekiel's Hierarchical World: Wrestling with a Tiered Reality*, edited by Stephen L. Cook and Corrine L. Patton, 73–89. SBLSymS 31. Atlanta: Society of Biblical Literature, 2004.

Person, Raymond F., Jr. *The Deuteronomic School: History, Social Setting, and Literature*. SBLSBL 2. Atlanta: Society of Biblical Literature, 2002.

Peterson, Brian Neil. *Ezekiel in Context: Ezekiel's Message Understood in Its Historical Setting of Covenant Curses and Ancient Near Eastern Mythological Motifs*. PTMS 182. Eugene, OR: Pickwick, 2012.

Pohlmann, Karl-Friedrich. *Das Buch des Propheten Hesekiel*, vol. 1, *Kapitel 1–19*. ATD 22/1. Göttingen: Vandenhoeck & Ruprecht, 1996.

Pohlmann, Karl-Friedrich. *Ezechielstudien: Zur Redaktionsgeschichte des Buches und zur Frage nach den ältesten Texten*. BZAW 202. Berlin: de Gruyter, 1992.

Polzin, Robert. *Moses and the Deuteronomist: A Literary Study of the Deuteronomic History I: Deuteronomy, Joshua, Judges*. New York: Seabury, 1980.

Pons, Jacques. "Le vocabulaire d'Ézéchiel 20: le prophéte s'oppose á la vision deutéronomiste de l'histoire." In *Ezekiel and His Book: Textual and Literary Criticism and Their Interrelation*, edited by J. Lust, 214–33. BETL 74. Leuven: Leuven University Press, 1986.

Poser, Ruth. *Das Ezechielbuch als Trauma-Literatur*. VTSup 154. Leiden: Brill, 2012.

Premstaller, Volkmar. *Fremdvölkersprüche des Ezechielbuches*. FzB 104. Würzburg, Echter, 2005.

Preuss, Horst Dietrich. "גלולים, *gillûlîm*." *TDOT* 3:1–5.

Preuss, Horst Dietrich. *Deuteronomium*. EdF 164. Darmstadt: Wissenschaftliche Buchgesellschaft, 1982.

Preuss, Horst Dietrich. *Old Testament Theology*. Translated by Leo G. Perdue. 2 vols. Louisville: Westminster John Knox, 1995.

Primeau, Ronald, ed. *Influx: Essays on Literary Influence*. Port Washington, NY: Kennikat, 1977.

Provan, Iain. *Hezekiah and the Book of Kings: A Contribution to the Debate about the Composition of the Deuteronomistic History*. BZAW 172. Berlin: de Gruyter, 1988.

Quick, Laura. *Deuteronomy 28 and the Aramaic Curse Tradition*. OTM. Oxford: Oxford University Press, 2018.

Rad, Gerhard von. *Deuteronomy: A Commentary*. Translated by Dorothea Barton. OTL. Philadelphia: Westminster, 1966. Original German *Das fünfte Buch Mose: Deuteronomium*. Göttingen: Vandenhoeck & Ruprecht, 1964.

Rad, Gerhard von. "The Form-Critical Problem of the Hexateuch." In *The Problem of the Hexateuch and Other Essays*, 1–78. New York: McGraw-Hill, 1966.

Rad, Gerhard von. *The Message of the Prophets*. Translated by D. M. G. Stalker. New York: Harper & Row, 1968. Trans. of *Die Botschaft der Propheten*. Siebenstern Taschenbuch 188. Munich: Gütersloher, 1967.

Rad, Gerhard von. *Old Testament Theology*, vol. 2, *The Theology of Israel's Prophetic Traditions*. Louisville: Westminster John Knox, 2001. Translation of *Theologie des Alten Testaments*, vol. 2, *Die Theologie der prophetischen Überlieferungen Israels*. Munich: Chr. Kaiser, 1960.

Rad, Gerhard von. "The Promised Land and Yahweh's Land in the Hexateuch." In *The Problem of the Hexateuch and Other Essays*, 79–93. Philadelphia: Fortress, 1966.
Rad, Gerhard von. *Studies in Deuteronomy*. SBT 9. London: SCM, 1953.
Rainey, Anson F. "The Ancient Hebrew Prefix Conjugation in the Light of Amarnah Canaanite." *HS* 27 (1986): 4–19.
Raitt, Thomas. *A Theology of Exile: Judgment/Deliverance in Jeremiah and Ezekiel*. Philadelphia: Fortress, 1977.
Rechenmacher, Hans. *"Außer mir gibt es keinen Gott!" Eine sprach- und literaturwissenschaftliche Studie zur Ausschließlichkeitsformel*. ATSAT 49. St Ottilien: EOS, 1997.
Renz, Thomas. *The Rhetorical Function of the Book of Ezekiel*. VTSup 76. Leiden: Brill, 1999.
Renza, Louis A. "Influence." In *Critical Terms for Literary Study*, edited by Frank Lentricchia and Thomas McLaughlin, 188. 2nd ed. Chicago: University of Chicago Press, 1995).
Reventlow, Henning G. *Wächter über Israel: Ezechiel und seine Tradition*. BZAW 82. Berlin: Töppelman, 1962.
Richter, Sandra L. *The Deuteronomistic History and the Name Theology:* lᵉšakkēn šᵉmô šām *in the Bible and the Ancient Near East*. BZAW 318. Berlin: de Gruyter, 2002.
Robertson, David A. *Linguistic Evidence in Dating Early Hebrew Poetry*. SBLDS 3. Missoula, MT: Society of Biblical Literature, 1972.
Rofé, Alexander. "The Covenant in the Land of Moab (Deuteronomy 28:69–30:20): Historico-Literary, Comparative, and Formcritical Considerations." In *Das Deuteronomium: Entstehung, Gestalt und Botschaft*, edited by Norbert Lohfink, 310–20. BETL 68. Leuven: Leuven University Press, 1985.
Rom-Shiloni, Dalit. "Deuteronomic Concepts of Exile Interpreted in Jeremiah and Ezekiel." In *Birkat Shalom: Studies in the Bible, Ancient Near Eastern Literature, and Postbiblical Judaism Presented to Shalom M. Paul on the Occasion of His Seventieth Birthday*, edited by Chaim Cohen et al., 1:101–23. Winona Lake, IN: Eisenbrauns, 2008.
Rom-Shiloni, Dalit. "Ezekiel and Jeremiah: What Might Stand behind the Silence?" *HeBAI* 1 (2012): 203–30.
Rom-Shiloni, Dalit. "Ezekiel as the Voice of the Exiles and Constructor of Exilic Ideology." *HUCA* 76 (2005): 1–45.
Rom-Shiloni, Dalit. "Facing Destruction and Exile: Inner-Biblical Exegesis in Jeremiah and Ezekiel." *ZAW* 117 (2005): 189–205.
Römer, Thomas C. "Book of Deuteronomy." In *The History of Israel's Traditions: The Heritage of Martin Noth*, edited by Steven L. McKenzie and M. Patrick Graham, 178–212. JSOTSup 182. Sheffield: Sheffield Academic, 1994.
Rooker, Mark F. *Biblical Hebrew in Transition: The Language of the Book of Ezekiel*. JSOTSup 90. Sheffield: Sheffield Academic, 1990.
Sanders, Paul. *The Provenance of Deuteronomy 32*. OtSt 37. Leiden: Brill, 1996.
Sandmel, Samuel. "Parallelomania." *JBL* 81 (1962): 1–13.
Schearing, L. S., and S. L. McKenzie, eds. *Those Elusive Deuteronomists: The Phenomenon of Pan-Deuteronomism*. JSOTSup 268. Sheffield: Sheffield Academic, 1999.
Schmidt, Brian B. "The Aniconic Tradition: On Reading Images and Viewing Texts." In *The Triumph of Elohim: From Yahwisms to Judaisms*, edited by D. V. Edelman, 75–105. CBET 13. Kampen: Kok Pharos, 1995.
Schniedewind, William M. *How the Bible Became a Book: The Textualization of Ancient Israel*. Cambridge: Cambridge University Press, 2004.

Schniedewind, William M. "Scripturalization in Ancient Judah." In *Contextualizing Israel's Sacred Writings: Ancient Literacy, Orality, and Literary Production*, edited by Brian B. Schmidt, 305–21. SBLAIL 22. Atlanta: SBL, 2015.

Schultz, Richard L. *The Search for Quotation: Verbal Parallels in the Prophets*. JSOTSup 180. Sheffield: Sheffield Academic, 1999.

Schwartz, Baruch J. "Ezekiel, P, and the Other Pentateuchal Sources." Paper presented at the annual meeting of the Society of Biblical Literature. Washington, DC, November 19, 2006.

Schwartz, Baruch J. "Ezekiel's Dim View of Israel's Restoration." In *The Book of Ezekiel: Theological and Anthropological Perspectives*, edited by Margaret S. Odell and John T. Strong, 43–67. SBLSymS 9. Atlanta: Society of Biblical Literature, 2000.

Schwartz, Baruch J. "A Priest Out of Place: Reconsidering Ezekiel's Role in the History of the Israelite Priesthood." In *Ezekiel's Hierarchical World: Wrestling with a Tiered Reality*, edited by Stephen L. Cook and Corrine L. Patton, 61–71. SBLSymS 31. Atlanta: Society of Biblical Literature, 2004.

Scurlock, JoAnn. "Oaths, ancient Near East." In *The Encyclopedia of Ancient History*, edited by Roger S. Bagnall et al., 9:4848–9. Oxford: Wiley-Blackwell, 2013.

Seely, David Rolph. "The Raised Hand of God as an Oath Gesture." In *Fortunate the Eyes That See: Essays in Honor of David Noel Freedman in Celebration of His Seventieth Birthday*, edited by Astrid B. Beck, 411–21. Grand Rapids: Eerdmans, 1995.

Skehan, Patrick W., and Eugene Ulrich. "4QDeut^q." In *Qumran Cave 4.IX: Deuteronomy, Joshua, Judges, Kings*, edited by E. Ulrich et al. DJD 14. Oxford: Clarendon, 1995.

Smith, George Adam. *The Book of Deuteronomy*. Cambridge Bible for Schools and Colleges. Cambridge: Cambridge University Press, 1918.

Smith, Mark S. "The Near Eastern Background of Solar Language for Yahweh." *JBL* 109 (1990): 29–39.

Smith-Christopher, Daniel L. *A Biblical Theology of Exile*. Minneapolis: Augsburg Fortress, 2002.

Sommer, Benjamin D. "Exegesis, Allusion and Intertextuality in the Hebrew Bible: A Response to Lyle Eslinger." *VT* 46 (1996): 479–89.

Sommer, Benjamin D. *A Prophet Reads Scripture: Allusion in Isaiah 40–66*. Stanford: Stanford University Press, 1988.

Spawn, Kevin L. *'As It Is Written' and Other Citation Formulae in the Old Testament: Their Use, Development, Syntax, and Significance*. BZAW 311. Berlin: de Gruyter, 2002.

Spottorno, María Victoria. "La omisión de Ez. 36:23b-38 y la transposición de capitulos en el papiro 967." *Emerita* 50 (1982): 93–8.

Stanley, Christopher D. "Rhetoric of Quotations." In *Exploring Intertextuality: Diverse Strategies for New Testament Interpretation of Texts*, edited by B. J. Oropeza and Steve Moyise, 42–62. Eugene, OR: Cascade, 2016.

Stavrakopoulou, Francesca. *King Manasseh and Child Sacrifice: Biblical Distortions of Historical Realities*. BZAW 338. Berlin: de Gruyter, 2004.

Stead, Michael R. *The Intertextuality of Zechariah 1–8*. LHBOTS 506. New York: T&T Clark, 2009.

Steins, Georg. *"Bindung Isaaks" im Kanon (Gen 22): Grundlagen und Programm einer Kanonisch-Intertextuellen Lektüre*. HBS 20. Freiburg: Herder, 1999.

Stiebert, Johanna. *The Exile and the Prophet's Wife: Historic Events and Marginal Perspectives*. Collegeville, MN: Liturgical, 2005.

Stiebert, Johanna. "Shame and Prophecy: Approaches Past and Present." *BibInt* 8 (2000): 255–75.

Stohlmann, Stephen. "The Judaean Exile after 701 BCE." In *Scripture in Context II*, edited by W. W. Hallo, J. C. Moyer, and L. G. Perdue, 147–75. Winona Lake, IN: Eisenbrauns, 1983.

Stökl, Jonathan. "'A Youth Without Blemish, Handsome, Proficient in All Wisdom, Knowledgeable and Intelligent': Ezekiel's Access to Babylonian Culture." In *Exile and Return: The Babylonian Context*, edited by Jonathan Stökl and Caroline Waerzeggers, 223–52. Berlin: de Gruyter, 2015.

Strine, C. A. "On the Compositional Models for Ezekiel 38–39: A Response to William Tooman." *VT* 67 (2017): 589–601.

Strine, C. A. "The Role of Repentance in the Book of Ezekiel: A Second Chance for the Second Generation." *JTS* 63 (2012): 467–91.

Strine, C. A. *Sworn Enemies: The Divine Oath, the Book of Ezekiel, and the Polemics of Exile*. BZAW 436. Berlin: de Gruyter, 2013.

Stromberg, Jacob. "An Inner-Isaianic Reading of Isaiah 61:1-3." In *Interpreting Isaiah: Issues and Approaches*, edited by David G. Firth and H. G. M. Williamson, 261–72. Downers Grove, IL: InterVarsity, 2009.

Stromberg, Jacob. "Observations on Inner-Scriptural Scribal Expansion in MT Ezekiel." *VT* 58 (2008): 68–86.

Stuhlmueller, Carroll. *Creative Redemption in Deutero-Isaiah*. AnBib 43. Rome: Pontifical Biblical Institute, 1970.

Sweeney, Marvin A. "Ezekiel: Zadokite Priest and Visionary Prophet of the Exile." In *Form and Intertextuality in Prophetic and Apocalyptic Literature*, 125–43. FAT 45. Tübingen: Mohr Siebeck, 2005.

Sweeney, Marvin A. *Isaiah 1–39: With an Introduction to Prophetic Literature*. FOTL 16. Grand Rapids: Eerdmans, 1996.

Tadmor, Hayim. "Treaty and Oath in the Ancient Near East: A Historian's Approach." In *Humanizing America's Iconic Book: Society of Biblical Literature Centennial Addresses 1980*, edited by Gene M. Tucker and Douglas A. Knight, 127–52. SBLBSNA 6. Chico, CA: Scholars Press, 1982.

Talmon, Shemaryahu. "The 'Desert Motif' in the Bible and in Qumran Literature." In *Biblical Motifs*, edited by A. Altmann, 31–63. Cambridge, MA: Harvard University Press, 1966. Repr. in *Literary Studies in the Hebrew Bible: Form and Content*, 216–54. Jerusalem: Magnes, 1992.

Taylor, Glen. *Yahweh and the Sun: Biblical and Archaeological Evidence for Sun Worship in Ancient Israel*. JSOTSup 111. Sheffield: JSOT, 1993.

Thelle, Rannfrid Irene. *Approaches to the "Chosen Place": Accessing a Biblical Concept*. LHBOTS 564. New York: T&T Clark, 2012.

Thiel, Winfried. *Die deuteronomistische Redaktion von Jeremia 1–25*. WMANT 41. Neukirchen-Vluyn: Neukirchener Verlag, 1973.

Thiessen, Matthew. "The Form and Function of the Song of Moses (Deuteronomy 32:1-43)." *JBL* 123 (2004): 401–24.

Tigay, Jeffrey H. דברים. *The Traditional Hebrew Text with the New JPS Translation*. JPS Torah Commentary. Philadelphia: Jewish Publication Society, 1996.

Tooman, William A. *Gog of Magog: Reuse of Scripture and Compositional Technique in Ezekiel 38–39*. FAT 2/52. Tübingen: Mohr-Siebeck, 2011.

Tooman, William A. "Transformation of Israel's Hope: The Reuse of Scripture in the Gog Oracles." Pages 50–105 in *Transforming Visions: Transformations of Text, Tradition, and Theology in Ezekiel*, edited by William A. Tooman and Michael A. Lyons. PTMS 127. Eugene, OR: Pickwick, 2010.

Tooman, William A., and Penelope Barter, eds. *Ezekiel: Current Debates and Future Directions*. FAT 112. Göttingen: Mohr Siebeck, 2017.

Tooman, William A., and Michael A. Lyons, eds. *Transforming Visions: Transformations of Text, Tradition, and Theology in Ezekiel*. PTMS 127. Eugene, OR: Pickwick, 2010.

Toorn, Karel van der. *Scribal Culture and the Making of the Hebrew Bible*. Cambridge, MA: Harvard University Press, 2007.

Torrey, C. C. *Pseudo-Ezekiel and the Original Prophecy*. New Haven: Yale University Press, 1930.

Tov, Emanuel. "Excerpted and Abbreviated Biblical Texts from Qumran." *RevQ* 16 (1995): 581–600.

Tov, Emanuel. "Recensional Differences Between the Masoretic Text and Septuagint of Ezekiel." In *The Greek and Hebrew Bible: Collected Essays on the Septuagint*, 397–410. VTSup 72. Leiden: Brill, 1999. Originally published in *ETL* 62 (1986): 89–101. Also reprinted in *Of Scribes and Scrolls: Studies on the Hebrew Bible, Intertestamental Judaism, and Christian Origins Presented to John Strugnell*, edited by Harold W. Attridge, John J. Collins, and Thomas H. Tobin, 43–56. Lanham, MD: University Press of America, 1990.

Tov, Emanuel. *Textual Criticism of the Hebrew Bible*. 3rd ed. Minneapolis: Fortress, 2012.

Troxel, Ronald L. *Prophetic Literature: From Oracles to Books*. Oxford: Wiley-Blackwell, 2012.

Tuell, Steven S. *Ezekiel*. NIBC. Peabody, MA: Hendrickson, 2009.

Turner, Kenneth J. *The Death of Deaths in the Death of Israel: Deuteronomy's Theology of Exile*. Eugene, OR: Wipf & Stock, 2011.

Vang, Carsten. "The So-Called '*Ur-Deuteronomium*': Some Reflections on Its Content, Size and Age." *Hiphil* 6 (2009): 1–22.

Varšo, Miroslav. "Das Deuteronomium mit Ezechiel lesen: eine intertextuelle Studie." Ph.D. diss., University of Vienna, 2002.

Vaughan, Patrick H. *The Meaning of* Bamah *in the Old Testament: A Study of Etymological, Textual, and Archaeological Evidence*. Cambridge: Cambridge University Press, 1974.

Vogt, Peter T. *Deuteronomic Theology and the Significance of* Torah: *A Reappraisal*. Winona Lake, IN: Eisenbrauns, 2006.

Watts, Rikk E. "Isaiah in the New Testament." In *Interpreting Isaiah: Issues and Approaches*, edited by David G. Firth and H. G. M. Williamson, 213–33. Downers Grove, IL: InterVarsity, 2009.

Weeks, Stuart. "Man-made Gods? Idolatry in the Old Testament." In *Idolatry: False Worship in the Bible, Early Judaism and Christianity*, edited by Stephen C. Barton, 7–21. London: T&T Clark, 2007.

Weinfeld, Moshe. *Deuteronomy 1–11: A New Translation with Introduction and Commentary*. AB 5. New York: Doubleday, 1991.

Weinfeld, Moshe. *Deuteronomy and the Deuteronomic School*. Oxford: Clarendon, 1972. Repr., Winona Lake, IN: Eisenbrauns, 1992.

Welch, Adam C. *The Code of Deuteronomy: A New Theory of Its Origin*. London: James Clark, 1924.

Welch, Adam C. *Deuteronomy: The Framework to the Code*. London: Oxford University Press, 1932.
Wellhausen, Julius. *Prolegomena to the History of Ancient Israel*. Translated by J. Sutherland Black and Allan Menzies. Cleveland: Meridian, 1965.
Wetzsteon, R. "Allusion." In *The Princeton Encyclopedia of Poetry and Poetics*, edited by Roland Greene et al., 42–3. 4th ed. Princeton: Princeton University Press, 2012.
Wevers, J. W. *Ezekiel*. NCB. London: Nelson, 1969.
Widengren, Geo. "Yahweh's Gathering of the Dispersed." In *In the Shelter of Elyon: Essays on Ancient Palestinian Life and Literature in Honor of G. W. Ahlström*, edited by W. Boyd Barrick and John R. Spencer, 227–45. JSOTSup 31. Sheffield: JSOT, 1984.
Wildberger, Hans. *Isaiah 1–12*. CC. Minneapolis: Augsburg Fortress, 1991.
Wilson, Ian. *Out of the Midst of the Fire: Divine Presence in Deuteronomy*. SBLDS 151. Atlanta: Scholars Press, 1995.
Wilson, Robert R. An Interpretation of Ezekiel's Dumbness." *VT* 22 (1973): 91–104.
Wilson, Robert R. *Prophecy and Society in Ancient Israel*. Philadelphia: Fortress, 1980.
Wiseman, D. J. "The Vassal-Treaties of Esarhaddon." *Iraq* 20 (1958): 1–99.
Wolff, Hans Walter. "The Kerygma of the Deuteronomistic Historical Work." In *The Vitality of Old Testament Traditions*, edited by Walter Brueggemann and Hans Walter Wolff, 83–100. Atlanta: John Knox, 1975. Translation of "Das Kerygma des deuteronomistischen Geschichtswerk." *ZAW* 73 (1961): 171–86. Also repr. in *Reconsidering Israel and Judah: Recent Studies on the Deuteronomistic History*, edited by Gary N. Knoppers and J. Gordon McConville, 62–78. SBTS 8. Winona Lake, IN: Eisenbrauns, 2000.
Wolff, Hans Walter. "The Kerygma of the Yahwist." In *The Vitality of Old Testament Traditions*, edited by Walter Brueggemann and Hans Walter Wolff, 41–66. Atlanta: John Knox, 1975. Translation of "Das Kerygma des Jahwisten." *EvT* 24 (1964): 73–98.
Wong, Ka Leung. *The Idea of Retribution in the Book of Ezekiel*. VTSup 87. Leiden: Brill, 2001.
Wright, Christopher J. H. *God's People in God's Land: Family, Land, and Property in the Old Testament*. Grand Rapids: Eerdmans, 1990.
Wright, David P. "Method in the Study of Textual Source Dependence: The Deuteronomic Code." In *Subtle Citation, Allusion, and Translation in the Hebrew Bible*, edited by Ziony Zevit, 159–81. Sheffield: Equinox, 2017.
Wright, G. Ernest. "Deuteronomy: Introduction and Exegesis." In *The Interpreter's Bible*, vol. 2. Nashville: Abingdon, 1953.
Wright, G. Ernest. "The Lawsuit of God: A Form-Critical Study of Deuteronomy 32." In *Israel's Prophetic Heritage: Essays in Honor of James Muilenburg*, edited by Bernhard W. Anderson and Walter Harrelson, 26–67. New York: Harper & Brothers, 1962.
Wu, Daniel Y. *Honor, Shame, and Guilt: Social-Scientific Approaches to the Book of Ezekiel*. BBRS 14. Winona Lake, IN: Eisenbrauns, 2016.
Yamauchi, Edwin M. "Tammuz and the Bible." *JBL* 84 (1965): 283–90.
Zevit, Ziony. "Echoes of Texts Past." In *Subtle Citation, Allusion, and Translation in the Hebrew Bible*, edited by Ziony Zevit, 1–21. Sheffield: Equinox, 2017.
Zevit, Ziony. *The Religions of Ancient Israel: A Synthesis of Parallactic Approaches*. London: Continuum, 2001.
Ziegler, Yael. *Promises to Keep: The Oath in Biblical Narrative*. VTSup 120. Leiden: Brill, 2008.

Zimmerli, Walther. "Das Phänomen der 'Fortschreibung' im Buch Ezechiel." In *Prophecy: Essays Presented to Georg Fohrer on his Sixty-Fifth Birthday*, edited by J. A. Emerton, 174–91. BZAW 150. Berlin: de Gruyter, 1980.

Zimmerli, Walther. *Ezekiel: A Commentary on the Book of the Prophet Ezekiel.* Translated by Ronald E. Clements. 2 vols. Hermeneia. Philadelphia: Fortress, 1979.

Zimmerli, Walther. "Le nouvel 'exode' dans le message des deux grands prophètes de l'Exil." In *Maqqél shâkedh: la branche d'amandier. Hommage à Wilhelm Fischer*, 216–26. Montpellier: Cause, Graille, & Castelnau, 1960. Repr. "Der 'Neue Exodus' in Der Verkündigung der Beiden Grossen Exilspropheten." In *Gottes Offenbarung: Gesammelte Aufsätze I*, 192–204. 2nd ed. TB 19. Munich: Kaiser, 1969.

Zimmerli, Walther. *Old Testament Theology in Outline*. Translated by David E. Green. Edinburgh: T. & T. Clark, 1978.

Zimmerli, Walther. "Promise and Fulfillment." In *Essays in Old Testament Interpretation*, edited by Claus Westermann, 89–122. London: SCM, 1963.

Index of References

Hebrew Bible/ Old Testament

Genesis
Ref	Page
1:26-27	44
12	170
12:7	170
13:15	170
13:17	170
14:22	151
15:7	170
15:18	170
17:8	170
18:19	112
22:16-18	112
24:7	170
26:3-4	170
26:3	170
28:4	170
28:13	170
34:5	135
35:12	170
43:11	69
48:4	170
48:21	152
49	98
49:9	98
49:10-14	99
49:10-12	99
50:24	113, 170

Exodus
Ref	Page
1:4	69
3:19	110
6:1	110
6:2-8	105, 156
6:4	170
6:6-8	156
6:6	110
6:8	113, 151, 152, 155, 170
12:25	170
13	128
13:5	150, 170
13:9	110
13:11	170
13:12-13	130
13:12	128
13:13	128, 130, 131
20:3	51
20:4	44
20:5	66, 98
21:12	100
23:13	51
25:9	68
25:40	68
32:11	110
33:1	113
34:14	98
34:15	51
34:16	51

Leviticus
Ref	Page
2	86
2:7	86
2:11-12	86
7:21	47
10:10-11	145
11	68, 70, 71
11:10	47
11:11	47
11:12	47
11:13	47
11:20	47
11:23	47
11:35	64
11:41	47
11:42	47
13	136
14:34	170
14:45	64
17–26	1
17	59, 131, 132
17:1-8	130
17:3	131
17:5	131
18	78
18:3	138
18:4	46
18:5	46, 104
18:22-30	49
18:24	119
18:26	46
19:4	42, 44, 46
19:26	62
19:37	46
20:2	42, 50, 100, 109
20:3	50, 109
20:4	50, 109
20:5	51
20:13	49
20:22-26	42
20:22	46
20:23	42
20:24	170
20:27	100
21:5	147
21:10	147
23:37	69
23:40	62
24:17	100

25:2	170	*Numbers*		1:39	170
25:18	46	5:23	20	1:43	107, 115
25:38	170	6:9	135	2:14-16	45
26	57, 59, 60,	11:12	170	3:24	110
	97, 141,	13–14	106	3:29	45
	142, 145,	13:2	106	4	12, 45, 52,
	146, 158,	13:16	106		57, 65, 66,
	163, 172,	13:17	106		68, 72–7,
	173, 188,	13:32	106		79, 143,
	196	14	155		148, 158,
26:1	42, 44, 46	14:7	106		159, 162,
26:3	46	14:8	170		163, 214
26:6	58	14:15-16	120	4:1-40	157
26:14-39	197	14:16	170	4:1-28	75
26:15	46	14:21	155	4:1-24	75
26:18	159, 196	14:28	155	4:1	46, 170
26:21	159, 196	14:30	150–2,	4:3-4	45
26:22-26	96		155	4:3	116
26:22	146, 147	14:36	106	4:5	46
26:23	159, 196	14:38	106	4:8	46
26:26	96	20:20	110	4:9-25	56
26:27	159, 196	22:7	52	4:14	46
26:30-31	43	23:23	52	4:15-24	143
26:30	42, 43, 57,	24:8	96	4:15-19	40
	59, 63	25:1-9	45	4:16-19	45, 75,
26:33	141, 142,	27:14	107		214
	144-47,	32:11	113, 151,	4:16-18	67–9
	154, 158,		170	4:16	44, 66, 74
	218	33:50-56	60	4:17-18	68, 71, 74,
26:34-39	141	33:50-53	42		77
26:34-35	141	33:52	44–6	4:17	69
26:36-39	141	35:16-34	100	4:19	42, 51, 68,
26:36	148	35:33-34	78		72–4
26:38	141, 146,			4:23-24	66
	147	*Deuteronomy*		4:23	44, 45
26:39	148	1–4	77	4:25-31	75, 163,
26:40-45	125, 194,	1–3	76, 116		190
	196, 197	1:8	112, 150,	4:25-28	74, 75,
26:40-42	188		170		79, 108,
26:42	173	1:9-15	110		137, 139,
26:44-45	173	1:21	170		144, 148,
27	130	1:26	107, 115		156–8,
27:9-10	130	1:31	116		160, 161,
27:28	130	1:32-45	45		163, 166,
36:30-31	59	1:33	106		172, 215,
		1:34-35	116		216, 218
		1:35	170	4:25-26	171

Deuteronomy (cont.)		7:4	42, 51	12	58, 59,
4:25	42, 44, 50,	7:5	44, 63, 64		109, 111,
	66, 160	7:6-8	105, 106,		131
4:26-28	158		113	12:1	46, 170
4:26-27	77	7:6	105	12:2-4	43
4:26	144, 158	7:7-8	113	12:2-3	60
4:27-28	53, 143	7:7	105	12:2	61, 62,
4:27	144, 145,	7:8	110, 113		123, 146
	147	7:13	150, 170	12:3	44, 63, 64
4:28-28	52	7:16	108	12:5	60, 64
4:28	53, 54, 56,	7:19	110	12:6	130
	57, 74,	7:23	57	12:7	63
	109, 124,	7:25-26	49	12:8-11	132
	144	7:25	48	12:17	130
4:29-31	75, 77,	7:26	47, 48	12:18	63
	163, 173,	8	87	12:20-21	131
	190, 194	8:1	112, 170	12:21	131
4:29-30	75	8:12	42	12:31	48, 50,
4:34	110	8:14-16	87		109
4:35	75, 76	8:15	116	13:2-19	42
4:36	144	8:19	51	13:3	51
4:37-38	106, 113	9:4-6	113	13:6-11 Heb.	100
4:37	105	9:5	112, 113,	13:7-12	100
4:39	75		170	13:7	51
4:40	119	9:6-29	45, 116	13:9	108
4:44-49	45	9:6-7	117	13:14	51
5–26	46	9:7	107, 116	13:14 Heb.	48
5	76	9:18	50	13:15	48
5:1	46	9:19	107	14	130, 132
5:7	51	9:23	107, 115	14:2	105
5:8	44	9:24	107, 116,	14:3	47
5:9	66		117	14:22-26	130
5:15	110	9:26	110	14:24-26	132
5:16	119	9:28	170	15:19	130
5:23	110	9:29	110	15:20	63, 130
5:33	119	10:11	170	16:22	44
6:1	46	10:13	46	17:1	47
6:2	46	10:15	105, 106	17:3	51, 72
6:3	170	10:16	117, 189	17:4	48
6:10	112, 150,	11:2	110	17:8	145
	170	11:5	116	17:9-12	20
6:13-14	42	11:9	150, 170	17:9	145
6:14-15	50	11:16	42, 51	18:10	50, 52,
6:14	51	11:19	119		109
6:18	170	11:21	170	18:12	47
6:21	110	11:28	51	18:14	52
6:23	170	11:32	46	18:20-22	111

18:20	51	28:36	51–4, 57,	29:28 Heb.	107, 144
19:8	170		74, 109,	29:29	192
19:12	110		124, 148	30	12, 173,
19:13	108	28:37	57		177–82,
19:21	108	28:41	143		184–90,
20:5-9	45	28:45-68	191		192, 197,
20:10-17	45	28:45	46, 57		212, 213,
20:18-26	45	28:47-68	163, 167		216, 218
20:18	48	28:47	166	30:1-20	190
21:1-9	111	28:58	166, 191	30:1-10	77, 184,
21:5	145	28:61	191		190–4,
21:18-21	111	28:64	51–4, 56,		196, 197
22	100		57, 74,	30:1-5	174
22:5	47, 48		109, 124,	30:1-2	125, 187
22:13-21	111		143–5,	30:1	143
22:21	100		147, 148	30:3-6	187
22:24	100	29–31	159	30:3-5	110, 177,
23:18 Heb.	47	29–30	77, 156		178, 180,
23:19	47	29	144, 159		184, 186,
24:4	47, 48	29:3	117		187, 190,
24:16	33	29:4	116		192, 193,
25:12	108	29:5 Heb.	116		212, 216,
25:13-16	47	29:9	111		218
26:3	150, 170	29:11	157	30:3-4	192
26:8	110	29:12-27	160	30:3	125, 144,
26:15	170	29:12	112		178, 179,
27:1	111	29:12 Heb.	157		181, 182,
27:3	170	29:13	157		185, 203
27:5	33	29:13 Heb.	112	30:4-5	180
27:15	44, 48	29:14 Heb.	157	30:4	181, 187
28	52, 57, 74,	29:15-16	138	30:5	125
	148, 160,	29:16-17 Heb.	138	30:6	161, 189,
	163, 166,	29:16	43, 47, 52,		192
	167, 169,		69, 106,	30:10	46, 191
	191, 196,		114	30:11	192
	197	29:17 Heb.	43, 47, 52,	30:15	104
28:11	150, 170		69, 106,	30:16	119
28:14	51		114	30:17	51
28:15	46, 166	29:22-28	77	30:18	119, 143
28:20	57	29:22-28 Heb.	160	30:19	104, 157,
28:22	57	29:22	107		158
28:26	57, 58	29:23 Heb.	107	30:20	112, 170
28:27-37	163	29:23-29 Heb.	77	31	159
28:36-37	143, 166,	29:24-27	143	31:7	170
	191	29:25-28 Heb.	143	31:9-11	20
		29:25	51	31:9	111
		29:27	107, 144	31:10-13	20

Deuteronomy (cont.)

31:16-20	159	32:36-43	91	8:5	56
31:16	51	32:36	88, 155	8:7	56
31:18	51	32:37	93	8:8	51
31:20	51, 170	32:39	93	8:20	56
31:21	102, 170	32:40-41	154, 155	12:14	107, 115
31:23	170	32:40	113, 151, 155	12:15	107, 115
31:27	107, 117, 159	32:41-43	88	15:23	52
31:28	158	32:41-42	97	26:19	51
31:29	50, 159	32:41	97	28:8	52
32	51, 81–5, 88–96, 99–102, 142, 145, 151, 155, 215	32:42	96, 97	*2 Samuel*	
		32:43	88	12:11	152
		32:47	119		
		33:24-26	113	*1 Kings*	
		34:4	170	2:3	33
		34:12	110	3:8	105
		37–31	155	8	191
32:1-43	80, 81, 88, 92, 95, 96, 217			8:42	110
		Joshua		8:46-53	190, 191
32:9-13	33	1:6	170	9:6	51
32:9	100	1:8	33	9:9	51
32:10-14	84, 85, 90	1:18	107, 115	11:4	51
32:10	82, 83, 85, 90, 116	8:24	82	11:5	47, 71, 114
		8:31	33		
32:11	85	13:22	52	11:7	47, 71, 114
32:12-14	85	21:43	170		
32:13	86, 100	22:28	68	11:10	51
32:15-18	81	23:6	33	11:35	152
32:15	86, 91	23:16	51	13:26	107, 115
32:16-17	86, 87, 91	24:2	51	14:9	50, 51
32:16	48, 50, 66, 87, 88, 91, 98	24:14	138	14:15	50
		24:16	51	14:22	98
				14:23	44, 61
		Judges		14:24	48
32:18	87, 91	2:12	50, 51	15:12	43
32:19-29	81	2:17	51	15:30	50
32:19-25	88	2:19	51	16:2	50
32:19	50	8:33	51	16:7	50
32:21	50, 66, 87, 88, 91, 98	10:13	51	16:13	50
				16:26	50
32:23-25	91, 96	*Ruth*		16:33	50
32:23	96	3:9	85	21	65
32:23:25	100			21:22	50
32:25	97	*1 Samuel*		21:26	43
32:30-31	96	6:2	52	22:54	50
32:35-36	88	8	56	23:21	33

2 Kings		*1 Chronicles*		136:11-12	110
3:2	44	22:2	186	147:2	186
5:17	51	28:11	68		
10:26	44			*Proverbs*	
10:27	44	*2 Chronicles*		15:1	107
14:6	33	19:8-11	20	15:18	107
16:3	48, 50, 109	33:7	66, 67	21:14	107
		33:15	66, 67	22:24	107
		35:12	33	27:4	107
16:4	61			29:22	107
16:10	68	*Ezra*			
17:1-23	169	3:4	33	*Ecclesiastes*	
17:6	169, 193	6:18	33	2:8	186
17:7-18	169			3:5	186
17:7	51	*Nehemiah*			
17:10	44, 61	8:8-9	20	*Isaiah*	
17:11	50	9:15	152	1–39	94
17:12	43	10:36	33	2:2-4	31
17:17	50, 52, 109	12:44	186	2:6-8	40
				2:8	44
17:35	51	*Job*		2:18	44
17:37	51	24:5-6	82	2:20	40, 44
17:38	51			4:2	114
18:4	44	*Esther*		8:2	20
19:18	52	4:16	186	10:10	44
21	72, 73			10:11	44
21:2	48	*Psalms*		11:11	180
21:3-5	73	3:7	186	11:12	179, 180, 194
21:6	50, 109	5:11	115		
21:7	66, 73	6:1	107	13:19	114
21:11	43, 48	10:12	149	14:1-2	180
21:15	50, 117	27:10	83	14:2	180
21:21	43	37:8	107	19	44
22	20	78	107	19:1	44
22:17	50, 51	78:38	107	19:3	44
23	109	78:56	115	19:13	69
23:5	73	78:58	66, 98	19:14 Heb.	69
23:6	67	96:5	44	19:15	69
23:10	50, 109	97:7-9	40	23:9	114
23:11	73	97:7	44	24:16	114
23:13	47, 48, 71, 114	105:28	115	27:12	179
		106	107	28:1	114
23:14	44	106:20	68	28:4	114
23:19	51	106:26-27	153	31:7	44
23:24	43, 47, 114	115:3-8	40	37:19	52
23:26-27	73	135:15-18	40		

Isaiah (cont.)

Reference	Page
40–66	94, 146, 192
40–55	179
40:18-20	40
43:5-6	179
43:19-20	82
44:9-20	40
46:1-7	40
49:1-13	179
49:10	179
49:12	179
49:14	207
49:22	149
51:17	66
52:7-12	179
52:8	179
52:11-12	179
55:11-13	179
58:11-14	33
58:14	100
62:8	151
66:3	47

Jeremiah

Reference	Page
1:16	51
2:2	117
2:8	20
2:20	61
2:27	52
3:6	61
3:9	52
3:19	114
4:1	47, 114
4:17	115
7:6	51
7:9-10	47
7:9	51
7:18	50, 51
7:19	50
7:20	107
7:30	47, 114
7:33	58
8:2	73
8:3	178
8:8	20
8:19	50
10:1-16	40
11:10	51
11:17	50
12:12	97
12:15	181
13:10	51
13:27	47, 114
14:14	44, 52
16:4	58
16:11	51
16:13	51
16:14-15	181
16:15	178
16:18	47, 48, 114
19:4	51
19:7	58
19:13	51
21:5	107
22:9	51
23:3	178, 181
23:8	178
23:21	52
24:6	181
24:8	198
24:9	178
25:6	50, 51
25:7	50
27:9	52
27:10	178
27:15	178
29:8	52
29:10	181
29:14	178, 181
29:18	178
30:3	181
30:10-11	181
31:8-10	181
31:28	73
32:10-12	20
32:29	50, 51
32:30	50
32:31	107, 110
32:32	50
32:34	47, 114
32:35	48, 50
32:37-41	206
32:37	181
33:5	107
33:26	181
34:20	58
35:15	51
36	16
36:7	107
40:11-12	198
40:12	178, 181
41:8	86
42:12	181
42:18	107
43:5	178
43:13	44
44:1	198
44:3	50, 51
44:4	48
44:5	51
44:6	107
44:8	50, 51
44:15	51
46:28	178
50:2	43

Lamentations

Reference	Page
4:11	107
5:7	73

Ezekiel

Reference	Page
1–24	203, 205
1:1-28	207
3:16-21	207
3:26-27	207
3:26	202
3:27	202
2:2–3:11	22
4:13	25, 178, 217
5:2	97, 140, 142
5:4-17	22
5:5-6	40
5:6-8	135
5:6-7	140
5:6	115
5:8	135
5:9	48

5:10	140	8:1–11:25	207	11:19	189
5:11	47–9, 78, 108, 117	8:1-18	161	11:21	47, 49
		8:1	110	11:25-26	206
5:12	97, 140, 142	8:3	65, 66, 98	11:27-29	206
		8:5-6	65, 66	12:14-15	140
5:13	107, 202	8:5	65, 66	12:14	69, 97, 142
5:15	69, 107	8:6	48, 49		
5:16-17	96, 100, 145	8:7-13	65, 69–71	12:15	143, 161, 202
		8:9	48, 49		
5:16	96	8:10	25, 43, 47, 67–9, 71, 77, 217	12:16	48
6	22, 58–60, 123			12:20	202
				13:6	52
6:1-14	109, 122	8:12	44	13:9	52, 202
6:1-7	57, 111	8:13	48, 49	13:13	107
6:3-7	59, 122	8:14-15	65, 71	13:14	202
6:3	59, 60	8:15-17	48	13:21	202
6:4-7	43	8:15	49	13:23	52, 202
6:4-6	43	8:16-18	65, 72	14	55, 111
6:4	43	8:16	72, 73	14:1-3	203
6:5	43	8:17	25, 49–51, 217	14:1	110
6:6	43, 60, 63			14:3	43, 55, 56, 111
6:7	202	8:18	108, 117		
6:8	140, 143	8:20	47	14:4	43
6:9	43, 49, 51	9	202	14:5	43
6:10	202	9:4	48	14:6	43, 48, 57, 189, 217
6:11-13	22	9:5	108, 117		
6:11	48	9:10	108, 117	14:7	43, 111
6:13-14	123	11	187	14:8	202
6:13	25, 43, 57, 60–2, 109, 111, 123, 146, 202	11:1-12	207	14:11	78
		11:10	202	14:16	49
		11:12	140, 202	15	5
		11:14-21	22, 203, 205, 207	15:7	202
6:14	202			15:52	183
7:3	48	11:14-17	206	15:63	183
7:4	48, 108, 117, 202	11:15	143	16	5, 25, 40, 51, 64, 80–5, 88–91, 96, 98, 100, 122, 131, 183, 188, 208, 215, 217, 218
		11:16-17	140, 206		
7:7	57	11:16	143, 205, 206		
7:8	48, 107				
7:9	48, 108, 117	11:17-18	126		
		11:17	143, 162, 175, 185, 187, 205, 206		
7:15	97				
7:20	44, 48, 49				
8–11	73, 111				
8	49, 51, 62, 65–7, 69, 70, 72–5, 77, 214	11:18	47, 49, 200, 206	16:1-43	80, 87, 90, 208
		11:19-20	140, 161, 189, 206	16:2	48
				16:3	100

Ezekiel (cont.)

16:4-14	218	16:53	89		126, 131, 133, 137–9, 141, 145, 149, 152–5, 158, 160, 172, 175, 189, 201, 203, 204, 207, 208, 215–17
16:4	100	16:54	89, 183		
16:5-6	82	16:55	89		
16:5	108, 117	16:58	48		
16:6	83, 90	16:59-63	80, 88, 200, 207		
16:7-13	84	16:59	200		
16:7	84, 90	16:61	183		
16:8	85	16:62	202		
16:9-13	84, 85, 90	16:63	201		
16:13-14	86, 91	17:16-17	22		
16:13	86	17:18	151	20:1-31	54, 177, 206
16:15-43	218	17:21	202		
16:15-34	91	18	41, 62, 122	20:1-26	54
16:15-22	86, 101			20:1-4	203
16:15	86, 91	18:2	73	20:1	110, 207
16:16	60, 122	18:5-8	41	20:2-31	53
16:17	44	18:6	43, 51, 62, 72, 109, 122	20:3-31	104
16:19	86			20:3	54, 207
16:20-36	40			20:4-26	54
16:20	131	18:9-12	48	20:4	49, 103, 111, 112, 138, 217
16:21	50, 109, 131	18:9	41		
		18:10-13	48		
16:22	48, 87, 91	18:11	62, 109, 122	20:5-31	122, 124
16:23-43	101			20:5-29	217
16:23-34	87	18:12	43, 48, 51, 72	20:5-26	41, 54, 55, 104, 107, 120, 121
16:24-25	122				
16:26	50, 87, 91	18:13	48		
16:31	122	18:15	43, 51, 62, 72, 109, 122	20:5-9	104
16:32	87			20:5-6	105, 106
16:35-43	88, 91, 100			20:5	105, 112, 133, 139, 151–3, 207, 215
		18:17	41		
16:36	43, 48, 49, 88	18:19	41		
		18:21-32	189		
16:38	100	18:21	41	20:6	106, 113, 114, 139, 151, 155, 156
16:39	64	18:24	48		
16:40-63	203	18:30-32	189		
16:43	48, 87, 91	18:31	189		
16:44-58	80, 88	19	5, 98, 99	20:7-8	138
16:44-55	188	19:2-9	98	20:7	43, 47, 78, 106, 114, 115
16:44-52	100	20	15, 22, 25, 40, 45, 53, 103–6, 109, 111, 112, 115, 118–20, 122, 125,		
16:47	48				
16:50	48			20:8	43, 47, 106, 107, 115, 139, 161, 207
16:51	48				
16:53-63	91, 200				
16:53-55	88				
16:53-54	200			20:9	120

20:10-17	104		139–41,	20:33-44	57, 64,
20:10-11	37, 40, 79, 115		143, 149–55, 156,		109, 203, 204, 207
20:10	116, 207		160, 161,	20:33-39	109
20:11-12	45		172, 207,	20:33-38	53–5, 124, 201
20:11	38, 119, 127, 133, 134, 136, 217	20:24	215, 216, 218 41, 43, 51, 127, 133,	20:33-34 20:33	109, 124, 139 55, 56,
20:12	134		134, 140		133, 207
20:13-21	119	20:25-26	104, 127,	20:34-35	175–7
20:13-17	45		129, 133,	20:34	110, 133,
20:13	106, 107, 115, 116, 119, 127, 133, 139, 140, 161, 207	20:25 20:26	134, 136–8 127–9, 134–7, 139, 215 50, 78,	20:35-38 20:35 20:36	140, 143, 175, 185, 206 125, 201 116 116
20:14	120		128–31,	20:38	207
20:15-16	41		135, 136	20:39	43, 78,
20:15	116, 153, 155, 207	20:27-29	22, 108, 111, 118–	20:40-41	207 206
20:16	41, 43, 51, 127, 133, 140, 151, 161, 214	20:27-28 20:27 20:28	24 121, 123 120–2 50, 61, 62, 108, 109,	20:40 20:41-42 20:41	58, 64, 65 22, 174–6 110, 133, 139, 140, 143, 185,
20:17	108, 116, 117, 139		122, 123, 139, 152,	20:42	202, 206 152, 202,
20:18-26	104, 122		207		207
20:18	37, 43, 45, 46, 78, 79, 116, 136	20:29 20:30-32	60, 120 54 78, 120,	20:43-44 20:43 20:44	200 200, 207 202
20:19	133	20:30-31	217	21	97, 100,
20:21	46, 106, 107, 115, 116, 119, 127, 133, 139, 140, 161, 207	20:30 20:31	47, 51, 55, 119, 189 40, 43, 50, 54, 109, 131, 133, 139, 207	21:1-14 21:3-5 Heb. 21:3-5 21:4 Heb. 21:5	142 78 97, 142 97 97 202
20:22	120		201, 206–	21:8-10	97, 142
20:23-26	122, 135, 137	20:32-44 20:32	8 53–6, 74,	21:9 21:9 Heb.	97 97
20:23-24	134		109, 124,	21:10 Heb.	97
20:23	74, 77, 79, 108, 116, 118, 120, 134, 137,		133, 139, 206, 214, 215, 218	21:11 Heb. 21:12 Heb. 21:14	97 97 97

Ezekiel (cont.)

21:15	97	23:38	121	30:8	202		
21:15 Heb.	97	23:39	43, 78, 131	30:11	97, 142		
21:16	97			30:13	43, 44		
21:17	97	23:49	43, 202	30:19	202		
21:20	97	24	202	30:23	140, 143, 161		
21:21 Heb.	52	24:1-14	207				
21:22 Heb.	52	24:2	21	30:25	97, 202		
21:23 Heb.	52	24:14	117	30:26	140, 143, 161, 202		
21:26	52	24:27	202				
21:27	52	25:5	202	32:10	97, 136		
21:28	52	25:7	146–8, 172, 202, 215	32:15	202		
21:28 Heb.	97			32:29	202		
21:29 Heb.	52			33:1-9	207		
21:33	97	25:9	114	33:10	55		
21:34	52	25:11	202	33:11	189		
22	62	25:14	107	33:22	202, 207		
22:2	48	25:17	202	33:24-29	206		
22:3	43, 78	26:6	202	33:24	106, 170		
22:4	43, 78	26:9	64	33:25	43, 51, 62, 72		
22:5	57	26:11	44				
22:7	22	26:12	64	33:26	48		
22:9	22, 62, 109, 122	26:14	202	33:29	48		
		27:17	86	34	63, 123, 181		
		28:7	97, 142				
22:10	22	28:20-23	206	34:1-10	123, 124		
22:11	48	28:22	202	34:3-4	123		
22:15	140, 143, 161	28:23	202	34:5	140		
		28:24	202	34:6	63, 109, 123, 140		
22:16	202	28:25-26	25, 208, 212, 217				
22:19	140			34:7-8	22, 123		
22:20	107	28:25	140, 143, 176, 177, 185	34:12	140		
22:22	202			34:13	126, 140, 176, 185		
22:25-29	99						
22:28	52	28:26	202	34:16	22		
23	40, 64, 131	29	204	34:17-24	22		
		29:5	58	34:23-24	124		
23:7	43, 78	29:6	202	34:27	202		
23:14	44	29:9	202	34:28	58		
23:25	107	29:12-13	140	34:30	202		
23:27	51, 72	29:12	143, 161	35:4	202		
23:30	43, 78	29:13	143, 176, 177, 185, 204	35:6	57		
23:36-49	121			35:9	202		
23:36	48, 49			35:12	202		
23:37-38	78	29:15	204	35:15	202		
23:37	40, 43, 50, 109, 131	29:16	202	36	206		
		29:21	208	36:3	57		

36:7	153	37:24-25	124	44:11	124		
36:11	202	37:24	41, 140	44:12	43, 124, 153		
36:16-23	209	37:26-28	65				
36:12	113, 176	37:28	202, 209, 210	44:13	48, 183		
36:18	43, 78			44:16	124		
36:19	140, 143, 161	38–39	208, 211, 212	44:20	147		
36:22-32	202	38:1–39:20	211	44:23-25	145		
36:22-23	200	38:1	209	47:14	152		
36:22	201	38:17	22	48:35	65		
36:23–37:28	209	38:18	107	*Daniel*			
36:23-38	208–11	38:23	202	5–6	211		
36:23-28	22	39:7	202	7–8	211		
36:23	202, 209, 210	39:8-10	22	9:13	33		
		39:21-29	211	12:7	151		
36:24-34	189	39:21	212				
36:24	126, 140, 176, 178, 185, 187	39:22	211	*Hosea*			
		39:23	211	2:7	69		
		39:24	211	2:17	117		
36:25	43	39:25-26	183	3:1	51		
36:26-27	161	39:25	181, 182, 211	4:6	20		
36:27	41, 140, 189			4:13	61, 62, 146		
		39:26	58, 183	8:12	20		
36:31-32	22, 200	39:27-28	140	9:10	45, 47, 83, 89		
36:31	48	39:27	176, 177, 185, 212				
36:32	183, 200			11:6	97		
36:33	200	39:28	25, 185, 186, 211, 217	12:2	25		
36:36	202			13:4-6	90		
36:37-38	203			14:1	115		
36:37	121	39:29	211				
36:38	202, 208	40–48	65, 207	*Joel*			
37	183, 208–11	40:46	124	1:19-20	83		
		43:1-9	207	2:22	83		
37:1	209	43:7-9	66				
37:6	202	43:7	43, 60, 65, 66, 78	*Amos*			
37:11	55			1	195		
37:13-14	22	43:8	48	6:1-7	71		
37:13	202	43:9	43				
37:14	202	43:10-11	183	*Micah*			
37:15-22	193, 194	43:10	68	1:6	195		
37:16	21	43:11	21	2:12-13	194		
37:21	126, 140, 176, 178, 185, 187	43:19	124	2:12	179, 180, 194		
		44:6	48				
		44:7	48	3:12	195		
37:23	43, 47, 78, 200	44:10-12	124	4:1-3	31		
		44:10	43, 51				

Micah (cont.)		**BABYLONIAN TALMUD**		*Babylonian Chronicle*	
4:6-7	194	*Megillah*		1:28	170
4:6	179, 180, 194	16b	95	*CAT*	
5:5	107	*Roš Haššanah*		1.114	71
5:12	44	31a	96		
5:13 Heb.	44			*Esarhaddon treaty*	
5:14	107	**JERUSALEM TALMUD**		iv 14-15	165
		Megillah			
Nahum		3:8, 74b	96	*Esarhaddon Vassal Treaty*	
1:6	107				
2:12-14	99	**MIDRASH**		ll. 292-95	165
		Sifre on Deuteronomy			
Habakkuk		321:1	96	*IIAB [CTA 4]*	
2:15	107	321:6	97	I, 23 Iv, 32	67
2:18-20	40				
		GREEK PAPYRI		*RS*	
Zephaniah		967	24, 208–11	17.352	165
3:3-4	99				
3:3	99			*Sefire*	
3:19	179, 180, 194	**INSCRIPTIONS**		I B l. 23	191
		ARAB		I B l. 28	191
		I, §114	168	I B l. 33	191
NEW TESTAMENT		I, §116	168		
Mark		I, §164	168		
1:2	33	I, §171	168		
		I, §318	167		
John		I, §321	167		
12:39	33	II, §172	167		
		II, §878	165		
1 Corinthians					
9:9	33				

INDEX OF AUTHORS

Ackerman, S. 66, 68–73
Ackroyd, P. R. 173
Albertz, R. 19, 128, 198
Albright, W. F. 60, 92
Allen, L. C. 19, 55, 63, 68, 80, 83, 96, 98, 104, 105, 121, 128, 199, 201, 205, 207, 210
Alster, B. 71
Alt, A. 11, 194
Altick, R. 30, 35
Andersen, F. I. 194
Anderson, B. W. 179

Bakhtin, M. 26
Barr, J. 24
Barrick, W. B. 60
Baxandall, M. 29
Beckimg, B. 169
Beentjes, P. C. 98
Beetham, C. A. 30, 32, 34, 35
Begg, C. 75
Ben-Porat, Z. 32, 38
Bergey, R. 94
Bergsma, J. S. 45, 104, 127, 129–31, 145, 154–6, 160
Bertholet, A. 163
Binger, T. 66
Block, D. I. 5, 18, 41, 43, 48, 49, 55, 56, 60, 63-65, 67, 71, 73, 80, 81, 95, 96, 98, 99, 103–5, 121, 125, 137, 141, 158, 183, 185, 189, 195, 196, 202, 203, 205–8, 210–12
Block, H. M. 27
Bloom, H. 26, 27
Boda, M. J. 188
Bodi, D. 43
Bogaert, P. M. 209
Braulik, G. 46, 75, 157
Brettler, M. Z. 187, 188, 192
Bright, J. 61
Brownlee, W. H. 205

Brueggemann, W. 170
Burrows, M. 1, 4, 5, 13, 84, 109, 145

Carley, K. W. 5, 13, 14, 63, 65, 80, 109
Carr, D. M. 8–10, 16, 20, 26, 37, 101, 193, 219
Cassuto, U. 94
Chance, J. K. 201
Cheney, P. 28
Childs, B. S. 3
Choi, J. H. 3, 111, 137
Christensen, D. 76, 166
Clayton, J. 28, 29
Clements, R. E. 2, 105
Coats, G. W. 154
Coggins, R. J. 11
Collins, T. 18, 19
Conklin, B. 151, 156
Cook, S. L. 10, 64, 65, 111, 183
Cooke, G. A. 68, 69, 205
Cornill, C. H. 62, 94
Crane, A. S. 210
Cross, F. M. 75, 76, 166, 169, 190
Crouch, C. L. 49

Davis, E. F. 7, 10, 19–21, 55, 103, 122, 127, 137
Day, J. 50, 66, 67, 72, 98, 138
Day, L. 84
Delcor, M. 158
Demsky, A. 21
Diepold, P. 170
Dohmen, C. 66
Dossin, G. 168
Driver, S. R. 33, 77, 138
Duhm, B. 194
Dürr, L. 195

Edenburg, C. 36, 194
Eichrodt, W. 17, 55, 56, 66, 67, 205, 208
Eissfeldt, O. 50, 92, 194

Elbogen, I. 96
Eliot, T. S. 26

Faur, J. 40
Fechter, F. 23
Filson, F. V. 208, 210
Finnegan, R. 8
Fishbane, M. 31, 35, 37, 94, 99, 100, 132, 153, 219
Fitzmyer, J. A. 156, 191
Fitzpatrick, P. 211
Fohrer, G. 85, 96-8
Freedman, D. N. 194
Freedy, K. S. 68
Friebel, K. G. 127, 133, 134
Friedman, R. E. 75, 77, 166, 190, 192, 196
Furniss, G. 8

Galambush, J. 80, 100, 101
Ganzel, T. 7, 42-4, 46, 47, 50, 54, 63, 65, 72, 73, 77, 78, 207
Garr, W. R. 116
Gehman, H. S. 208, 210
Gese, H. 129
Gibson, J. 29, 34, 35
Gile, J. 80, 162, 205
Ginsberg, H. L. 196
Gleis, M. 60
Goody, J. 8
Götze, A. 168
Graffy, A. 206
Grayson, A. K. 170
Greenberg, M. 3, 5, 17, 18, 45, 49, 55, 56, 58, 62, 65, 66, 68, 69, 73, 80, 83, 84, 88, 96, 98, 99, 105, 109, 122, 128, 154, 160, 161, 201, 203, 205, 206
Greenfield, J. C. 152
Greenspahn, F. E. 40
Guillén, C. 27
Gunkel, H. 83
Gurney, O. R. 71

Habel, N. C. 170, 171
Hahn, S. W. 45, 104, 127, 129-31, 145, 154-6, 160
Halbertal, M. 39
Halperin, D. J. 56, 77, 169
Haran, M. 12
Hartin, P. 163

Harvey, J. 158
Hassan, I. H. 28
Hays, C. B. 35
Hays, R. 29, 34, 37
Heider, G. C. 50, 128
Heiser, M. 76
Hendel, R. S. 39
Hermerén, G. 27, 28, 30, 34, 35
Herrmann, S. 22, 193, 199, 205
Hillers, D. R. 164, 166, 167, 169, 191
Holladay, W. H. 61, 94, 123
Hollander, J. 29, 30
Hölscher, G. 22, 194
Hoppe, L. J. 111
Hopper, P. J. 115, 116
Horst, P. W. van der 127
Hossfeld, F.-L. 22, 23, 175, 177, 205
Huffmon, H. B. 158
Humbert, P. 48
Hurvitz, A. 186
Hwang, J. 112
Hyatt, J. P. 171

Irwin, W. 209

Jacobsen, T. 71, 72
Johnson, A. C. 208, 210
Joyce, P. M. 2, 16, 18, 21, 23, 55, 59, 113, 115, 125, 128, 161, 182, 188, 202, 203, 205, 210, 220
Judge, T. A. 40

Kase, E. H. 208, 210
Kasher, R. 61, 85, 96-8
Kaufmann, Y. 6, 12, 58, 59, 66, 73, 92
Keck, E. 59
Keiser, T. 94
Kelly, J. R. 34, 35
Kim, B. 98
Kim, H. C. P. 94
Kitchen, K. 164, 165, 167-69
Klawans, J. 77, 78
Klein, A. 123
Knapp, D. 157
Knohl, I. 132
Knoppers, G. N. 194
Konkel, M. 15, 17
Krašovec, J. 159, 191, 197
Kristeva, J. 26
Krüger, T. 83, 87, 121, 128

Kruger, P. A. 85
Kugler, G. 128, 154, 163
Kutscher, R. 72
Kutsko, J. F. 3, 13, 39, 40, 43, 47, 51, 54, 87
Kuyvenhoven, R. 181, 186, 187

LaRocca-Pitts, E. C. 44, 48, 49, 60, 61
Labuschagne, C. J. 152
Lapsley, J. E. 161, 183, 201
Lawrence, P. J. N. 164, 165
Leene, H. 182
Leonard, J. M. 34-6, 89, 90, 188
Leuchter, M. 92, 94
Levenson, J. D. 75, 77, 157, 166
Levinson, B. M. 111
Levitt Kohn, R. 5, 6, 15, 24, 46, 47, 54, 77, 96, 103, 104, 106-8, 144, 145, 156
Lichtheim, M. 102
Lilly, I. E. 210, 211
Liwak, R. 22, 197, 205, 206
Lohfink, N. F. 75, 157, 162
Longman, T., III 195
Lundbom, J. R. 57
Lust, J. 24, 55, 103, 105, 110, 118, 121, 138, 139, 141, 149, 150, 155, 161, 174, 181, 186, 187, 192, 193, 197, 198, 204, 205, 209, 210
Lutzky, H. C. 67
Lyons, M. A. 1, 4, 6, 7, 17, 28, 33, 34, 37, 43, 56, 59, 62, 63, 79, 82, 96-8, 104, 117, 122, 126, 135, 136, 142, 146-8, 159, 172, 183-5, 187-9, 196, 219

MacDonald, D. R. 19, 34-6
MacDonald, N. 76
Machacek, G. 26, 31
Mackie, T. P. 24, 186, 217
Magnetti, D. L. 156, 158
Malul, M. 83, 101
Margalit, A. 39
Mason, R. 36
Matties, G. H. 46
Mayes, A. D. H. 75, 76, 157
Mays, J. L. 194
McCarthy, D. J. 157, 164, 166
McConville, J. G. 57, 160, 191
McGarry, E. P. 151
McKane, W. 17
McKenzie, S. L. 23

McLaughlin, J. L. 70, 71
Meek, R. L. 29, 219
Meer, M. N. van der 210
Mein, A. 7, 21, 39, 40, 46, 55, 59, 60, 64, 70, 71, 78, 122, 128, 188, 189
Mendecki, N. 192
Mendenhall, G. E. 92, 157
Meyer, H. 30
Middlemas, J. 39, 40, 42, 50, 67, 68, 70, 71, 73, 87
Milgrim, J. 47, 49, 50, 57, 58, 60, 63, 65-67, 73, 103, 128, 173
Milgrom, J. 12, 13, 42
Millar, J. G. 160
Millard, A. R. 164
Miller, G. D. 34
Miller, P. D. 170
Miller, R. S., II 8
Miner, E. 35, 89
Moughtin-Mumby, S. 80, 85
Müller, D. H. 99
Müller, R. 194

Nelson, R. D. 75-7, 166, 169, 170, 190
Newsom, C. A. 12
Nicholson, E. W. 11, 46, 171, 190, 192, 193
Niditch, S. 7-9
Nielsen, E. 157, 162
Nigosian, S. A. 92, 93
Nihan, C. 59
Noble, P. R. 36
Nogi, K.-i. 13
Noort, E. 50
North, C. R. 40
Noth, M. 11, 75, 76, 163, 171, 190

O'Brien, K. S. 35, 38
O'Hare, D. 24
Oded, B. 165, 167-69, 193
Odell, M. S. 66, 68, 69, 71, 105, 211
Ohnesorge, S. 175, 193, 205
Olson, D. 46
Olyan, S. M. 66, 201
Ong, W. 8
Otten, H. 168
Otto, E. 11

Pakkala, J. 11, 12
Pardee, D. 70

Parpola, S. 156, 164, 165
Patton, C. L. 4, 13, 23, 43, 105, 107, 109, 128, 139
Person, R. F., Jr 11
Peterson, B. N. 57
Pohlmann, K.-F. 18, 80, 161, 198, 199
Polzin, R. 77
Pons, J. 104–6, 110–14, 116–20, 124, 126
Poser, R. 183
Premstaller, V. 17
Preuss, H. D. 43, 105
Provan, I. 60

Quick, L. 164

Rad, G. von 4, 11, 75, 163, 170, 171, 190, 192, 194, 196, 220
Rainey, A. F. 93
Raitt, T. 188, 199–202, 205
Rechenmacher, H. 76
Renz, T. 100
Renza, L. A. 26
Reventlow, H. G. 119, 138
Richter, S. L. 64
Robertson, D. A. 92, 93
Rofé, A. 156, 157, 160
Rollston, C. 20
Römer, T. C. 162
Rom-Shiloni, D. 32, 52, 54–6, 58, 61, 63, 143, 145, 166, 169, 171, 177, 182, 188
Rooker, M. F. 186
Rothstein, E. 28, 29

Sanders, P. 92, 93, 96, 157
Sandmel, S. 34
Schearing, L. S. 23
Schmidt, B. B. 39
Schniedewind, W. M. 21, 79
Schultz, R. L. 6, 29–31, 33, 34, 37, 38, 99
Schwartz, B. J. 2, 14, 42, 144, 182, 183, 188, 201
Scurlock, J. 156, 157
Seely, D. R. 151
Skehan, P. W. 95
Smith, G. A. 169
Smith, M. S. 72
Smith-Christopher, D. L. 164, 166
Sommer, B. D. 29, 34, 36, 37, 94, 146, 219
Spawn, K. L. 30, 33

Spottorno, M. V. 209–11
Stackert, J. 11
Stanley, C. D. 38
Stavrakopoulou, F. 49, 50
Stead, M. R. 31, 34, 38
Steins, G. 15
Stiebert, J. 12, 201
Stohlmann, S. 169
Stökl, J. 3, 4
Strine, C. A. 151–3, 188, 212
Stromberg, J. 24, 36
Stuhlmueller, C. 179
Sweeney, M. A. 7, 180

Tadmor, H. 156
Talmon, S. 117
Taylor, G. 72
Thelle, R. I. 58, 61
Thiel, W. 193
Thiessen, M. 95, 96
Thompson, S. A. 115, 116
Tigay, J. H. 52, 92
Tooman, W. A. 1, 7, 186, 211, 212
Toorn, K. van der 8, 16, 17, 20, 30, 197
Torrey, C. C. 5
Tov, E. 24, 51, 68, 95
Troxel, R. L. 24
Tuell, S. S. 130, 131, 133
Turner, K. J. 160

Ulrich, E. 95

Vang, C. 76
Varšo, M. 14, 15, 48, 61
Vaughan, P. H. 60
Vogt, P. T. 132

Watanabe, K. 156, 164, 165
Watts, R. E. 32
Weeks, S. 40
Weinfeld, M. 43, 45–8, 50, 52, 61, 62, 75, 77, 105, 117, 129, 157, 164, 166, 167, 194
Welch, A. D. 163, 169, 193
Wellhausen, J. 59, 162
Wetzsteon, R. 31
Wevers, J. W. 68, 205, 208
Widengren, G. 141, 195, 196, 212
Wildberger, H. 169, 194
Wilson, R. R. 13, 18, 24, 64, 202, 203

Wiseman, D. J. 165
Wolff, H. W. 75, 77, 171, 190, 192
Wong, K. L. 39, 57, 78, 96
Wright, C. J. H. 170, 171
Wright, D. P. 35, 36
Wright, G. E. 81, 92, 94, 96, 192
Wu, D. Y. 183

Yamauchi, E. M. 71

Zevit, Z. 9, 67
Ziegler, Y. 157
Zimmerli, W. 1, 19, 21, 23, 37, 40, 43, 51, 52, 54, 55, 60, 62, 63, 68, 80, 83, 87, 88, 99, 105, 120–3, 125, 171, 199, 203, 205–8